Comparative Labor Relations Law

MARVIN J. LEVINE

UNIVERSITY OF MARYLAND, College Park

Comparative Labor Relations Law

GENERAL LEARNING PRESS

250 James Street

Morristown, New Jersey 07960

To Tali and Mark

Manufactured in the United States of America.

Published simultaneously in Canada.

Library of Congress Catalog Card Number 74–81170.

ISBN 0–382–18086–0

PREFACE

Developments in labor relations during the past decade have highlighted the increasing militancy of public employee labor organizations. Constant inflation and the standard of equitable comparison with the progress achieved by unionized workers in private industry have caused teachers, nurses, garbage collectors, firemen, and policemen to relegate the blanket of conventional security that formerly covered public employment to the proverbial dustheap. Despite federal, state, and local legislative prohibitions, the incidence and duration of strikes and work stoppages by public employees have greatly intensified. This conflict situation has generated exhaustive analyses in the literature, with a number of books drawing comparisons with the private sector.

However, in reviewing the literature, this writer has been impressed with the need for further description and analysis of the legal aspects of public sector labor relations. In an effort to fill this need, a casebook approach with accompanying textual information seemed most appropriate as an explanatory vehicle for students of labor law; government administrators and officials of public employee unions engaged in negotiations; practitioners in arbitration, mediation, and fact finding; and interested laymen.

Moreover, the book, if utilized as a basic or supplementary text at the college level, should prove highly valuable for undergraduate and graduate business administration and economics courses in labor law, labor relations, and collective bargaining. It also has substantial interdisciplinary relevance for courses in public personnel administration in the political science area and professional negotiation workshops in schools of education. The discussion questions after each case, particularly, should elicit meaningful discussions.

The chapter headings represent those areas at the federal, state, and local levels of public employment where the bulk of labor law problems have arisen. By comparing administrative rulings and court decisions with National Labor Relations Board determinations in the private areas, similarities and differences between the two fields are emphasized.

The author wishes to express his thanks to the labor relations boards of Oregon, Pennsylvania, Michigan, New Jersey, New York, and Rhode

Island; to the Office of Collective Bargaining in New York City for furnishing unpublished case materials; and to Mr. Sylvester Garrett of Pittsburgh, Pennsylvania, for the arbitration material.

It is my hope that this book will be a meaningful contribution in a rapidly evolving sector of labor relations.

Marvin J. Levine
College Park, Maryland

CONTENTS

Chapter 4–*The Collective Bargaining Process*

Chapter 5–*Unfair Labor Practices*

Chapter 6–*Impasse and Grievance Resolution Techniques*

TABLE OF CASES

1 | Jurisdictional Prerequisites

THE IDENTIFICATION of employers and employees in private industry was relatively clear-cut, posing few problems, until the advent of conglomerates. The distinction between employees and management becomes apparent when the conventional supervisory functions involving decision making that shape the employment structure and create a superior-subordinate relationship (that is, on-the-job training, discipline, discharge, production standards, and so on) are set in motion. This dichotomy between management and the work force is not as apparent in the public sector, primarily because of the diffusion of responsibility for decision making among various governmental agencies or levels of supervision within one agency.

Yet the definition of *employer* and *employee* in public sector labor relations is crucial. A failure to conform to definitional requirements could bar either party from an administrative or judicial review when legal questions stemming from representation elections, unit determination, and unfair labor practice charges require resolution. The delineation of public employment status also acts to interpret who will represent public management in collective bargaining negotiations and which public employees will be represented by a labor organization in the formal bargaining process.

The following quotations illustrate the broad scope of public employment and the potential difficulties inherent in a definition of employer and employees. The Advisory Commission on Intergovernmental Relations drafted a comprehensive, model state public employee relations bill that includes the following definitions:

1. "Public employee" means any person employed by any public agency excepting those persons classed as legislative, judicial, or supervisory public employees; elected and top management appointive officials; and certain categories of confidential employees including those who have responsibility for administering the public labor-management relations law as a part of their official duties."

4. "Public agency" or "public employer" means the State of [   ] and every governmental subdivision; school and non-school special district; public and quasi-public corporation; public agency; town, city, county, city

1

and county, and municipal corporation; and authority, board, or commission, whether incorporated or not and whether chartered or not.[1]

Milton Derber provides an example of the proliferation of public employers in one populous state:

> The public employer is not a single type. It assumes a wide variety of legal and structural forms which need to be treated quite differently. In the state of Illinois there are roughly 6,000 separate governmental units, including 1,200 municipalities, 1,100 school districts, including airport, drainage, housing, park, and sanitary authorities, to name only the most numerous. This listing, moreover, counts the huge and intricate state government as a single unit despite the diversity of its segments, such as the code departments (finance, labor, public works, public safety, and public aid), the several public university and college systems, the state toll highway commission, the state library, etc. . . .[2]

The cases in this chapter will not deal with the problems surrounding the inclusion or exclusion of supervisory, managerial, or professional employees from bargaining units. That topic will be thoroughly discussed later in the book. Initial case materials will be concerned with the elements involved in determining whether certain governmental units qualify as public employers and whether certain groups of employees are properly classified as public employees.

Section 1. Definition of Public Employer and Public Employees

This recent case illustrates the lack of unanimity between courts and administrative agencies in the determination of public employment status. The issues center around whether medical interns, residents, and postgraduate fellows associated with a state university medical center are to be treated as public employees and whether a state university is a public employer. The court's reversal of an employment relations commission ruling also affects a representation election sought by the affected individuals for collective bargaining purposes.

Regents of the University of Michigan v. MERC [3]
Michigan Court of Appeals, 1972

VAN VALKENBURG, J.: Appellant regents of the University of Michigan seek review of the March 16, 1971 decision and order of appellee Michigan Employment Relations Commission, whereby a representation election was ordered to be conducted among the interns, residents, and postdoctoral fellows working for the appellant at the University of

Michigan Medical Center for the purpose of determining whether said individuals wished to be represented for collective bargaining purposes by the University of Michigan Interns-Residents Association.

The genesis of this story goes back to the fall of 1966, when a group of interns and resident doctors connected with the University Hospital, desiring to bargain with the regents of the University of Michigan concerning wages, rates of pay, and conditions of employment, decided to band together and form the University of Michigan Interns-Residents Association. The regents, however, refused to recognize this newly formed organization as a bargaining agent. The association thereafter filed an election petition with the commission in April 1970.

An extensive hearing was held in June and July of 1970 before a trial examiner. Briefs were filed and oral arguments were presented to the full commission on March 2, 1971, whereupon the commission issued its order of March 16, 1971, setting the election for April 21, 22, and 23, 1971. Prior to the election the regents sought to stay the election. This court denied the motion . . . "but without prejudice to the plaintiff's right to decline to bargain with the bargaining agent until a decision by this court on the application for leave and until further order of the court."

The election was held and resulted in 296 votes in favor of representation, 115 against, and 4 challenged ballots. The association soon after the election requested of the regents that negotiations be instituted, but this was refused on the theory that the matter was still pending before this court. Leave to appeal was granted and an order was issued staying all proceedings among the parties until such time as a final decision could be made.

The factual setting having been laid, we must now look at the issues raised: May the Public Employment Relations Act be applied to the regents of the University of Michigan in the present matter without contravening their authority under Const. 1963, Article 8, Section 5?

The question of whether the constitutional grant of authority to supervise, direct, and control university affairs insulates the governing bodies of state universities from regulation as a public employer has now been laid to rest. The Michigan Supreme Court in *Board of Control of Eastern Michigan University* v. *Labor Mediation Board,* 384 Mich. 561, 565, 566 (1971), while recognizing that "The powers and prerogatives of Michigan Universities have been jealously guarded not only by the boards of those universities but by this court in a series of opinions running as far back as 1856," nonetheless held that

> Here we find no plenary grant of powers which, by any stretch of the imagination, would take plaintiff's operations outside of the area of public employment. "Public employment" is clearly intended to apply to employment or service in all governmental activity, whether carried on by the state or by townships, cities, counties, commissions, boards, or other gov-

ernmental instrumentalities. It is the entire public sector of employment as distinguished from private employment. The public policy of this state as to labor relations in public employment is for legislative determination.

We therefore hold that, while the regents continue to enjoy the entire control and management of their affairs and property, they are a public employer and thus are subject to regulation as a public employer.

Hence, we are confronted with the crucial issue: Are interns, residents, and postdoctoral fellows serving at the university and affiliated hospitals of the University of Michigan Medical Center public employees within the meaning of 1965 P.A. 379?

Two members of the commission, who comprised the majority, decided that, although the persons who sought to be included in the bargaining unit were students of the University of Michigan Medical School, they nonetheless also had an employment relationship with the university and were entitled to unite for collective bargaining purposes. The majority determined the appropriate unit to be "All interns, residents, and fellows employed by the regents of the University of Michigan possessing the equivalent of a minimum of an M.D. or D.D.S. degree, and postdoctoral fellows in the clinical and basic sciences, EXCLUDING pharmacy interns, dietetic interns, nurse anesthetist trainees, chaplaincy interns, and all other employees."

The third member of the commission dissented, holding that

> I would find on the basis of the record as a whole that interns and residents are not employees in the traditional or legal sense but are in fact postgraduate students. Their activities represent a continuation of their medical study and are, therefore, primarily educational rather than employment in nature. I would find, contrary to my colleagues, that the interns and residents are not public employees for whom this commission should direct an election.

Appellees maintain that the findings of fact made by the majority of the Employment Relations Commission are final, and that the reviewing court may not substitute its judgment for that of the administrative agency if such findings by the agency are supported by competent, material, and substantial evidence. . . .

In 1947 the legislature enacted 1947 P.A. 336, commonly referred to as the Hutchinson Act, for the purpose of preventing strikes among public employees and creating a procedure by which to mediate grievances. . . . The statute does not, however, define what is meant by the words *public employees*. Some help is found in *Hillsdale Community Schools* v. *Labor Mediation Board,* 24 Mich. App. 36, 41 (1970), where it was held that

The words "public employee" are to identify the employees other than private and do not define public employees so as to exclude supervisory personnel.

The word "employee" is quite flexible in meaning and subject to different interpretations in accordance with the intent of the statute in which it is used. Illustrative of this point, we quote the language found in 30 CJS, Employee, p. 672:

> "Employee" has neither technically nor in general use a restricted meaning by which any particular employment or service is indicated, and that it may have different meanings in different connections admits of no doubt. The word "employee" has no fixed meaning which must control in every instance, and it is not a word of art, but takes color from its surroundings and frequently is carefully defined by the statute where it appears.

Since the term "employee" is nebulous in nature and undefined in the statute, what then was the intent of the legislature with regard to interns, residents, and postgraduate fellows acting as such at hospitals associated with state universities? It is first necessary to look at the nature of these persons' positions. *Webster's Third New International Dictionary* defines the word "intern" as "An advanced student or recent graduate in a professional field; one trained in a profession allied to medicine who undergoes a period of practical clinical experience prior to practicing his profession."

The same dictionary defines "resident" as "A physician serving a residency," with "residency" being defined as "A period of advanced medical training and education that normally follows graduation from medical school and completion of internship and that consists of supervised practice of a specialty in a hospital and its out-patient department and instruction from specialists on the hospital staff." "Fellow" is defined as "A young physician who has completed training as an intern and resident and has been granted a stipend and position allowing him to do further study and research in a specialty."

The relationship between these persons and the regents thus assumes a unique blend of the aspects of both employer-employee and teacher-student. Neither can we overlook the fact that a state university is a unique public employer, because its powers, duties, and responsibilities are derived from the Constitution rather than from enactments of legislation. See *Regents of University of Michigan* v. *Labor Mediation Board,* 18 Mich. App. 485, 490 (1969).

The regents have exclusive control of all matters dealing with the education of the student. To this end, the legislature cannot enact any law which will regulate or direct the manner in which the educational processes are to be conducted. The wisdom of this independence was well stated in *Brannum* v. *Board of Regents of University of Michigan,* 5 Mich. App. 134, 138 (1966):

> This court recognizes that such independence must be maintained in educational matters in order to provide the highest quality education for the students of Michigan, and in order to maintain the outstanding national reputation of the university.

The educational and employment aspects of the relationship of the interns, residents, and postgraduate fellows with the regents are inextricably mixed. To hold that these persons are employees within the meaning of the statute would impinge, to some degree, upon the constitutional authority of the regents to control and manage the educational affairs of the university. Absent some clear expression by the legislature that they intended to exercise their constitutional authority to regulate labor relations among public employees in such a manner as to so impinge upon the regents' constitutional authority, this court will assume that the legislature did not intend such a result. If the legislature had intended that graduate students were to be included as public employees within the meaning of the statute, they would have clearly indicated such an intent.

Courts cannot be oblivious to the consequences of their decisions. If the interns, residents, and postgraduate fellows associated with the University Medical Center were to be classified as herein requested, the assistants in all other departments, working part-time at their trade or profession for a small stipend, would, in order to avoid discrimination, conclude that they were entitled to the same treatment. Such a result could well wreak havoc on the very ability of the regents to control and manage the educational affairs of the university. It is further noted that the legislature, itself, considers interns and other assistants as students rather than employees, for the purpose of determining the amount of annual appropriation made to the university.

This case is apparently one of first impression, not only in Michigan, but in the entire United States. While the attorneys for both sides filed long and exhaustive briefs, which clearly indicate the importance of this litigation, none of the cases therein cited offers any real help in the determination of this issue. It would be of little value to review all the citations, since, in the final analysis, all can be distinguished. We would also note that in New York interns and residents may organize for purposes of collective bargaining; however, such bargaining units are specifically provided for by statute. The legislature of that state has spoken on the question; the legislature of Michigan has not.

Therefore, for the reasons stated herein, it is the conclusion of this court that the interns, residents, and postgraduate fellows associated with the University of Michigan Medical Center are not public employees within the meaning of 1965 P.A. 379; (MCLA 423.201 *et seq.;* MSA 17.455(1) *et seq.*).

The decision of the Michigan Employment Relations Commission is hereby reversed and set aside, but without costs, a public question being involved.

MC GREGOR, J. (Concurring in part and dissenting in part):

I concur in my brothers' conclusion that the University of Michigan Board of Regents is a public employer. However, I am constrained to dissent from my brothers' holding that the interns, residents, and post-doctoral fellows are not "public employees" within the meaning of 1965 P.A. 379 (MCLA 423.201 *et seq.;* MSA 17.455(1) *et seq.*).

The majority opinion holds that the interns, residents, and postdoc-toral fellows cannot be characterized as employees because they are students. The fact that the members of the Interns-Residents Association are "students" does not thereby preclude them from also maintaining their status of employees of the university. In short, this is not a situation where the interns-residents are either students or employees; the terms "student" and "employee" are not mutually exclusive.

The regents cannot refute the fact that the interns and residents do not participate in classroom work, but are instead engaged in clinical work in the hospital. Furthermore, the interns and residents treat patients in a clinical context, although under the supervision of hospital personnel. This fact further serves to emphasize the employee status of the interns and residents, as it is directly analogous to the supervisory capacity which is present in the normal employer-employee relationship. Each year the resident or intern signs a one-year agreement deemed as binding by both parties; they receive compensation and are subject to federal tax thereon. The benefits provided by the hospital to its regular employees are provided to the members of the association as well. Indeed, interns and resident physicians have been considered employees for various purposes by the many courts of the United States. In *Martin* v. *Roosevelt Hospital,* 426 F.2d 155 (1970), the Court of Appeals held that a resident physician is an employee under the reemployment provisions of the selective service statute. The court also noted that the position of resident physician is not so temporary as to be regarded as casual employment. In *Woddail* v. *Commissioner of Internal Revenue,* 321 F.2d 721 (1963), a doctor was employed as a resident physician and his salary was denominated as a stipend. The doctor then excluded his tax-exempt fellowship amount from his gross income. The Commissioner of Internal Revenue ruled that the doctor, not being a candidate for a degree at an educational institution, was therefore not a recipient of a scholarship excludable under Section 117 of the Internal Revenue Code. The court agreed with the commissioner and found that the examination of the position of a resident physician vis-à-vis the hospital results in a perfect example of an employer-employee relationship.

In negligence cases, particularly malpractice cases, interns and resident physicians have long been determined as employees of the hospital, working directly under its supervision and control and acting on behalf of the hospital. See *Stuart Circle Hospital Corp.* v. *Curry,* 173 Va. 136, 3 S.E.2d 153 (1939); *Post* v. *Crown Heights Hospital, Inc.* 173 Misc. 250, 17 N.Y.S.2d 409 (1940); *City of Miami* v. *Oates,* 152 Fla. 21, 10 So.2d 721 (1942); *Moeller* v. *Hauser,* 237 Minn. 368, 54 N.W.2d 639 (1952); *Parmerter* v. *Osteopathic General Hospital,* Fla. App., 196 So.2d 505 (1967).

Hospital interns and resident physicians have also been held to be employees within the context of Workmen's Compensation Acts. In *Bernstein* v. *Beth Israel Hospital,* 236 N.Y. 268, 140 N.E. 694 (1923), the court, analyzing the position of interns and resident physicians, held that "He was a servant or employee by every test of permanence of duty, of intimacy of contact, and of fullness of subjection." See also *Nordland* v. *Poor Sisters of St. Francis,* 4 Ill. App. 2d 48, 123 N.E.2d 121 (1954).

The aforementioned cases necessitate the conclusion that, for the purposes of collective bargaining, the members of the Interns-Residents Association possess the requisite degree of employee status as to come within the scope of public employees, within the meaning of 1965 P.A. 379. Therefore, I dissent from the majority opinion and vote to affirm the order of the Michigan Employment Relations Commission without costs.

Discussion Questions

1. Discuss the factors considered by the court in resolving the issue of whether the state university is a public employer.
2. Why did the court reverse the commission's decision that the students were public employees?
3. What repercussions did the court fear would follow a determination that the interns, residents, and postgraduate fellows were public employees?
4. What effect does the court ruling have on the goal of the affected individuals to secure representation for collective bargaining purposes?
5. Indicate in which respects the dissenting opinion differed from the majority viewpoint.

Section 2. Status of State Employees

In the preceding case, a state appellate tribunal ruled that individuals in a state-university-student relationship do not qualify as public employees seeking representation in collective bargaining. The following case describes a jurisdictional question that develops when the employment status of state-college faculty members is placed in doubt because of statutory considerations. Once again the evolution of a collective bargaining relationship hinges on the outcome.

In the Matter of

Board of Trustees of State Colleges, Rhode Island College of Education (employer) *and* **Rhode Island Chapter of the American Federation of Teachers** *and* **The American Association of University Professors (petitioner)**

Case No. EE–1768

(State of Rhode Island and Providence Plantations, Providence, Sc. before the State Labor Relations Board, Rhode Island State)

STATEMENT OF THE CASE

At the formal hearing held on February 6, 1968, the issue before the board was the question of its jurisdiction. The following testimony was received by the board in the following order:

William J. Sheehan, Esquire, representing the Board of Trustees of State Colleges, pointed out to the State Labor Relations Board that there was a question of its statutory jurisdiction and that the Board of Trustees of State Colleges was not waiving the jurisdictional issue but wanted the State Labor Relations Board to decide whether it had jurisdiction or not. He further noted that the General Laws of Rhode Island created the Board of Trustees of State Colleges spelling out its powers and exclusions from the Administrative Procedure Act, and so on, and pinpointed the powers of the board as set forth in 16–31–12:

> 16–31–12 Employees Exempt from Merit System: Certification of Teachers: The appointment, promotion, salaries, tenure, and dismissal of administrative, instructional, and research employees, and secretarial employees not exceeding ten in number, of the state colleges shall not be subject in any manner or degree to control by the personnel administrator or by any officer or board other than the Board of Trustees of state colleges. The certification of teachers at the University of Rhode Island is hereby abolished, except for such teachers as elect to come or remain under it.

He further noted that the General Laws give the Board of Trustees of State Colleges the same powers over the University of Rhode Island, Rhode Island College, and Rhode Island Junior College.

Dr. Alfred D. Sumberg of the American Association of University Professors stated that his organization doubted if the Labor Relations Board, which in his opinion was designed for industrial purposes, had jurisdiction in this matter. He explained to the board that his organization's 1940 Statement of Academic Freedom and Tenure, which had been adopted by and incorporated in the faculty manuals of Rhode Island College and the University of Rhode Island, had been reaffirmed by the Board of Trustees of State Colleges. Dr. Sumberg attempted to show historically that there was no similarity between faculty and industry in that in industry the union members cannot choose the corporation president, set the policy, order materials, or tell management what to manufacture, and so on; the faculties in universities go far beyond what unions can do in representation and participation in the operation of the universities, and in the sharing of responsibilities, duties, and liabilities between the faculty and the university. It was his belief that a bargaining agent would be in violation or in conflict with the charter of the Faculty Council of Rhode Island and a fundamental principle of shared responsibility that had been widely adopted in American higher education; that the establishment of a bargaining agent would create an adversary relationship on the Rhode Island campus; that collective bargaining would increase administrative costs for the Board of Trustees and increase payments of dues for the faculty; that the faculty members' traditional individual freedom might be lost; and that collective bargaining would violate sound principles of academic freedom. Collective bargaining in colleges and universities is against national trends he felt, and as a result thereof, the board should not assume jurisdiction over higher education, particularly at Rhode Island College.

Harold Adams, Esquire, the attorney for the Committee of Concerned Faculty, filed a motion to dismiss the petition based on the jurisdictional grounds spelled out in 16–31–12. Mr. Adams suggested that a conflict would exist between the laws governing the Board of Trustees of State Colleges (in which they are free to exercise their duties without any authority of any other board) and the State Labor Relations Board. If the State Labor Relations Board tried to enforce 36–11, it would create many problems for the Board of Trustees and probably would be in violation of the law establishing said board.

Mr. Adams further suggested that Title 36, Chapter 11 deals with state employees. Said chapter does not distinguish between classified and unclassified personnel. He contended that some funds and grants to Rhode Island College faculty members are not from the state of Rhode Island and, as such, the Board of Trustees cannot regulate or control the manner in which these funds are to be appropriated or spent. Therefore, the

Board of Trustees would be without authority to negotiate with the collective bargaining agent on these funds. He further attempted to show that the makeup of the Board of Trustees of State Colleges was different from most boards in that the representatives of the alumni of the University of Rhode Island and Rhode Island College were not appointed or elected by state officials or the people, but in fact were selected by the alumni of the schools and as such do not fall within the definition of state officials.

Julius Michaelson, Esquire, attorney for the petitioning union, stated that objections to the question of jurisdiction should be raised by a party or intervenor to the proceedings and that no objections were raised by a party or intervenor. His inference was that the Committee of Concerned Faculty and the American Association of University Professors were not parties or intervenors. He suggested that the Teachers Arbitration Act in Rhode Island, pertaining to collective bargaining, gives rights to employees of cities and towns and thereupon has no bearing on this matter. Under the Organization of State Employees Act, 36–11, the only exclusion was state police; that the paychecks of the members of the faculty were from the state of Rhode Island and Providence Plantations; that Chapter 36–11, Organization of State Employees Act, is the most recent statute dealing with state employees and should be given the most weight and consideration; and if they had intended to exclude the college professors, the state legislature would have excluded them the same as they did the state police. He further contended that the Board of Trustees of State Colleges was created by an act of the state legislature; and because most of their members were appointed by the Governor, they are state officials.

CONCLUSIONS OF LAW

1. The employer, the Board of Trustees of State Colleges, is a duly constituted department within the government of the state of Rhode Island. Said Board of Trustees of State Colleges qualifies as an employer and has its offices and principal place of business at . . . .

2. It was undisputed on this record, and we find and conclude, therefore, that in fact and within the meaning of the act: The Petitioner is a labor organization under the provisions of 28–7 of the General Laws of Rhode Island, 1956, as amended, and the unit appropriate for the purposes of collective bargaining is the Rhode Island College of Education.

3. That the American Association of University Professors is an association of college faculty members.

4. That the Committee of Concerned Faculty is a committee made up of some of the faculty members of Rhode Island College.

5. That the faculty members of the State University and colleges are not excluded from the Organization of State Employees Act, 36–11.

6. That the faculty members of Rhode Island College are state employees as defined under the Organization of State Employees Act, 36–11.

7. The Rhode Island State Labor Relations Board has jurisdiction to entertain the petition of the Rhode Island Chapter of the American Federation of Teachers.

ORDER

By virtue and pursuant to the power vested in the Rhode Island State Labor Relations Board by the Rhode Island State Labor Relations Act IT IS HEREBY DIRECTED that upon the basis of the foregoing Conclusions of Law, Testimony, and General Laws of the State of Rhode Island, the Rhode Island State Labor Relations Board finds it has jurisdiction to entertain this petition filed by the Rhode Island chapter of the American Federation of Teachers and orders that the State Labor Relations Board hold an election on March 21, 1968 for: All instructional and research faculty of Rhode Island College including Henry Barnard School; excluding deans, administrative, and all other personnel. All motions to dismiss are hereby denied.

Dated: Rhode Island State Labor Relations Board
        March 22, 1968

Discussion Questions

1. Are the arguments of the AAUP officials against collective bargaining rights for state-college faculty members convincing in the light of recent trends?
2. In the final analysis, which statute among those cited was given the most weight in a definition of state employees?

Section 3. Definition of Federal Employees

Executive Order 11491 governs labor–management relations in the federal government. Normally, the distinction between federal and state employment status is easily drawn. However, in the instant case, the Assistant Secretary of Labor for Labor–Management Relations, who is authorized to rule on petitions for representation and questions involving the appropriateness of bargaining units, must decide whether civilian technicians employed by a state's Army and Air Force National Guard are state employees for labor relations purposes and outside the jurisdiction of the executive order. Two representation petitions were consolidated for hearing because of the similarity of the issues involved.

In the Matter of

Mississippi National Guard, 172nd Military Airlift Group (Thompson Field) (activity) *and* **International Union of Electrical, Radio, and Machine Workers, AFL-CIO and Its National Army–Air Technicians Association, Local 676 (petitioner)**

Case No. 41–1723 (RO)[4]

Mississippi National Guard (Camp Shelby) (activity) *and* **American Federation of Government Employees, AFL-CIO, Local 3151 (petitioner)**

Case No. 41–1741 (RO)

(United States Department of Labor before the Assistant Secretary for Labor–Management Relations)

DECISION AND REMAND

Upon petitions duly filed under Section 6 of Executive Order 11491, a consolidated hearing was held before Hearing Officer Seymour X. Alsher. The hearing officer's rulings made at the hearing are free from prejudicial error and are hereby affirmed.

Upon the entire record in these cases, including briefs filed by all the parties, the Assistant Secretary finds

1. The labor organizations involved claim to represent certain employees of the activity.

2. A possible question concerning the representation of certain employees of the activity exists within the meaning of Section 10 of Executive Order 11491.

3. In Case No. 41–1723 (RO), the International Union of Electrical, Radio, and Machine Workers, AFL-CIO and its National Army–Air Technicians Association, Local 676, herein called IUE, seeks an election in a unit of all nonsupervisory Wage Board employees employed by the 172nd Military Airlift Group, Mississippi National Guard, at the activity's Thompson Field installation. In Case No. 41–1741 (RO), the American Federation of Government Employees, AFL-CIO, Local 3151, herein called AFGE, seeks a unit of all employees in the Annual Train-

ing Equipment Pool, Combined Support Maintenance Shop, Organization Maintenance Shop No. 6, and the United States Property and Fiscal Office at the activity's Camp Shelby installation. At the hearing, the activity declined to take a position concerning the appropriateness of the units sought by the IUE and the AFGE. In this respect, the activity contended, among other things, that the provisions of Executive Order 11491 did not apply in this matter because the employees involved are under the operational control of The Adjutant General of the state of Mississippi, who is appointed and employed pursuant to state law and that the executive order is neither binding upon nor applicable to employees of the state of Mississippi.

The Adjutant General of the state of Mississippi administers the Army and Air National Guard technicians' program within regulations and guidelines established by the secretaries of the Department of the Army and Department of the Air Force and the chief of the National Guard Bureau, which is a joint bureau of the above-named departments. The Adjutant General is appointed by the Governor of the state of Mississippi. Neither the National Guard Bureau nor the secretaries of the departments of the Army or the Air Force have the authority to veto the selection of an individual chosen by the Governor to be The State Adjutant General. However, in order for a State National Guard program to be recognized, federally, a State Adjutant General must comply with certain prescribed standards established by outstanding agency regulations issued by the above-named secretaries.

In support of the activity's position that the provisions of Executive Order 11491 were inapplicable in the matter, the following contentions were made:

1. Public Law 90–486, which allegedly granted National Guard employees federal employee status, was, in fact, enacted solely for the purpose of granting retirement benefits and protection under the Federal Torts Claims Act to excepted National Guard technicians.

2. The terms and provisions of Executive Order 11491 are not binding upon nor applicable to the sovereign state of Mississippi.

3. Certain portions of National Guard Regulations No. 51 and Air National Guard Regulations, No. 40–01, which were issued on March 1, 1970 by the secretaries of the Departments of the Army and the Air Force for the purpose of providing guidance for the organization, functions, and responsibilities with respect to civilian personnel administration within the Army and Air National Guard, including the implementation of Executive Order 11491, circumvent the intent of Congress and were never contemplated by the Public Law 90–486.

4. The laws of the state of Mississippi do not grant The Adjutant

General any authority to negotiate or enter into contracts with labor organizations.

With respect to the first contention, the activity asserted that close scrutiny of the legislative history of Public Law 90–486 reveals that National Guard technicians were conferred federal employee status only for those specifically enumerated purposes set forth in the legislative history. In this regard, it is contended that these limited purposes were to grant retirement benefits and coverage under the Federal Torts Claims Act to excepted National Guard technicians.

With respect to the second contention, the activity asserted that Executive Order 11491 is not applicable to the state of Mississippi because National Guard technicians are engaged in a state rather than a federal function. In support of this contention, the activity notes that Public Law 90–486 amended Section 2105(a) of Title 5 of the United States Code which defines what constitutes a federal employee, by providing that an individual can be appointed to the civil service by, among other specifically named officials, a state Adjutant General. In this regard, it is contended that for National Guard technicians to be found to be federal employees, they must meet all three of the criteria, outlined in Section 2105(a), including the requirement that they be engaged in the performance of a federal function. (The other two requirements include being appointed to the civil service by a federal official and being subject to supervision by a federal official.) Because Mississippi National Guard technicians are allegedly performing a state function in that they are appointed and supervised by a state Adjutant General, it is argued that they are not federal employees.

In regard to the activity's third contention, it appears that the activity objects to Section 7 of National Guard Regulations No. 51 and Air National Guard Regulations No. 40–01 which were issued on March 1, 1970, by the secretaries of the Departments of the Army and the Air Force. The purpose of the regulations was to provide guidance with respect to personnel administration including the implementation of Executive Order 11491 by state Adjutants General in their respective jurisdictions. It is asserted by the activity that personnel administration is exclusively a state function, and therefore, Executive Order 11491 cannot be imposed upon the state through regulations.

In support of its fourth contention, it is asserted that the activity's Adjutant General can exercise only those powers which are specifically granted him by the laws of the state of Mississippi. Because the laws of the state of Mississippi do not specifically and expressly grant the state Adjutant General the authority to negotiate or enter into a contract with a labor organization, it is contended that the state Adjutant General is powerless in implementing the provisions of Executive Order 11491.

In contrast to the position of the activity in this case, it should be noted that the Department of Defense's interpretation of Public Law 90–486 finds National Guard technicians to be federal employees and accordingly, in that department's view, Executive Order 11491 is applicable to National Guard technicians.

Thus, the record reveals that Assistant Secretary of Defense Kelly, in a memorandum dated March 26, 1970, to Major General Wilson, the chief of the National Guard Bureau, stated in part, that

> I have learned . . . that the Governor and Adjutant General of Mississippi contend that National Guard technicians are not federal employees for the purpose of Executive Order 11491, Labor–Management Relations in the Federal Service. . . . National Guard technicians in the fifty states became federal employees as a result of Public Law 90–486 (32 U.S.C. § 709). . . . Please inform The Adjutant General of the state of Mississippi that National Guard technicians under his jurisdiction are federal employees for the purposes of Executive Order 11491, and instruct him as to the necessity for observing and implementing the policy of this department, as described above, with respect to those technicians. . . .

Based on the foregoing, I find that National Guard technicians are employees within the meaning of Section 2(b) of the order. As noted above, the record reveals that the Department of Defense has interpreted Public Law 90–486 to mean that the National Guard technicians, as defined therein, are employees of the federal government. Consistent with its interpretation of the law, regulations have been issued, specifically National Guard Regulations No. 51 and Air National Guard Regulations No. 40–01, to implement the terms and provisions of Executive Order 11491. Moreover, under Executive Order 11491, I have issued two representation decisions involving National Guard technicians units and the activities in those cases made no contention that Executive Order 11491 was inapplicable to their Adjutants General because of their capacity as state officials or because National Guard technicians are state employees.

With respect to the contention that Public Law 90–486 constitutes National Guard technicians to be federal employees for certain enumerated, limited purposes, the legislative history of Public Law 90–486 reveals that its proposed scope was broader than merely granting retirement benefits and protection under the Federal Torts Claims Act to excepted National Guard technicians. In this regard, the Senate Armed Services Committee's Report, issued in 1968, concerning Public Law 90–486 states, in part, that

> This bill implements the purpose by converting the technicians to *federal employee status* with certain controls on administration and supervision which would as a matter of law remain at the state level. In effect, the

technicians will become *federal* employees receiving the salaries, fringe and retirement benefits, but with certain administrative control regarding employment supervision remaining with The Adjutant General of the jurisdiction concerned under regulations prescribed by the secretary concerned. . . .

Thus, contrary to the view of the activity, I find that there is no indication in Public Law 90–486 or in the legislative history which preceded it that federal employee status was granted to National Guard technicians solely for the purpose of granting these employees federal retirement benefits or coverage under the Federal Torts Claims Act.

I also have considered the contention that the laws of Mississippi do not permit The Adjutant General to negotiate with a labor organization. The applicable regulations issued by the secretaries of the Army and Air Force and certain sections of Title 32 of the U.S. Code indicate that The Adjutant General of a state, in effect, has been designated as an agent of the secretaries of the Army and the Air Force as well as of the chief of the National Guard Bureau, to insure that personnel and labor relations policies are administered in conformity with accepted federal standards. Acting as an agent of the secretaries of the Army and the Air Force and the chief of the National Guard Bureau, it appears that sufficient enabling authority is found in outstanding regulations issued by the secretaries of the Army and the Air Force to insure that state Adjutants General will comply with the terms and provisions of Executive Order 11491. Consequently, I find that the provisions of the executive order are applicable to the activity and that the National Guard technicians in the sought unit are employees within the meaning of Section 2(b) of Executive Order 11491.

With respect to the appropriateness of the units sought, the record shows that both the IUE and the AFGE seek units composed of National Guard technicians employed at two separate installations of the activity in the state of Mississippi. Neither the representative of the Department of Defense nor the representative of the activity presented any evidence at the hearing with respect to the claimed units. Indeed, the activity's Adjutant General left the hearing room shortly after reading his formal statement of position concerning jurisdiction into the record. There were no other representatives of the activity remaining in the hearing room who sought to present evidence concerning the appropriateness of the claimed units. . . .

Since, in my view, the record does not provide an adequate basis on which to determine the appropriateness of the claimed units, I shall remand the subject cases to the appropriate regional administrator to reopen the record solely for the purpose of receiving evidence concerning the appropriateness of the units sought.

ORDER

IT IS HEREBY ORDERED that the subject cases be, and they hereby are, remanded to the appropriate regional administrator.

Dated: April 2, 1971   /s/ W. J. Usery, Jr., Assistant Secretary of
    Washington, D.C.   Labor for Labor–Management Relations

Discussion Questions

1. State the arguments advanced by the activity to support the view that the National Guard civilian technicians are state employees.
2. Trace the rebuttal arguments of the Assistant Secretary in advancing the thesis that the technicians are federal employees.
3. To what degree did the Assistant Secretary rely on precedent in disagreeing with the state of Mississippi's position?
4. Why was the unit determination issue remanded to lower level officials for resolution?

Section 4. Essential Elements of the Employment Relationship

In the first case of its kind recorded in the United States, a labor organization composed of inmates in a New York State correctional facility sought recognition from the state as the collective bargaining representative for the entire Green Haven prison population.

The New York Public Employment Relations Board, in facing this novel request, explored the various criteria that must be satisfied before a valid employer-employee relationship can be said to exist at the state level.

In the Matter of

State of New York (Department of Correctional Services) (party in interest) *and* Prisoners Labor Union at Green Haven (petitioner)

Case No. C–0794 [5]

(State of New York Public Employment Relations Board)

STIPULATED FACTS

The New York State Department of Correctional Services (herein referred to as the department) maintains and operates 21 correctional facilities with a total prisoner population of about 15,000. One such institution is the Green Haven Correctional Facility, a maximum security prison in Dutchess County with about 1,700 male adult prisoners. All prisoners have been convicted of felonies in the state and sentenced to a term of imprisonment or death.

Article 7 of the Correction Law governs the work experience of prisoners during their incarceration. About 1,379 prisoners are "employed" within the Green Haven prison pursuant to Section 171:

> The commissioner of correction and the superintendents and officials of all penitentiaries in the state may cause inmates . . . who are physically capable thereof, to be employed. . . . Such labor shall be either for the purpose of production of supplies for said institutions, or for the state, or any political subdivision thereof, or for any political institution owned or managed and controlled by the state, or any political division thereof; or for the purpose of industrial training and instruction, or partly for one, and partly for the other of such purposes.

Apart from those who are temporarily disabled, prisoners who are not "employed" fall into one of three categories: "unemployed" (prisoner willing to work but no assignments available), "idle" (prisoner refuses to work), or "temporarily restricted" from working for disciplinary reasons.

Work assignments to one of four programs issue from the Job Assignment Classification Committee, comprised solely of prison supervisory officials. Such assignments may, but need not, reflect a specific prisoner request.

Enlisted in the vocational and academic educational programs are about 138 and 400 prisoners, respectively. . . .

About 533 prisoners participate in the maintenance program for Green Haven buildings, grounds, and equipment. Through this program, prisoners are provided an opportunity to learn various crafts, trades, and maintenance skills. The industrial program, in which about 308 prisoners are involved, is designed to develop other work skills and habits.

"Idle" prisoners and those under disciplinary restrictions receive no compensation. For the rest, payment varies as follows: "unemployed" and "student" prisoners are paid 20 and 25 cents a day, respectively; working (and disabled) prisoners in occupational grade 1 receive 25 cents a day; while those in occupational grades 2 to 4 are paid on sliding scales, to a maximum of $1 per day in the highest grade. Incentive payments are made to certain prisoners in the industrial program.

All "employed" prisoners work a regular schedule of not more than eight hours a day excluding Sundays and holidays. For work in excess of this, they are paid at the rate of one and one half times their regular compensation. . . .

CONTENTIONS OF THE PARTIES

This case presents for decision the novel issue of whether prisoners in state institutions are "public employees" under the Public Employees Fair Employment Act, colloquially known as the Taylor Law, and thus entitled to have an employee organization of their choice negotiate terms and conditions of prison "employment" with the state. The petitioner and the *amici curiae* argue in the affirmative, while the state takes the contrary position.

The central thesis of petitioner's argument is that the Correction Law and the economic realities of the prisoners' work experience both proclaim the existence of an employer-employee relationship between the state (through its Department of Correctional Services) and the individual Green Haven prisoners. To establish its first point, that "the work relationship is defined by law as one of employment," petitioner relies heavily upon Section 171 of the Correction Law. Petitioner notes that prior to 1970, Section 171 mandated work by prisoners at hard labor. During 1970, the legislature amended Section 171 to merely permit prisoners to be "employed."

According to petitioner, this amendment signified a fundamental change in the nature of the work experience of prisoners: where formerly they were compelled to labor, now they were free to contract or withhold their services as in any traditional employment relationship. The introduction of the element of volition into the work equation and the use of the word "employed" are evidence to petitioner of a legislative intent to confer employee status on the prisoners.

Other statutory indicia of legislative intent to create an employment relationship which petitioner cites are the use of the terms "compensation" and "graded wage schedules" in Section 187 of the Correction Law and the use in Section 183 of the term "employ(ment)" to describe the work status of inmates both while incarcerated and following their discharge. ("It shall be the duty of the commissioner . . . to employ the prisoners . . . in occupations in which they will be most likely to obtain employment after their discharge. . . .")

In support of its contention that the prisoners have a de facto employer-employee relationship with the Department of Correctional Services, petitioner marshals the following evidence traditionally considered indicative of such status: prisoners may give or withhold their services; if they choose to work they are paid on a graded wage scale, with time and one-half for overtime; they are permitted to apply for specific jobs; their work is supervised and controlled by officials of Green Haven and of the department; and the products of their labor, if not used in the institution, are sold by the department at competitive prices to other agencies.

Petitioner's next argument is addressed to the point that "there is nothing inherent in the nature of a prisoner's status which compels the exclusion of the union from the coverage of a law such as the Taylor Law." Thus, prisoners are not specifically excluded from the law's definition of "public employee" as are, for example, members of the state militia.

Proceeding from its premise that prisoners are employees of the state, petitioner further contends that Article I, Section 7 of the New York State Constitution, providing that "employees shall have the right to organize and to bargain collectively," mandates the extension of negotiating rights under the Taylor Law to the prisoners. Along this line, petitioner alleges that recent court decisions cited in its brief have broadened the constitutional rights of prisoners, extending to them the right of assembly, the right to petition the government for redress of grievances, the right to free exercise of religion, and other First Amendment rights. It has been held, according to petitioner, that the enjoyment of these rights is subject to restriction only upon evidence of a clear and present danger to prison security or of substantial interference with orderly prison administration. From these developments, petitioner concludes that the Green Haven prisoners have an unfettered constitutional right to union representation because the state has failed even to interpose a claim of interference with prison security or discipline. Moreover, contends petitioner, the formation and operation of a prisoners' labor union would be a constructive innovation for both the state and the prisoners because it would be a medium for securing the existence of a harmonious relationship heretofore lacking.

The petitioner's final point is to discount the significance of Sections 79 and 79(a) of the state civil rights law, which revokes the civil rights of prisoners sentenced to life imprisonment ("civil death") and suspends the civil rights of those imprisoned for a lesser term. Petitioner attacks this as an archaic holdover which, in any event, is irrelevant to a proceeding like the instant one involving as it does the exercise of constitutional, and not merely civil, rights. As petitioner puts it:

> [C]ertification is but another method, adopted by the legislature in the Taylor Law, of enforcing and regulating the constitutional right to form a union and to negotiate collectively. Both the prisoners and the state can benefit from having the exercise of this right so protected and regulated.

The state vigorously denies that prisoners, because of their work activities, are employees of the Department of Correctional Services, or "public employees" under the Taylor Law. It takes the position that the work programs in which prisoners participate simply carry out the rehabilitative mission of the department.

The state argues that the recent deletion of the "hard labor" requirement from Section 171 of the Correction Law was merely a technical change. In support of this proposition, it relies upon language in the Governor's memorandum regarding L. 1970, Chap. 476 which amended Section 171 and other sections of the Correction Law.

Moreover, according to the state, the Correction Law itself contains evidence that the legislature did not, through the amendment of Section 171, mean to establish an employment relationship between the department and its prisoners. Section 470 of that law provides retirement benefits for department employees, defined as "any person[s] employed under the commissioner. . . ." It is hardly to be expected, argues the state, that the legislature would have intended prisoners to benefit from this provision, yet such would be the consequence of a finding that they enjoyed employee status in the department. Further, the labor law in general, and specifically the protections afforded therein, has been held inapplicable to prisoners in *Beale* v. *State of New York,* 46 N.Y.S.2d 824 (Ct. Cl. 1944).

The state also disagrees with the petitioner that a de facto employer-employee relationship exists. Such a relationship historically results from a wholly voluntary agreement between two parties. The necessary element of volition is missing in the present situation even though prisoners can accept or refuse work. The state has determined that its rehabilitative program will best be served by permitting prisoners the option of working or remaining idle. Prisoners thus have a choice about working only because the state has deemed it advisable to give them one; the state could decide, even within the permissive framework of the existing Section 171 of the Correction Law, to adopt a different work system. The option, in reality, is the state's, not the prisoners'. Similarly, employees receive "compensation" in furtherance of the Correction Law's rehabilitative goals, not because the state must fulfill its part of a contract for hire.

Directing its attention to the application of the Taylor Law to prisoners, the state argues that a finding that prisoners are "public employees" would be incompatible with the stated public policy of the law. As expressed in Section 200, the law exists "to promote harmonious and cooperative relationships between government and its employees and to protect the public by assuring, at all times, the orderly and uninterrupted operations and functions of government." But, says the state, "the only 'function of government' in which the inmates of Green Haven participate is that which is embodied in their own incarceration"; furthermore, all their activities "are entirely incidental to the maintenance by the state of a correctional system designed to facilitate the return of the inmates to the community."

As further evidence that the legislature did not intend that prisoners be "public employees," the state calls attention to the following dilemma. All persons in the service of the state (except the militia) are specifically included in the "civil service" of the state under Civil Service Law Section 2.5. Pursuant to Article V, Section 6 of the state Constitution, appointments and promotions in the "civil service" are to be made according to merit and fitness based upon competitive examinations as far as practicable. The state thus concludes that "the Civil Service Law itself reduces petitioner's argument to absurdity."

The *amici curiae* address their brief to the argument that formation of a union representing prisoners is in the public interest and will promote the policy objectives of the Taylor Law. The following language from their brief aptly summarizes this position:

> The formation of the prisoners' union at Green Haven will promote the stated goals of the Taylor Law and is welcome. It is welcome because it furthers the public interest in securing peaceful resolution of labor disputes; because it is a positive step toward stemming the ever-rising tide of prison riots; because it promises to promote the meaningful rehabilitation of criminal offenders. Unionism and collective bargaining are capable of sufficient adjustment to accommodate the special conditions which the status of being a prisoner imposes upon state prisoner employees. And it is in the interest of the people of New York State in a far more vital way that promising rehabilitative methods be tried than that the present failing status quo in corrections be perpetuated.

DISCUSSION

The Taylor Law propelled public employment labor relations in the state into the mid-twentieth century. Public and private employees had for years prior to 1967 enjoyed the constitutional right to organize and bargain collectively through representatives of their own choosing. However, in the absence of a statute obligating public employers to negotiate with recognized or certified employee organizations, practical implementation of this constitutional guarantee was dependent upon a public employer's whim.

With the advent of the Taylor Law in 1967, collective negotiations for public employees became an enforceable reality. Briefly stated, it required for the first time that public employers negotiate and enter into written agreements with incumbent employee organizations over terms and conditions of employment. Mandatory impasse resolution procedures were included to assist parties who were unable to reach agreement at the negotiating table. In addition, the prohibition against strikes by public employees was continued.

The immediate beneficiary of the Taylor Law, the "public employee," is defined in Section 201.6(a) as "any person holding a position by appointment or employment in the service of a public employer. . . ." The state of New York is specifically designated in Section 201.6(a) as a "government" or "public employer."

The instant case, apparently one of first impression in this country, raises expressly or by implication fundamental policy questions in the area of criminal justice. However, the sole issue presented for decision herein is a narrow one: is a prisoner in a state correctional institution who performs work while incarcerated "holding a position by . . . employment in the service of a public employer" and therefore entitled to the protections and privileges of the Taylor Law? . . .

The Taylor Law provides a working definition, not an exact equation, for ascertaining who is a "public employee." In deciding whether particular persons or classes of individuals are encompassed within the definition, traditional concepts of employees status deserve consideration as do the realities of the working relationship. . . .

I have previously stated that the Taylor Law definition of "public employee," as set forth in Section 201.7 "does not appear to be used in an all-embracing sense." Two New York Court of Appeals decisions interpreting the scope of the term "employee" in the Workmen's Compensation Law offer significant assistance in further construing the Taylor Law.

Goldstein v. *State of New York,* 281 N.Y. 396, 401 (1939), presented the question of whether service in the National Guard constituted employment by the state, thus making the volunteer an "employee" under the Workmen's Compensation Law. The court of appeals answered the question in the negative, as follows:

> It seems to us to be apparent that the statute was never intended to cover militiamen while engaged in active service. There are many reasons which lead to that conclusion.
>
> Working men and women, employees of others, under our system of government are free men and women. They have the same standing, rights, and privileges possessed by other members of our body politic. They may work or not according to their own free will. If engaged in work they may quit working at any time if they desire without liability therefor unless prevented by the terms of some express contract. They may organize labor unions for the purpose of improving their working conditions. They may engage in strikes against their employers to compel their employers to grant them certain rights or privileges which they deem themselves entitled to. They may even engage in peaceful picketing of their employers' places

of business to induce their employers to grant them the rights which they claim.

Upon the other hand, when a man becomes a member of the state militia he must, when in active service, surrender for the benefit of the state certain of the privileges enjoyed by working men who are employees. . . . Members of the state militia do not become members for the purpose of receiving the small per diem allowances awarded them by the state while they are in active service. . . . It seems clear that one who joins the state militia and is engaged in active service therein is in no sense an employee of the state. He is simply performing a duty which he owes to the sovereign state as a resident and citizen. It makes no difference whether he does that voluntarily in time of peace or in response to the call of the Governor in time of trouble.

The parallels between *Goldstein* and the instant case are striking. Neither the Taylor Law nor the Workmen's Compensation Law contains a definitional answer to the issue, thus inviting reference to traditional usage. By tradition, an employment relationship requires a working commitment freely given, not one performed out of legal or moral compulsion. Volunteer National Guardsmen are not free agents because their service is hedged with special regulations and restrictions not shared by other (nonmilitary) individuals, and their "volunteer" status derives from the performance of "a duty which the volunteer . . . owes to the sovereign state as a resident and citizen." Prisoners are confined in the custody and care of the state following conviction for a crime. The circumstances of their confinement, by definition, restrict and regulate their freedom of movement, of decision, and of independent action. The fact that prisoners may now choose to work or remain idle does not transform them into free agents, for all functions which they perform are still a consequence of their confinement. . . . The work programs in which they participate have rehabilitation as their optimum goal. Thus, the "service" the state derives from the work of prisoners is incidental to the service the state is performing for society and for the prisoners in advancing their rehabilitation. Given these parallels, *Goldstein* provides clear precedent for finding that prisoners are not "public employees" under the Taylor Law.

The second illuminating case, *Matter of Toomy* v. *New York State Legislature,* 2 N.Y.2d 446 (1957), involved the application of the same term in the Workmen's Compensation Law ("any employment by the state . . .") to services rendered by a member of the State Assembly. The court of appeals, in holding that such services were outside the statute, pointed out that the concept of "public official" was traditionally "repugnant" to the concept of "employee" and found special significance, therefore, in the fact that the duties of members of the legislature were omitted from the law. . . . *Toomy* instructs that specific evidence of legislative intent must exist to justify a statutory construction reconciling two such customarily hostile concepts as "employee" and "public official." Similarly, the concepts of "employee" and "prisoner" have an inherent repugnance. Thus, without express legislative sanction there can be no basis for reading the term "public employee" to include prisoners. . . .

Indeed, it is highly doubtful that the legislature even contemplated such a possibility. Section 209(a) of the Taylor Law forbids employers and employee organizations from engaging in certain conduct under penalty of committing an improper practice. One such improper practice is the unilateral imposition by an employer of terms and conditions of employment. But, following tradition, the state enjoys the right (subject to constitutional considerations) to exercise control over all tangible aspects of prison life.

Thus, a finding that prisoners are "public employees" would result under the law as now structured in a severe curtailment of this traditional prerogative and a concomitant transfer of significant powers to prisoners. Such a radical restructuring of the criminal justice system should not spring forth full-grown like Athena from the head of Zeus.

The above considerations warrant a finding that prisoners do not come within the definition of "public employee" in the Taylor Law. As the ensuing discussion will reveal, the petitioner's specific arguments to the contrary are not persuasive.

Petitioner's first argument rests on the Correction Law itself. By definition, it is claimed, the legislature has established an employment relationship between the prisoners and the department, and through it the state. Proper evaluation of the currently applicable Correction Law provisions regarding prisoner labor requires an examination of that statute prior to the 1970 amendment to Section 171.

Authorization for prisoner labor comes from Article 3, Section 24 of the state constitution which, since 1938, has read as follows:

> The legislature shall, by law, provide for the occupation and employment of prisoners sentenced to the several state prisons, penitentiaries, jails, and reformatories in the state; and no person in any such prison, penitentiary, jail, or reformatory shall be required or allowed to work, while under sentence thereto, at any trade, industry or occupation, wherein or whereby his work, or the product or profit of his work, shall be farmed out, contracted, given, or sold to any person, firm, association, or corporation. This section shall not be construed to prevent the legislature from providing that convicts may work for, and that the products of their labor may be disposed of to, the state or any political division thereof, or for or to any public institution owned or managed and controlled by the state, or any political division thereof.

The legislature implemented this mandate through a number of provisions of the Correction Law, most importantly for this case Article 7, headed, "Labor in Correctional Institutions." Prior to its 1970 amendment, Section 171, then entitled, "Prisoners to Be Employed; Products of Labor of Prisoners," required the "commissioner of correction" and other officials to "cause all the prisoners in the state correctional institutions and such penitentiaries who are physically capable thereof, to be employed at hard labor. . . ." That section also fixed the prisoner work week ("not to exceed eight hours of each day, other than Sundays and public holidays"). Section 183 ordered the commissioner "to employ the prisoners . . . in occupations in which they will be most likely to obtain employment after their discharge. . . ." Section 187, entitled "Earnings of Prisoners," authorized, but did not mandate, the payment of "compensation for work performed"; however, for those prisoners who were paid, the department was required to prepare "graded wage schedules . . . based upon classifications according to the value of work performed by each."

In 1970, the "hard labor" requirement in Section 171 was replaced by the following language: "The commissioner of correction . . . may cause inmates . . . to be employed. . . ." This was the only substantive change in Section 171 or any of the other above noted provisions of the Law.

Analyzing these sections of the Correction Law, the petitioner concludes that the legislature has deliberately created an employment relationship between prisoners and the department. It relies particularly upon the fact that the legislature chose to use the concept of "employment" rather than of "occupation" in carrying out the constitutional mandate, selected the terms "compensation" and "graded wage schedule," and has now made the performance of work by prisoners a matter of choice rather than compulsion. The petitioner's conclusion is not warranted.

Both the constitution and Article 7 of the Correction Law omit any mention of the words "employer" and "employee," the most obvious and specific words of art to use in establishing the existence of such a relationship. Further, as the above chronology reveals, legislative use of the words "employed" (Section 171), "employ" (Section 183), and "compensation" and "graded wage schedules" (Section 187) dates to a time when "hard labor" was legislatively mandated for prisoners. Penal servitude and "employee" status are in any normal sense mutually exclusive conditions; the former denies, while the latter demands, the exercise of free will. Reason and logic thus preclude any finding that the legislature, in characterizing penal servitude prior to 1970 as being "employed at hard labor," or in directing the commissioner to "employ" prisoners in certain occupations, thereby forged a contract of hire and an employment relationship. To the contrary, these words make sense only if interpreted to mean "put to work," "occupied," or "used." Similarly, in the context of compelled labor, the words "compensation" and "graded wage schedules" carry no connotation of "employee" recompense; they merely signify the concept and manner of token payments for participation in a rehabilitative program.

Quite obviously, none of these words assumed a different meaning in 1970 simply because the legislature dropped the "hard labor" requirement in favor of a provision giving the commissioner the option of causing prisoners to be employed and determining what form of work they should do. The particular formulation used by the legislature is also significant. The commissioner was not empowered "to employ" them as he chose but only to "cause them . . . to be employed." Thus, no new forms of the term "employ" were introduced into the law by this amendment.

In any event, the existing evidence regarding the genesis and purpose of the amending legislation conclusively demonstrates that no radical departure, such as would be the case if "employee" status were being conferred on prisoners, was intended by its passage.

. . . It is instructive to contrast the language of the Correction Law concerning the work experience of prisoners on prison premises (that is, those involved herein) with that used in Article 26, the addition to the Correction Law in 1969 authorizing "work release" programs. Under such programs, eligible inmates may leave the prison premises during the day for a variety of functions (Section 851.3). Of particular interest in this proceeding is Section 855, entitled, "Application of Labor Laws," which provides that the laws of the state "with respect to employment conditions shall apply to inmates participating in work release programs." By this specific action, the legislature demonstrated its awareness that inmates did not enjoy any of the perquisites of employee status and that its specific intervention was needed to remove this disability. The absence of any similar provision from the 1970 amendment to Section 171 can only indicate legislative intent not to create an employment relationship for inmates working in the prisons.

The New York Civil Rights Law looms as a further impediment to the conclusion urged by petitioner. Section 79(a) revokes the civil rights of all inmates serving a life term, while Section 79 suspends them for the duration of sentence in the case of all inmates serving a lesser term. The right to enter into such a contract of hire would seem to be one such right denied inmates. . . .

Accordingly, for the reasons set forth above, I conclude that the Correction Law has not granted to prisoners "employee" status and thus has not established an employment relationship between prisoners and the department or through it the state.

As its second argument, petitioner urges that an examination of the facts of the prisoners' present working experience in the light of traditional tests of employer-employee status reveals the existence of a de facto employment relationship. I agree with petitioner, as I have previously noted, that traditional concepts and the practical realities of the situation are proper sources of inquiry in construing the term "public employee" as it appears in the Taylor Law. Nevertheless, . . . I once again disagree on the merits with the petitioner.

The record, as the petitioner points out, shows that prisoners may choose whether to work or remain idle; they may request but not demand a work assignment; prisoners working or studying, or unassigned through no fault of their own, are paid a daily wage on a graded wage scale; those working receive time and a half for overtime and may receive incentive payments; and prison authorities control work performance.

These factors do not exist in isolation, however. The programs of work or study in which prisoners are engaged seek to accomplish their rehabilitation, as the 1968 committee report makes clear; even when unsuccessful in that endeavor, they still are intended to amount only to methods of utilizing inmate time for constructive purposes. The primary nexus between prisoners and the state is a custodial, not a work, relationship; the latter is incidental to the prisoners' incarceration. How then could it be said, absent specific authorization, that in working they hold positions by "employment in the service of a public employer?"

Finally, of significance is the fact that participation in these programs has been made voluntary only to the extent of accepting or rejecting the assignment made by prison authorities. A prisoner cannot reject the assignment and look elsewhere for work; he must in that situation remain "idle" and unpaid. In reality, then, an element of compulsion does still characterize the work experience.

CONCLUSION

For the reasons set forth above, I find that prisoners are not "public employees" as defined in the Taylor Law. I thus have had no occasion to pass upon petitioner's remaining arguments concerning the constitutional rights of prisoners as "employees" to organize and bargain collectively; or the many arguments of the amici curiae . . . devoted to proving why collective negotiations for prisoners would benefit the prisoners. These penological and sociological arguments, to bear fruit, must be presented to the lawmaking arm of the state; the significant and complex public policy questions which they raise can only be resolved by appropriate legislative action.

Accordingly, the petition herein should be, and hereby is, dismissed.

Dated: December 18, 1972   /s/ Paul E. Klein
      Albany, N.Y.   Director of Public Employment
                                  Practices and Representation

Discussion Questions

1. What influence does the New York Civil Rights Law have on the decision in this case?
2. As a matter of public policy, do you feel that prison inmates should be granted organizational and collective bargaining rights?
3. Was the judicial rationale in the *Goldstein* and *Toomy* cases relevant to a determination of the basic issue in this case? If so, how?
4. What single most important characteristic of a traditional employment relationship is missing here?

Section 5. Determination of the Proper Public Employer(s)

Two apparently conflicting state statutes separated in time by nearly a quarter of a century posed several jurisdictional questions for resolution by Michigan's highest court. One concerned statutory jurisdiction over labor relations, and the second concerned which public employer among several county agencies would properly represent public management in the development of collective bargaining relationships with county employees.

Civil Service Commission for the County of Wayne v. Wayne County Board of Supervisors and Wayne County Labor Relations Board *and* Wayne County Board of Road Commissioners[6]
State of Michigan Supreme Court

BEFORE THE ENTIRE BENCH. *Per Curiam.* Two admittedly conflicting statutes compete in litigious depth for jurisdiction over the process of collective bargaining by Wayne County employees with their employer (or employers). As two courts already have come to know in painful and dissentient succession (see *Wayne County Civil Service Commission* v. *Wayne County Board of Supervisors*, 22 Mich. App. 287), the competition presents that most difficult of all appellate problems: the ascertainment of legislative intent when there is no evidentiary or other reasonably authoritative guide to pertinent meaning or purpose of the legislators. . . .

The first of these competing statutes P.A. 370 (1941); MCLA 38.401, *et seq.;* CL 38.401, *et seq.* (1948); MSA 5.1191(1) stated and now states expressly its purpose. Section 1 thereof reads, in full:

> Section 1. Civil Service Act; purpose. The purpose of this act is to guarantee to all citizens a fair and equal opportunity for public service; to establish conditions of service which will attract officers and employees of character and capacity, and to increase the efficiency of the county governmental departments, commissions, boards, and agencies, by the improvement of methods of personnel administration.

The second of these statutes P.A. 379 (1965); MCLA 423.201, *et seq.;* MSA 17.455(1) correspondingly stated and now states the legislative purpose; this time by a redesigned title of that which previously was known as the Hutchinson Act of 1947 (No. 336). The new title:

> An act to prohibit strikes by certain public employees; to provide review from disciplinary action with respect thereto; to provide for the mediation of grievances and the holding of elections; to declare and protect the rights and privileges of public employees; and to prescribe means of enforcement and penalties for the violation of the provisions of this act.

A majority of three judges of the circuit court concluded that "the employer of all county employees is the county of Wayne and that the board of supervisors is the legally constituted body authorized to act for and on behalf of the county as the public employer." As for the status of the defendant Wayne County Board of Road Commissioners and its employees, the same majority ruled "that the Wayne county road commission is *not* an employer separate and distinct from the county of Wayne, *and that the public employer is the county of Wayne,* acting through and by the Board of Supervisors." . . .

On appeal a majority of the assigned panel of the Court of Appeals ruled that plaintiff Wayne County Civil Service Commission is possessed of statutory power to classify positions in the county employment service and to submit uniform pay plans for the standardization of salaries but does not have exclusive control over such classification and standardization, since all such must be approved by the County Board of Supervisors. To its reasoning the panel, having finally made a judgment, added this declaration of heartfelt relief (p. 299):

> While this is not the simplest solution to the difficult problem with which we are faced, and though it may even tend to confuse and complicate the area of collective bargaining within Wayne County, it is the only plausible solution under the confines of the present statutory law.

This court granted leave (383 Mich. 782) to settle if possible what was regularly termed below a "chaos of legislation."

The plaintiff Civil Service Commission contends that Act 370 has made it the exclusive bargaining agent for all employees of the county of Wayne, subject only "to concurrence of the Board of Supervisors on salaries and wages," and that it is entitled to a judicial declaration that "collective bargaining shall be conducted by the Civil Service Commission for all county employees and in accordance with the requirements of Act 370."

The defendant County Board of Supervisors, searching the involved statutes in somewhat greater depth, contends that

> 3. Act 379, to the extent that it places rates of pay, hours of work, and other conditions of employment of public employees, including employees of Wayne county, into the area of collective bargaining supersedes *pro tanto* those provisions or parts of Act 370 dealing with the same subject matters.

Finally, the defendant Wayne County Board of Road Commissioners, depending in part upon a separate constitutional provision and statute, contends that it is the "public employer" of its own employees for the purposes of Act 379.

Having arrayed these contentions for scrutiny, our ensuing views doubtless will be understood better by an outset declaration of specific decision. We disagree with the stated position of the plaintiff Civil Service Commission. We agree with what in our view is the generally dispositive contention of the defendant Wayne County Board of Supervisors, and we agree finally with the stated position of the defendant Wayne County Board of Road Commissioners.

First. To read the act of 1941 carefully, in conjunction with the act of 1965, is to understand the judicial difficulty. The earlier act was conceived and enacted immediately after the people had adopted the Civil Service Amendment of 1940, effective January 1, 1941 for state employment. . . . Designed as that act was for adoption by counties having a *population of 300,000 or more,* the measure strove in applicable terms to provide the same rights for employees of such counties, and the same betterment of public service in such counties, as the people had just approved hopefully with respect to the state service. In neither instance could collective bargaining by public employees have been in the minds of the people, or of the legislators. The thought of strikes by public employees was unheard of. The right of collective bargaining, applicable at the time to private employment, was then in comparative infancy and portended no suggestion that it ever might enter in—the realm of *public* employment.

However, the act of 1941 brought within its purposefully inclusive as well as exclusive purview "all positions not specifically included by this act in the unclassified service." . . . Then, by Section 27, headed, "Scope," it provided that *all* of its declared aims should apply to the employees of *all* boards, commissions, and departments of each statute-adopting county. So, upon adoption of the act by Wayne County, there came into being a Wayne County Civil Service Commission, the authority of which in important if not exclusive part extended to control of the relation of public employer and public employee within the county.

The view taken here of these separate statutes is that they cannot be harmonized. . . . The attempts and counterattempts made below do not prove that premise. In the course of our review of the act of 1965, the conviction grows that it did not occur to the legislators that the manifestly well thought out provisions of the act would both encroach upon and impair, to some extent, the previously assigned authority and duty of a civil service commission operating under the act of 1941, and that serious trouble might arise on account of that fact.

The drafting and enacting legislature of 1965 . . . did not foresee what since has come to pass. It did not include that needed exclusory clause or proviso, as Judge Fitzgerald noted (22 Mich. App. 287, 294), and therefore left no specific evidence of intent either way. In the words of Cardozo, we are left to *guess* what the 1965 legislature would have done had the point come to attention, and our *guess* is that it would have advised all established county civil service commissions as we now do by today's judgment.

This is not to say that the act of 1965 repeals outright the act of 1941. Respecting as always our long since declared and regularly maintained rule that repeals by implication are not favored, and that it is only when the two measures in view are so incompatible that both or all cannot fully stand, we can only find that this is a striking instance for application of that rule which, back in 1877, was written into the court's opinion of *Breitung* v. *Lindauer,* 37 Mich. 217, 233 (1877):

> The rule is that the latter act operates *to the extent of the repugnancy,* as a repeal of the first, or, if the two acts are not in express terms repugnant, yet if the latter *covers the whole subject of the first,* and contains new provisions showing that it was intended as a substitute, it will operate as a repeal.

In short shrift this means that the purposed thrust of the act of 1965, that of prohibiting strikes by public employees and providing collective bargaining, negotiation, and enforced mediation of labor disputes arising out of public employment coming within the scope of the act, must be implemented and administered exclusively as provided therein. Hence, the original authority and duty of the plaintiff Civil Service Commission was diminished *pro tanto,* by the act of 1965, to the extent of free administration of the latter according to its tenor.

Second. Thus far, in the course of this litigation, that status under the act of 1965 of specific divisions or classes of Wayne County employees has not been pleaded or considered. There is one exception. It was decided in circuit this way:

> It is our conclusion, therefore, that the Wayne County Road Commission is not an employer separate and distinct from the county of Wayne, and that the public employer is the county of Wayne, acting through and by the Board of Supervisors.

This ruling was reversed by Division 1, 22 Mich. App. 297, 298. Our reasons for agreeing with Division 1 are much the same as were written there by Presiding Judge Fitzgerald.

While not alone of controlling force, it is of piquant moment to recall that the quoted determination in circuit was filed March 12, 1968, and that within 104 days thereafter an apparently galvanized legislature added two new subsections to Section 10(a) of Chapter IV of the county road law (MCLA) 224.10(a); MSA 9.110 and provided immediate effect thereof. The first of these subsections (5) communicates an extra measure of legislative purpose in near double compound. It proceeds:

> (5) Nothing in this section shall prohibit or restrict a board of county road commissioners who have prior to January 1, 1968 entered into a collective bargaining agreement from participating in a pension or insurance program for those of its employees who are members of a collective bargaining unit, as determined pursuant to Section 13 of Act No. 336 of the Public Acts of 1947, as added, being Section 423.213 of the Compiled Laws of 1948, which complies with and is established under the then existing requirements of Section 302(c) of the National Labor Relations Act, as amended, 29 U.S.C. 186(c), and the applicable provisions of the internal revenue code, notwithstanding the failure of such pension or insurance program to (a) provide benefits in the form of endowment policies or annuities, (b) provide benefits within the dollar limitations of this section, (c) provide benefits in accordance with the conditions of eligibility of this section, (d) provide for vesting of benefits before the employee commences retirement, or (e) provides for coverage of employees outside the bargaining unit covered by such collective bargaining agreement.

From as far back as 1909 P.A. 283, Section 10 of the county road law has authorized each board of county road commissioners to "employ" its necessary "servants and laborers." This section leaves no doubt of original and present intent that each board of county road commissioners shall be the employer of its employees, and that such employees shall be employees of that same board.

Such are our reasons for previously declared agreement with the defendant road commission that it is, within the act of 1965, the "public employer" of its employees and it alone is the duty bound employer particularly within the meaning and purpose of Section 15 of the act of 1965.

To Summarize and Restrict

1. Our instant rulings are limited to

(a) Determination that the plaintiff Civil Service Commission has no lawful part in the administration, directly or indirectly, of the act of 1965, and

(b) Determination of the independent status under the act of 1965 of the county road commission and its employees.

2. This action was instituted under GCR 1963, Section 521, to obtain a declaratory judgment. It seems to have been tried summarily, without testimony and upon the pleadings and stipulations of the parties. Necessarily the main and probably controlling question, considered in division "First" above, was the focal point of inquiry. Excepting as found above, the status if any of other divisions or classes of county employees, under the act of 1965, was *not* considered and now is *not* determined.

3. Further litigation may indeed be necessary to settle the status of other such divisions or classes. Whatever the fact in that regard, it is believed that our central holding above will permit the warring agencies of Wayne County government to proceed more comfortably with their respectively assigned legislative functions.

Reversed in part and remanded for further proceedings consistent with the foregoing declaratory views. No costs.

Discussion Questions

1. Under the provisions of 1965 P.A. 379, who is the "public employer" required to recognize unions as exclusive representatives of employees in the service of Wayne County?
2. Is there more than one "public employer" in the county government? If so, who are they?
3. Which body of the county government has the right and responsibility to carry out the requirements of Act 379 in determining adequate bargaining units and the recognition of exclusive agents of employees?
4. Which body of the county government has the right and responsibility to represent the county in matters dealing with the establishment of salaries, wages, and terms and conditions of employment of employees in the classified service?

5. Has Act 379 terminated or otherwise modified the power and authority of the Civil Service Commission under Act 370?

CHAPTER 1

1 51 *Government Employee Relations Reporter* 211 (Washington, D.C.: Bureau of National Affairs, Inc., 1971).

2 Milton Derber, "Who Negotiates for the Public Employer?" *Perspectives in Public Employee Negotiations,* Public Employee Relations Library (Chicago, Ill.: Public Personnel Association, 1969), p. 54.

3 68 Labor Cases 52, 767–768 (Chicago, Ill.: Commerce Clearing House, Inc., 1972).

4 21 GERR 5065–5068 (RF-22) (Washington, D.C.: Bureau of National Affairs, Inc., 1971).

5 GERR (No. 486) E1–E6 (Washington, D.C.: BNA, Inc., Jan. 15, 1973).

6 GERR (No. 393) E1–E3 (Washington, D.C.: BNA, Inc., March 22, 1971).

2 | Appropriate Bargaining Unit Determination

IN both public and private employment, before recognitional rights are to be conferred on a labor organization, there must be a determination as to precisely which classifications of employees will be represented in the collective bargaining process. Unit determination is the term used to describe the procedure of delineating the scope or parameters of the employee group to be so served. Moreover, meaningful collective negotiations require that the employee representative be brought face-to-face with the management representatives who will be dealing authoritatively with the problems to be discussed. Therefore, appropriate units should lie within some ascertainable organizational boundary, within which the management representative can make authoritative decisions on a significant range of probable topics for negotiation.

Several important differences characterize bargaining structures in public and private labor-management relations. Prasow thus explains the reasons for the dissimilarities:

> Broad uniformity is traditional in public sector employment. In private industry, however, a major factor that has made for narrow units has been the competitive nature of the industry. Management and employees faced with different market constraints must remain relatively free to consider their separate problems. In the public sector, however, with the treasury uniformly governing all financial aspects of the situation, the problem of competition between different groups in the industry is not a factor. Also, in both the private and the public sectors, employee election districts often have been influenced largely by strategic consideration of the employer and the union. That is, unions and management have traditionally maneuvered for larger or smaller units primarily to improve their chances of success in the election. If management prefers a certain group to win the election, it may favor a unit size that would result in a successful election of that union or association. Thus, the size and composition of the unit may have an important bearing on who wins the election.[1]

37

The Twentieth Century Fund Task Force on Labor Disputes in Public Employment has recommended that the broadest possible unit in public employment "consistent with viable negotiations should be provided. Serious distortions in public services can occur if one agency or department negotiates cost items without regard to other agencies and departments under the same budgetary or taxing authority." [2]

In the private sector, the NLRB, following the guidelines set by Section 9(b) of the Labor Management Relations Act, determines whether the appropriate unit shall be "the employer unit, craft unit, plant unit, or subdivision thereof." However, the statute allows the board considerable latitude in its interpretations because there is no requirement that the bargaining unit be the "*only* appropriate unit, or the *ultimate* unit, or the *most* appropriate unit; the act requires only that the unit be 'appropriate.' " [3] Wellington and Winter argue that this flexibility is not relevant for the public sector:

> The National Labor Relations Board long ago held that a bargaining unit need only be *an* appropriate unit rather than *the* most appropriate unit. Even though state public employee relations statutes seem greatly influenced by the private sector analogy and do not explicitly nullify this long-standing rule, the feasibility of its use in the public sector has been challenged. . . .[4]

One such challenge occurred under New York's Taylor Law, where a bargaining unit must meet the following qualifications before it will be approved by the New York State Public Employee Relations Board (PERB). First, the employees involved must have a community of interest. Secondly, the public employer at the level of the unit must have the authority to agree or to make effective recommendations with respect to the terms and conditions to be negotiated. Attilio Di Pasquale has made the following comment with reference to the New York experience:

> It is reported that the PERB has construed this statutory criterion to require the designation of as few units as possible, consistent with the overriding requirement that employees be permitted to form or join employee organizations of their own choosing.[5]

Stated differently, the PERB policy is that the fragmentation of public employer's employees into small units is to be avoided. To avoid fragmentation, the board has adopted the "most appropriate unit" policy.

This differs significantly from the approach in the federal government adopted under Executive Order 10988. In that order any unit, so long as it was appropriate under the community-of-interest guideline, was to be approved, even though more appropriate units might be conceived. For example, this policy led to the "albatross" of fragmented units that now threatens to blunt managerial effectiveness in the Navy Department.[6]

Small, fragmented units were recognized under the old executive order when the scope of bargaining was considerably narrower than it is today.

In the private sector, the NLRB has established certain criteria for determining whether a particular unit is appropriate. Among the principal variables considered are the following: the similarity of duties, skills, wages, and working conditions of the employees; the pertinent collective bargaining history, if any, among the employees involved; the extent and type of union organization; the employees' own wishes in the matter; and the appropriateness of the units proposed in relation to the organizational structure of the company itself.[7]

Presently, in the federal service, one of the criteria established by Section 10(b) of Executive Order 11491 for the determination of an appropriate bargaining unit for purposes of exclusive recognition indicates that "a unit may be established on a plant or installation, craft, functional, or other basis which will ensure a clear and identifiable community of interest among the employee concerned . . . ." Any unit should include individuals who have skills, working conditions, common supervision, or functions, in common to such a degree that it makes sense for them to deal collectively with management through a single voice. Conversely, no unit can be appropriate if its members are so divided by different interests arising from their work, skills, or functions that it is unreasonable to assume that they can speak with a single voice. The interests of the employees should be of prime importance in unit determinations. Employees in the same or closely related jobs and employees having similar wages, hours, and working conditions have the same collective bargaining interests. The purposes of the present executive order apparently will be realized most fully if the employees grouped in the unit have a mutual interest in the objects of collective bargaining to be sought by the labor organization that will represent them in negotiations. One expert in public sector labor relations goes so far in these remarks as to predict that national unit bargaining will be the trend of the future:

> It is all too easy to say that the existing units are appropriate considering the limited scope of bargaining, since there is not now bargaining over wage rates or pensions on an agency-wide or government-wide basis and there, is, therefore, little harm in establishing units on a departmental or agency basis. But what will happen when the scope of bargaining is expanded, as it will be some day, along the lines established under the postal corporation act. Will it be possible at that time to establish broad occupational units, or at least, agency-wide units so that you would have the equivalent of national bargaining on such items as salaries, pensions, welfare plans, vacations, holidays, and sick-leave policies? [8]

In fact, as a subsequent case will demonstrate, the trend toward national units at the federal level has already been initiated.

Municipalities are also confronted with the difficult task of proper bargaining unit determination. Once again the basic problem to be resolved involves the decision that fragmentation of bargaining units will or will not be preferable to the establishment of broad all-inclusive units. The experiences of Philadelphia and New York City graphically demonstrate the consequences of following the very broad or narrow unit model. One observer has noted that

In Philadelphia, all city employees, with the exceptions of police, fire, teachers, and transit workers, were established in one bargaining unit, represented by the American Federation of State, County, and Municipal Employees (AFSCME). This was a very broad unit of approximately 50,000 workers. In sharp contrast, New York City has approximately 900 bargaining certifications of employee organizations; hundreds of which are established on the basis of job title alone. These job classifications are grouped into about 200 different bargaining relationships with about 90 different employee associations representing these employees. It is little wonder that the Office of Collective Bargaining in New York City says the task of restructuring negotiation units will be a difficult and time-consuming one for many years.[9]

Another basic problem area concerns the inclusion or exclusion of certain occupational classifications in a bargaining unit. In the private sector the NLRB will usually rule that plant guards, watchmen, supervisors and foremen, managerial and confidential employees, and professional employees are to be excluded from units of production and maintenance workers. At the federal government level, Section 10(b) seems to draw from private sector experience by excluding from the proposed bargaining unit any management official or supervisor, employees engaged in personnel work in other than a purely clerical capacity, guards, and both professional and nonprofessional employees, unless a majority of the former vote for inclusion in the unit.[10] If an individual participates in decisions that affect personnel by making or implementing policy or does "effectively recommend important actions with respect to personnel in such matters as promotion, transfer, discipline, pay increases, and the like," [11] he will be termed a managerial or executive employee not eligible for inclusion in the same bargaining unit with the employees he regulates.

With respect to the status of supervisory employees, this writer has previously made the following comments:

The inclusion of supervisory employees in bargaining units is apparently more complicated in the public sector than in private employment. Spokesmen for some public employee organizations, particularly in the uniformed services, in education, and in some employee associations, suggest that the conventional distinction between the functions of management and employees which prevails in the private sector is not applicable in public service. They argue that supervisors in public employment have a community of interest with the employees they supervise which outweighs any conflicts of interest they might have in the direction of the work force.[12]

The cases in this chapter will explore various aspects of unit determination questions at the federal, state, and local levels previously discussed here.

Section 1. The Community of Interest Test

Of the following four cases, two involve law enforcement personnel at the county and municipal levels and two concern federal government employees. In the county case, the rationale of the hearing examiner will be examined and immediately thereafter the decision of the state employment relations commission that affirmed his ruling will be described. These decisions involve the determination of appropriate bargaining units. The reader is invited to note similarities and differences in the standards that are applied.

In the Matter of

Defense Supply Agency, DCASR Boston–Quality Assurance (activity) *and* **National Association of Government Employees, Local R1–202 (petitioner)** *and* **American Federation of Government Employees, AFL–CIO, Local 1906 (intervenor)**

Case No. 31–4300(EO)[13]

(United States Department of Labor before the Assistant Secretary for Labor–Management Relations)

SUPPLEMENTAL DECISION AND DIRECTION
OF ELECTION

Upon a petition duly filed under Section 6 of Executive Order 11491, a hearing was held in this case. Thereafter, on May 7, 1971, I issued my decision and remand, in which I affirmed the hearing officer's denial of the intervenor's motion to present evidence challenging the adequacy and validity of the petitioner's showing of interest and in which I remanded the case to the appropriate regional administrator to reopen the record solely for the purpose of receiving evidence concerning the appropriateness of the unit sought. On June 8, 1971, a further hearing was held before Hearing Officer Anthony D. Wollaston. The hearing officer's rulings made at the reopened hearing are free from prejudicial error and are hereby affirmed.

Upon the entire record in this matter, including the facts developed at both hearings, I find

1. The labor organizations involved claim to represent certain employees of the activity.

2. The NAGE seeks an election in a unit of all employees of the Defense Contract Administration Services Region Boston–Quality Assurance Directorate, Operations Division, of the Defense Supply Agency, excluding those employees located at the Boston Army Base, 666 Summer Street, Boston, Massachusetts, management officials, employees engaged in federal personnel work in other than a purely clerical capacity, professional employees, and supervisors and guards as defined in the order.

The Defense Supply Agency was established on October 1, 1961, and is responsible for providing supplies and services used in common by the military services. Defense Supply Agency facilities are located at strategic points throughout the country, with its headquarters located in Alexandria, Virginia. These facilities include supply centers, distribution depots, service centers, and Defense Contract Administration Services Regions.

The Defense Contract Administration Services Region (DCASR), Boston, Massachusetts, was established in August, 1965. The mission of a DCASR is to provide contract administration services in support of, among others, the Army, Navy, Air Force, and the Defense Supply Agency. The DCASR, Boston, is under the direction of a regional commander, who is a commissioned officer in the Navy stationed at Regional headquarters located at 666 Summer Street, Boston, Massachusetts.

The DCASR, Boston, is divided geographically into a headquarters operations area in Boston and two districts. Eight plant offices, located at the plants or facilities of suppliers, and four area offices, are subordinate to the headquarters and the two districts. Functionally, the DCASR, Boston, is divided into several offices and directorates. One of the directorates is the Directorate of Quality Assurance, which contains five divisions, including the Operations Division.

Quality assurance employees are responsible for insuring that the quality of commodities produced by a contractor complies with the standards outlined in the procurement contract. There are approximately 250 employees, including quality assurance representatives and clericals, in the petitioned for unit of the Operations Division. These employees work in approximately 120 locations outside of Boston regional headquarters, are classified as quality assurance specialists and quality inspection specialists, and their grades range from GS–7 for quality inspection specialists to GS–9 or GS–11 for quality assurance specialists. There are resident and nonresident types of employees within this group. The nonresident employees, although assigned to a duty station, travel on a regular schedule to a number of plants within their own area. The resident quality assurance employees are assigned to certain areas while others are assigned to offices in particular plants of contractors and, as a rule, do not travel. All quality assurance specialists engage in similar duties and are under common supervision. Those who are employed in offices located in particular plants also report to a Defense Contract Administration Services Office (DCASO) plant chief who is in charge of the offices of the particular plant and who reports directly to the regional commander. There is one central personnel office located within the regional headquarters from which administrative matters, work assignments, and a central payroll originate. The record reveals that there is transfer and interchange of the quality assurance employees among the various locations.

The record indicates that on November 13, 1967, the activity accorded exclusive recognition to the AFGE, covering the same unit as that petitioned for herein by the NAGE. On December 27, 1968, the activity and the AFGE entered into a negotiated agreement. At the hearing held on March 23, 1971, the parties agreed that the NAGE's petition was filed in a timely manner and that there existed no agreement bar to any election which might be directed.

The parties do not dispute the appropriateness of the unit sought, nor was any evidence offered by the parties to establish that the claimed unit would not promote effective dealings and efficiency of agency operations within the meaning of Section 10(b) of Executive Order 11491.

Under all the circumstances, I find that the employees in the unit sought have a clear and identifiable community of interest in that they share the same general working conditions and salary schedules; have common supervision; engage in similar duties; and are subject to transfer and interchange among the various locations of the division.

Accordingly, I find that the following employees constitute a unit appropriate for the purpose of exclusive recognition under Executive Order 11491:

All employees of the Defense Contract Administration Services Region Boston–Quality Assurance Directorate, Operations Division, of the Defense Supply Agency, excluding those employees located at the Boston Army Base, 666 Summer Street, Boston, Massachusetts, employees engaged in federal personnel work in other than a purely clerical capacity, professional employees, management officials, and supervisors and guards as defined in the order.

DIRECTION OF ELECTION

An election by secret ballot shall be conducted among the employees in the unit found appropriate, as early as possible, but not later than forty-five days from the date below. The appropriate area administrator shall supervise the election, subject to the assistant secretary's regulations.

Eligible to vote are those in the unit who were employed during the payroll period immediately preceding the date below, including employees who did not work that period because they were out ill, or on vacation, or on furlough, including those in the military services who appear in person at the polls. Ineligible to vote are employees who quit or were discharged for cause since the designated payroll period and who have not been re-hired or reinstated before the election date. Those eligible shall vote whether they desire to be represented for the purpose of exclusive recognition by National Association of Government Employees, Local Rl–202; or by American Federation of Government Employees, AFL-CIO, Local 1906; or by neither.

Dated: August 31, 1971   /s/ W. J. Usery, Jr., Assistant Secretary of
       Washington, D.C.   Labor for Labor–Management Relations

Discussion Questions

1. Which factors in this case were considered to have satisfied the community of interest standard used to determine the appropriate bargaining unit?
2. List the occupational categories to be excluded from the bargaining unit.
3. What is the objective of the NAGE petition?

In the Matter of

Bergen County Board of Chosen Freeholders (public employer) *and*
Bergen County Detectives and Investigators Association (petitioner)

Docket No. RO–88

(State of New Jersey before the Public Employment Relations Commission)

HEARING OFFICER'S REPORT
AND RECOMMENDATIONS

. . . The petitioner seeks to represent a unit of detectives and in-vestigators employed in the prosecutor's office in the county of Bergen. The employer takes the position that such a unit is inappropriate and that the appropriate unit should include all law enforcement personnel employed by the county.

. . . On or about February 17, 1970 the petitioner requested recognition as the exclusive negotiating representative for the employees in the requested unit. On that date the public employer orally refused to grant such recognition. Accordingly, a question concerning representation exists and the matter is appropriately before the commission.

The public employer is a county in the northern part of New Jersey. It is administered by the Board of Chosen Freeholders and its agent, the County Administrator.

The county employs among others approximately 48 in the prosecutor's office, 6 weights and measures investigators, 88 sheriff's officers, 73 court attendants, 107 county traffic police, 18 in the Identification Bureau in the sheriff's office, and 14 sergeants-of-arms at the district court. The appointing authority in all cases is the Board of Freeholders. All personnel matters are based upon specific recommendations made by the prosecutor, the sheriff, the chief of county police, the supervisors of the Weights and Measures Department and by the judge of the district court. Each of the aforementioned submits its own departmental budget requests to the freeholders, who make the final decision. All salaries are paid from the same fund. Personnel records are kept in a central location. There is a uniform schedule of all fringe benefits, that is, vacations, sick leave, and so on, for all county employees. There is no history of collective negotiations as the freeholders have used meetings at budget time with the representatives of the various groups on a sounding board basis only.

The prosecutor's office is under the supervision of the county prosecutor, who is appointed by the Governor with the consent of the Senate. It contains one first assistant, ten assistant prosecutors, several clerks, one chief of detectives, two captains, four lieutenants, seven county detectives and seventeen investigators. There are also twenty-one employees on "lend-lease" from the police department, four from the sheriff's department, and two on leave of absence from other police departments. The employees on "lend-lease" receive their instructions from the prosecutor's office and on a day-by-day basis are responsible to him. They are paid by their old department, that is, the police department or sheriff's office, though they are not under their control in any way. Lend-lease personnel have been with the prosecutor's office for anywhere from four months to two years.

The men from the prosecutor's office are divided into six groups. Their work is mostly of an investigatory nature of alleged crimes. The matter under investigation may be initiated from the prosecutor's office or it may be the result of a preliminary investigation performed by police of the various municipalities within the county or the county police. In any event, the final investigation is performed by the prosecutor's office, at which time a determination is made as to whether or not to present the matter to the grand jury for possible indictment. If an indictment is returned, the detective and investigator may assist the assistant county prosecutors in the actual preparation for trial.

The county police department is mostly responsible for traffic control in the county. Occasionally they do preliminary investigation of a crime and then turn the matter over to the prosecutor's office. This investigatory work that is performed is similar to the work done by the several communities within the county. The police department is under the supervision of the chief of police. If a superior officer is lend-leased to the prosecutor's office he takes his assignment from personnel in that office regardless of his rank.

The sheriff's department is supervised by the sheriff. Its main duties are (1) to keep order in the court, (2) to act as guards in the county penitentiary, and (3) to act as process servers in civil matters. The Identification Bureau within the sheriff's office is composed of technicians who are responsible for identifying fingerprints and other evidential matters that may be useful in the investigation and trial of a criminal matter. This office also contains files concerning other related matters. The prosecutor's office is the bureau's best customer though the prosecutor's office occasionally uses the facilities of the FBI. Also employed in the sheriff's department are employees designated "Sheriff's Office Assigned Detectives," who perform under direction varied investigational and other work involved in the detection and apprehension of criminals.

The weights and measures employees have the responsibility to inspect and check all types of weighing and measuring devices in the county. They do not carry a hand weapon. If they find a violation of a statute or a town ordinance, they file a complaint similar to a traffic summons which is processed by the prosecutor's office.

The aforementioned departments have their own supervisors. The county detectives, investigators, and lend-lease personnel assigned to the office report to the prosecutor. The police department has its own chief of police. The sheriff's officers including those who work in the courts, as process servers and as prison guards, report to the sheriff. The weights and measures personnel are under the supervision of the county freeholders. The sergeants-at-arms are under the supervision of the judges.

The county prosecutor's office is in the court house. The police department employees report to the police department which is in a different location than the court house. The sheriff's employees report either to the county jail, the old county jail, or the court house. The police department is an around-the-clock operation as is the sheriff's department operation at the penitentiary. The members of the prosecutor's office are theoretically to work from 8:30 to 4:30 but, in fact, depending upon the case load and the matter under investigation, work much longer. The sheriff's department employees who act as process servers may be required to work at night to serve papers.

The sheriff's employees assigned to the court house work when court is in session. In the summertime, when they are not needed in the court house, four to ten of them have been assigned to the prosecutor's office to work as investigators. Occasionally, when a raid is planned and additional personnel is needed, members of the several departments are combined.

County detectives and county investigators are covered under the "County Detectives and County Investigators Act (Revision of 1959)." This act provides in part that the prosecutor may appoint county detectives who upon their employment shall be in the classified service of civil service. The act also provides for the creation of the position of county investigator which shall be in unclassified service and who serves at the pleasure of the county prosecutor subject to removal by him at any time.

The lieutenant and the captain in the prosecutor's office supervise the *work product* of the investigator and detective and the lend-lease personnel. They do not hire, fire, or discipline. They may not and have never *effectively* recommended any of the aforementioned. They may make such recommendations, but the chief of detectives would then perform his own investigation and make his recommendation to the first assistant county prosecutor who may, in turn, make his own investigation and recommendation to the prosecutor who, in turn, makes his recommendation to the freeholders when necessary. The chief of detectives is also responsible for the clerical staff. His recommendations as to any personnel matter with that group are followed by the first assistant prosecutor and the prosecutor without any additional investigation. Both the chief, the first assistant prosecutor, and the prosecutor may suspend an employee up to five days without a hearing. Accordingly, I find that the chief of detectives is a supervisor *within the meaning of the act* but that the captain and/or lieutenant are not (emphasis supplied).

The public employer takes the position as stated above that the only appropriate negotiating unit within Chapter 303 is all positions within law enforcement of the county. It would include personnel in weights and measures, the sheriff's office, the county police department, the Identification Bureau, the prosecutor's office, and the sergeant-at-arms in the county district law court. Petitioner, on the other hand, takes the position that even though the prosecutor's office is classified as law enforcement, it is entirely different from any of the groups as proposed by the employer; that the jobs are different; that the responsibilities of the job required are far different; and that the appropriate unit is the county detectives and the investigators employed in the prosecutor's office excluding lend-lease personnel.

The act does not require the commission to find the *most* appropriate unit or the *only* appropriate unit but calls for a finding that, after giving due regard for the community of interest among the employees concerned, a unit is *an* appropriate unit. In the instant case there is a community of interest among all law enforcement personnel employed in the prosecutor's office including lend-lease personnel, lieutenants, and captains but excluding the chief of police and all other personnel.

Those employed in the prosecutor's office have a similarity of duties, requiring distinct skills and working conditions. The day-by-day control of operations and managerial functions is within the prosecutor's office. There is little or no contact with other county personnel and a minimum of interchange. The promotional ladders for the employees, supervisory hierarchy, and immediate common supervision are unique to the prosecutor's office. Though employee benefits are at present identical, such benefits were unilaterally promulgated prior to the enactment of Chapter 303, Laws of 1968, and is therefore inapposite.

Concerning the lend-lease personnel, I shall pierce the civil service regulation veil and include them in the unit. They have a community of interest with the detectives and investigators in the prosecutor's office. There is in fact no difference between them and county investigators.

Accordingly, based upon the foregoing and the record as a whole, I recommend that an election be directed among all law enforcement personnel employed by the Bergen County Board of Chosen Freeholders in the county prosecutor's office including captains, lieutenants, and lend-lease personnel, but excluding office clerical, professional and craft employees, managerial executives, the chief of detectives, supervisors within the meaning of the act, and all other county employees.

Dated: December 24, 1970 /s/ Howard M. Golob
            Trenton, N.J.   Hearing Officer

DECISION AND DIRECTION OF ELECTION

. . . The commission has considered the entire record, the hearing officer's report and recommendations, and the exceptions and, on the facts in this case, finds

.   .   .

3. The board has refused to recognize the association as the exclusive negotiating representative for certain of its employees; therefore, a question concerning the representation of public employees exists and the matter is properly before the commission for determination.

4. Petitioner seeks to represent a unit of all detectives and investigators employed in the Bergen County prosecutor's office. The employer contends that the unit sought is inappropriate because it includes supervisors and because the only appropriate unit would include all law enforcement personnel in Bergen County. The hearing officer recommended that an election be directed in a unit of "all law enforcement personnel employed

by the Bergen County Board of Chosen Freeholders in the county prosecutor's office including captains, lieutenants, and lend-lease personnel, but excluding office clerical, professional and craft employees, managerial executives, the chief of detectives, supervisors within the meaning of the act, and all other county employees. . . ."

5. No exceptions were filed to the finding of the hearing officer regarding the unit placement of lieutenants, captains, and the chief of county detectives. His recommendations that the lieutenants are not supervisors within the meaning of the act and captains are not supervisors within the meaning of the act are adopted *pro forma.*

6. The employer takes exception to several elements of the hearing officer's report. First, it excepts to the hearing officer's approach to the unit question, that is, his view that the act does not require a finding of the most or only appropriate unit, but merely a finding that the unit be appropriate. The employer posits, for argument's sake, the appropriateness of both the unit found by the hearing officer and the unit claimed by the employer, then questions how a choice can be made in the absence of statutory guidelines, and finally concludes that logic dictates that the selection be made on the basis of the "most" appropriate unit. This approach presents an issue not involved in this case. The only issue there is whether or not the unit in which petitioner seeks certification is appropriate for collective negotiations. No party seeks to be certified in the "employer's unit" so there is no requirement to determine its appropriateness. Conceivably a unit sought by an employee organization may be found inappropriate and in so doing the unit contended for by the employer may by inference be considered appropriate. But that is not the case the employer argues. It attacks a selection between several appropriate units when in fact no such selection was made.

The commission is in basic agreement with the hearing officer's determination limiting the unit to law enforcement personnel within the prosecutor's office. In addition to certain factors cited by the hearing officer to support that conclusion, the commission especially relies on another significant factor, a statutory provision which makes the office of county prosecutor a unique one in an employer-employee relations context. N.J.S.A. 2A:158–1 provides for the appointment "for each county, by the Governor with the advice and consent of the Senate . . . some fit person . . . who shall be the county prosecutor. . . ." The expenses of the prosecutor, including his staff, are to be approved by the Board of Chosen Freeholders. However, N.J.S.A. 2A:158–7 provides

> The amount or amounts to be expended shall not exceed the amount fixed by the Board of Chosen Freeholders in its regular or emergency appropriation, unless such expenditure is specifically authorized by order of the assignment judge of the superior court for such county.

Thus, a county prosecutor, unlike the sheriff, the chief of county police, or any other county functionary within or outside of the area of law enforcement, has available to him an appeal from decisions of the board of freeholders. The prosecutor may request of the assignment judge funds beyond those provided by the freeholders, and the assignment judge is empowered to authorize additional expenditures. . . . As a consequence there exists a potential for treatment of employees in the prosecutor's office which differs from that accorded to other law enforcement personnel in the county regarding certain terms and conditions of employment. And in fact this potential has been realized, although not in this particular county.

It is our judgment that this factor, coupled with others cited by the hearing officer, justifies the conclusion that a unit of law enforcement personnel of the county prosecutor constitutes an appropriate unit.

On one aspect of the unit question the commission differs with the hearing officer, namely, his inclusion of so-called "lend-lease" personnel. Both parties take exception to that inclusion. As noted by the parties at the hearing, there was a suit then in progress relating to the validity of the arrangement whereby employees of the county police department were temporarily assigned for investigative work in the prosecutor's office. The Appellate Division of the Superior Court of New Jersey ruled on July 7, 1971 that such transfers had not been validly made because they ignored applicable civil service regulations. That decision would seem to remove lend-lease personnel as an issue. Those in the classified service, that is, county patrolmen and sheriff's officers, who had been temporarily assigned to the prosecutor, will presumably either return to their home department or submit to civil service regulations and qualify for permanent assignment in the prosecutor's office. As to the one individual from Palisades Interstate Park Commission and another from South Hackensack Police Department, it appears that they are not within the term "lend-lease." They are not considered to be on temporary assignment, but rather have been, so far as the employer is concerned and the testimony indicates, permanently assigned to the prosecutor's office and thus indistinguishable from other staff personnel not in dispute.

The remaining exceptions, all by the employer, have been considered and are found to be without merit. Thus, the employer contends that the hearing officer disregards evidence of the interchange of personnel between law enforcement units. Except for "lend-lease" personnel whose status was resolved above, the only evidence of interchange of employees between the prosecutor's office and other law enforcement personnel is that sometimes on an informal basis men have been made available for the purposes of raids. The employer also excepts to the hearing officer's finding that the county police department's principal function is traffic control. The record, especially the testimony of the first assistant prosecutor, clearly supports the finding. Finally, the employer claims the hearing officer ignored various factors which the employer contends demonstrate an inappropriateness of a unit limited to the prosecutor's office. It is clear from the hearing officer's report that he was aware of these factors and considered them; he found them insufficient to support the employer's contention, a treatment with which we agree. The employer concludes by way of argument that the hearing officer's recommendation, if followed, would adversely affect and otherwise substantially restrict law enforcement activities in Bergen County. This argument no longer has force so far as "lend-lease" personnel are concerned. To the extent it relates to the question of a limited unit versus a countywide enforcement unit, we find this conclusion to be unsupported by the record.

7. The unit appropriate for collective negotiations is "All law enforcement personnel employed by the Bergen County Board of Chosen Freeholders in the county prosecutor's office including captains and lieutenants, but excluding office clerical, professional and craft employees, managerial executives, the chief of detectives, supervisors within the meaning of the act, and nonpolice employees." . . .

By order of the commission.

Dated: April 6, 1972
   Trenton, N.J.

/s/ Charles H. Parcells
Acting Chairman

Discussion Questions

1. The commission did not explore the issue of whether the unit should be the *most* appropriate one possible. Discuss this omission.
2. What limitations were imposed on the scope of the bargaining unit?
3. What significance did the state statute dealing with the funding of the prosecutor's office have in the determination of the appropriate unit?
4. Why were the lieutenant and captain in the prosecutor's office considered nonsupervisory personnel while the chief of detectives was viewed as a supervisor?
5. Describe the duties of "lend-lease" personnel. Did the commission agree with the hearing officer's disposition of such personnel's bargaining unit status?

In the Matter of

City of East Providence, Police Clerks (employer) *and* **International Union of District 50, UMWA (petitioner)**

Case No. EE–1835

(State of Rhode Island and Providence Plantations, Providence, Sc. before the State Labor Relations Board, Rhode Island State)

DECISION

DIRECTION OF ELECTION

The International Union of District 50, UMWA, hereinafter called the petitioner, filed its petition, pursuant to the General Laws of Rhode Island, 28–7–16 (1956), as amended.

STATEMENT OF THE CASE

A hearing was duly held before the Rhode Island State Labor Relations Board of January 16, 1969. At the hearing, the International Union of District 50, UMWA was represented by Mr. William Foley.

The petition requested that the six people designated as police clerks working for the police department in the city of East Providence be organized as a bargaining unit.

The city solicitor for East Providence contended that the police clerks were not separate and distinct from the other clerks and the appropriate unit should be a unit comprised of all the clerks employed by the city of East Providence. The city of East Providence was not objecting to the petition filed by the union but to the unit that the petition was seeking.

Testimony regarding the duties of the clerks was given by the personnel director and the city manager of the city of East Providence in which they agreed that the duties of all the clerks in the city of East Providence are typing, answering the phone, and filing.

Mr. Richard F. Ogden, a representative for the police clerks, testified that he was a police clerk for the city of East Providence for a period of eight years; that the police clerks were required to wear uniforms and badges supplied to them by the city of East Providence; that they had to escort prisoners from their cells to different rooms in the police station for purposes of arraignment; that they had to relieve officers who were off duty and take the incoming complaints; that they needed licenses from the Federal Communications Commission in order to handle the radio calls; and that the police clerks worked on a rotating shift of forty hours a week while the other clerks worked a regular shift of thirty-five hours a week.

The police clerks are hired through the Division of Personnel which also establishes the qualifications for other classifications; for example, accountant clerks and clerk typists.

Prior to a recent survey by Yarger Associates, the police clerks were classified as Group 4. The Yarger report abolished the classification Group 4 and reclassified the clerks in the police department to police clerks. However, the qualifications and duties of the police clerks were not affected.

CONCLUSIONS OF LAW

1. The employer, the city of East Providence, is a municipal corporation duly organized under the laws of Rhode Island. The city of East Providence conducts no interstate business and makes no sales to points outside of Rhode Island. Said city qualifies as an employer and has its offices and principal place of business at City Hall, East Providence, Rhode Island.

2. The International Union of District 50, UMWA is a labor organization within the meaning of the provisions of the State Labor Relations Act, as amended.

3. That the clerks are hired through the Division of Personnel.

4. The duties performed by the police clerks are different from those performed by the clerks in other departments.

5. That all the police clerks, approximately six, within the police department of the city of East Providence, should be included in one unit and the request of the city of East Providence to include all clerks in one unit is denied. . . .

Entered as Order of the
Rhode Island State Labor Relations Board
Dated: January 28, 1969

/s/_____
Chairman

/s/_____
Member

/s/_____
Member

Discussion Question

1. As in the New Jersey case immediately preceding, the proponents of the narrower bargaining unit were sustained in their position. In this case what factors influenced the board's decision that the police clerks should be in a bargaining unit separate from the other clerical employees?

In the Matter of

Federal Aviation Administration, Department of Transportation (activity)[14] and National Association of Air Traffic Specialists (petitioner) and National Association of Government Employees (intervenor) and American Federation of Government Employees, AFL–CIO (intervenor)

Case No. 22–2145(RO)

Federal Aviation Administration, Department of Transportation (activity) *and* **National Association of Government Employees, Local R3–22 (petitioner)**

Case No. 20-2414(RO)

(United States Department of Labor before the Assistant Secretary for Labor–Management Relations)

DECISION, ORDER, AND DIRECTION OF ELECTION

. . . The hearing officer's rulings made at the hearing are free from prejudicial error and are hereby affirmed.

Upon the entire record in these cases . . . the Assistant Secretary finds

1. The labor organization involved claims to represent certain employees of the activity.

2. In Case No. 22–2145(RO), petitioner, National Association of Air Traffic Specialists, herein called NAATS, seeks a nationwide unit of all flight service specialists (FSS) employed at flight service and at international flight service stations, excluding all air traffic control specialists (ATCS) employed at centers and terminals, management officials, evaluation and proficiency specialists, teletype operators, electronic technicians, supervisory employees, employees engaged in federal personnel work, and guards. In Case No. 20–2414(RO), the petitioner, National Association of Government Employees, Local R3–22, herein called NAGE, seeks a unit similar to that sought by the NAATS but limited to FSS assigned to the Wilkes-Barre, Pennsylvania flight service station.

The NAGE and the American Federation of Government Employees, AFL–CIO, herein called AFGE, contend that the petition filed by the NAATS improperly includes the FSS covered by current negotiated agreements and the FSS presently included in units where a bargaining representative obtained exclusive recognition and/or certification as exclusive representative within the twelve-month period preceding the filing of the NAATS petition. The NAGE and the AFGE further contend that the NAATS petition is barred from including the FSS at each location where a valid election was held within the twelve-month period preceding the filing of the petition. In these circumstances, it is urged that the NAATS petition should be dismissed. The NAATS asserts that negotiated agreements which cover units which were established prior to the effective date of Executive Order 11491 do not constitute a bar to the inclusion of the employees in such units in its proposed broader unit because the appropriateness of those units was determined by the activity under Executive Order 10988 and not by the Assistant Secretary. The NAATS contends further that while it may be argued that negotiated agreements and certification and election bars preclude the inclusion of units established after the effective date of Executive Order 11491, in the circumstances of this case involving a petition for a nationwide unit, it would promote labor relations stability to invalidate the above-mentioned bars and include such units in its proposed unit. The activity did not take a position on the bar issues.

I. Alleged Bars to the NAATS Petition

The history of collective bargaining on an exclusive basis involving the activity's flight service stations is limited to stationwide units and, currently, the employees at 48 of the approximately 346 flight service stations are represented by exclusive bargaining representatives. The employees at 40 of these 48 facilities are represented by the NAGE and employees at the remaining 8 are represented by the AFGE. The record reveals that the activity and the NAGE are parties to current negotiated agreements which cover employees employed at the four facilities located at Boston, Massachusetts; Buffalo, New York; Morgantown, West Virginia; and Windsor Locks, Connecticut. In addition, the activity has current negotiated agreements with the AFGE which cover employees at the two facilities located at Fort Worth, Texas and Deming, New Mexico. The evidence establishes that the NAATS petition herein was not timely filed within the meaning of Section 202.3(c) of the Assistant Secretary's regulations, insofar as it encompassed employees included in the above-noted units covered by negotiated agreements, with the exception of the unit at Windsor Locks, Connecticut, where the agreement was executed subsequent to the filing of the petition.

Based upon a review of the negotiated agreements, I find that those negotiated agreements which were in existence at the time the NAATS filed its petition . . . constitute bars to an election in the units they cover. Thus, where, as here, a petition for a broad unit seeks to include employees who are already represented exclusively in an existing, less comprehensive unit and who are covered by an existing negotiated agreement, absent unusual circumstances not present here, I will not permit the existing unit to be disturbed based on the agreement bar principle. . . . Accordingly, I conclude that those exclusive employee bargaining units which were covered by negotiated agreements at the time the NAATS filed its petition herein may not be included in the unit sought by NAATS.

The evidence establishes that at the activity's facilities in Windsor Locks, Connecticut; Springfield, Missouri; Chicago, Illinois; La Crosse, Wisconsin; New Orleans, Louisiana; and Wichita Falls, Texas, the exclusive bargaining representative involved obtained exclusive recognition within the twelve-month period immediately preceding the filing of the NAATS petition in the subject case. In these circumstances, I find that in accordance with Section 202.3(b) of the Assistant Secretary's regulations, the NAATS petition was untimely filed with respect to the above-noted facilities. Thus, to disturb exclusive recognition status that has been in existence for less than one year would create, in my view, unwarranted instability and uncertainty in labor relations and, therefore, would be inconsistent with the purposes and policies of the executive order.

With respect to the remaining facilities of the activity covered by exclusive recognition and included within the NAATS petition, there is no evidence that the employee bargaining units at these facilities were covered by negotiated agreements at the time the NAATS filed its petition. . . . Moreover, it appears that exclusive recognition at these locations had been in existence for a period in excess of twelve months prior to the filing of the NAATS petition. Under these circumstances, I find the following policy is applicable in order to effectuate the purposes and policies of the executive order:

1. With respect to those exclusively recognized units in which the evidence establishes the existence of a collective bargaining history—that is, such units have been covered by negotiated agreements which either still exist or have recently expired—and establishes further that the NAATS petition was timely filed either in the "open period" of an existing agreement or subsequent to its recent termination, I am persuaded that employees in such units should have the opportunity to vote in a self-determination election. Thus, the employees in such existing units would vote whether or not they desire to continue to be represented in their unit by their current exclusive bargaining representative. If a majority indicate such a desire, their existing unit would remain intact. However, if a majority of these employees do not vote for the labor organization which represents them currently, their ballots would then be pooled with those of the employees voting in any unit found appropriate as a result of the NAATS petition herein.

2. With respect to those exclusively recognized units in which the evidence does *not* establish the existence of a collective bargaining history— that is, such units have not been covered by a negotiated agreement or a recently expired negotiated agreement—I am of the view that the appropriateness of such a unit for the purpose of exclusive recognition under the executive order may be considered, without regard to a prior grant of exclusive recognition, upon the filing of a petition encompassing that unit. Thus, if such exclusively recognized units are deemed to be inappropriate, the employees in these units would be included properly under the NAATS petition and, accordingly, would vote in any election conducted pursuant to

that petition, without regard to their prior inclusion in less comprehensive exclusively recognized units. . . .

II. Appropriate Unit

The activity contends that the appropriate unit herein should include all of the FSS at flight service stations and international flight service stations, as petitioned for by the NAATS, as such employees share a clear and identifiable community of interest and their inclusion in a single nationwide unit would promote effective dealings and efficiency of operation. The NAGE and the AFGE contend that there is a clear and identifiable community of interest among the FSS at the stationwide level and that the nationwide unit sought by the NAATS is inappropriate. They further contend that the unit sought by the NAATS is inappropriate because it excludes teletype operators. Additionally, the NAGE argues that a unit which includes all the FSS at flight service stations also should include the ATCS employed at combined station-towers and the AFGE contends that any nationwide unit of the FSS should include ATCS, as well as all clericals and evaluation and proficiency specialists. In this latter regard, the activity and the NAATS contend that the evaluation and proficiency specialists should be excluded from any unit found appropriate as managerial employees. Finally, the AFGE states that the unit sought by the NAATS is based upon its extent of organization as shown by the fact that it includes only the FSS and that the NAATS limits its membership to such employees.

The Federal Aviation Administration is engaged in providing for the safe and expeditious flow of air traffic. Its operations are divided into several operating divisions, including the Air Traffic Division, the division involved in this proceeding, which is responsible for supervising air traffic control towers, air traffic control centers, flight service stations, and combined station-towers. Control towers are located near airports and the ATCS employed therein are responsible for controlling the movement of air traffic within the immediate vicinity of the airports. Control centers are located along airway routes, and the ATCS employed therein are responsible for controlling the movement of air traffic between airports and over certain oceanic routes. Flight service stations, which employ approximately 3,312 FSS, are located from about 50 to 100 miles apart along airway routes, at landing areas, and similar locations, and are engaged in providing helpful information to the flying public on such matters as weather, favorable flight altitudes, and visual flight aids along flight routes. The service stations also contact the proper authorities in cases of actual or potential accidents, and initiate search and rescue missions for lost aircraft. In addition, these facilities receive flight plans for both visual and instrument flights and transmit them to the appropriate air traffic facilities. There are also combined station-towers which perform the functions of both control towers and flight service stations. The evidence reveals that the approximately forty-five combined station-towers are considered to be air traffic control facilities, as are the towers and centers, and that the specialists at these facilities are considered to be ATCS. The record indicates that while these employees spend about half of their time performing duties which are flight service in nature, the remainder is spent performing air controller functions for which only the ATCS are qualified.

The Air Traffic Division, which is headquartered in Washington, D.C., is divided into eleven regions, each of which is headed by a regional division chief. Each division chief is responsible for the operation of the control towers, control centers, and combined station-towers as well as the flight service stations located in his region. The division chief reports to a regional director, who is responsible for all of the activity's operating divisions in a particular region and who reports to the Federal Aviation Administrator at the national headquarters. Immediately beneath the division chiefs are the facility chiefs who supervise the day-to-day operations of the individual facilities. The facility chiefs may be aided by assistant chiefs, watch supervisors, and other supervisory personnel depending on the size of the work force. The record reveals that the flight service facility chiefs have the authority to make recommendations on employee personnel actions such as transfers, promotions, and demotions, but the final authority for such actions is vested at the regional level.

The activity's personnel, labor relations, and operating policies are determined at the national headquarters. The personnel policy is the same for all flight service stations and any differences that exist with respect to such matters as work shifts or vacation scheduling result from the demands of local conditions. The activity's personnel policy includes a national merit promotion plan for all employees, and although the regions have authority to develop guidelines for merit promotions, such guidelines are required to conform to the national policy. In addition, the activity has a national policy on working hours, and holiday and overtime pay, and while the application of the policy may differ from one facility to another, the evidence establishes that such differences are not permitted to deviate from the national policy.

The activity's national labor office is responsible for the activity's overall labor-relations program and it provides guidelines and instructions for the labor-relations offices which exist in each regional office. The national office aids the regions in resolving labor-relations problems, and participates in all collective bargaining negotiations along with representatives from the regions and facilities involved. While a national representative may or may not act as the spokesman during negotiations, all negotiated agreements, whether negotiated at the regional or facility level, are subject to approval by the national office.

As noted above, the FSS and the ATCS are classified as air traffic control specialists and are included in the same civil service classification series. Recruiting is carried out on a national basis and all recruits are hired at the same grade level and are required to attend the activity's training academy where the first three weeks of training are the same for all employees regardless of their ultimate assignment. Thereafter, the training is specialized for each of the two groups. The journeyman level for the ATCS is GS-13, whereas the journeyman level for the FSS at the service stations is either GS-9, -10, or -11, depending on the skills required at the particular facility.

There are substantial differences in the duties and skills of the FSS and the ATCS. Thus, the primary function of the FSS is informational and they are not "true" controllers as they do not control or separate aircraft as do the ATCS employed at the centers, towers, and combined station-towers. The FSS provide preflight information to pilots on flight conditions along their planned flight routes and they may provide information and advice to pilots in flight which may prove helpful in guiding them to a safe destination. However, any instructions they provide are strictly advisory. On the other hand, the ATCS employed at the towers, centers, and combined station-towers have the authority to control aircraft in flight and pilots operating under instrument flight plans are required to obey their instructions except in emergency situations. Further, the ATCS are required to be able to separate and direct the flight of aircraft through the use of radar, whereas the FSS are trained only in the use of weather radar.

The evidence establishes that the area of consideration for filling vacancies in the work force at a flight service station of the activity is generally at the facility level. However, the record reveals that there is a substantial amount of transfers of the FSS between flight service stations, most of which are occasioned by employees from stations with the lower journeymen grades transferring to those with a higher grade structure. There is also a certain amount of transfers between flight service stations and controller facilities because of a greater opportunity for advancement at those facilities than at the service stations. In this latter regard, the evidence established that the FSS who transfer from flight service stations to controller facilities may require as much as twenty months of training in controlling and separating aircraft through the use of radar and other electronic equipment before qualifying as ATCS, while any ATCS who transfer from control facilities to flight service stations require from six to nine months of training, depending on prior experience, before qualifying as FSS. The activity treats the FSS who seek to transfer between stations in the same manner as it does any other job applicants and those who transfer are required to achieve an area rating at their new duty station prior to their becoming fully accredited specialists. Those who transfer between flight service stations may achieve an area rating after a comparatively short period of from one to ninety days, during which time they become familiar with the terrain, landmarks, rivers, and other visual flight aids in the vicinity of their new duty station as well as equipment which did not exist at the former duty station.

The activity provides manuals for the FSS which differ from those provided the ATCS. It also provides for stricter and more frequent physical examinations for the ATCS than for the FSS. Further, in this regard, all of the activity's operating manuals, which set forth in detail the function of the activity's various air traffic facilities and the duties and responsibilities of the various employee classifications, are prepared and distributed from the national office. Moreover, the activity's program for training non-supervisory employees, as well as supervisors, is determined at the national level.

The record shows that the work force at most of the activity's flight service stations is restricted to the FSS and supervisors. However, thirty-three of the stations employ evaluation and proficiency specialists, while an indeterminate number of stations employ teletype operators and clericals. Also, electronic technicians work at the stations. The evaluation and proficiency specialists are assigned to the larger flight service stations and are charged with training, rating, and certifying the competence of the rank and file FSS. They make determinations as to the skills and competence of the FSS and make recommendations to the respective facility chiefs as to whether the employees evaluated should be trained, promoted, demoted, transferred, or dismissed. Also, they may serve as facility chief in his absence. The evidence established that the functions of the evaluation and proficiency specialists are performed by the facility chiefs at those stations which do not have such specialists.

Generally the teletype operators are employed only at the flight service stations which have more than fourteen professional employees. They work in the same area and under the same supervision as the FSS. They are classified as clericals and neither give any preflight assistance to the flying public, nor perform any of the other duties performed by the FSS. The duties of the teletype operators, which consist mostly of sending and receiving messages with teletype equipment, are performed by the FSS at stations which do not have such operators. The activity employs also an unspecified number of clericals at some of the flight service stations. They perform such functions as typing and filing. While these clericals work along with the FSS and under the same supervision, they neither give preflight assistance to the public nor do they perform any of the other functions of the FSS.

The activity employs also approximately 8,000 electronic technicians, who are responsible for maintaining the equipment at flight service and controller facilities. While some of these technicians perform their duties in areas normally occupied by the FSS and the ATCS, their supervision and duties differ from that of the FSS and the ATCS, and they do not perform any of the informational services performed by the FSS, or control functions performed by the ATCS. Moreover, electronic technicians are not in the same division of the activity as the FSS and the ATCS.

Based on all of the foregoing circumstances and noting the limitations discussed above with respect to agreement bar, certification bar, and recognition bar, I find that a unit comprised solely of the FSS at flight service stations is appropriate for the purpose of exclusive recognition. Thus, the record establishes that the FSS employed at flight service stations have skills which differ substantially from the skills possessed by all other occupational groups, including the ATCS, employed by the activity. Moreover, while the record reveals that the FSS have certain interests in common with other occupational groups which may be employed at flight service stations, such as teletype operators and clericals, it demonstrates that the FSS have overall interests which are separate and distinct from such employees. Thus, while teletype operators and clericals may perform some of the nontechnical functions which the FSS might perform in the absence of teletype operators and clericals, the evidence establishes that the recruitment and training of the FSS and the basic work they perform is distinct and different from that of the teletype operators and clerical employees. In addition, while the clericals and teletype operators may share the same supervision as the FSS, their grade structure and opportunities for advancement differ and follow different progressions. With respect to the electronic technicians, while the FSS in some instances work at the same physical location as these technicians, the record shows that by training, background, and job progression the two groups do not share such a community of interest as to require their inclusion in the same unit. With respect to the thirty-three evaluation and proficiency specialists, I find that the record establishes that these employees effectively evaluate the job performance of the FSS and that their duties place their interests more closely with personnel who formulate, determine, and oversee policy than with personnel in the proposed unit who carry out the policy. In these circumstances, I find that they are supervisory and/or managerial employees and, therefore, I shall exclude them from the unit found appropriate.

Finally, with respect to the ATCS, while there is some similarity in the training and skills of the FSS at flight service stations with that of the ATCS at the controller facilities, it is clear that their skills are not interchangeable. Thus, neither the FSS nor the ATCS can transfer between their two respective different types of facilities without a substantial amount of training. On the other hand, it is clear that the FSS may transfer between flight service stations with only a minimum amount of training. Further, the record establishes that the basic duties of the two groups differ substantially. Thus, the ATCS control and separate aircraft, whereas the FSS perform what is essentially an informational service for the flying public.

With respect to the question of the appropriateness of a nationwide unit, the record establishes that all of the FSS are recruited nationally, have similar skills, training, functions, and interests, and perform essentially the same kind of work on a day-to-day basis. Also, the skills of these employees at different service stations are interchangeable and the evidence reveals that a substantial number of FSS transfer between flight service stations. Moreover, there is one central training facility for all specialists and the program is established at the national level. In addition, the labor relations and personnel policies for the FSS are established at the national level. In this connection, although there may be variations in labor relations and personnel policies to conform to regional or local conditions, it is clear that variations are subject to approval by the national office. Significantly, the activity's labor relations policy provides that negotiated agreements, whether negotiated at the regional or station level, are subject to national approval.

In these circumstances, I conclude that the employees sought by the NAATS have a clear and identifiable community of interest and that such a unit will promote effective dealings and efficiency of agency operations. Accordingly, with the exception of those units of FSS in which the NAATS petition was filed untimely, or in which, as discussed above, separate self-determination elections are warranted, I find that the following employees constitute a unit appropriate for the purpose of exclusive recognition under Executive Order 11491:

> All air traffic control specialists, GS–2152 series, employed at flight service stations and at international flight service stations; excluding GS–21 series personnel employed at centers, terminals, and combined station-towers; GS–2152 series employees employed in flight service stations at Boston, Massachusetts; Buffalo, New York; Morgantown, West Virginia; Windsor Locks, Connecticut; Fort Worth, Texas; Deming, New Mexico; New Orleans, Louisiana; Springfield, Missouri; Chicago, Illinois; La Crosse, Wisconsin; and Wichita Falls, Texas; teletype operators, clericals, electronic technicians, evaluation and proficiency specialists, employees engaged in federal personnel work in other than a purely clerical capacity, other management officials and supervisors, and guards as defined in the order.

I also find that the unit sought by the NAGE in Case No. 20–2414(RO) consisting of all air traffic control specialists employed at the Wilkes-Barre, Pennsylvania flight service station is not appropriate. Thus, as noted above, the record establishes that the policies and regulations which affect the employees at Wilkes-Barre are established above the station level. Further, it is clear that the final authority for personnel and labor relations decisions, which affect the employees' terms and conditions of employment, is vested at a higher level of management. In addition, there is no history of collective bargaining at the activity's Wilkes-Barre facility and no evidence that employees at the facility have an interest different from that of other FSS of the activity in the unit I have found appropriate. In these circumstances, I find that the establishment of a unit on a station-wide basis would not promote effective dealings and efficiency of agency operations. Accordingly, and considering also the fact that the FSS in Wilkes-Barre will have the opportunity to vote in a more comprehensive unit, I find that the unit sought by the NAGE is not appropriate, and I shall order that its petition be dismissed. In connection with this latter unit determination, I find also that in the circumstances described above, exclusively recognized units of FSS encompassed by the NAATS petition, where there is no evidence of a collective bargaining history, similarly would be inappropriate.

ORDER

IT IS HEREBY ORDERED that the petition in Case No. 20–2414 (RO) be, and it hereby is, dismissed.

DIRECTION OF ELECTION

An election by secret ballot shall be conducted among the employees in the unit found appropriate as early as possible, but not later than forty-five days from the date below. . . .

Dated: December 27, 1971 /s/ W. J. Usery, Jr., Assistant Secretary of
      Washington, D.C.   Labor for Labor-Management Relations

Discussion Questions

1. Discuss the factors cited by the Assistant Secretary to support his ruling in favor of a national unit of flight service station specialists.
2. How was the NAGE petition at the Wilkes-Barre facility handled?
3. Why were teletype operators, clerical employees, and electronic technicians excluded from the FSS unit?
4. By what rationale did the Assistant Secretary decide on the inclusion or exclusion in the national unit of facilities where exclusive recognition had already been granted another labor organization?
5. What argument did the NAATS utilize against contract, election, and certification bars to their petition?
6. Did the activity take a position vis-à-vis the unit determination issue?

Section 2. Severance from an Existing Unit

In the private sector, the Labor-Management Relations Act (LMRA) allows the NLRB to conduct so-called craft severance elections that allow skilled craftsmen to disaffiliate themselves from broader units of production and maintenance employees in order to seek separate representation.[15] The NLRB utilizes a number of criteria in determining the validity of this bid for a separate identity, including the following: "The craft identity of the employees sought; the history of bargaining at the plant and in the industry involved; the degree of integration of the disputed employees in the employer's production process; past efforts on the part of the employees in the proposed unit to maintain separate identity and representation; the qualification of the petitioning union as representative of the type of craftsmen sought. . . ."[16] The next decision involves an attempt by a group of school nurses to break away from a bargaining unit of teachers with whom they share a common bargaining agent. The influence of private sector guidelines is ascertainable as the state's Employment Relations Commission overrules the hearing officer's recommendations. The second case, at the federal level, establishes the "Davisville" rule, whereby "carve-outs" from existing units are to be discouraged except in the most unusual circumstances.

In the Matter of

South Plainfield Board of Education (public employer) *and* **New Jersey State Nurses Association (petitioner)** *and* **South Plainfield Education Association (intervenor)**

Docket No. R–89

(State of New Jersey Public Employment Relations Commission)

REPORT AND RECOMMENDATIONS

A petition was filed with the Public Employment Relations Commission June 17, 1969 by the New Jersey State Nurses Association. Pursuant to a notice of hearing to resolve a question concerning representation of nurses of the South Plainfield Board of Education, hearings were held before the undersigned on December 2 and December 16, 1969 at which all parties were given an opportunity to examine and cross-examine witnesses, to present evidence, and to argue orally. Briefs were filed by two of the parties on January 28, 1970. Upon the entire record in this proceeding, the hearing officer finds

. . .

3. The public employer having refused to recognize the New Jersey State Nurses Association as the majority representative of the nurses employed by the South Plainfield Board of Education, a question concerning representation exists and the matter is appropriately before the undersigned for report and recommendations.

ISSUES

There are two main issues in this case: first, whether or not the petition is timely; second, if it is timely, do the nurses constitute an appropriate unit.

The act is silent with respect to the timeliness of petitions, although the rules and regulations of the commission do treat this subject. It should be noted, however, the August 29, 1969 effective date of the rules postdates the filing of the petition in this case by almost two and one half months.

Section 6(d) of the act does empower the commission "to resolve questions concerning representation of public employees" and to decide in each instance "which unit of employees is appropriate for collective negotiation. . . ."

Section 7 of the act provides the only specific guideline regarding appropriate units: "The negotiating unit shall be defined with due regard for the community of interest among the employees concerned. . . ."

TIMELINESS OF THE PETITION

The record indicates that negotiations between the public employer and the intervenor commenced in early November, 1968. On December 9, 1968, the public employer and the intervenor agreed upon the unit which was to be recognized. Nurses were included in the unit. On January 14, 1969, the board passed a resolution recognizing the South Plainfield Education Association as the majority representative for a unit which included teachers, nurses, and several other groups. At least up until this time, there was a nurse who attended some of the meetings including the meeting of January 14, 1969.

Apparently there was no question concerning the majority status of the education association at the time of recognition. The South Plainfield Education Association had represented the teachers for at least six or seven years. The board did not ask for authorization cards and the education association did not solicit them from their members. There is no evidence that the nurses did not want to be included in the unit at the time of recognition.

In November, 1968, when the education association made their first proposal to the board, they asked that nurses be placed on the teachers' salary guide. On January 14, 1969, the board negotiator made an offer with respect to nurses. The nurses were dissatisfied with this offer and urged the negotiating representative to attempt to get a better offer. Several meetings were held at which the salary guide of nurses was discussed. The education association attempted at least until March to negotiate a better guide for the nurses. These efforts were not successful. Finally, on June 11, 1969, a contract was signed by representatives of the board and the education association. The contract clearly covers nurses and it includes Schedule B, nurses' salary guide, which is incorporated by reference into the contract as is Schedule A, the guide for teachers.

In February, 1969—apparently because they were frustrated in their efforts to get a better guide—the nurses joined the New Jersey State Nurses Association. The education association agreed in March to release the nurses. This release was contained in a letter dated March 21, 1970 from Mr. Jayson, president of the education association to Mr. Harper of the state nurses' association. There is no evidence that the Board of Education was officially informed of this action until October 31, 1969, when Mr. Jayson wrote a letter to Dr. Vansant, superintendent.

The action of the education association may not have been completely consistent. On one hand, they released the nurses from the negotiating unit. On the other hand, they concluded and signed a collective agreement which covers the nurses.

It should also be noted that the contract was signed before the petition was filed, although it is true that the New Jersey State Nurses Association did ask for recognition on April 11, 1969.

The undersigned regards stability—but not inflexibility—as an important consideration in the development and implementation of the policy desired by the legislature when Chapter 303, Laws of 1968, was enacted.

To deny a recognized negotiating agent—such as the South Plainfield Education Association in the instant case—a reasonable opportunity to negotiate a contract after being recognized would not contribute to stability. This conclusion is not based upon the rules and regulations of the commission, which became effective August 29, 1969—several months *after* the petition in this case was filed. However, it is evident that the commission recognized this consideration because the rules which they did adopt do make provision for a protected period during which negotiations may take place following recognition.

Nevertheless, the hearing officer agrees with the petitioner that the rules should not be applied retroactively. To find otherwise would require a finding that the South Plainfield Education Association is *not* entitled to a protected period because the conditions precedent thereto set forth were not satisfied in this instance.

The Board of Education acted in good faith in recognizing the unit which included nurses. They signed this agreement which covered nurses. The majority representative of the employees also signed an agreement covering nurses.

The case cited by Mr. Harper on page 11 of his brief differs from this one in that, in this case, not only did negotiations take place, but an agreement was signed. Furthermore, the contract does contain substantive terms and conditions of employment. The only difference in coverage between nurses and teachers is the salary guide. All other items including the grievance procedure apply equally to teachers and nurses.

Based upon the above, the undersigned finds that the contract signed June 11, 1969 by the board and the education association should continue in effect. However, this finding does not preclude the possibility of a recommendation that an election be directed at some future time *if* the unit is found to be appropriate.

APPROPRIATE UNIT

We now turn to the question of whether or not the eight nurses constitute an appropriate unit.

Teachers and nurses have much in common. They share many aspects of the employment relationship. The two groups do have a community of interest and there is no apparent conflict of interest. In an earlier case, *Garfield Board of Education* v. *Garfield Education Association,* PERC, No. 16, the commission found appropriate a unit which included teachers and nurses.

However, this may not be the *only* appropriate unit. It is *an* appropriate unit. There are a number of factors which set the nurses off and make them a separate, recognizable group with a unity based upon factors unique to nurses. They must wear uniforms. They must be registered nurses. They are concerned primarily with the health of the students and with performing tests and other functions related thereto. The teaching that they do pertains to the health functions which they perform.

These facts do satisfy the undersigned that the nurses have a community of interest and that they do constitute an appropriate unit . . . .

Dated: March 26, 1970 /s/ Jeffrey B. Tener
      Trenton, N.J. Hearing Officer

DECISION

. . . The commission has considered the record, the hearing officer's report and recommendations, and the exceptions and, on the facts in this case, finds

.　　　.　　　.

3. The petition seeks to establish a separate negotiating unit for school nurses; they were previously represented by the intervenor in a unit of teachers, nurses, counselors, and librarians, pursuant to the employer's grant of recognition. The hearing officer found that the one-year contract, covering the unit above and executed before the filing of the instant petition, should be given effect for the duration of its term and thereby bar an election during its term. He further found, however, that school nurses could be separated from the existing contract unit and would constitute a separate appropriate unit unto themselves. He therefore recommended that an election be directed in a unit of nurses at a time following the expiration of the one-year contract. The employer excepts to the hearing officer's recommended unit finding. The petitioner also excepts, essentially on the grounds that the employer was notified, well in advance of the contract's execution, that the intervenor was relinquishing its status as negotiating representative for the nurses, that the nurses had designated a new representative, namely the petitioner, that the contract subsequently executed did not, and was not intended by intervenor to, cover nurses, and therefore it could not operate to bar an election in a nurses' unit during its term. In support of its position, petitioner notes the absence of objective evidence indicating that the intervenor ever represented a majority of the nurses and further notes that their inclusion within the unit recognized by the employer resulted solely from the intervenor's representation that the nurses were in the unit for which it had majority support.

After due consideration, the commission finds petitioner's exceptions to be without merit. Any attempt to cast doubt upon the validity of the employer's initial grant of recognition to the intervenor for a unit including nurses cannot be sustained. The hearing officer found, and there is no evidence to the contrary, that the employer's grant of recognition to the intervenor as majority representative was made in good faith. Furthermore, intervenor's president affirms that at the time of recognition no one questioned the absence of written authorizations from a majority of the employees: "everyone was obviously supporting this at this particular moment." The record is quite clear that what triggered the nurses' dissatisfaction was not a claim that they had never authorized the intervenor to negotiate for them, but that having agreed to this spokesman (by whatever means then sufficient for the purpose), they were no longer satisfied with the results achieved. It was then that they sought release from the teachers' association and representation by the nurses' association. But the employer, having granted exclusive recognition in good faith, pursuant to Chapter 303, was not obligated to yield to the nurses' request for severance. Nor was it obligated to recognize the intervenor's attempted disclaimer of representation for nurses. In the absence of a petition to this commission raising a question concerning representation, the employer, under the circumstances of this case, was free to pursue contract negotiations to a conclusion. The contention that the intervenor no longer spoke for the nurses and did not intend the contract to cover them is immaterial in view of the employer's refusal to depart from the boundaries of the recognition it had granted. Moreover, the contract does encompass nurses and no evidence of a contrary intent can operate to alter the express terms of the agreement.

The bilateral agreement of the parties to include nurses in the unit covered by the contract is not altered by the statement that the nurses will seek to appeal to this commission their inclusion in such unit. In the opinion of the commission, the statement regarding the nurses' intent to appeal is not a reservation by the signatories to the contract whereby the nurses' status is undetermined or held in abeyance pending the commission's determination.

This is not, therefore, a situation where the parties to this contract, the public employer and the South Plainfield Education Association, have inserted a unit reservation. Rather, the provision merely sets forth a fact relating to a third-party beneficiary of the contract. We do not construe this provision in the agreement as creating any infirmity in the binding nature of the contract relating to the nurses, nor do we conclude that this requires the granting of a severance election to the nurses.

It is axiomatic in labor relations that in determining an appropriate unit or in achieving an agreement, the specific wishes of each group may not always be satisfied. If the desires of each group of employees were to be given controlling weight, complete chaos would result since, in any appropriate unit, there are groups whose interests are of some variance to the total complement of the unit and there are employees or categories of employees who do not want the designated representative to represent them for purposes of collective negotiations. However, one of the principles of labor relations is that employees who are found to constitute an appropriate unit are governed by the contract negotiated by their exclusive negotiating representative. . . . The representative in seeking to meet the desires of the majority, in some instances, alienate a minority or may fail to satisfy the needs of some particular group. Were all such groups whose needs were not met permitted to obtain separate representation or none at all, the concepts of an appropriate unit of exclusivity of majority representation and of collective negotiations would soon disappear to be replaced by individual or group dealings. Whether this unit is one established by this commission or is one agreed upon by the parties to a contract is not material providing it is basically an appropriate unit. Thus, where as here, the parties to a contract have agreed upon an appropriate unit without a reservation, the existence of some dissatisfaction by members of the unit will not constitute a basis to separate or sever a dissatisfied group from an appropriate unit. . . .

The commission concludes, under all the circumstances of this case, that it is not appropriate to permit the separation of nurses from the contract unit. It is not enough to observe that nurses enjoy a community of interest among themselves. Any group having common qualifications, duties, and conditions of employment will meet this test. The issue is whether their interests are so distinct from those with whom they were formerly grouped as to negate a community of interest. It is true that a nurse's training and qualifications differ from those of a teacher but she is not limited thereby, for the school nurse functions in both the medical and educational spheres. And even where she performs purely medical duties, her professional service is directed toward the maintenance and betterment of the educational process, whether it be an annual physical examination or a home visit to determine the cause of a student's school behavior problem. The medical characteristics of the job are dominated by educational interests and integrated with the teaching process in order to achieve a common object, the education of students. In addition to this overriding interest, nurses share with teachers a variety of common conditions such as hours, fringe benefits, daily supervision by the school principal, as well as formal classroom instruction duties. Under all the circumstances, the commission concludes that the interests of the nurses are so closely related to the educational process that the factors distinguishing nurses from teachers are submerged in recognition of the broader community of interest shared by the two groups. Furthermore, in this case, the nurses have been included with the teachers for purposes of representation for approximately six years. This history of prior representation constitutes an additional factor in determining their community of interest. Accordingly, the nurses should not be removed from the existing unit. The petition is dismissed . . . on our finding that the nurses may not, under the facts in this case, constitute a separate unit.

By order of the commision.

Dated: August 28, 1970   /s/ William L. Kirchner, Jr.
      Trenton, N.J.   Acting Chairman

Discussion Questions

1. Why are the wishes of a group of employees toward a specific type of representation not allowed to be the controlling factor in unit determination cases?
2. The commission overruled the hearing officer's finding that the nurses could be severed from the existing unit. Discuss the rationale here.
3. For what reasons did the commission reject the contention of the state nurses' association that the education association was not the exclusive bargaining agent for the school nurses?
4. In your opinion, who presents the strongest argument, the commission or the hearing officer?
5. Why was the education association disclaimer of representation for the nurses rejected by the commission?

In the Matter of

United States Naval Construction Battalion Center (activity) *and* American Federation of Government Employees, Local 1422, AFL–CIO (petitioner) *and* National Association of Government Employees, Local R1–14 (intervenor)

Case No. 31–3246(EO) [17]

(United States Department of Labor before the Assistant Secretary for Labor–Management Relations)

DECISION AND ORDER

. . . The hearing officer's rulings made at the hearing are free from prejudicial error and are hereby affirmed.

Upon the entire record in this case . . . the Assistant Secretary finds

.   .   .

3. Petitioner seeks a unit composed of all nonsupervisory Wage Board employees at the United States Naval Construction Battalion Center, Davisville, Rhode Island, but excluding all management officials or supervisors, all employees engaged in federal personnel work in other than a purely clerical capacity, all guards, all professional employees, and all ungraded nonsupervisory Wage Board employees who are employed in the administration and comptroller, FASCO (Facilities System Office) and security departments of the activity. It is the petitioner's position that the employees it seeks to represent constitute an appropriate unit because they

have a clear identifiable community of interest in that they work under an identical wage system and have similar working conditions. Moreover, in most cases, they have similar skills and occupations. The petitioner also asserts that in the private sector the National Labor Relations Board has found appropriate similar separate units of clerical employees and production and maintenance employees.

The activity contends the unit sought by the petitioner is inappropriate because Wage Board employees do not constitute either a craft or a distinct functional group who have special interests sufficiently different from graded employees to warrant their severance from an existing unit that has been in existence since January, 1963. Its position is that ungraded and graded employees share a substantial community of interest which is shown by the fact they work together, many of them side-by-side, under common supervision and share common benefits. Further, the activity states that separate units will not promote effective dealings and efficiency of agency operations within the meaning of Section 10(b) of the executive order, but rather will lead to general labor unrest. In this regard, the activity believes separate units would necessitate separate contracts which may result in different working conditions, benefits, and personnel policies. In turn, this would tend to confuse employees and promote jealousy which would impair the efficient operations of the activity. Moreover, it is asserted that the present flexibility of assigning employees from one group to another, that is, graded to ungraded and vice versa, would be substantially curtailed if not eliminated.

The intervenor is in agreement with the activity that the unit sought by the AFGE is inappropriate. It points out that all the employees are currently covered by the same personnel offices, personnel policies, and the identical grievance procedures and that the work integration and work flow are such that the stability of the operation demands an activitywide unit. Further, in agreement with the activity, it points to the employees' community of interest and history of the parties' bargaining relationship which has produced stability in labor relations.

The activity is engaged in preserving, storing, and providing shipping facilities for mobilization, advance base stock, servicing naval construction units, and has facilities to provide engineering and technical services as required. Its operations are conducted at Davisville, Rhode Island. . . . The total employee complement consists of approximately 719 employees, which includes approximately 59 graded supervisors; 303 graded employees; 35 ungraded supervisors; and 322 ungraded employees. The chief office at the activity is the command office, which has under it 14 departments or offices, which in turn, depending on their size, are split into divisions, branches, or sections.

The employees who sought to be severed by the petitioner from the existing unit, with four individual exceptions, are concentrated in the Supply Department, where there are employed approximately 163 Wage Board employees, and the Construction Equipment Department, herein called CED, where there are employed approximately 155 Wage Board employees. The record also reveals that there are approximately 94 graded employees in the Supply Department and approximately 17 graded employees in CED.

CED consists of four divisions: Administrative Division; Production and Quality Control Division; Equipment Overhaul and Repair Division; and Transportation Equipment Maintenance Division. . . .

With respect to the work performed in CED, the record reveals the graded schedulers hand deliver their orders to ungraded inspectors, and schedulers and inspectors work together several hours a day. Further, in connection with their work, the schedulers contact Wage Board supervisors in the shop about the status of work and also talk to Wage Board mechanics in the shops about details of the work being done. Production scheduling clerks, who are graded, schedule equipment being processed through the shop and it is necessary that they have contact with ungraded employees. The graded preventive maintenance clerk schedules work that is to be done in the shop (primarily by ungraded employees), and handles calls such as tire and battery trouble calls and then transmits instructions directly to the tire man or battery man, who are ungraded, as the case may be. Ungraded employees in the repair and maintenance branches make contact with graded warehouse employees or supervisors when they go into the warehouse to work on equipment. After CED repairs or overhauls equipment, it is brought to the completed line from which it is taken to its ultimate destination by storage or supply area employees. Graded employees in the Supply Department have occasion to enter shop areas where ungraded employees work to check or search for equipment. Countermen, who are graded and who work in the Supply Department, come into contact with mechanics who are ungraded, when mechanics come to them for parts. The countermen and mechanics both work in the shops. A production controller, who is graded, works in the same office as the ungraded inspectors and has contact with the inspectors on a continuing basis as to the status of equipment.

With respect to working conditions in CED, the Wage Board employees generally work in shop areas which are as large as 100 feet by 100 feet, whereas the graded employees generally work in or out of offices. The shop areas are heated by steam heat with blowers and the office areas are heated by radiators. The office areas are cooled by fans in the summertime, but the only fan in the shop is located near the welders. Shop doorways open to the outside and, in bad weather when the doors are required to be open to let pieces of large equipment through, rain or snow may come through the door openings, whereas the office areas do not have this problem. Shop employees wear safety equipment when required. Some Wage Board employees, such as mechanics, wear coveralls or rent working clothes, but other Wage Board employees, such as inspectors, wear regular street clothes. The noise level in the shops is higher than that in the office areas and shop employees are subject to various fumes, but there are exhaust fans to carry these fumes out of the shops. However, fumes and element problems are not exclusive with Wage Board employees, as on occasion graded employees also work in the shops. Shop employees, in varying degrees, are subject to industrial accidents, and on occasion work in the shops requires climbing for both graded and ungraded employees. At times, shop employees are required to work outside in bad weather, although this work is kept at a minimum. The work in the shop areas is dirtier than that encountered by office employees, but both groups have wash-up time.

With respect to labor relations in CED, the record reveals that according to provisions in their agreement, the activity meets with NAGE representatives on a monthly basis. It is department policy that supervisors have the authority to settle grievances. On occasion, labor or personnel problems are taken up directly with the civilian head of the department, and in other instances, problems go to him if they are not resolved at a lower level. The evidence reveals that the majority of union complaints or problems involve Wage Board employees, although the procedures apply equally to graded and ungraded employees.

The second department in which the petitioner is seeking to represent employees is the Supply Department. This department is responsible for the receipt, storage maintenance, shipment, preservation, packing, and shipment of preposition war reserve stocks, and for outfitting the Atlantic battalions. It contains 8 divisions, 11 branches, and 14 sections, including 39 storage buildings, plus about 12 other office and work areas located throughout the base.

Although the Supply Department has a relatively large structure the record in the subject case is confined mainly to the functions of the Material Division, where both graded and ungraded employees are employed in the five following branches: Freight Terminal Branch; Storage Branch; Labor and Equipment Branch; Shop Stores Branch; and Packing and Preservation Branch. These five branches have a total of ten sections. . . .

The record reveals that within the Supply Department there is a substantial amount of interchange of employees from one job to another, as well as interrelationships between graded and ungraded employees. With respect to the Freight Terminal Branch, graded employees arrange for the shipping, and ungraded employees do the physical loading and actual shipping. There is a liaison section of three graded employees who are assigned to the Receipt Control Branch of the Control Division, but who work in the Receiving, Inspection, and Delivery Section of the Freight Terminal Branch. These graded employees have a record of all materials due to come in, and when the material is received, the ungraded receiving employees unload the truck, place the material on the receiving floor, pull the vendor's slip, and give it to the graded liaison employees, who, in turn, based on the purchase order number, pull the corresponding paper work so that the receiving employees can ascertain where the material is to be delivered. An ungraded supervisor in the receiving building supervises a graded supply clerk in his office, and a graded traffic clerk supervises ungraded stock men in the transit shed.

Although most of the employees in the Storage Branch are ungraded and work throughout the thirty-nine warehouses, employees from the Technical Requirements Division, who are all graded, work with and assist them. In addition, there are three graded equipment specialists assigned to the Storage Branch who perform the same type of work as the ungraded employees in the Storage Branch. These equipment specialists are supervised by a Wage Board supervisor.

The record establishes that the ungraded employees in the Labor and Equipment Branch work with all of the various departments on the base and on occasion are assigned to graded jobs where backlogs exist. Further, in the Ship Stores Branch, there are employees, both graded and ungraded, who work together. Also, a graded supervisor supervises ungraded employees in the holding room where if orders cannot be filled, they are held until they are filled. . . .

With respect to over-all working conditions at the activity the record reveals that the hours of work are the same for graded and Wage Board employees. Snack bar or cafeteria facilities are available to both graded and Wage Board employees, as are restroom facilities. All facilities or privileges accorded to graded employees are accorded to Wage Board employees. The activity has a merit promotion program which applies to both graded and Wage Board employees, and the same criteria are used in granting merit promotions to both classes of employees. The activity has a performance rating system in which a supervisor rates employees, and the next higher supervisor reviews the rating and a rating is given. If an employee is not satisfied with his rating he can appeal to a Performance Rating Board whose members are appointed by the commanding officer of the base. The members of the board who are graded and Wage Board employees pass judgment on both graded and Wage Board employees. The record shows that in two reductions in force, one on December 18, 1969, and one on June 17, 1970, there were some fifteen transfers from graded to Wage Board positions, and from Wage Board to graded positions. Both groups are paid by check, the graded employees every other Tuesday, and the Wage Board employees every other Friday. Wage Board employees and graded employees up to a certain grade punch a time clock.

The evidence also establishes that the last negotiated agreement between the activity and the NAGE was signed on behalf of the NAGE by six employees: three Wage Board employees and three graded employees. An extension of this agreement was signed by the local president of the NAGE, a Wage Board employee. In regard to the current officers of the NAGE at the activity, there are three graded and five Wage Board employees. Also, at the activity, there are four regional directors of the NAGE, two from each group; and on the Board of Directors, there are five graded employees and one Wage Board employee. There are three graded and eight Wage Board stewards in the Supply Department and all eight stewards in CED are Wage Board employees. In the seven-year period that the NAGE has represented the employees, approximately twenty-five grievances reached the hearing stage, and of this number approximately fifteen involved Wage Board employees. The record shows that if problems are not resolved at the lowest possible level (as most of them are), they are taken to the division head; from the division head they are taken to the Board of Directors; from there to the commanding officer and then on to either the Civil Service Commission or the Secretary of the Navy, according to the agreement.

Based on the foregoing, I find the employees in the unit sought by the petitioner do not possess a clear and identifiable community of interest that would entitle them to separate representation.

In reaching this conclusion I have taken into consideration the fact that where, as here, a petitioner is seeking to sever a group of employees from an established, represented unit there are various interests which are affected and must be taken into account. These include the effect severance would have on the effectiveness of employee representation; the past history of bargaining; the stability of labor relations as related to effective dealings and the efficiency of agency operations; the appropriateness and distinctness of units; and the overall community of interest of the employees involved.

In the subject case the NAGE has represented the graded and the Wage Board employees at the activity for approximately seven years. The record indicates Wage Board employees play a prominent role in the administration of the NAGE and there is no indication that the AFGE is either more or less qualified than the NAGE to represent the employees in the proposed unit. At best, it would be speculative as to how the AFGE would represent the employees in the proposed unit whereas the record shows that the manner in which the NAGE has represented employees on an activity-wide basis for seven years has resulted in stable labor relations at the activity. In these circumstances, the introduction of an additional agreement, would, in my view, tend to promote neither effective dealings nor efficiency of agency operations.

Further, I do not agree with the petitioner's claim that the unit it seeks to represent will insure a clear, identifiable community of interest among the employees concerned. The petitioner is seeking to exclude specifically some of the Wage Board employees while otherwise seeking to include all the Wage Board employees. Further, the petitioner is not seeking a distinct, homogeneous group of craftsmen or employees, but instead, as the record reveals, is seeking a group possessing varying degrees of assorted skills. There is no evidence of uniform separate supervision, and in fact, some Wage Board employees work directly under the supervision of graded supervisors and some graded employees work directly under the supervision of Wage Board supervisors. In some cases, graded and Wage Board employees work side-by-side doing the same type of work and in cases of temporary absences or work load, graded employees do the work of Wage Board employees, or vice versa. Further, graded and Wage Board employees share the same working areas in some instances, and the record gives numerous examples of necessary day-to-day contact between graded and Wage Board employees. Various facilities on the base are used in equal manner by graded and Wage Board employees. Moreover, Wage Board and graded employees have transferred categories when reductions in force have occurred, and there have been assignments from one group to the other in order to maintain the efficiency of the activity.

In sum, there are a number of pertinent factors present in this case which support a finding that an activity-wide unit of Wage Board and graded employees is appropriate. These include the fact that all employees have the same benefits and hours, and that there is employee interchange and transfer within the unit, common labor policies, integrated operations, bargaining history, and centralized administration.

In reaching a decision in a proposed severance case as this, a determination must be made as to whether the benefits that might reasonably accrue to the employees being sought for severance exceed the benefits to be derived from maintaining an existing relationship. The relevant factors in this case cited above convince me that the advantages of continuing the existing bargaining relationship at the activity exceed the possible consequences of separate representation sought by the petitioner. . . .

Although each case can be expected to have its individual differences, the general theory of a severance case remains the same. Therefore, for future guidance, I conclude it will best effectuate the policies of the executive order that where the evidence shows that an established, effective, and fair collective bargaining relationship is in existence, a separate unit carved out of the existing unit will not be found to be appropriate except in unusual circumstances.

As there are no unusual circumstances present which preclude applying the criteria set forth above to the facts of this case, I find the interests of all employees and the agency would be better served by continuing the existing bargaining relationship. Accordingly, I find the unit sought by the petitioner is inappropriate for the purpose of exclusive recognition, and shall therefore dismiss the petition.

ORDER

IT IS HEREBY ORDERED that the petition in Case No. 31–3246 (EO) be, and it hereby is, dismissed.

Dated: January 15, 1971   /s/ W. J. Usery, Jr., Assistant
          Washington, D.C.   Secretary of Labor for Labor-
                                               Management Relations

Discussion Questions

1. Summarize the main arguments presented in the petitioner's request for a separate bargaining unit.
2. Discuss the activity's position opposing severance.
3. Describe the history of the past bargaining relationship involving the Wage Board employees.
4. Why did the intervenor oppose a separate unit?
5. How would you describe the amount of interchange between graded and ungraded personnel? Minimal? Substantial? Illustrate your choice.
6. Which criteria did the Assistant Secretary emphasize in rejecting the bid for separate representation?

Section 3. The Distinction Between Guards and Other Employees

Section 9(b) of the LMRA sets out in precise language the restrictions on the inclusion of plant guards in bargaining units with other employees in the following language:

> if it includes, together with other employees, any individual employed as a guard to enforce against employees and other persons rules to protect property of the employer or to protect the safety of persons on the employer's premises.

> No labor organization shall be certified as the representative of employees in a bargaining unit of guards if such organization admits to membership or is affiliated directly or indirectly with an organization which admits to membership employees other than guards.[18]

The upcoming case deals with the determination of whether firemen perform functions that would classify them as guards within the meaning of Executive Order 11491 (which governs the labor relations status of federal employees).

In the Matter of

United States Department of the Air Force, 910th Tactical Air Support Group (AFRES) Youngstown Municipal Airport, Vienna, Ohio (activity) *and* **International Association of Fire Fighters, AFL–CIO, Local F–154 (petitioner)**

Case No. 53–2973(RO) [19]

(United States Department of Labor before the Assistant Secretary for Labor–Management Relations)

DECISION AND DIRECTION OF ELECTION

Upon a petition duly filed under Section 6 of Executive Order 11491, a hearing was held. . . . The hearing officer's rulings made at the hearing are free from prejudicial error and are hereby affirmed.

Upon the entire record in this case, including the petitioner's brief, the Assistant Secretary finds:

1. The labor organization involved claims to represent certain employees of the activity.

2. A question concerning the representation of certain employees of the activity exists within the meaning of Section 10 of Executive Order 11491.

3. Petitioner, International Association of Fire Fighters, AFL-CIO, Local F–154, herein called IAFF, seeks an election in a unit of all fire fighters employed at the Youngstown Municipal Airport, Vienna, Ohio.

The activity questioned whether the fire fighters, who perform certain incidental security functions in addition to fire fighting, are "guards" within the meaning of Section 2(d) of Executive Order 11491.

The 910th Tactical Air Support Group (AFRES), Youngstown Municipal Airport, Vienna, Ohio, is one of eleven different Air Force bases in the United States which comprise Headquarters Air Force Reserve, a major component of the United States Air Force. The mission of the activity is to train Air Force ready reservists to maintain combat proficiency for recall to active military duty in the event of a national emergency or a war.

Of the approximately 198 civilian employees employed at the Youngstown Municipal Airport, there are twenty-two fire fighters including supervisors. The duties performed by the fire fighters include (1) general maintenance of the fire fighting department's equipment and physical plant; (2) checking buildings for fire hazards; (3) repairing fire extinguishers; (4) performing stand-by duty while engines on aircraft are started and also while fuel is removed from aircraft; and (5) responding to military and civilian aircraft and structural fires at the base and municipal airport terminal.

In 1969 the activity found it necessary to assign certain security or guard work to the fire fighters. By February, 1970, the fire fighters were performing all of the security work at the base, which consists primarily of gate duty and installation patrols. The fire fighters currently work scheduled shifts of 24 hours on and 24 hours off duty, 72 hours a week. A typical 24-hour shift includes 4 hours of gate duty at the main gate guardhouse, 4 hours of installation patrol duty, 8 hours of fire fighting duty, and 8 hours of stand-by duty at the firehouse. There are approximately 8 or 9 fire fighters on each shift. Of that number, 6 of the fire fighters perform both fire fighting and security duties during each shift.

In merging the fire fighting and security functions, the activity designated 6 of the 22 fire fighters to perform security work. In actual practice, however, all of the fire fighters perform both functions.

Currently, the fire fighters stand watch at the main gate from 6:30 A.M. to 5:15 P.M., and 11:30 P.M. to 12:15 A.M., Monday through Friday. Their duties while on gate watch include checking visitors in and out of the airport, issuing visitor passes, controlling traffic, and giving out information. In the event of a fire, a fire fighter on gate duty is instructed to lock the gate and respond to the fire alarm. There are 6 installation patrols made every 24 hours. In addition to checking buildings for potential fire hazards, the fire fighters check to see that the doors of the buildings are locked. The total amount of time expended by the fire fighters in performing the additional security functions represents approximately 8 percent of the total man-hours worked by them during an average month.

All of the fire fighters work out of the base firehouse under the direct supervision of the fire chief or the assistant chiefs, even while performing security work. None of these employees have received any training or have participated in drills to enable them to perform security work.

The fire fighters wear regulation fire fighters' uniforms while performing security work, are not armed, and have not received any training to gain proficiency in the use of fire arms. Nor do fire fighters have the authority to detain or arrest individuals. The record also reveals that they have never issued traffic tickets and have not had to investigate or make reports concerning incidents of pilferage.

Prior to the merging of the fire fighting and security functions, the activity employed a regular guard force. Each guard wore a distinctive guard uniform as well as a side arm carried in a gun holster. Although they did not possess arrest authority, they could detain an individual until local law enforcement authorities or federal marshals arrived at the base to pick up a suspect. Also, they issued visitor passes at the gate and were authorized to issue citations for traffic infractions. The guards worked out of the base security office under the direct supervision of a security chief and they worked forty hours a week with three scheduled shifts each day of eight hours' duration.

Based on the foregoing facts, I find that the evidence demonstrates that the added security functions performed by the fire fighters in the subject case do not bring them within the meaning of "guards" as set forth in Section 2(d) of the executive order. In performing the security functions, the fire fighters wear their regular fire fighter uniforms; they are not armed or deputized; they have not received instructions or training in checking the installation for the presence of unauthorized persons, or for the loss of property, or the enforcement of rules established by the activity; they are supervised by the fire chief and not by the chief of security; and their performance of the security duties appears to be temporary. Moreover, their security duties are clearly subordinate to their duties and responsibilities as fire fighters.

The subordinate nature of their security duties is evidenced by, among other things, the limited amount of time spent in this regard and the fact that if a fire occurs, their primary responsibility is to answer the fire alarm notwithstanding the fact that they are engaged at the time in a security function.

In the particular circumstances of the case, I find that the performance of certain limited security duties by the fire fighters does not in any real sense give rise to a conflict of loyalty between the activity on the one hand, and their fellow employees on the other. Accordingly, I find that the petitioned-for employees are not "guards" within the meaning of Section 2(d) of Executive Order 11491 and that the following unit appropriate for the purpose of exclusive recognition:

> All fire fighters employed by the 910th Tactical Air Support Group (AFRES), Youngstown Municipal Airport, Vienna, Ohio, excluding all employees engaged in federal personnel work in other than purely clerical capacity, professional employees, management officials, and supervisors and guards as defined in the order.

DIRECTION OF ELECTION

Election by secret ballot shall be conducted among the employees in the voting unit described above, as early as possible, but not later than thirty days from the date below. . . .

Dated: February 12, 1971   /s/ W. J. Usery, Jr., Assistant Secretary of
        Washington, D.C.   Labor for Labor-Management Relations

Discussion Questions

1. Describe the security functions performed by fire fighters in this case.
2. Why were the fire fighters not considered to be guards within the meaning of the executive order?
3. What is the basic reason why guards are not included in the same bargaining unit with regular activity employees?

Section 4. The Exclusion of "Managerial" Employees from Supervisory Units

In private employment the NLRB has consistently excluded so-called managerial employees from regular bargaining units on grounds that such an employee is either (1) one who, while not a supervisor, is so closely related to or aligned with management as to present a potential conflict of interest between employer and employees; or (2) one who formulates, determines, or effectuates an employer's policies, and who has discretion in the performance of his job, but not if the discretion must conform to the employers established policies.[20] In public employment, managerial employees, by definition, could not be included in the same unit with nonsupervisory personnel. However, because supervisory units are allowed in certain instances, the question then becomes one of whether managerial employees can be part of supervisory bargaining units. Such an issue does not arise in private industry, although foremen and supervisors are allowed to organize, because their employers are not required to negotiate with them, whereas public management must bargain with units of supervisors in certain cases. The following cases involve these issues and again indicate that (1) the rulings of hearing officers are subject to reversal by public employment relations commissions, and that (2) commission findings can be overturned by appellate courts.

———————

In the Matter of

City of Newark (public employer) *and* **Professional Fire Officers Local 1860 International Association of Fire Fighters, AFL–CIO (petitioner)** *and* **Newark Fire Officers Association (intervenor)**

Docket No. R–124

(State of New Jersey Public Employment Relations Commission)

REPORT AND RECOMMENDATIONS

. . . The main issue in this case is whether or not the petition filed by Local 1860 is timely filed or whether it should be dismissed in light of the fact that the intervenor has been recognized by the city of Newark as the negotiating agent for the employees in question. If the petition is found to be timely filed, an issue arises as to the appropriate unit. . . .

It is the position of the petitioner that the petition is timely filed and that an election should be directed to determine the majority representative of the employees in the unit sought. The intervenor contends that it was accorded recognition on June 23 or 24, 1969, and that, therefore, the petition should be dismissed. The public employer, while maintaining that the Fire Officers Association has been recognized, indicates a desire to cooperate in this proceeding and a willingness to abide by whatever decision the commission renders. . . .

. . . The . . . meeting which took place on June 23 and 24, 1969, in the conference room of the City Council chambers . . . was called by Mr. Biunno, the business administrator, and attended by representatives of the Fire Officers Association as well as by representatives of three other employee groups: the Firemen's Mutual Benevolent Association, the Patrolmen's Benevolent Association, and the Police Superior Officers Association. . . . At this meeting, Mr. Biunno agreed to "recognize" the four employee organizations as the exclusive negotiating agents for their respective units. Recognition was granted on the basis of the majority status of the FOA as documented by dues checkoff records. Approximately 213 of the 230 superior officers in the unit were having dues deducted from their pay by the city. This "recognition" did not take written form either at this time or subsequently. It was conveyed orally to the parties. . . . Local 1860 was not invited to nor aware of this meeting. . . .

The question before the hearing officer is whether or not the "recognition" which was accorded to the FOA on June 23 or 24, 1969 was valid. . . .

The authority of the business administrator in the area of "recognition" is unclear. The Optional Municipal Charters Act, N.J.S.A. 40:69A–44(e), provides that "the business administrator shall, *subject to the direction of the Mayor,* supervise the administration of each of the departments established by ordinance. For this purpose, he shall have the power to investigate the organization and operation of any and all departments, to prescribe standards and rules of administrative practice and procedure . . ." (emphasis supplied). There is nothing in the record to indicate that the Mayor directed the business administrator to recognize the FOA and the other organizations.

Testimony on this issue is ambiguous. The business administrator stated that, "In my opinion, it (recognition) would be binding. And, I would say the city—meaning the members of the Municipal Council—would recognize it as binding." However, he also stated that no organization has been granted recognition other than oral recognition because we are "refering to a formal declaration in writing, which cannot be done by me alone." The rules and regulations of the commission specifically call for *written* recognition in Section 19:11–14.

The rules and regulations of the commission did not become effective until August 29, 1969. These rules set forth five criteria in Section 19:11–14, which are to be followed if the grant of recognition thereunder is to be considered by the commission as tantamount to certification by the commission. In May, 1969, before these rules and regulations became effective, proposed rules and regulations were made available and discussed. Mr. Biunno testified that he personally picked up a copy of the proposed rules and regulations and that he and his staff went over them. He also stated on the record that he did not remember specifically the provision relating to recognition. These provisions were identical in the proposed rules and regulations and in the rules and regulations as finally adopted.

Briefly, the facts surrounding the recognition of the FOA fall into two groups. On the one hand, the FOA had represented the superior officers for many years. At the time of recognition, they were actively seeking to assure the availability of additional funds from the state which would permit the City Council to provide salary increases. Over 90 percent of the superior officers were having their FOA dues deducted from their pay by the city. The FOA had asked the city for recognition.

On the other hand, the IAFF had also asked for recognition. The Mayor had assured them that the city would recognize no employee organization until the rules and regulations of the commission became available. These rules and regulations became effective over two months after the recognition of the FOA. The rules and regulations were not followed in granting recognition to the FOA. The proposed rules and regulations contained identical criteria regarding recognition. These rules were not followed, although the city was aware of the existence of these proposed rules. The IAFF was not told of the meeting at which the FOA was recognized. While the FOA had a membership of over 90 percent of those eligible, the fact is that membership in the two organizations is widely overlapping. Testimony at the hearing regarding the procedure for chartering new locals of the IAFF indicated that Local 1860 had signed up over 50 percent of the superior officers by June, 1969, when the recognition of the FOA was granted.

On the basis of these facts, the hearing officer finds the petition of Local 1860 to be timely. This finding should not be interpreted as a rebuff to the city. There is nothing in the record to indicate that the city intentionally violated Chapter 303 in recognizing the FOA. The act was very new in June, 1969, and the commission had not adopted rules and regulations. Nevertheless, the proposed rules were not followed and Local 1860 had a substantial membership and had been assured that no organization would be recognized until rules were adopted. Under these circumstances, it seems that the best way to clear the air and to find out which of these organizations the employees want to represent them for the purposes of collective negotiations would be through a secret-ballot election.

THE APPROPRIATE UNIT

The positions included in the petition are fire chief, deputy fire chief, superintendent of fire alarms and radio, battalion fire chief, chief inspector of combustibles, chief communications officer, supervisor of apparatus, assistant superintendent of fire alarms and radio, fire captain, assistant chief inspector of combustibles, chief fire alarm operator, and foreman, fire alarms and radio.

All parties stipulated that this unit was an appropriate one. Furthermore, the parties stipulated that all of the positions included in the petition were supervisory, that is, occupants of these positions are supervisors as defined in the act. (The act defines a supervisor as one "having the power to hire, discharge, discipline, or to effectively recommend the same. . . ." Section 7)

The undersigned will not go beyond the stipulations of the parties except to the extent necessary to conform with statutory requirements. The positions in question are found to be supervisory and the occupants of these positions are found to be supervisors as defined in the act.

Similarly, the unit is found to be appropriate in that it has been "defined with due regard for the community of interest among the employees concerned . . ." as specified in Section 7 of the act.

However, not all of the positions are appropriately included in a negotiating unit. Section 3 of the act defines public employee as "any person holding a position, by appointment or contract, or employment in the service of a public employer, except elected officials, *heads and deputy heads of departments* and agencies, and members of boards and commissions . . ." (emphasis supplied).

The terms "head" and "deputy head" are not defined in the act. But they are specifically excluded from the definition of public employee. While it is recognized that there is a director of the fire department, the job description of fire chief provides that, "Under the direction of a designated member of the local governing body he has charge of the fire department." The deputy fire chief, "Under the direction of the fire chief assists in the management and discipline of the fire department" and "has charge of the fire department in the absence of the fire chief. . . ." These job descriptions lead the hearing officer to the conclusion that the incumbents of these positions are "head" and "deputy heads" of departments as provided in the act and that they are not public employees as defined in the act. Therefore, they may not be included in an appropriate unit since only public employees are covered by the act (Section 7).

Furthermore, the act specifically provides that "managerial executives" are not to receive the rights which the act confers (Section 7). Again, the term "managerial executive" is not defined, but the job descriptions of the fire chief and deputy fire chief would seem to indicate a managerial function: the chief has charge of the department and the deputy chief has charge of the department in the absence of the chief.

The job description of the battalion fire chief, who is under the deputy chief in the chain of command, states that he "assists in the management and discipline of the municipal uniformed fire department" but it specifies that he does so by "supervising a group of fire companies. . . ." This is different from managing or assisting in the management of the fire department. Battalion fire chiefs are not found to be managerial executives.

In a group as large as this one—with over 230 superior officers—one would expect to find more than one "managerial executive" at the top. Based upon the above, the undersigned finds that the titles of fire chief and deputy fire chief are held by "managerial executives." Thus, these positions are not entitled to coverage under the act.

The appropriate unit is found to be all superior officers of the Newark Fire Department including battalion chief and captains but excluding fire fighters and other nonsupervisors, managerial executives, craft employees, professional employees, and policemen.

RECOMMENDATIONS

It is recommended that an election be directed among the employees in the unit described above to determine whether the employees of the

Newark Fire Department wish to be represented for purposes of collective negotiations by Local 1860, IAFF, by the Newark Fire Officers Association, or by neither organization. The recognition which has been granted to the FOA should not constitute a bar to an election because the rules which provide for such a bar were not adhered to in granting recognition to the FOA. The chief and deputy chief should be excluded from the unit because they are not "public employees" and because they are "managerial executives." The election should be conducted in accordance with the rules and regulations of the Public Employment Relations Commission.

Dated: January 17, 1970 /s/ Jeffrey B. Tener
        Trenton, N.J. Hearing Officer

DECISION AND DIRECTION OF ELECTION

. . .

3. The employer refuses to recognize petitioner as the exclusive negotiating representative for certain of its employees; accordingly, a question concerning the representation of public employees exists and the matter is properly before the commission for determination.

4. The hearing officer found that notwithstanding the employer's "recognition" of intervenor, the petition was timely filed and not barred by such recognition. No party has taken exception to that finding and the commission hereby adopts it. The hearing officer further found that, notwithstanding the agreement of all parties to the appropriateness of a unit of fire officers, including chief and deputy chiefs, the latter two titles could not properly be included in the unit because they were, respectively, the head and deputy heads of the department and thus statutorily excluded from the definition of public employee; the hearing officer also found that these employees were managerial executives, a class excluded from the act's coverage. He therefore concluded that the appropriate unit consisted of all superior officers excluding chief and deputy chiefs. Both petitioner and intervenor except to the exclusion of the deputy chiefs. Neither takes exception to the exclusion of the chief.

The record reveals that the parties had stipulated to the inclusion of the chief and deputy chiefs and that no evidence was taken concerning their status. The record does disclose that there is a director, a chief, 16 deputy chiefs, and a total complement of approximately 230 officers. In his report, the hearing officer sets forth the job description of the deputy chief: "Under the direction of the fire chief he assists in the management and discipline of the fire department . . . has charge of the fire department in the absence of the fire chief. . . ." It was in reliance principally on this description that the hearing officer concluded as he did regarding the deputy chiefs. The commission considers such description an inadequate basis for finding that the deputy chief is either a managerial executive or a deputy head. Furthermore, in view of the fact that there are two positions, namely, chief and director, above the position of deputy chief, the commission is equally unable to conclude from that additional fact that the deputy chief should be considered a deputy head. In the absence of more compelling evidence, the commission declines to find that deputy chiefs are either managerial executives or deputy heads. They shall be included in the unit in accordance with the parties' initial stipulation. Regarding the status of the chief, the commission makes no determination at this time. The parties initially agreed to include him. By their exceptions, petitioner and intervenor, have, in effect, agreed to exclude him. The employer filed no exceptions; it states it will abide by the commission's decision. The record is inadequate for a determination. He will be permitted to vote subject to challenge.

The appropriate unit is "All superior officers employed by the Newark Fire Department, including deputy chiefs, but excluding all fire fighters and other nonsupervisory employees, managerial executives, craft and professional employees, and policemen."

The parties stipulated that all those included in the unit agreed to were supervisors within the meaning of the act. The record discloses that Local 1860, IAFF was specifically chartered for the purpose of representing Newark fire officers and that a separate local, 1846, IAFF, was chartered for the purpose of representing rank-and-file firemen. The intervenor has for years limited its membership to officers. Since in this case the term officer denotes supervisor and since both Local 1860 and the intervenor admit only officers, that is, supervisors, to membership, either organization may, in accordance with the provisions of the act, represent the supervisors of the fire department.

5. The commission directs that a secret-ballot election shall be conducted among the employees in the unit found appropriate. . . .

By order of the commission.

Dated: April 22, 1970
      Trenton, N.J.

/s/ Walter F. Pease
      Chairman

Discussion Questions

1. Describe the circumstances leading to the initial recognition of the FOA as an exclusive bargaining agent.
2. Did the prior recognition of the FOA constitute a bar to a subsequent election involving the IAFF?

3. Why did the commission disagree with the hearing officer's recommendation that the fire chief and deputy fire chief were "managerial executives"?
4. Are managerial executives public employees?

Board of Education of the Town of West Orange in the County of Essex (a corporation) v. Elizabeth Wilton and Administrators Association of West Orange Public Schools
Supreme Court of New Jersey, A–36 September Term, 1970 [21]

The opinion of the court was delivered by FRANCIS, J.

After the legislature adopted the New Jersey Employer-Employee Relations Act, L. 1968, c. 303 . . . certain administrative employees of the West Orange Board of Education organized the Administrators Association of the West Orange Public Schools and requested the board to recognize it as the collective negotiating unit for all supervisory personnel, except the superintendent of schools. . . . On February 10, 1969, the board recognized the association as negotiating representative for principals, assistant principals, subject matter directors, and administrative assistants but excluded from the unit "Directors who act in supervisory capacity" over such personnel. Pursuant to this resolution, the board refused to accept the association as the appropriate negotiating unit for Elizabeth Wilton, who holds the supervisory position of director of elementary education.

The association then filed a petition with the Public Employment Relations Commission asking that it be designated as the exclusive representative of all supervisory personnel of the board, including Miss Wilton. . . . Miss Wilton, who had become a member of the association, joined in the petition. By way of answer, the Board of Education admitted that it had accepted the association as the negotiating unit for the employees in the described categories. However, it asserted that the unit was not appropriate for Miss Wilton because her status as director of elementary education invested her with supervision over the other employees included therein and such intimacy with the managerial aspects of the board's operation that she should be excluded. The commission referred the matter to a hearing officer for the taking of testimony and the making of a report and recommendation.

At the hearing, the board's position was that Miss Wilton is a top echelon supervisor and as such does not belong in the same negotiating unit with principals, assistant principals, subject matter directors, and administrative assistants because her duties require her to supervise them in the interest of the board's management and control of the school system. On the other hand the association . . . contended that all employees of the public school system, including those who have supervisory duties over teachers, excepting only the superintendent of schools, are eligible under the act to join an employee organization. Section 13A3(d) provides among other things that the term "employee" shall include any person holding "employment in the service of a public employer . . . provided that in any school district this shall exclude only the superintendent of schools or other chief administrator of the district." And under Section 13A–5.3 public employees are granted the right to join an employee organization, provided, however, that the right shall not extend to "any managerial executive" except that in a school district such executive "shall mean the superintendent of schools or his equivalent." It is provided also that "except where established practice, prior agreement, or special circumstances dictate the contrary," no "supervisor having the power to hire, discharge, discipline, or to effectively recommend the same" shall "have the right to be represented in collective negotiations by an employee organization that admits nonsupervisory personnel to membership, and the fact that any organization has such supervisory employees as members shall not deny the right of that organization to represent the appropriate unit in collective negotiations. . . ." The section further directs that the "negotiating unit shall be defined with due regard for the community of interest among the employees concerned. . . ."

. . . Substantial evidence was adduced before the hearing officer to show Miss Wilton's place in the administrative structure of the school system. Under Article V, Section 1 of the *Board of Education Policy Manual,* the board appoints a director of elementary education and a director of secondary education "who shall be directly responsible to the superintendent of schools in the performance of all duties." To qualify for such appointment, the directors must have experience at their respective levels in teaching, supervision, and administration, and "a broad knowledge of educational problems." The board's organization chart shows the director of elementary education (Miss Wilton) on a higher plane in the administrative hierarchy than elementary school principals. In the chain of authority, it positions the director on a direct line above the principals, below whom it places the "teachers, nurse, pupils, secretaries, and custodians." The director of secondary education is shown on the chart on the same plane as the director of elementary education. In a direct line below the director of secondary education (and on the same level as the elementary principals) are the secondary principals, below whom appear assistant principals, administrative assistant, department chairman, counselors, teachers, nurse, pupils, secretaries, custodians, and cafeteria staff. The board's policy manual . . . reveals that among other things the directors have the duties (1) of making recommendations and advising the superintendent as to "needed extensions or readjustments of the educational program, services, and activities of the school"; (2) of assisting "teachers, principals, and other members of the professional staff in the improvement of instruction"; (3) of encouraging the "continuous study of curriculum problems by principals" and promoting "all efforts for curriculum development and improvement in keeping with the best current practices and thought"; and (4) of assisting "the superintendent in the recruitment, selection, assignment, and transfer of teachers."

Each elementary or secondary school principal is in charge of a school building, and he in turn is "directly responsible to either the director of elementary education or the director of secondary education." Each principal has the further duty of making "all reports for his school as required by law or by the directors of education, and the superintendent." In the area of secondary education where assistant principals are appointed, such persons are directly responsible to the building principal who is charged with the assignment of their duties.

In his testimony, the superintendent of schools outlined Miss Wilton's position as a supervisor in the administrative hierarchy of the West Orange schools. He said that as director she is responsible for the administration of the elementary schools; she supervises the work of each of the nine elementary school principals and evaluates their performance for purposes of recommending tenure and salary increments for them to the superintendent of the Board of Education. . . .

. . . The superintendent also pointed out that, as director, Miss Wilton holds regularly scheduled monthly meetings with the elementary school principals and she is responsible for the instructional program and curriculum development in the elementary schools. She reviews the budget proposals of all principals. She recruits teachers for elementary schools, interviews the candidates and recommends them to the superintendent for appointment; she recruits and screens the staff personnel of the schools and recommends them to the principal. In turn, the principals will interview and observe candidates recommended by Miss Wilton, but if she recommends a person for a teaching post in a particular school and the principal does not wish such person, she would have the final say in the matter, subject, of course, to approval of her recommendation by the superintendent or the Board of Education.

The superintendent gave a number of examples of Miss Wilton's exercise of the duties and authority he described, including written evaluation reports of principals. Although she does not have the final power to either hire or discharge or to deny either tenure or a salary increment, no one in the case cited a single example of the refusal of the superintendent or the board to accept her recommendation. In this connection, also, it may be noted that as an incident of her assigned tasks she is a regular attendant at the public meetings of the Board of Education. . . .

. . . After reviewing the testimony and noting the fact that her salary for the year 1969–1970 was computed on a basis different from that of the teachers and principals, the hearing officer found that Miss Wilton was a "top level managerial employee rather than a rank-and-file supervisory employee," and that of the "top echelon managerial group" she was the only member of the association. He agreed that the evidence weighed heavily in favor of the board's view that to have Miss Wilton "in the same negotiating unit as the people she supervises constitutes a conflict of interest that could seriously reduce her effectiveness as an administrator." He concluded, and so reported to the commission, that it would be "inappropriate for her to be included in the same negotiating unit as administrators whom she supervises." . . .

After filing of the hearing officer's report and prior to decision by PERC, the exceptants sought to supplement the record by an affidavit of Miss Wilton to the effect that after the hearer's report, the superintendent of schools hired an assistant superintendent of curriculum and instruction as of July 1, 1969, whom she described as "commonly referred to as director of education for grades K–12." She asserted that this hiring resulted in the elimination of her direct relationship with the superintendent; that it made her "an assistant for elementary education to this new assistant superintendent"; and that it had the effect . . . of placing her on the same administrative level as elementary and secondary principals. She claimed, therefore, that the proposed change provided further reason for including her in the negotiating unit proposed by the administrators' association.

Thereafter, the superintendent of schools filed an additional affidavit asserting that the Board of Education had never adopted the transitional organization chart which was prepared and discussed on or about March 6, 1969, prior to the hearing before the hearing officer. He asserted that the alleged position of director of education referred to in Miss Wilton's affidavit did not exist, and further that her relationship to the elementary principals had not changed "one iota." Her supervisory duties as detailed above remained the same and, as director of elementary education, "the nine elementary principals will continue to be directly responsible to Miss Wilton." His affidavit said, however, that she would report in the future to the "new assistant superintendent of schools in charge of curriculum and instruction, K–12." . . . On July 2, 1969, PERC reversed the holding of the hearing officer and ruled as a matter of law that Miss Wilton had such a "community of interest" with the other members of the association as warrants her inclusion in the collective negotiating unit. In doing so, it said,

The act provides that supervisors may not be represented by an organization that admits nonsupervisory personnel and that supervisory personnel and nonsupervisory employees may not be combined in the same unit in the absence of established practice, prior agreement, or unusual circumstances. The act is clear and unambiguous in not proscribing the right of various ranks of supervisors to be combined in the same unit or belong to the same organization.

Therefore, PERC declared that the director of elementary education may be included in the specific "unit of supervisors and administrators and may be represented by the association." . . .

In reaching its decision, PERC construed Sections 13A–3(d) and 13A–6(d) to mean that in school districts only the superintendent of schools is excluded from an employees' unit and that all persons who qualify as supervisors may properly be assigned to an organization of supervisors, irrespective of their relation to each other, the nature of the authority of one or more over the others, or whether the public employer has placed one employee on a higher plane of authority and supervision in the organizational structure of the school system than other supervisors. We cannot agree with such a broad interpretation. If followed unqualifiedly in all situations, it might seriously weaken the effectiveness of the statute as an instrument of meaningful public employer-employee relations. In some situations, obviously, it might put the *employer,* in the form of a high echelon supervisor, on both sides of the negotiating table, to the detriment of the *employees* in the unit; in other situations it might put an employee on both sides of that table and deprive the employer of the loyalty he has the right to expect from an employee entrusted with administration of management supervisory policy.

In seeking out the proper solution for the present case, two factors, apparently considered to have been significant by PERC, should be evaluated. First, it pointed out that despite a degree of supervision by principals over assistant principals both classes are included in the association negotiating unit. That fact has no particular bearing here because . . . both grades of supervisors are members of the association and the Board of Education has raised no issue with respect to their membership. Secondly, PERC referred to Miss Wilton's desire and consent to be a part of the unit. Her consent is an element which may be considered but as in the private employment sector, it should not be deemed controlling. . . . The determinative factor, so far as Miss Wilton is concerned, in ascertaining the appropriateness of a unit is neither what she wants nor what the public employer wants, but rather whether her inclusion in the unit will serve and not subvert the purpose of the act, that is, establishment and promotion of fair and harmonious employer-employee relations in the public service.

There is no doubt that the legislature intended to authorize appropriate independent negotiating units for supervisory employees (except the superintendent of schools or his counterpart) of the Board of Education. But there is no clear and unqualified direction in Section 13A–5.3 and 13A–6 (d) to permit all such supervisory employees to join a single negotiating unit and to require the board to recognize it as their exclusive negotiating representative, regardless of gradations of duties of particular supervisors.

Ordinary considerations of employer-employee relations make it sensible to say that if performance of assigned duties by a particular supervisor bespeaks such an intimate relationship with the management and policy-making function as to indicate actual or potential substantial conflict of interest between him and other supervisory personnel in a different or lower echelon of authority, such supervisor should not be admitted to the same negotiating unit. Admission would not be fair either to the other supervisory employees or to the employer. Obviously no man can serve two masters. . . .

. . . Whether the matter under discussion is concerned with the propriety of supervisors joining the same organization as ordinary employees, or the propriety of supervisors in various degrees of managerial proximity in relation to the employer and each other belonging to the same organization, the issue would seem to be substantially the same. Are the duties, authority, and actions of the employee in question, vis-à-vis the other employees in the association, primarily related to the management function? To what extent does the reasonable and good faith performance of the obligations a supervisor owes to his employer have capacity, actual or potential, to create a conflict of interest with other supervisors whose work he is obliged to oversee and evaluate for his employer?

Unfortunately, it cannot be said that the language used in Sections 13A–5.3 and 13A–6(d) regarding the appropriate negotiating unit for supervisors in a school system clearly expresses the solution intended by the legislature. The superintendent of schools or his equivalent is excluded beyond question. Further, except where "established practice, prior agreement, or special circumstances dictate the contrary" no "supervisor having the power to hire, discharge, discipline, or to effectively recommend the same" shall "have the right to be represented in collective negotiations by an employee organization that admits nonsupervisory personnel to membership. . . ."

. . . Our statute in its totality is ambiguous as to whether all grades of supervisors in a local school system, except the superintendent of schools, or his equivalent, may be included in the same unit. But it is not wholly without direction. Except where established practice, prior agreement, or special circumstances dictate the contrary, inclusion of nonsupervisory personnel in the same unit as supervisors who have "the power to hire, discharge, discipline, or to effectively recommend the same" is prohibited. Aside from these specifications, the nature of the negotiating unit is to be determined generally "with due regard for the community of interest among the employees concerned. . . ."

. . . In dealing with Miss Wilton specifically, PERC considered her simply as another supervisor and, as such, entitled by unquestionable statutory prescription to a determination that the association is an appropriate unit for her. The nature of her authority over the other supervisors or of her obligations to the employer vis-à-vis the others in the unit, or the fact that her compensation was fixed on a basis different from the others, was not felt to be significant. We cannot agree. . . .

In the present case, PERC made no evaluation, in terms of conflict of interest, of the facts relating to Miss Wilton's position as director of elementary education and the nature of the supervision she was obliged to exercise over other supervisors, such as elementary school principals in the lower echelon of authority. There is no doubt that it was her duty, among other things, to supervise the work of the principals of the nine elementary schools and to evaluate their performance for the purpose of reporting and making recommendations to the superintendent of schools with respect to salary increases and tenure for them. In the performance of such tasks she owed undivided loyalty to the Board of Education. If she were joined in an employees unit which included the principals whose work she was duty bound to appraise in the board's interest, would she be under pressure, real or psychological, to be less faithful to the board and more responsive to the wishes of her associates in the negotiating unit? She is obliged, of course, to be fair and nondiscriminatory in evaluating the principals, and if the association felt that she was consciously or unconsciously in error in doing so, presentation of a grievance would undoubtedly result. In that event she would have to defend against a complaint made by an organization of which she was a member.

In this connection it must be noted that the bylaws of the association provide for a grievance committee. Section 2 thereof says that the committee shall be a representative body "to include but not be limited to: one director; one secondary principal; one junior high; two elementary; one assistant principal." Thus, while the record is silent on the point, it appears that Miss Wilton may well be a member of the committee designed to process grievances against her own actions. . . .

. . . On the basis of our discussion in this case, we are satisfied, despite the ambiguity in the statute, that PERC was in error in declaring that all the supervisors, regardless of their status with respect to each other, per se possess the community of interest which requires or justifies their inclusion in the same negotiating unit. . . . We hold that where a substantial actual or potential conflict of interest exists among supervisors with respect to their duties and obligations to the employer in relation to each other, the requisite community of interest among them is lacking, and that a unit which undertakes to include all of them is not an appropriate negotiating unit within the intendment of the statute. . . .

Here, however, PERC did not perform its fact-finding function. It assumed existence of the necessary community of interest between Miss Wilton and the other supervisors in the unit simply because she was classified as a supervisor. Adequate treatment of the problem required an evaluation of the specific nature of the authority delegated to her as director of elementary education to supervise and review the work of other supervisors and to make responsible and effective recommendations to the superintendent of schools with respect to the hiring, salary, and tenure of principals, as well as the operation of the elementary schools. If good faith performance of the obligation to the Board of Education arising from the authority delegated to her gives rise to a substantial potential for conflict of interest, the fact that she desires to join the same unit as those she must supervise cannot be deemed sufficient warrant for her membership therein. PERC must decide whether, on a fair appraisal, her role puts her on the management side of the negotiating table. If so, a temporary or short-term advantage to the association that might come from allowing her to be in the supervisors' unit would be more than outweighed by the long-term disadvantage to effective and healthy labor relations.

Under the circumstances the determination of PERC and the affirmance thereof by the Appellate Division are reversed. The matter is remanded to PERC for a specific fact finding and statement of the reasons therefor, as to whether Miss Wilton's obligations to her employer as they now exist are sufficiently indicative of potential conflict of interest between her and the other supervisors to require her exclusion from the administrators' association negotiating unit. . . .

Discussion Questions

1. As described in the organization chart of the Board of Education, what are the duties of the director of elementary education?
2. Did the hiring of an assistant superintendent of curriculum and instruction affect Miss Wilton's status?
3. In what respects did the commission differ with the hearing officer's findings? What was the statutory base for its disagreement?
4. Discuss the relationship between elementary school principals and Miss Wilton.
5. Why did the New Jersey Supreme Court reverse the commission ruling that included Miss Wilton in the supervisory unit?
6. Can supervisory and nonsupervisory employees ever be included in the same unit?

7. What significance did the court place on the fact that Miss Wilton desired inclusion in the supervisory unit?
8. Which specific fact demonstrated the conflict of interest that would arise if Miss Wilton were included in the broad unit?

In the Matter of

Civil Service Forum Local 300, SEIU, AFL–CIO *and* **District Council 37, AFSCME, AFL–CIO** *and* **City Inspectors Guild** *and* **The City of New York and Related Public Employers (principal consumer affairs inspector)**

Decision No. 8–72

(Office of Collective Bargaining Board of Certification)

DECISION AND ORDER MODIFYING DIRECTION OF ELECTION

By motion dated December 10, 1971, the city requested this board to reconsider its decision "to the extent that it holds the title principal consumer affairs inspector is not managerial." None of the parties to this proceeding has objected to the city's motion.

It is the city's contention that the record supports a finding and conclusion that the single employee in the title of Principal Consumer Affairs Inspector (Greenspan) employed in the Department of Consumer Affairs is a managerial employee. In support of its contention, the city cites and refers to various portions of the testimony in this record.

We have reviewed the record and find that the record supports a finding that the principal consumer affairs inspector is a managerial employee.

An analysis of the testimony credited by the trial examiner, concerning the managerial status of Mr. Greenspan, discloses that proposals made by him to the director of field operations or to the executive assistant to the commissioner are invariably accepted; that Mr. Greenspan represents the department in talks with the National Bureau of Standards, and also represents the department at national conferences of weights and measures; that the commissioner and top staff consult with Mr. Greenspan in any area that involves weights and measures; that Mr. Greenspan directed the administration of a training program for the new department's inspectional employees, and developed the curriculum for this training course; that Mr. Greenspan serves as the department's chief training officer, and had a very important part in the preparation of the first draft of the department's administrative manual; that he was given the responsibility "and also the power" to consult directly with budget and other departments involving the capital budget, specifically with respect to the construction and outfitting of a central testing laboratory expected to cost $722,500; and that he had initially recommended the construction of such laboratory. The testimony also established that Mr. Greenspan participated in the site selection of a testing station, working with the first deputy commissioner to accomplish this objective, and dealt directly with the executive assistant to the commissioner and Commissioner Myerson.

A significant portion of Mr. Greenspan's actual duties and activities is not precisely within the examples of typical tasks set forth in his job description. Thus the record established his orientation toward management interests and his importance to the department as a managerial employee.

Having found that the title of principal consumer affairs inspector in the Department of Consumer Affairs as performed by the incumbent employee is managerial, it is our conclusion that he be excluded from the supervisory unit heretofore found appropriate. Therefore, our Certification of Representative heretofore issued under Decision No. 81–71 will be modified by the order entered below.

ORDER

IT IS HEREBY ORDERED that the Certificate of Representative heretofore issued under Decision No. 81071 be, and the same hereby is, modified by deleting from the unit description therein the title of principal consumer affairs inspector and by amending said Certificate of Representative as follows: "IT IS HEREBY CERTIFIED that Civil Service Forum, Local 300, SEIU, AFL–CIO, is the exclusive representative for the purposes of collective bargaining of all supervising consumer affairs inspectors, supervising inspectors of ports and terminals, principal inspectors of ports and terminals, and employees in restored Rule X titles who are serving in positions equated thereto, employed by the city of New York and related public employers subject to the jurisdiction of the Board of Certification, and subject to existing contracts, if any," and IT IS FURTHER ORDERED that except as so modified, the Certificate of Representative heretofore issued under Decision No. 81–71 shall, in all respects, remain the same.

Dated: March 15, 1972
    New York, N.Y.

/s/ Arvid Anderson
    Chairman

/s/ Walter L. Eisenberg
    Member

/s/ Eric J. Schmertz
    Member

Discussion Question

1. List the reasons the Board of Certification considered Mr. Greenspan to be a managerial employee.

Section 5. The Exclusion of Supervisory Personnel at the Municipal Level

Normally an employee will be considered to be a supervisor if his job duties include at least two of the following:

(a) performing such management control duties as scheduling, assigning, overseeing, and reviewing the work of subordinate employees;
(b) performing such duties as are distinct and dissimilar from those performed by the employees supervised;
(c) exercising judgment in adjusting grievances, applying other established personnel policies and procedures, and in enforcing the provisions of a collective bargaining agreement; and
(d) establishing or participating in the establishment of performance standards for subordinate employees and taking corrective measures to implement those standards.[22]

In the instant case, the principal issue to be resolved is whether foremen can be considered supervisors under the New Jersey law and thereby be excluded from a unit of municipal employees.

In the Matter of

City of East Orange (petitioner) and Communications Workers of America, AFL–CIO (certified representative)

Docket No. CU–50

(State of New Jersey before the Public Employment Relations Commission)

DECISION

. . . The undersigned has considered the record and the hearing officer's report and recommendation and on . . . the facts in this case finds . . .

.   .   .

3. The employer seeks clarification of a unit previously certified by the commission, which unit excluded supervisors. Specifically the question

is whether certain "foremen" titles are supervisory within the meaning of the act. Because the parties are unable to resolve this unit question, the matter is properly before the undersigned for determination.

4. In the absence of exceptions to the report and recommendations, the undersigned adopts the hearing officer's findings and recommendations *pro forma*. The titles street foreman, sewer foreman, and traffic maintenance foreman are supervisory and excluded from the certified unit.

Dated: September 17, 1971   /s/ Maurice J. Nelligan, Jr.
      Trenton, N.J.   Executive Director

REPORT AND RECOMMENDATIONS OF HEARING OFFICER

QUESTION AT ISSUE

Are the street foremen, sewer foremen, and the traffic maintenance foremen supervisors within the meaning of the act?

BACKGROUND

The parties herein are in the process of negotiating a contract, and among the union's original demands was a request for inclusion of foremen in the unit to be covered. During the course of negotiations, the parties were able to agree to the designation of certain foremen as supervisors within the meaning of the act, and to their exclusion from the unit. However, the status of three foremen job titles, to wit, street foreman, sewer foreman, and traffic maintenance foreman remained unresolved. As to the latter three job titles, the union was prepared to agree that they should be excluded from the unit provided that their salaries would be modified to reflect commensurate duties and responsibilities, and, secondly, that their actual supervisory responsibilities be more clearly defined vis-à-vis the civil service job descriptions. The public employer granted salary increases to the foremen (higher than to other employees) but apparently was unable to satisfy the union with respect to the supervisory functions of said foremen. . . . The undersigned notes . . . that six of the eight foremen in dispute signed a statement in which they indicated a desire to be excluded from any nonsupervisory unit.

DISCUSSION AND FINDINGS

C34:13A–5.3 provides in part: *"nor, except where established practice, prior agreement, or special circumstances dictate the contrary, shall any supervisor having the power to hire, discharge, discipline, or to effec-*

tively recommend the same, have the right to be represented in collective negotiations by an employee organization that admits nonsupervisory personnel to membership." Assuming a statutory, supervisory status for the instant foremen, the record does not reveal any degree of established practice, prior agreement, or special circumstances to warrant a recommendation favoring their right to be represented by an employee organization comprised of nonsupervisory personnel. Instead, however, the record clearly delineates that they do discipline, and effectively recommend discharge. Witness D'Altillo, head engineer, testified that the foreman "has the right to suspend without review up to and including five days. The foreman has the right to recommend, and I say effectively recommend dismissal." . . . The witness stated that this description of foremen's authority applied to the instant foremen at issue. Exhibit P–2, a survey of suspensions of nonsupervisory employees made in the street, sewer, shade tree, and traffic divisions during 1968–1970, reveals that ten of twenty-six suspensions were ordered by foremen. Witness D'Altillo stated, too, that a foreman's recommendation pertaining to the retention of temporary employees was never rejected by the superintendent or the assistant superintendent. . . . *No part of this testimony was contradicted by the Intervenor.* (CWA)

The undersigned believes that the record adequately satisfied the pertinent requirements of C34:13A–5.3 vis-à-vis the power to discipline and effectively recommend discharge. Accordingly, the hearing officer finds that the instant foremen, to wit, five street foremen, two sewer foremen, and one Traffic Maintenance Department foreman are supervisors within the meaning of the act and shall be excluded from the instant collective negotiation unit as hereinafter defined.

RECOMMENDATIONS

1. The foremen in the Street Department, Sewer Department, and the Traffic Engineering Department shall be found to be supervisors within the meaning of the act, and shall not have the right to be represented in collective negotiations by an employee organization that admits nonsupervisory personnel to membership.

2. The appropriate unit for purposes of collective negotiation shall be all employees of the city of East Orange in the Department of Recreation; building maintenance; engineering; dog warden, division of the Health Department; excluding officers, clericals, professional and craft employees, managerial executives, police, and supervisors within the meaning of the act.

Dated: August 16, 1971   /s/ Bernard J. Manney
      Trenton, N.J.   Hearing Officer

Discussion Question

1. What criteria of supervision did the foremen in this case satisfy that warranted their exclusion from the unit of nonsupervisory employees?

Section 6. The Inclusion of Supervisory Personnel at the Municipal Level

In a recent Connecticut case involving a psychiatric guidance clinic for children in the New Haven area, the state's Board of Labor Relations, although expressing certain reservations, found that supervisors should be included in the same unit as nonsupervisors "even though potential conflicts of interest cannot be dismissed as fanciful." [23] The board indicated that "the course of the law in Connecticut has been almost the exact opposite of the course of federal law" with regard to the inclusion of supervisors.[24] The following criteria were relied on to support what is definitely a minority viewpoint in the United States:

> We find, though not without some doubts and misgivings, that supervisors should be included in the same unit as nonsupervisors. This is a small, closely-knit group of employees. Their relationship with each other is intimate. All the witnesses who testified to the point expressed a wish to have a single unit. None expressed a fear that prejudice would result from the inclusion of supervisors and nonsupervisors. The ratio of supervisors to nonsupervisors is high; the groups to be supervised are small (in some cases apparently nonexistent); supervision within the group is sometimes diffused. The supervisors have common backgrounds (in terms of education and qualifications) with the professional nonsupervisors. . . . All these factors lead us to favor a single unit.[25]

The board stated that if problems developed the unit would be reconsidered, and, in any event, professionals and clericals would be allowed to vote on whether they desired to be included with both supervisors and nonsupervisors.[26]

The following case in New York City also concluded allowing supervisors to be included in the same units with nonsupervisors.

In the Matter of

The City of New York *and* **City Employees Union, Local 237, IBT**

Decision No. LO–72

(Office of Collective Bargaining Board of Certification)

DECISION AND ORDER

On October 28, 1971, the city of New York filed its motion herein requesting the merger and consolidation of the following certifications previously issued to City Employees Union, Local 237, International Brotherhood of Teamsters; Decision No. 85–70 covering pipe laying inspector and senior pipe laying inspector; 4 NYCDL No. 60 . . . covering blasting inspector and senior blasting inspector; 7 NYCDL No. 73 . . . covering transportation inspector; CWR–90/67 covering water use inspector and senior water use inspector; and CWR–91/67 covering supervising water use inspector and principal water use inspector. The union has consented to the city's motion. . . .

It may be noted that the city's motion included a request for a self-determination election among the supervisory employees to ascertain their desires with respect to their inclusion in a combined unit consisting of supervisory and nonsupervisory employees. The city's request was consistent with the requirement of NYCCBL at the time the motion was made. (NYCCBL Section 1173–3.01) . . .

However, effective January 12, 1972, the NYCCBL was amended and, insofar as it is pertinent hereto, the requirement of a self-determination election for the purpose of securing a combined unit of supervisory and nonsupervisory employees is conditioned upon the employer interposing an objection to such a unit: Section 5, Subdivision 1, omitting the requirement of a self-determination election and Section 12, Subdivision b(1) requiring a self-determination election when a petition for a combined unit is filed "and the public employer objects thereto. . . ."

As noted, the public employer (the city) has not only not objected to a combined unit of supervisory and nonsupervisory employees but has, in fact, initiated the proceeding for the attainment of such a unit and the union, as representative of all of the employees concerned, has consented. Under the circumstances we decide this case on the basis of the law as it exists today and we hold that the unit requested is appropriate and that there being no objections there is no need for a self-determination election.

ORDER

Pursuant to the powers vested in the Board of Certification by the New York City Collective Bargaining Law, IT IS HEREBY ORDERED that . . . the consolidated unit shall consist of pipe laying inspectors, senior pipe laying inspectors, blasting inspectors, senior blasting inspectors, water use inspectors, senior water use inspectors, and employees in restored Rule X titles equated thereto, employed by the city of New York. . . .

Dated: March 20, 1972   /s/ Arvid Anderson
New York, N.Y.   Chairman

Discussion Question

1. What apparently was decisive in the board's determination to include both supervisors and nonsupervisory personnel in the same unit?

Section 7. The Exclusion of Supervisors at the Federal Level

In the Federal Service there is little room for ambiguity concerning the bargaining unit status of supervisors. Section 10(b) of Executive Order 11491 specifically states,

> (b) A unit may be established on a plant or installation, craft, functional, or other basis which will ensure a clear and identifiable community of interest among the employees concerned and will promote effective dealings and efficiency of agency operations. A unit shall not be established solely on the basis of the extent to which employees in the proposed unit have organized, nor shall a unit be established if it includes . . . (1) any management official or *supervisor* . . . (emphasis supplied).

Section 2(c) further defines what a supervisor is,

> "Supervisor" means an employee having authority, in the interest of an agency, to hire, transfer, suspend, lay off, recall, promote, discharge, assign, reward, or discipline other employees or responsibly to direct them, or to evaluate their performance, or to adjust their grievances, or effectively to recommend such action, if in connection with the foregoing the exercise of authority is not of a merely routine or clerical nature, but requires the use of independent judgment. . . .

Of course, as at other levels of public employment, the job description and job duties of apparent supervisory occupations must be carefully evaluated to determine whether the integral components of supervision are present in the employment setting. The status of head nurses in a Veterans Administration (VA) hospital is next examined to ascertain whether or not they normally carry out the duties of supervisors in an effort to clarify their bargaining unit status.

In the Matter of

Veterans Administration Hospital, Buffalo, New York (activity) *and*
**New York State Nurses Association, affiliated with the American
Nurses Association (petitioner)**

Case No. 35–1196 [27]

(United States Department of Labor before the Assistant Secretary for
Labor–Management Relations)

DECISION AND ORDER

. . . The hearing officer's rulings made at the hearing are free from prejudicial error and are hereby affirmed.

Upon the entire record in this case . . . the Assistant Secretary finds

. . .

2. The petitioner, New York State Nurses Association, affiliated with the American Nurses Association, herein called NTSNA, seeks an election in the following unit: all registered nurses employed as head nurses at the VA Hospital, Buffalo, New York, excluding all supervisory and managerial registered nurses employed at Buffalo VA Hospital.

The activity contends that head nurses are clearly supervisors and that a separate unit of head nurses would be inappropriate under Executive Order 11491.

The activity is a general medical and surgical hospital which also supplies, among other things, outpatient services. The hospital has twenty-four wards for inpatient care, plus an operating room and an outpatient department. All nurses ultimately are responsible to the chief of nursing services, who has two associate chiefs. Under the chief and associate chiefs are ten clinical supervisors, six on the day shift, three on the evening shift, and one on the night shift. Under the immediate supervision of the clinical supervisors are twenty-six head nurses, one in each of the twenty-four wards, and one each in the operating room and the outpatient department. On each ward there are several nursing teams consisting of staff nurses, licensed practical nurses, and nursing assistants.

The record indicates that the head nurse has administrative and clinical responsibility for providing continuity of nursing care on a twenty-four-hour basis, assigns the ward staff to nursing teams, assigns tours of duty, assigns duties to the staff nurses, licensed practical nurses, and nursing assistants and assigns patients to a team for care. In addition, the head nurse develops goals and objectives for her unit and provides for staff development through consultation and in-service training programs to meet individual and group staff needs.

Typically, the tour of duty for the head nurse is the day tour. The record discloses that staff nurses on the evening and night shifts operate the unit within the framework of the overall plan for providing nursing care established by the head nurse. In this regard, any problems which arise on the evening or night shifts are handled by the clinical supervisors on those shifts, who discuss the problems with the head nurse at the first opportunity. Control of the wards' twenty-four-hour operation is maintained by the head nurse through meetings and discussions with the incoming evening shift and the outgoing night shift.

Although the head nurse spends a great deal of her time in patient care, she is responsible for a certain amount of administrative work and must finish such work each day before she leaves, even if this requires that she remain after her shift is completed. In addition, the head nurse attends periodic meetings and training sessions with higher supervisors and training personnel, as well as meetings with other head nurses and subordinate personnel.

The head nurse makes an annual proficiency rating on each staff nurse, licensed practical nurse, and day tour nursing assistant under her direction. The head nurse's rating cannot be changed by any of her supervisors. Thus, if a clinical supervisor disagrees with a rating prepared by a head nurse, she can only note her disagreement. The record reveals that the head nurses' ratings are accepted approximately 95 percent of the time. The record indicated further that the proficiency rating made by the head nurse is one of the important factors considered by the Nurse Professional Standards Board in recommending promotions. Thus, when a member of her staff is eligible for promotion, the head nurse must give an affirmative recommendation, or the processing of the promotion is carried no further.

The head nurse also initiates recommendations for awards to members of her staff. Such recommendations pass through successive levels of higher supervision for endorsement and, if concurred in, are sent to the final approving authority.

The evidence establishes that the head nurse may discipline members of her staff by issuing an admonishment, without recourse to higher authority; she may also recommend other types of disciplinary actions, such as reprimand or discharge. In this respect, the record indicates that a head nurse's recommendation for discharge has, on several occasions, been effectuated without further independent investigations being conducted.

The head nurse also handles certain employee grievances. If she cannot resolve such grievances, the record reveals that she refers them to higher authority and that she participates in the matter as it goes through the grievance procedure to final resolution.

Based on the foregoing, I find that head nurses are "supervisors" within the meaning of the order, inasmuch as they responsibly direct the work of ward employees by planning the goals and objectives of the ward, assign subordinate nursing personnel, and assign patients to respective teams for care. In addition, the record establishes that the head nurse uses independent judgment in the exercise of the above-mentioned authority; plays an important role in evaluating the performance of staff members; has an effective role with respect to promotions of staff members; initiates merit awards procedures, in which her recommendation plays an important part; has the authority to discipline staff members and may effectively recommend discharge in appropriate instances; and is involved in the handling of employee grievances.

Since a unit of employees classified as head nurses, as sought by the NYSNA, would include supervisors as defined by Section 2(c) of the executive order and since Section 10(b)(1) of the order prohibits the establishment of a unit if it includes any management official or supervisor, I find that the petition herein should be dismissed.

ORDER

IT IS HEREBY ORDERED that the petition in Case No. 35–1196 be, and it hereby is, dismissed.

Dated: August 30, 1971   /s/   W. J. Usery, Jr., Assistant Secretary of
        Washington, D.C.   Labor for Labor-Management Relations

Discussion Question

1. Review the duties of the head nurses in the VA hospital. Do they meet the supervisory criteria established by Executive Order 11491?

Section 8. The Exclusion of Supervisors from a Unit of Firemen

The next case is unusual in that the public employers involved are a city and four counties in the state of Hawaii, all interested in the question of whether fire captains and lieutenants are supervisory personnel not to be included in the same unit with rank-and-file fire fighters. As in other cases, the proper construction of relevant statutes is crucial. Here, too, one member of the employment relations board disagrees with his colleagues in maintaining that the preceding classifications, along with several others, are in reality not supervisory in nature and should be included in the same unit as nonsupervisory employees.

In the Matter of

Hawaii Fire Fighters Association Local 1463, IAFF, AFL–CIO (petitioner) *and* **Hawaii Government Employees Association, Local 152, HGEA/AFSCME (petitioner)** *and* **City and County of Honolulu, County of Hawaii, County of Maui, County of Kauai (employers)**

Case No. R–11–3 [28]

(State of Hawaii Public Employment Relations Board)

FINDINGS OF FACT, CONCLUSIONS OF LAW, AND DIRECTION OF ELECTION

. . . The Hawaii Fire Fighters Association and the Hawaii Government Employees Association, respectively, petitioned the board on January 4 and January 5, 1971, for an optional appropriate bargaining unit of all firemen throughout the state. The Hawaii Government Employees Association withdrew its petition on September 15, 1971, without objections from the public employers.

Petitioner requested an optional appropriate bargaining unit of all employees in the respective fire departments of the public employers in the following classes: fire fighter, fire fighter-fire apparatus operator, fire apparatus operator, senior fire apparatus operator, fire search and rescue squadman, fire equipment operator I, fire equipment operator II, fire lieutenant, fire captain, battalion chief, fire division commander, fire alarm operator, fire alarm shift supervisor, fire alarm superintendent, assistant fire prevention inspector, fire prevention inspector I, fire prevention inspector II, fire prevention assistant bureau chief, fire prevention bureau chief, fire safety education specialist I, fire safety education specialist II, fire safety and training bureau chief, fire boat engineer, fire boat pilot, helicopter pilot and fire fighting plans and training officer.

Petitioner requested the exclusion of the following classes of employees in the respective fire departments of the public employers: fire chief, deputy fire chief, departmental staff executive assistant, fire suppression operations commander and all office clerical employees, professional employees, confidential employees, and part-time or temporary employees.

All above-named parties in interest stipulated that the following positions of the respective fire departments of the public employers should be excluded from the bargaining unit: fire chief, fire deputy chief, fire division commander, fire battalion chief, fire administrative services officer, fire suppression operations commander, and fire fiscal and personnel officer. It was also stipulated that Fire Captain Lionel Muller of the city and county of Honolulu and Fire Equipment Operator Edward T. Kozuki and Chief

Mechanic Hiromu Matsunami of the county of Hawaii should be excluded from the bargaining unit.

The parties further stipulated that the following positions are supervisory: fire prevention bureau chief, fire alarm superintendent, fire safety and training bureau chief, and fire division commander.

The parties further stipulated that the following positions are nonsupervisory: fire fighter, fire search and rescue squadman, fire apparatus operator, fire equipment operator I, fire equipment operator II, fire alarm operator, fire prevention inspector I, fire prevention inspector II, fire safety education specialist I, fire safety education specialist II, fire boat engineer, fire boat pilot and helicopter pilot.

The county of Hawaii and petitioner stipulated that persons in positions of fire captain and fire lieutenant, including fire prevention inspector II, are supervisory.

The city and county of Honolulu allege that persons in positions of (1) captain and lieutenant in fire suppression, (2) fire alarm bureau shift supervisor, and (3) fire prevention inspector II are not supervisors.

The counties of Kauai and Maui stipulated that persons in positions of fire captain and fire lieutenant are within the statutory definition of supervisory employees pursuant to Section 89–2(18), Hawaii Revised Statutes, but in view of the nature of their work, which is spent as part of a crew a major portion of the time, captain and lieutenant are not supervisors.

The issues in the instant case are (1) the supervisory or nonsupervisory status of captain and lieutenant in fire suppression, fire alarm bureau shift supervisor, and fire prevention inspector II of the city and county of Honolulu and (2) whether or not fire captain and fire lieutenant of the counties of Kauai and Maui spend a major portion of their time as part of a crew.

With respect to captain of fire suppression in the city and county of Honolulu, he is commander of his fire station and, therefore, has complete charge of the station. He has the responsibility for the maintenance of the building and the apparatus under his command. He assigns the employees on his shift to duties of maintaining the building and apparatus. He is not required to perform such duties of maintaining the building and apparatus, although he may do so.

The captain is also in charge of first response fire fighting. In an initial fire response he controls the operation of a fire as first officer on the scene. Upon the arrival of a senior officer, he then returns to his company so that he may supervise the work of members of his company and may operate the equipment. The captain is at all times in complete command of his company.

It is the captain's obligation to see that the rules and regulations of the fire department are obeyed by the men on his shift at the fire station. He administers the training programs to those employees under his command. Although six training programs are regularly scheduled by the department, the captain can schedule additional drills and conduct further training as he deems necessary. He also conducts preplanning inspections and must see that they are carried out.

There are numerous rules and regulations pertaining to the maintenance and conduct of firemen and also many training manuals. The record shows that 90 percent of the duties of fire fighters are spelled out in the various manuals and rules and regulations. The training manuals are canned manuals, but in order that the captain may effectively train his men in current and modern fire fighting methods, he must do independent research.

The captain has complete control of all personnel at his fire station. He is required to enforce discipline of the employees he commands. He can effectively recommend transfer of a fire fighter out of his command. He can grant a fire fighter relief before his regular release time. He can permit fire fighters on his shift, as well as fire fighters of different shifts, to exchange "J" days.

The captain annually evaluates the work performance of his men. He can effectively recommend promotion. If he should give a fire fighter a poor performance rating, the fire fighter will not receive his annual incremental raise. The captain also evaluates probationary fire fighters. If the evaluation is a poor performance rating, the probationary fire fighter may not get permanent status. There is no evidence in the record that the evaluations of the captain have not been accepted by the fire chief.

The record further discloses that captain represents management at the fire station. The *Rules and Regulations Governing the Fire Department* defines commanding officers as captain and lieutenant. In the interest of the public employer, the captain effectuates the policies of the fire department. He must have knowledge of the principles and practice of a supervisor. The City and County of Honolulu Civil Service Department conducts training programs for captains to become supervisors.

With respect to lieutenant in fire suppression in the city and county of Honolulu, he is classified like the captain as a commanding officer under the *Rules and Regulations Governing the Fire Department,* revised. The record indicates that the lieutenant acts as captain 75 percent of his time on duty and the remaining 25 percent of his time as fire equipment operator II.

The record is uncontroverted that when the lieutenant acts in the capacity of captain, all the authority and duties of a captain inures to the lieutenant. He is in complete charge of the fire station and has the responsibility for the maintenance of the building and the apparatus. He is in charge of first response fire fighting. In the initial fire response, he controls the operation of a fire as first officer on the scene. He returns to his company to supervise the work of members of his company and may operate equipment when a senior officer arrives. The lieutenant, in the captain's absence, is at all times in complete command of his company.

While acting as captain, the lieutenant can grant fire fighters privileges such as exchange of shifts, relief before change of platoons, change of "J" days, and short absences from quarters. He can effectively discipline his men. He can effectively adjust their grievances. He can effectively recommend merit awards. He is often consulted by the captain in rating the performance of the men under his command. If the captain is on extended leave, the lieutenant evaluates the work performance of his men.

With respect to fire alarm bureau shift supervisor, he directs and assigns work to employees under his command. He regularly evaluates the work performance of men under his command. He can effectively recommend transfer of personnel on his shift to another shift. There is no evidence in the record that such direction, assignment, or evaluation performed by the fire alarm shift supervisor has not been accepted by the fire chief.

The fire alarm bureau shift supervisor relieves the fire alarm superintendent during his absence and acts in the capacity of fire alarm superintendent. In view of the evidence of the record, it is obvious that all fires are not the same and when an unusual fire situation occurs, which is not covered by the departmental manual, the fire alarm superintendent, or the fire alarm shift supervisor in his absence, is required to use his independent judgment to handle the situation.

With respect to fire prevention inspector II, he directs and assigns work to fire prevention inspector I. He can deny a request for annual leave whenever, in his judgment, there is a shortage of personnel. He can permit his men not to report back to the office at regular quitting time. He can grant overtime and approve requests for gas mileage.

The fire prevention inspector II makes annual evaluations of men under his command. He can effectively recommend promotion. He can effectively recommend suspension and when the employee is disciplined, he can effectively recommend leniency. There is no evidence in the record that any of the authority and duties exercised by the fire prevention inspector II —direct and assign employees, deny annual leave requests, permit employees not to report back to the office, grant overtime and gas mileage, or evaluate employees, including recommendation for promotion—has been denied by the fire chief.

The city and county of Honolulu offered no evidence that fire suppression captain, fire suppression lieutenant, and fire prevention inspector II spend a major portion of their time as part of a crew. Deputy Fire Chief

Aiu testified that he did not know whether a captain spent more than 50 percent of his time at the fire station doing the same thing as a fire fighter. The evidence is conflicting whether fire alarm shift supervisor spends a major portion of his time doing the same thing as rank-and-file employees.

The county of Kauai stipulated that captain and lieutenant are supervisory employees, but contended that they should be considered nonsupervisory since a major portion of their time is spent as part of a crew. However, the county of Kauai did not offer any evidence in support of its contention that due to the nature of a captain's or lieutenant's work, a major portion of their working time is spent as part of a crew or team with nonsupervisory employees.

The county of Maui offered evidence that because of the nature of work of captain and lieutenant, they are nonsupervisory employees. The thrust of the county of Maui's evidence is that captain and lieutenant spend a major or "greater" portion of their time as part of a crew. However, the record clearly discloses that the evidence proffered by the county of Maui to show that captain and lieutenant spend a greater part of their working time as part of a crew is just an estimate, which is not derived from thorough study.

CONCLUSIONS OF LAW

In determining the supervisory status of a public employee the board is compelled to adhere to the statutory definition of a supervisor. Section 89–2(18) . . . states,

> "Supervisory employee" means any individual having authority in the interest of the employer, to hire, transfer, suspend, lay off, recall, promote, discharge, assign, reward, or discipline other employees, or the responsibility to assign work to and direct them, or to adjust their grievances, or effectively to recommend such action, if, in connection with the foregoing, the exercise of such authority is not of a merely routine or clerical nature, but requires the use of independent judgment. . . .

A statute should be construed, if practicable, so that its component parts are consistent and reasonable. Every word used is presumed to have meaning and purpose, and should be given full effect if so doing does not violate the obvious intent of the legislature. Inconsistent phrases are to be harmonized, if possible, so as to reach the legislative intent. When we follow these guidelines, it is obvious that we must construe both Sections 89–2(18) and 89–6(a) . . . to give meaning and purpose to both sections to arrive at the legislative intent of who are supervisory employees in the public service.

The phrase "major portion" has a clear and definite meaning and we, in interpreting Section 89–6(a) . . . must give this phrase the ordinary meaning, which is defined to be, greater or larger. We are of the opinion that the legislature intended the clause "major portion of the working time of a supervisory employee is spent as part of a crew or team with nonsupervisory employees," as found in Section 89–6(a) to mean that the supervisory employee must spend a greater or larger portion of his time in a nonsupervisory capacity with nonsupervisory employees in order to harmonize Sections 89–2(18) and 89–6(a), Hawaii Revised Statutes.

It is our opinion that the legislature in its wisdom directed the board not to be misguided by class titles in its determination of the supervisory status of an employee. Also, it is our opinion that the legislature mandated the board to direct the parties to produce evidence regarding the nature of an employee's work to determine whether he is or is not a supervisor. Such evidence shall include whether a major, greater, or larger portion of the working time of a supervisory employee is spent as part of a crew with nonsupervisory employees in a nonsupervisory capacity.

Public employees perform their functions and services through elected and appointed officials and employees hired by the public employers. In the broadest sense, any employee receiving compensation for services performed by him on behalf of a public employer can be said to be an employee of the public employer. Such interpretation would encompass the Governor, all the mayors, the department heads, division heads, and surely they all work as part of a crew or team in carrying out their administrative, managerial, and other functions. It would lead to an absurd situation where there would be no supervisory employees in the public sector if we do not interpret Section 89–6(a) to mean as time spent in a nonsupervisory capacity.

We also look to the *Rules and Regulations Governing the Fire Department,* revised, of the city and county of Honolulu and manuals outlining the duties and responsibilities of captain and lieutenant. The facts in the instant case attest to their authenticity and we cannot believe that they may have been written in response to the union's petition.

> Company commanders are the only officers whose command is at all times under their immediate supervision and control. Consequently, their position is one of the utmost importance in the enforcement of discipline and the promotion and maintenance of efficiency. Therefore, they will consider it their indispensable duty to be constantly vigilant and, while setting an especially good example, require that their command measure up to the standard of departmental requirements.

Section 130 of the rules and regulations states,

Company commanders shall be in control of their respective companies while on duty and shall be responsible for putting into effect the policy, rules and regulations, practices, and procedures of the department.

The above cited sections of the *Rules and Regulations Governing the Fire Department* of the city and county of Honolulu and the facts of the instant case enumerating the authority and duties, lead us to conclude that captain and lieutenant perform their duties in the interest of the public employer and which require the use of independent judgment.

There is no hard-and-fast rule that can be established at this time declaring that a given classification or job title should *ipso facto* be classified as supervisory. Rather, each case must be determined on its individual facts.

Under the facts of the instant case pertaining to the fire suppression captain and fire suppression lieutenant, we find that they represent the public employer at the fire station and that they direct and assign work to men under their command. We find that they can adjust the grievances of men under them. We find that the captain and, at times, the lieutenant evaluate the employees under them. Such evaluation becomes part of the employee's personnel record and is a determinative factor in deciding whether the employee receives his annual wage increment. We find that they can effectively recommend promotion, transfer, reward, and discipline. We further find that such aforementioned authority exercised by the captain and the lieutenant in the interest of the public employer is not merely routine or clerical in nature, but requires the use of independent judgment.

Under the facts of the instant case pertaining to fire alarm shift supervisor, we find that he directs and assigns work to men under his command. We find that he can effectively recommend transfer. We find that he evaluates his men and that such evaluation function creates a sharp conflict of interest between the fire alarm shift supervisor and the "rank-and-file" subject to his authority. We further find that such aforementioned authority exercised by the fire alarm shift supervisor in the interest of the public employer is not merely routine and clerical in nature, but requires the use of independent judgment.

Under the circumstances of the instant case pertaining to fire prevention inspector II, we find that he directs and assigns work to men under his command. We find that he can effectively recommend transfer, promotion, suspension, and discipline; that he can deny annual leave and grant overtime to his men; and that he evaluates his men. We further find that such authority exercised by the fire prevention inspector II in the interest of the public employer is not merely routine or clerical in nature, but requires the use of independent judgment. . . .

The city and county of Honolulu produced no evidence that either the fire suppression captain, the fire suppression lieutenant, or the fire prevention inspector II spend a major, larger, or greater portion of their time as part of a crew or team of fire fighters in a nonsupervisory capacity. We are of the opinion that the fire alarm shift supervisor spends a major, greater, or larger portion of his time as a supervisory employee.

Therefore, we conclude that captain and lieutenant in fire suppression, fire alarm shift supervisor, and fire prevention inspector II of the city and county of Honolulu are supervisors within the meaning of Chapter 89, Hawaii Revised Statutes.

The county of Kauai stipulated that its captain and lieutenant are supervisory within the meaning of Chapter 89–2(18), Hawaii Revised Statutes. It further contends that its supervisors spend a greater portion of their time as part of a crew and should, therefore, be considered nonsupervisory. However, the county of Kauai produced no evidence and submitted no brief to substantiate its position that captain and lieutenant spend a major, larger, or greater portion of their time as part of a crew or team of fire fighters in a nonsupervisory capacity. Therefore, we have no alternative but to conclude that the county of Kauai has either waived or abandoned its position. We summarily find that captain and lieutenant of the fire department of the county of Kauai are supervisors within the meaning of Chapter 89, Hawaii Revised Statutes.

The county of Maui stipulated that its captain and lieutenant are supervisors within the meaning of Section 89–2(18), Hawaii Revised Statutes. However, its position is that since captain and lieutenant spend a major, greater, or larger portion of their time in a nonsupervisory capacity, they are not supervisors. In support thereof, the county of Maui produced evidence indicating the captain and lieutenant spend 46 percent of their working time as supervisors and 54 percent of their time in a nonsupervisory capacity. However, the record unmistakably shows that such evidence is based on very rough estimates and is not the result of a thorough study. Furthermore, the record discloses that the inaccuracy of these figures was admitted in testimony. It is our opinion that we cannot give weight or credence to the evidence submitted by the county of Maui.

Under these circumstances, we find that the county of Maui has failed to produce relevant convincing evidence that its captain and lieutenant spend a major portion of their working time as part of a crew or team of fire fighters in a nonsupervisory capacity. Therefore, we conclude that captain and lieutenant of the fire department of the county of Maui are supervisors within the meaning of Chapter 89, Hawaii Revised Statutes.

Hawaii Public Employment Relations Board

/s/ Mack H. Hamada, Chairman
/s/ John E. Milligan, Board Member

DISSENTING OPINION

I dissent from my colleagues' majority decision that captains and lieutenants are supervisory employees.

The testimony and exhibits clearly show that while captains and lieutenants have important and high-rank sounding titles, they are supervisors at the working foreman and/or leadman level. Thus, they should be designated as nonsupervisory employees as this board did in the representation cases involving blue collar employees.

In those cases, working foremen were designated nonsupervisory employees.

I feel my colleagues are strictly adhering to the definition of a supervisory employee pursuant to Section 89–2(18), Hawaii Revised Statutes, and have not given sufficient consideration to the intent of the provision in Section 89–6(a) . . . which states,

> In differentiating supervisory from nonsupervisory employees, class titles alone shall not be the basis for determination, but in addition, the nature of work, *including whether or not a major portion of the working time of a supervisory employee is spent as part of a crew or team with nonsupervisory employees,* shall also be considered (emphasis added).

I believe such strict adherence to the definition of Section 89–2(18) alone in determining who are supervisors is not consistent with the intent and purposes of the Hawaii Collective Bargaining Law. Both sections of the law—Sections 89–2(18) and 89–6(a)—must be considered together in determining whether an employee is supervisory or not.

The intent of the legislature is quite clear as to where the line should be drawn between supervisory and nonsupervisory employees. It is apparent that the legislature intended to follow the long-standing policy of the National Labor Relations Board, since it used a definition of supervisory employees that is nearly identical to the definition of supervisors contained in the National Labor Relations Act. In the application of that act supervisors at the working foreman and leadman level are included in the collective bargaining unit with rank-and-file workers. I contend that if the legislature had intended otherwise, it could easily have so indicated. On the contrary, Hawaii Legislature went further and included the above-cited provision of the act, Section 89–6(a), to clarify the question of where the supervisory exclusion line is to be drawn; that is, that working foremen level employees are nonsupervisory employees for the purpose of rank-and-file unit eligibility.

In the instant case, all of the time of captains and lieutenants is spent as part of a crew or team—they live, eat, work, and fight fires together, always as a team. Together they make up the crew on each piece of fire fighting equipment. No other work force has a closer knit crew or team relationship than the members of a fire engine or ladder company in a fire department. I believe that such a close community of interest which exists among captains, lieutenants, and nonsupervisory employees should not be overlooked in differentiating supervisors from those who are not supervisors. Therefore, I agree with the positions of the city and county of Honolulu and the counties of Maui and Kauai that since a major portion of the time of captains and lieutenants is spent as a part of a crew or team with nonsupervisory employees, they should be considered nonsupervisory employees in conformity with Section 89–6(a) of the act.

I find merit in the contention of the city and county of Honolulu that nearly all of the supervisory duties and responsibilities of a captain or a lieutenant are routine or clerical in nature. In my judgment, captains and lieutenants are assignors and overseers of work rather than of personnel; their supervisory duties are not sufficiently important and distinct to justify denying them their right under the act to bargain collectively with their teammates, through representatives of their own choosing. The testimony and exhibits reveal that practically every move initiated or action taken by a captain or lieutenant is predetermined; it is spelled out in detail in the operations manual or rules manual or in directives from superior officers. The captains and lieutenants have no authority to deviate from them. Their main functions are to lead the team or crew and to see that they do their exercises, including fire drills, and are prepared to fight a fire, in much the same manner as a corporal or sergeant in the army leads his squad or company. The captain has some paper work to take care of, but most of it, if not all, is routine filling out of forms and reports, attendance records, equipment usage reports, and so on. He receives instructions and work specifications from superiors and transmits them to the crew.

I find the following definitions of leadman in the *Dictionary of Occupational Titles* . . . published by the U. S. Department of Labor, and guidelines for working foremen to be a fairly accurate description of the duties and responsibilities of a captain and a lieutenant:

> Leadman (any ind.) group leader; leader. A term applied to a worker who takes the lead and gives directions to workers in his group while performing same duties as workers. Receives instructions and work specifications from supervisor and transmits them to worker. Motivates workers to meet production standards, and helps workers or supervisors to solve work problems. Regularly performs all tasks of workers in group. May assign and explain tasks to workers. May inspect machines, equipment, incoming materials, and completed work. May record information such as time and production data. Is not responsible for final decisions regarding quality and quantity of work produced or for personnel actions, such as releases, transfers, up-grading, or disciplinary measures. Supervisory functions are secondary to the production duties he performs.

I direct attention to the Hawaii State *Guideline for Evaluation of Blue Collar Supervisory Classes Instruction,* p. 23, which reads as follows:

> *Evaluation Criteria—Working Foreman.*
> 1. *Summary of Concepts.* Supervises and participates in the activities of a work unit.
> 2. *Characteristic Duties and Responsibilities.* Has immediate accountability and responsibility for the work of subordinate nonsupervisory employee(s); participates in the work for a substantial portion of the time; sets work pace to assure satisfactory work progress; provides technical assistance to subordinates; maintains and prepares reports of job activities; estimates job requirements; provides on-the-job techniques; may recommend personnel action on leave requests, promotions, performance evaluation, and so on.
> 3. *Controls over Work.* Under general supervision, is accountable for assigned projects or work activities in a single occupation or closely related occupations, and the daily work of assigned subordinate(s). Work is assigned through oral and written instructions on a daily or project basis, subject to spot check and review by a foreman.

To further illustrate the low level of supervisory authority of captains and lieutenants, which I construe to be no more than that of a working foreman or leadman, I call your attention to some of their duties and responsibilities which are spelled out in the *City and County Manual of Operations,* Honolulu fire department. . . .

Based on the aforementioned considerations and the evidence in the record, I cannot agree with my colleagues decision that fire department captains and lieutenants are supervisors. I find the differentiation of supervisory and nonsupervisory employees as submitted by the city and county of Honolulu and the counties of Maui and Kauai, rather than that of petitioner, to be appropriate in accordance with the intent of Sections 89–2(18) and 89–6(a), Hawaii Revised Statutes, which are not ambiguous.

Therefore, I conclude that captain, lieutenant, fire alarm bureau shift supervisor, and fire prevention inspector II positions are not supervisors and should, therefore, be considered as nonsupervisory employees for the purposes of determining the nonsupervisory firemen's collective bargaining unit.

/s/ Carl J. Guntert, Board Member

DIRECTION OF ELECTION

IT IS HEREBY ORDERED that an election, by secret ballot, shall be conducted among the supervisory and nonsupervisory employees in the above-described employee group. . . .

IT IS FURTHER ORDERED that the eligible employees shall vote whether or not they desire to have an optional appropriate bargaining unit, whether supervisory and nonsupervisory employees shall be included in the same bargaining unit, and whether or not they desire to be represented for collective bargaining purposes by the Hawaii Fire Fighters Association, Local 1463, IAFF, AFL–CIO or no representation.

Hawaii Public Employment Relations Board

Dated: January 3, 1972   /s/ Mack H. Hamada, Chairman
      Honolulu, Hawaii   /s/ Carl J. Guntert, Board Member
                         /s/ John E. Milligan, Board Member

Discussion Questions

1. Something more than a job title provides a conclusive indication that an occupation is supervisory or nonsupervisory in nature. Discuss this factor.
2. What example did the board use to illustrate the spurious logic implicit in overstating the "crew" or "team" concept of public service?
3. State the rule of statutory construction as set out by the board.
4. What error in statutory interpretation did the dissenting board member allege was committed by his colleagues?
5. Cite the evidentiary problems encountered by the counties of Kauai and Maui that influenced the board's findings.
6. How did the dissenter support his contention that captains and lieutenants should be included in the nonsupervisory unit?
7. Follow the line of reasoning of the board in its ruling that captains and lieutenants carried out duties that classified them as supervisors.

Section 9. Definition of Supervisors in a Police Department

The preceding decision involved the unit status of captains and lieutenants in a fire department; here we are faced with a determination of whether police sergeants are supervisors to be excluded from a unit of rank-and-file patrolmen. Once more, careful scrutiny of actual job functions turns out to be more important for purposes of unit determination than the job title itself.

In the Matter of

Township of Hanover (public employer) *and* **Local 128, PBA (petitioner)**

Docket No. RO–49

(State of New Jersey before the Public Employment Relations Commission)

DECISION AND DIRECTION OF ELECTION

. . . The undersigned has considered the entire record, the hearing officer's report and recommendations and the exceptions and on the facts in this case finds

.   .   .

3. Petitioner seeks to represent a unit of all policemen, excluding only the chief. The unit petitioned for would include the following: the deputy chief, six sergeants, including a detective sergeant, and seventeen patrolmen, including two detectives. The hearing officer found the petitioner to be an employee representative within the meaning of the act and further found that an appropriate unit for collective negotiations should include all patrolmen and sergeants. Excluded from that unit is the chief and the deputy chief. The hearing officer came to that unit determination based upon his conclusion that the sergeants were not supervisors within the meaning of the act, and that the deputy chief came within C34:13A–3(d) of the statute which defines public employee and specifically excepts from that definition "heads and deputy heads of departments."

The employer excepts to the findings of the hearing officer as to the appropriate unit, with specific regard to the inclusion of sergeants and patrolmen in a single unit, and also to the finding that petitioner is an appropriate employee representative.

In the absence of any exception to the finding of the hearing officer as to the status of the deputy chief as a deputy department head, the undersigned adopts that finding *pro forma.*

With regard to the sergeants, the employer contends that these personnel be excluded from the unit based upon their status as either supervisors or managerial executives within the meaning of the act, or their lack of community of interest with the patrolmen.

By statutory construction a supervisor is one exercising the authority to hire, discharge, discipline, or effectively recommend the same. The exercise of any one of these authorities is sufficient to qualify that person as a supervisor within the meaning of the act.

A review of the record in this case indicates that with regard to the hiring and firing of personnel, the sergeants have neither the power to do so themselves, nor the power to recommend effectively such courses of action. While there is some testimony to the effect that sergeants are on occasion informally requested by the chief to render a verbal opinion as to the performance of a probationary patrolman, and that such an opinion would be given "serious" consideration, it is clear that the ultimate determination as to the weight to be accorded this opinion, and in fact whether or not the employee is to be retained, remains solely within the discretion of the chief. The consideration of an opinion which is subject to independent analysis does not constitute the high order of reliance necessary to meet the test of effective recommendation. It is the chief who makes recommendations to the township committee which exercises final authority on permanent appointments.

In the township of Hanover police department an employee may be discharged only after charges are filed and a hearing is held before the township committee and only by authority of that body. The chief has the sole authority to suspend any member of the department pending a hearing, and such suspension may be with or without pay in the discretion of the chief. While there is testimony that the desk officer might send a patrolman home who was out of uniform or otherwise unable to serve, this action would be immediately reported to the chief who would make the determination as to whether or not pay loss should be involved. Additionally it is undisputed in the record that the "desk officer" to whom this responsibility would fall is in fact a patrolman rather than a sergeant approximately 50 percent of the time during the summer months and 10 percent of the time during the balance of the year. In any event, it is clear that this emergency action would depend for its disciplinary nature upon the determination of the chief, and therefore does not demonstrate the disciplinary power of the desk personnel, be they sergeants or patrolmen.

A second issue is that of the alleged "managerial executive" status of the sergeants. If, as the employer urges, sergeants are managerial executives within the meaning of the act, they must be excluded since the act provides that the rights accorded public employees do not extend to managerial executives. While the act does not define a managerial executive, the essential characteristics of the term as utilized in the field of labor relations denote one who determines and executes policy through subordinates in order to achieve the goals of the administrative unit for which he is responsible or for which he shares responsibility. It is the final responsibility to formulate, determine, and effectuate policy that distinguishes the managerial executive from other staff or line positions.

In the instant case the facts demonstrate that the sergeants do not formulate or determine policy. Their role is limited to routine assignment of patrolmen to certain patrol areas determined by the chief and deputy chief, and the assignment of police to cover situations called in to the department while they are on desk duty. Even here though, these assignments are made on a rotational system. While the sergeants are required to exercise a certain amount of independent judgment in making these assignments, it is clear that this does not measure up to the high levels of responsibility implicit in the term managerial executive.

The other allegation made by the employer to bolster its managerial executive argument is that the desk officer is in "full and sole control of the department over 50 percent of each workday. . . ." While it is un-disputed on the record that the desk officer is physically alone in the sta-tion from the time the chief and deputy chief leave until they return the following morning, it is equally clear the desk officer has no power to "control" the department beyond the duties already described above. The desk sergeant has already been found to have no power to discipline or effectively recommend same in either the presence or absence of the chief; his desk duties are pursuant to a routine established by the chief and deputy chief and consist of the same activities whether or not his superior officers are present; finally, there is a regulation or memorandum from the chief ordering that he and the Mayor be notified if certain serious emer-gencies arise. In view of this regimentation, there is no basis for a finding that the sergeants are managerial executives and that they are thus to be excluded from representation.

The final exception of the employer going to the merits of the unit determination deals with an alleged lack of community of interest between the sergeants and the patrolmen. In this regard consideration must be given to the guidelines for unit determination laid down by the Supreme Court in *Board of Education of the Town of West Orange* v. *Elizabeth Wilton et al.* (1971). There, the Court, in discussing a unit of all super-visory personnel which included the highest ranking supervisor below the superintendent of schools, held "where a substantial, actual, or potential conflict of interest exists among supervisors with respect to their duties and obligations to the employer in relation to each other, the requisite community of interest among them is lacking, and that a unit which under-takes to include all of them is not an appropriate negotiating unit within the intendment of the statute."

In the instant case, while there is no problem with ranks of super-visors within a supervisory unit, nonetheless it is the opinion of the undersigned that the same fundamental considerations of unit determina-tion must be looked to. If, as the Court found in *Wilton,* a unit need not be appropriate merely because all employees within it are supervisory, then it would follow that a mere showing that the sergeants are non-supervisory would not in itself demonstrate the appropriateness of a unit consisting of those employees and the rank-and-file patrolmen absent a showing that no "substantial, actual or potential conflict of interest" exists between the two groups.

In *City of Camden, Department of Public Safety, Division of Fire,* PERC No. 52, the commission was faced with the question of unit place-ment of nonsupervisory superior officers and in that case determined that by virtue of their responsibility and authority in matters of hiring, pro-bation, and discipline the superior officers were so closely associated and identified with the employer's interests that a substantial conflict of interest existed with relation to the firemen. In the instant case, the record does not demonstrate that the sergeants have such authority and responsibility to create a substantial, actual, or potential conflict of interest. The sergeants play no role in hiring of personnel, have no unique or significant responsibility in the disciplining of personnel, and with respect to evaluation, are consulted only occasionally on an informal basis by the chief for an oral statement as to how a new man is doing. In further mitigation of the sergeants' responsibility in this area is the fact that new men are assigned on a buddy system with a veteran patrolman and this man may also be called upon by the chief to make a similar evaluation.

In summary then, the role of the sergeants in the Hanover police department is not such as to constitute them as either supervisory or managerial executives, and while their duty at the desk does place them in a position where they direct the patrolmen from place to place as a dispatcher might, any conflict arising therefrom is considered *de minimus* and not substantial within the framework of the Court's rationale in the *Wilton* case. . . .

4. Upon consideration of the record, it is found that Policemen's Benevolent Association, Local 128 is an employee representative within the meaning of the act, and further that the appropriate unit for collective negotiations is "All patrolmen and sergeants employed by the township of Hanover, but excluding the Chief, Deputy Chief, all supervisors within the meaning of the Act, managerial executives, craft, professional and office clerical employees."

5. It is directed that an election in the unit described above be held within thirty days of the date of this decision. . . .

Dated: December 23, 1971   /s/ Maurice J. Nelligan, Jr.
       Trenton, N.J.   Executive Director

Discussion Questions

1. How was the status of the deputy chief resolved?
2. Why were sergeants ruled to be nonsupervisory employees eligible for inclusion in the same unit with patrolmen?
3. If not considered supervisors, could sergeants be considered "managerial executives," who also are excluded from nonsupervisory units?
4. Indicate the rule regarding the appropriateness of supervisory units as formulated in the *Wilton* case. Distinguish it from the ruling in this case.

Section 10. Conditions for the Inclusion of Professional and Nonprofessional Employees in One Unit

In private employment, Section 2(12) of the LMRA, defines professional employees to mean:

(a) any employee engaged in work (i) predominantly intellectual and varied in character as opposed to routine mental, manual, mechanical, or physical work; (ii) involving the consistent exercise of discretion and judgment in its performance; (iii) of such a character that the output produced or the result accomplished cannot be standardized in relation to a given period of time; (iv) requiring knowledge of an advanced type in a field of science or learning customarily acquired by a prolonged course of specialized intellectual instruction and study in an institution of higher learning or a hospital, as distinguished from a general academic education or from an apprenticeship or from training in the performance of routine mental, manual, or physical processes; or

(b) any employee, who (i) has completed the courses of specialized intellectual instruction and study described in clause (iv) of paragraph (a), and (ii) is performing related work under the supervision of a professional person to qualify himself to become a professional employee as defined in paragraph (a).[29]

The NLRB is forbidden by Section 9(b) of the LMRA to "decide that any unit is appropriate . . . if such unit includes both professional employees and employees who are not professional employees unless a majority of such professional employees vote for inclusion in such unit." [30]

In government employment at the federal level, Executive Order 11491 uses almost the identical standard in Section 10(b)(4):

no unit shall be established for purposes of exclusive recognition which includes . . . (4) both professional employees and nonprofessional employees unless a majority of such professional employees vote for inclusion in such unit.

The same standard seems to be used at the state level. For example, New Jersey Statutes Annotated, Section 34:13A–6, states that the Public Employment Relations Commission will determine the appropriate unit. However, no unit will be appropriate that includes "both professional and nonprofessional employees, unless a majority of such professional employees vote for inclusion in such unit."

In summary form the essentials of professional status are (1) varied, intellectual work; (2) the consistent exercise of discretion or judgment; (3) nonstandardizable work, in terms of time; (4) study in a specialized discipline ordinarily taught in a university or a hospital; or (5) work done in preparation for a professional career, under a professional person, by one who has completed the courses of specialized study mentioned in (4).

In any event, the characteristics of professional status seem to be easily distinguishable from those of nonprofessionals; and because of a lack of community of interest both groups should not be included in the same negotiating unit. However, as will next be demonstrated at the federal and state level, this exclusion is not automatic and, in fact, only by voting to do so will professionals in certain fact situations be allowed to disassociate themselves from nonprofessionals.

In the Matter of

United States Army Engineer Division, New England (activity) *and* American Federation of Government Employees, AFL–CIO, Local 2995 (petitioner)

Case No. 31–3177 (EO)[31]

United States Army Engineer Division, New England (activity) *and* National Federation of Federal Employees, Local 1164 (petitioner)

Case No. 31–3214 (EO)

(United States Department of Labor before the Assistant Secretary for Labor–Management Relations)

DECISION, ORDER, AND DIRECTION OF ELECTION

. . . The hearing officer's rulings made at the hearing are free from prejudicial error and are hereby affirmed.

Upon the entire record in this case (the petitions were consolidated) the Assistant Secretary finds

. . .

3. In Case No. 31–3177 (EO), petitioner, American Federation of Government Employees, AFL–CIO, Local 2995 (hereinafter referred to as AFGE), seeks an election in a unit of all nonprofessional, nonsupervisory employees of the United States Army Engineer Division, New England (hereinafter referred to as the activity), "stationed" at the activity's Headquarters in Waltham, Massachusetts. In Case No. 31–3214 (EO), petitioner, National Federation of Federal Employees, Local 1164 (hereinafter referred to as NFFE), seeks an election in a unit of all nonsupervisory professional and nonprofessional employees of the United States Army Engineer Division, New England, assigned to the activity's headquarters in Waltham, Massachusetts, and its field facilities. At the hearing, the activity took a neutral position with respect to the appropriateness of the units proposed by the petitioners.

The main function of the United States Army Engineer Division, New England, is the construction, operation, and maintenance of flood control and local flood protection structures, as well as the improvement and maintenance of navigable waterways. The activity's headquarters, located in Waltham, Massachusetts, has 14 organizational components and employs approximately 453 employees. It is responsible also for the administration and operation of five additional field facilities. These field facilities, excluding the Cape Cod Canal, employ approximately 107 employees. General responsibility for the administration of the entire operation rests with the division engineer who is located in the executive office at the activity's headquarters. The Personnel Office, the Office of the Comptroller, the Office of Administrative Services, the Engineering, Construction, and Operations divisions, and other administrative offices are located at the activity's Waltham, Massachusetts headquarters.

The Personnel Office handles all personnel matters, including employee grievances arising in the headquarters and the field. The Office of Administrative Services and the activity's other administrative offices provide the work force with transportation, supplies, and other necessary services. The Engineering Division, which is the largest component, performs some of the activity's essential technical functions. These include the obtainment of technical data through periodic surveys which are conducted in the field by teams composed of professional and nonprofessional personnel.

With respect to the bargaining history prior to the filing of the subject petitions, the activity accorded exclusive recognition to the AFGE under Executive Order 10988, covering a unit of maintenance and operating employees at the Cape Cod Canal. Also, formal recognition was granted by the activity to the AFGE under Executive Order 10988 in a unit composed of nonprofessional employees stationed at the activity's headquarters.

The record discloses that the field facilities are separated geographically from the activity's headquarters. However, supervision of employees assigned to the activity's headquarters and the various field facilities is maintained through a well-defined chain of supervision which begins with the executive office at the activity's headquarters.

According to the classification standards which apparently are applied uniformly throughout the activity, the engineers and other professional employees comprise more than one-third of the entire work force. Engineers are assigned to the Engineering Division as well as to other components at the activity's headquarters and in the field. This situation is true also with respect to technicians and clerical employees.

The record further shows that employees have "bumping rights," which they can exercise against other employees on a division-wide basis; that there has been transferring of employees between the activity's headquarters and its field components; that cafeteria and parking facilities at the activity's headquarters are used by both professional and nonprofessional employees; and that the activity publishes a newspaper which contains items of interest to all of its employees. As indicated above, all personnel matters, including the processing of grievances, are handled by the Personnel Office at the activity's headquarters.

It is clear from the record that the unit sought by the AFGE covering all nonprofessional, nonsupervisory employees "stationed" at the activity's headquarters in Waltham, Massachusetts, would encompass not only the employees who work solely at headquarters but also certain employees who spend a substantial portion of their working time in the field. The establishment of such a unit would result in the inclusion of some employees assigned to the field, while excluding other field personnel. In these circumstances and considering the activity's centralized administrative and supervisory structure, the integration of its work processes within the various headquarters and field segments, the similarity of job classifications at headquarters and in the field, the fact that there have been transfers of employees between headquarters and its field components, and the fact that "bumping rights" are on a division-wide basis, I find that the unit sought by the AFGE is not appropriate.

I also find, based on the foregoing, that the division-wide unit of professional and nonprofessional employees, as proposed by the NFFE, is appropriate. As noted above, the record reveals that there is substantial integration of functions between the activity's headquarters and its field facilities. Supervision of employees assigned to the various organizational components in the headquarters and field facilities is maintained through a chain of supervision which begins with the executive officer in the division's headquarters. The Engineering Division, which is the activity's largest component, includes both professional and nonprofessional technical employees who, in many instances, perform duties both at the activity's headquarters and in its field facilities. Also, there is evidence that employees have transferred from job to job within the division and that they have "bumping rights" on a division-wide basis. In these circumstances, I find that there is a clear and identifiable community of interest among the employees petitioned for by the NFFE. Moreover, such a comprehensive unit will, in my view, promote effective dealings and efficiency of agency operations.

I find that the following employees of the activity may constitute a unit appropriate for the purpose of exclusive recognition under Executive Order 11491: all headquarters and field professional and nonprofessional employees of the United States Army Engineer Division, New England, excluding employees assigned to the Cape Cod Canal, all employees engaged in federal personnel work in other than a purely clerical capacity, management officials, and supervisors and guards as defined in the order.

As stated above, the unit found appropriate includes professional employees. However, the Assistant Secretary is prohibited by Section

10(b)(4) of the order from including professional employees in a unit with employees who are not professional unless a majority of the professional employees vote for inclusion in such a unit. Accordingly, the desires of the professional employees as to inclusion in a unit with nonprofessional employees must be ascertained. I shall therefore direct separate elections. . . .

ORDER

IT IS HEREBY ORDERED that the petition filed in Case No. 31–3177 (EO) be, and it hereby is, dismissed.

DIRECTION OF ELECTION

An election by secret ballot shall be conducted among the employees in the unit found appropriate, as early as possible, but not later than thirty days from the date below. . . .

Dated: January 15, 1971   /s/ W. J. Usery, Jr., Assistant Secretary of
       Washington, D.C.   Labor for Labor-Management Relations

Discussion Questions

1. Which elements of the employment relationship were emphasized as creating a community of interest between the professional and nonprofessional employees?
2. Why was the AFGE petition denied?
3. Why was the NFFE petition approved?

In the Matter of

Jefferson Township Board of Education (public employer) *and* **Local 866, affiliated with the International Brotherhood of Teamsters (petitioner)** *and* **Jefferson Township Education Association (intervenor)**

Docket No. RO–180

Jefferson Township Board of Education (public employer) *and* **American Federation of States, County, and Municipal Employees, AFL–CIO (petitioner)** *and* **Jefferson Township Education Association (intervenor)**

Docket No. RO–183

(State of New Jersey before the Public Employment Relations Commission)

DECISION

. . . The commission has considered the entire record, the report and recommendation of the hearing officer, the exceptions, and, on the facts in this case finds

.   .   .

3. On September 17, 1970, the Teamsters requested recognition from the board and the board refused to grant such recognition in the unit described below unless and until the petitioner was certified by the commission. Similarly, on March 11, 1970, AFSCME requested recognition unless and until the petitioner was certified by the commission. Accordingly, there is a question before the commission concerning representation and the matter is appropriately before the commission for determination.

4. The Teamsters seek to represent all bus drivers employed by the board. AFSCME seeks to represent clericals, custodial, maintenance, cafeteria workers, and head custodials. The association has represented the employees sought by the Teamsters and by AFSME as well as teachers and other employees in a single unit. Contracts between the board and the association covering the employees in the overall unit were in effect from July 1, 1969 to June 30, 1970 and from July 1, 1970 to June 30, 1971. The board and the association contend that the petitions filed herein should be dismissed.

The hearing officer recommended that the units sought by the Teamsters and AFSCME be found inappropriate and that the petitions be dismissed. Furthermore, he found that the unit defined in the recognition clause of the 1970–1971 contract between the board and the association was an appropriate unit.

Both the Teamsters and AFSCME are seeking to remove from an existing unit certain segments of employees. The commission, in considering these attempts to sever certain groups of employees from an extant unit, must determine whether the facts justify the fragmentation of a unit into several smaller allegedly appropriate units.

The uncontroverted evidence reveals that prior to the establishment of the existing unit, separate elections were conducted among the several groups of employees including bus drivers, secretaries, custodians, cafeteria personnel, and so on, in which majorities of each of those groups voted to be represented by the association. The professional employees, who were already represented by the association, voted to include these nonprofessional groups in a single unit with themselves. Following these elections, the association requested and received recognition from the board as the sole and exclusive representative for collective negotiations for the employees described above. In accordance with the recognition, a contract was entered into April 14, 1969 between the association and the board for the term July 1, 1969 to June 30, 1970. This agreement specifically included in the recognition clause the bus drivers as well as the employees sought by AFSME. That contract contains specific articles and provisions which relate to bus drivers and custodians as well as the other groups sought by AFSME including salary schedules for secretaries, custodians, and maintenance personnel, bus drivers, and the cafeteria staff. On February 9, 1970, the board and the association signed another agreement for the period July 1, 1970 to June 30, 1971. Like its predecessor, this agreement specifically included the nonprofessional employees sought by the petitioners herein, contained contract provisions which applied uniquely to several of the groups including custodians and bus drivers, and included salary schedules for secretaries, custodians and maintenance employees, bus drivers, and the cafeteria staff. . . .

There is no evidence, nor is there even a contention, that the association in any way defaulted on its statutory obligation to be "responsible for representing the interests of all such employees without discrimination and without regard to employee organization membership." There is no claim that the association did not provide effective and fair representation to all employees in the unit. In fact, as described above, the record indicates that the association did make a responsible effort to represent all elements in the negotiating unit.

In its exceptions the Teamsters contend first that the hearing officer erred by disposing of the petitioned-for, smaller unit on the basis that the larger, existing unit was appropriate. It argues that the only issue is the appropriateness of the unit sought, that consideration of the existing unit would not be dispositive unless such unit was the only one found appropriate, and that the existing unit is, if anything, patently inappropriate.

We do not agree that the existing unit is, on its face, inappropriate by any statutory reference. The alleged defects are said to exist because the unit contains what the employer describes as three supervisors "within the meaning of the act" and because it mixes professional and nonprofessional employees. Yet the statute carries no absolute proscription to such arrangements, and in fact contemplates the possibility of such mixtures in certain situations. Whether or not the commission, upon request for certification in an overall unit, would have found appropriate the unit that later came to be is not the issue. No one here is asking for a *de novo* definition of a comprehensive unit. The unit was established through recognition and is not, on its face, inappropriate. For purposes of this proceeding no further examination of the unit's appropriateness need be made. . . .

The underlying question is a policy one: assuming without deciding that a community of interest exists for the unit sought, should that consideration prevail and be permitted to disturb the existing relationship in the absence of a showing that such relationship is unstable or that the incumbent organization has not provided responsible representation. We think not. To hold otherwise would leave every unit open to redefinition simply on a showing that one subcategory of employees enjoyed a community of interest among themselves. Such a course would predictably lead to continuous agitation and uncertainty, would run counter to the statutory objective and would, for that matter, ignore that the existing relationship may also demonstrate its own community of interest.

Here we have a unit created by recognition, not demonstrated to be inappropriate, covered by two successive agreements, and represented by an organization not shown to have provided less than responsible representation. Under these circumstances, the commission is not prepared to upset that relationship on the single premise that bus drivers enjoy a variety of common interests. The commission concludes that the unit sought is not one appropriate for collective negotiations in these circumstances. In view of this disposition, the remaining exceptions of the Teamsters fall.

The Teamster petition for a unit of bus drivers and the AFSCME petition are dismissed for the foregoing reasons.

By order of the commission.

Dated: October 22, 1971   /s/ William L. Kirchner, Jr.
       Trenton, N.J.   Acting Chairman

Discussion Questions

1. Describe the bargaining history between the association and the Board of Education. Was it a significant factor in the outcome of the case?
2. Why did the commission rule against fragmentation of the existing unit?
3. What is the important policy issue involved in this case?

CHAPTER 2

[1] Paul Prasow, "Principles of Unit Determination—Concept and Problems," in *Unit Determination—Recognition and Representation Elections in Public Agencies,* Proceedings of a Conference on Public Sector Labor Management Relations, September 23–24, 1971 (Los Angeles: University of California, Institute of Industrial Relations, 1972), p. 3.

[2] *Pickets at City Hall* (New York: Twentieth Century Fund, 1970), p. 11.

[3] *Labor Relations Expediter* 30b (Washington, D.C.: Bureau of National Affairs, 1970).

[4] Harry H. Wellington and Ralph K. Winter, Jr., *The Unions and the Cities* (Washington, D.C.: The Brookings Institution, 1971), p. 104.

[5] Comments by Attilio Di Pasquale, head of the Labor and Employee Relations Division of the Department of the Navy's Office of Civilian Manpower Management, at the Federal Bar Association Council on Labor Law and Labor Relations Conference on Collective Bargaining in the Federal Sector, Washington, D.C., April 29–30, 1971.

[6] *Ibid.*

[7] *Labor Relations Expediter, loc. cit.*

[8] Arvid Anderson, chairman of the New York City Office of Collective Bargaining, in an address to the Federal Bar Association Council on Labor Law and Labor Relations Conference on Collective Bargaining in the Federal Sector, Washington, D.C., April 29–30, 1971.

[9] Prasow, *op. cit.*, p. 2.

[10] *Labor-Management Relations in the Federal Service, Executive Order 11491*, Oct. 29, 1969, effective Jan. 1, 1970.

[11] Arvid Anderson, "The Structure of Public Sector Bargaining," in *Public Workers and Public Unions*, ed. by Sam Zagoria, The American Assembly (Englewood Cliffs, N.J.: Prentice-Hall, Inc., 1972), pp. 40–42.

[12] Marvin J. Levine, "Labor Relations Status of Supervisors in the Federal Government," *Public Personnel Review* (January, 1972), p. 25.

[13] 21 *Government Employee Relations Report* 5277–5278 (RF-31) (Washington, D.C.: Bureau of National Affairs, Inc., Aug. 31, 1971).

[14] 21 GERR 4085–4089 (RF-40) (Washington, D.C.: BNA, Inc., 1972).

[15] LRX 33 (Washington, D.C.: BNA, Inc., 1970).

[16] *Ibid.*

[17] 21 GERR 4011–4015 (RF-39) (Washington, D.C.: BNA, Inc., 1972).

[18] Labor Relations Expediter 28a (Washington, D.C.: BNA, Inc., 1971).

[19] 21 GERR 5039–5040 (RF-18) (Washington, D.C.: BNA, Inc., 1971).

[20] LRX 32a (Washington, D.C.: BNA, Inc., 1970).

[21] GERR (No. 390) E1–E8 (Washington, D.C.: BNA, Inc., March 1, 1971).

[22] In the Matter of State of Rhode Island, Department of Administration, Employer and Rhode Island State Employees Association Petitioner and Rhode Island Public Employees Council 70 AFSCME, AFL–CIO, and Service Employees International Union, AFL–CIO, Intervenor. Case No. EE–1714, March 24, 1971.

[23] GERR (No. 493) B11–B14 (Washington, D.C.: BNA, Inc., March 5, 1973).

[24] *Ibid.*, B-12.

[25] *Ibid.*, B-13.

[26] *Ibid.*, B-11.

[27] 21 GERR 5275–5276 (RF-31) (Washington, D.C.: BNA, Inc., 1971).

[28] GERR (No. 427) E1–E6 (Washington, D.C.: BNA, Inc., January 31, 1972).

[29] LRX 28b, 29 (Washington, D.C.: BNA, Inc., 1970).

[30] *Ibid.*, 28b.

[31] 21 GERR 5015–5017 (RF-15) (Washington, D.C.: BNA, Inc., 1971).

3 | Selection of a Bargaining Agent: Election and Certification

ONCE the appropriate bargaining unit has been determined, a representation election is the conventional means for determining negotiation rights. Considerable experience concerning the implementation of the election process has been gained from the private sector model, which is more or less emulated by the federal executive order now in operation and by most state statutes, and from which public agency election and certification procedures are basically derived.

A brief description of the union certification process in private industry is appropriate at this point because the procedures followed are often duplicated in public employment.

Section 9 of the NLRA provides for representation elections. A petition for an election, which can be filed with the NLRB by either the employees, any individual or labor organization acting on behalf of the employees, or employers who have been presented with representation claims by competing unions, contains a description of the unit of employees in which an election is sought, the approximate number of employees in the unit, and the names of all unions that claim to represent the employees in the unit. The petitioner must be acting on behalf of a substantial number of employees. "Substantial" has been defined to mean that at least 30 percent of the employees involved have indicated, by authorization cards, petitions, or other means, that they would vote in favor of union representation. An employer requesting an election must demonstrate only that some union has made a claim to representing his employees.

The board usually specifies that the employees eligible to vote are those who were employed during the payroll period immediately preceding the date of its decision in the case. The employer is asked to furnish an alphabetized payroll so that any question of voting eligibility can be settled

133

in advance. The board's order customarily directs that employees who did not work during the payroll period designated because they were ill, temporarily laid off, or on vacation are eligible to vote.

If it is determined that a legitimate question concerning representation exists, the board ordinarily will direct a secret ballot election to be held within thirty days. The election details are left to the board, which devises rules designed to encourage the workers' participation in the election.

Wellington and Winter have pointed out the similarities in procedures in public employment at the state level:

> The rules of the New York PERB are typical of the major state agencies. There must be a 30 percent showing of interest by employees in a union before the PERB will hold a representation election. . . . The petitioning union must prove that membership in the union is for the purposes of representation in collective bargaining. . . .[1]

Finally, in both the public and private realms, if a union is victorious in the balloting, the appropriate board or commission will certify it as the exclusive bargaining representative for the group of employees in the designated bargaining unit. This certification removes all doubt of the union's majority status for at least one year. Moreover, if the employees have rejected the union's offer of representation, no further election can be held for a period of at least one year.

The cases in this chapter are designed to demonstrate the varying degrees of conformity with the private sector model that exist in public employment.

Section 1. The Pre-election Campaign

Union organizational activity normally involves efforts to solicit union membership and to distribute union literature on company property. In private industry, several recent NLRB decisions have established guidelines for permissible activity in these areas.[2] The rules may be stated as follows:

1. Employees are free to engage in oral solicitation on behalf of a labor organization anywhere on the employer's premises during nonworking time.

2. Employees are free to distribute union literature in nonworking areas of the employer's premises.

3. Rules limiting solicitation and distribution, presumptively valid under the foregoing principles, may be rendered invalid if adopted for a discriminatory purpose.

The following case in the federal service illustrates the close adherence to private sector rules; however, it also indicates that NLRB and court rulings will not necessarily have the force of binding precedent.

In the Matter of

Charleston Naval Shipyard (respondent) *and* **Federal Employees Metal Trades Council, Metal Trades Department, AFL-CIO (complainant)**

Case Nos. 40–1940 (CA), 40–1950 (CA)[3]

(United States Department of Labor before the Assistant Secretary for Labor–Management Relations)

DECISION AND ORDER

. . . The Assistant Secretary has reviewed the rulings of the hearing examiner made at the hearing and finds that no prejudicial error was committed. The rulings are hereby affirmed. The Assistant Secretary has considered the hearing examiner's report and recommendations and the entire record in the subject cases, including the exceptions, statements of position, and briefs, and hereby adopts the findings, conclusions, and recommendations of the hearing examiner only to the extent consistent herewith.

The complaints in the instant cases filed by the Charleston Metal Trades Council (herein called the union) against the Charleston Naval Shipyard (herein called the shipyard) alleged violations of Sections 19(a) (1) and 20 of Executive Order 11491 based on the shipyard's notice of February 18 and its subsequent memoranda of March 16 and 27, 1970. The union contends that the notice and memoranda effectively coerced, restrained, and intimidated employees in the exercise of their rights assured under Executive Order 11491. The shipyard, on the other hand, defends its conduct in issuing the above-mentioned directives on the basis that it was merely acting in accordance with outstanding instructions of the Civil Service Commission which provide, in part, that during the period subsequent to the filing of a valid challenge requiring a redetermination of exclusive status, an "agency should not authorize the use of agency facilities to either the incumbent exclusive or the challenging organization(s) to conduct membership or election campaigns." In this respect, the shipyard contends that the Assistant Secretary of Labor is without authority to find that a directive, regulation, order, or policy issued by the Civil Service Commission, Department of Defense, or any other "higher authority" over the shipyard is invalid because such a determination would violate Sections 4(b) and 25(a) of the order.

The hearing examiner concluded that the directives governing union electioneering activities promulgated by the shipyard interfered with, restrained, or coerced employees in the rights assured by Executive Order 11491 since such rules infringed on the employees' right under Section 1 of the order to "assist a labor organization."

In reaching his recommendation, the hearing examiner relied on precedent developed under the National Labor Relations Act. He reasoned that in view of the similarity of language between Sections 7 and 8(a)(1) of the act and Sections 1 and 19(a)(1) of the order, that "the decisions under the statute dealing with employee rights in solicitation and distribution of literature are applicable under the order. . . ." The hearing examiner also rejected the shipyard's contention that in issuing the disputed regulations it was acting under a legal obligation to follow the directives of the Civil Service Commission and the Department of Defense. In this regard he stated that rights of employees established under the executive order "are not diminished by erroneous rulings of the Civil Service Commission or the Department of Defense."

There is no indication in the reports and recommendations which preceded Executive Orders 10988 and 11491 that the experience gained in the private sector under the National Labor Relations Act would necessarily be the controlling precedent in the administration of labor-management relations in the federal sector. Thus, many of the provisions of Executive Order 10988 constituted clear attempts to take into account situations peculiar to federal sector labor-management relations. Moreover, in 1969, when it was determined that improvements in the federal labor-management relations program were warranted, it was made clear by the study committee that the proposed changes dealt only with deficiencies found to exist under Executive Order 10988, and there was no intention to adopt some other model for federal labor-management relations.

Based on the foregoing, it is my belief that decisions issued under the Labor–Management Relations Act, as amended, are not controlling under Executive Order 11491. I will, however, take into account the experience gained in the private sector under the Labor–Management Relations Act, as amended, policies and practices in other jurisdictions, and those rules developed in the federal sector under the prior executive order. Accordingly, I reject the reasoning of the hearing examiner in the instant case insofar as he implies that all of the rules and decisions under the Labor–Management Relations Act, as amended, would constitute binding precedent on the Assistant Secretary with respect to the implementation of his responsibilities under Executive Order 11491.

Also, I reject the shipyard's assertion that I am without authority to determine whether directives or policy guidance issued by the Civil Service Commission, Department of Defense, or any other agency are violative of the order when those directives or policies are asserted by the activity as a defense to allegedly violative conduct. Both the study committee's report and recommendations and the order itself clearly indicate the role which the Assistant Secretary was intended to play in the processing of unfair labor practices complaints under the order. Thus, the study committee's report and recommendations stated that the lack of a third-party process in resolving unfair labor practice charges was a serious deficiency under the prior federal labor–management program. To rectify this deficiency, it was recommended that the Assistant Secretary of Labor for Labor–Management Relations be authorized to issue decisions to agencies and labor organizations subject to a limited right of appeal to the Federal Labor Relations Council. The study committee stated that as the Assistant Secretary issues decisions a body of precedent would be developed from which interested parties could draw guidance. The recommendations of the study committee culminated in Section 6(a)(4) of the order which provides, in part, that the Assistant Secretary of Labor for Labor–Management Relations shall "decide complaints of alleged unfair labor practices and alleged violations of the standards of conduct for labor organizations." Hence, neither the study committee's report and recommendations nor the order itself requires that in processing unfair labor practices complaints I am bound to accept as determinative those directives or policies of the Civil Service Commission, the Department of Defense, or any other agency which in my view contravene the purposes of the order.

Accordingly, I reject the shipyard's contention that I am without authority to find a violation in the instant case because its conduct was based on directives issued by the Civil Service Commission and the Department of Defense.

As did Executive Order 10988, Executive Order 11491 guarantees to employees of the federal government the right "to form, join, and assist" a labor organization "without fear of penalty or reprisal." Section 19(a)(1) of Executive Order 11491 states that "agency management shall not interfere with, restrain, or coerce employees in the exercise of the rights assured by this order." That provision raises the basic issue to be resolved herein, that is, were the shipyard's attempts to control employee electioneering on its premises, as evidenced by its February 18 notice to employees and its subsequent memoranda of March 16 and 27 in derogation of expressly guaranteed employee rights under Executive Order 11491?

In attempting to resolve this issue, I have carefully reviewed the policy and practice developed in the federal sector under Executive Order 10988 pursuant to the Civil Service Commission's Personnel Manual Letter 711–6. As noted above, such policy and practice was adopted to cover a particular period prior to the execution of an election agreement when a valid and timely challenge had been filed with respect to an incumbent labor organization's exclusive representative status. During this period, agencies were counseled not to authorize the use of their facilities to either the incumbent exclusive representative or the challenging organization for the purpose of conducting membership or election campaigns.

The Civil Service Commission contended that this procedure represents "the most reasonable approach we have discovered to achieving among the contending unions the requisite fairness or equality of opportunity which alone can guarantee a genuinely free and representative election."

The shipyard and the Department of Defense offered further justification for the Civil Service Commission policy on the grounds that the government, as an employer, is "more neutral" in these matters than private employers and that there exists a substantial past practice under this policy which, if changed, would result in instability in federal labor–management relations.

The basic rules governing employee solicitation and distribution were established by the Supreme Court in *Le Tourneau Co. of Georgia* v. *NLRB,* 324 U.S. 793 (1945) and *Republic Aviation Corp.* v. *NLRB,* 324 U.S. 794 (1945). The Court held that the enforcement of no-distribution and no-solicitation rules against employees during their nonworking time was unlawful except where there were unusual circumstances present.

In the instant cases there is no evidence to establish that employee solicitation activity with respect to the forthcoming election or their distribution of campaign literature had the effect or would have had the effect of creating a safety hazard or interfering with work production or the maintenance of discipline in the shipyard. Moreover, the argument that a moratorium on electioneering prevents the incumbent from exercising its natural advantage over the challenger is likewise unpersuasive since equality also can be maintained by granting full communication rights to both unions. A prohibition on any reasonable form of solicitation or election campaigning works not only to the detriment of unit employees who may seek to become informed, but also to the detriment of the challenging union, which, unlike the incumbent, has not enjoyed the advantage of a prior relationship among the unit employees. I conclude, therefore, that the purposes sought to be achieved by the operation of the shipyard's rules are neither attained nor do they justify limiting the employees' right established under Executive Order 11491 "to assist a labor organization."

Accordingly, in the absence of any evidence of special circumstances which would have warranted the shipyard's limiting or banning employee solicitation during nonwork time and the distribution of campaign materials on its premises during employee nonwork time and in nonwork areas, I find that the shipyard's notice of February 18, 1970 and its subsequent memoranda of March 16 and 27, 1970, interfered with employee rights assured under Executive Order 11491 and were therefore violative of Section 19 (a)(1) of the order.

CONCLUSION

Through promulgating and maintaining a rule which prohibits employees from engaging in solicitation on behalf of the union or any other labor organization during nonwork time and from distributing literature for the union of any other labor organization on activity premises in nonwork areas during nonwork time, the shipyard has violated Sections 19(a)(1) of the executive order.

THE REMEDY

Having found that the shipyard has engaged in certain conduct prohibited by Section 19(a)(1) of Executive Order 11491, I shall order the shipyard to cease and desist therefrom and take specific affirmative action . . . designed to effectuate the policies of the order.

ORDER

Pursuant to Section 6(b) of Executive Order 11491 and Section 203.23(a) of the regulations, the Assistant Secretary of Labor for Labor-Management Relations hereby orders that the Charleston Naval Shipyard shall:

1. Cease and desist from:
(a) Promulgating or maintaining a no-solicitation rule which restricts shipyard employees from engaging in solicitation on behalf of the union or any other labor organization at the workplace during their nonwork time providing there is no interference with the work of the agency.
(b) Promulgating or maintaining a rule which prohibits shipyard employees from distributing literature on behalf of the union or any other labor organization on shipyard premises in nonwork areas during their nonwork time. . . .

Dated: November 3, 1970 /s/ W. J. Usery, Jr., Assistant Secretary of
     Washington, D.C.   Labor for Labor-Management Relations

Discussion Questions

1. How did the Assistant Secretary rebut the contention that he could not contravene the ruling issued by the Civil Service Commission, the Department of Defense, and the like?
2. Why did the Assistant Secretary contend that labor relations decisions in the federal sector were not irrevocably tied to private sector precedents?
3. Was there close reliance on private sector guidelines in this case?
4. Compare the rules governing electioneering under the two executive orders.
5. What was the key issue in this case?

Section 2. The Proper Conduct of Elections

In the private sector, conduct on the part of an employer or union during an election campaign that makes the free choice of a bargaining representative unlikely will result in the invalidation of the balloting even though such activity would not be sufficient to justify the filing of an unfair labor practice charge by itself. In election cases the NLRB must determine whether the employees had an opportunity to cast uncoerced ballots representing their true desires on the union issue. If it finds conduct impairing a free choice, the board will nullify the election and direct that a new one be held. Public sector cases follow basically the same standards of conduct, as the following decision demonstrates.

In the Matter of

City of Providence, Rhode Island (employer) *and* **Laborers International Union of North America, on Behalf of Local Union 1033 (petitioner)** *and* **Rhode Island Public Employees, Council 70, AFSCME, AFL-CIO (intervenor)**

Case No. EE–1751

(State of Rhode Island before the State Labor Relations Board)

DECISION AND ORDER

STATEMENT OF THE CASE

On February 9, 1968, the employer, the city of Providence, and the unions, the Rhode Island Public Employees, Council 70, AFSCME, AFL-CIO, and the Laborers International Union of North America, AFL-CIO, executed an agreement for a consent election to be conducted among all employees employed by the city of Providence, excluding office and clerical employees, supervisory personnel, professional and technical employees, teachers, policemen, firemen, and school custodians on March 8, 1968.

On the day of the election, the board issued and served its report upon secret ballot, which showed that of 810 ballots cast, 416 votes were in favor for representation by the Laborers International Union; 154 ballots cast for Rhode Island Public Employees; 211 ballots for no unions; and 9 ballots were challenged.

On March 14, 1968, the Rhode Island Public Employees, Council 70, AFSCME, AFL-CIO, filed objections to the election pursuant to Section 11 of the board's general rules and regulations.

On March 20, 1968, the Laborers International Union, AFL-CIO, filed a motion to dismiss the Rhode Island Public Employees, Council 70, AFSCME's objections to the election.

A hearing to determine the merits of the objections was duly held on April 11, 1968 before the Rhode Island State Labor Relations Board. Briefs were filed by both parties.

Upon consideration of the entire record and the briefs, the board renders the following decision.

THE OBJECTIONS

1. The intimidation and threats of the employees' physical well-being upon the job premises.

2. The intimidation and threats to the employees' free choice by preventing the free entrance to the polling place by the act of physically stopping the employees' vehicles.

3. The violation of the administrative rules of the State Labor Relations Board by distributing literature at and around the polling place within the hours of voting.

4. The violation of the State Labor Relations Board Administrative rules politicking within the twenty-four hours prior to the election by means of posting or causing to have posted throughout the politicking area, large signs on trees urging the support and vote of Local 1033.

5. The picketing of the Commissioner of Public Works Department on March 7, 1968 and other acts and statements implying company unionism on the part of this protestor.

Objection No. 1

There was no testimony or evidence presented on Objection No. 1.

Objection No. 2

Mr. Peter F. Barchi, a Providence city employee, testified that he was stopped at the gates, which are outside the 200-foot mark, by people blocking passage in the roadway, and given a marked ballot indicating a vote for Local 1033. (This ballot was marked exhibit No. 1 and placed into evidence.) Mr. Barchi was also asked if this stoppage influenced his voting in any respect. He replied that it did not, nor did it prevent him from going into Roger Williams Park, or from going to the voting polls.

We find the evidence insufficient to sustain this portion of the objection, nor is there any showing that such threats, if made, influenced the employees in casting their votes at the election.

Accordingly, we shall overrule this objection.

Objection No. 3

Both unions were advised that literature could be distributed within the twenty-four hour limit and that they could electioneer beyond the 200-foot mark.

The administrative rules of the State Labor Relations Board, pertaining to distribution of literature at and around the polling place within the hours of voting, were not violated. Therefore, we shall overrule this objection.

Objection No. 4

Mr. Ronald J. Gizzarelli, employed as an international organizer for the state, county, and municipal employees, testified that he took photographs of the said violations.

The first slide showed a Volkswagen truck with a sign attached thereto with the words, "March 8, Vote 278." In the same photograph another sign was held by two men stating, "March 8, Vote 278." There were other vehicles with signs and markings and men holding signs which were not distinguishable by any members of the board.

The board found that the second photograph showed a man holding a sign near the center of the road but the markings on the sign were not distinguishable to any members of the board.

Mr. Rene Berthiaume, international representative for the Rhode Island Public Employees, testified that he was familiar with the 200-foot rule. Mr. Berthiaume could not state that any of the alleged violations took place within the 200-foot mark.

Mr. Arthur E. Coia, international representative for the Laborers International Union of North America, testified that the vehicles from his Local and Local 278 were parked outside the 200-foot mark.

Mr. Arthur A. Coia, business manager for the Laborers International Union of North America, testified that the vehicles with signs on them for Local 1033 were 240 feet from the polling place.

The bulk of the evidence developed at the hearing concerned Local 1033's electioneering during the election and whether it occurred within

200 feet of the polling place. The evidence is clear, and needs not be re-stated in detail here, that Local 1033 did engage in electioneering beyond the 200-foot mark. Such electioneering was lawful, did not violate the board's rules governing the conduct of the election, and would not be material unless it occurred within 200 feet of the entrance to the building in which the election is being conducted.

One of the purposes of this rule of the board is to create a neutral area within which voters should be free from approach by any party. The area surrounding the gates provided such a neutral area prior to the time the voters entered the building in which the election was being held. All electioneering by the unions stopped 200 feet from the voting area.

Although the evidence adduced by the Rhode Island Public Employees at the post-election hearing indicates that several instances of electioneering took place within 200 feet of the polling place, during the election no one ever complained to the board's agents or policemen stationed in the area that electioneering was taking place within the prohibited area. Members from both unions were intermingling outside the 200-foot mark throughout the polling hours. There was no evidence to substantiate the charges of posting of large signs, urging the support and vote of Local 1033, through-out the polling area and on trees within the twenty-four hours prior to the election. The board finds that the photographs were taken in an area be-yond the 200-foot mark.

We find that, for practical purposes, the gate was beyond the 200-foot mark from the entrance of the building where the election was being held, and that electioneering, near the entrance gate, was not in violation of the board's rules.

There being no evidence that any electioneering occurred within the 200-foot mark, or disbursement of literature within the 200-foot mark, we shall overrule this objection.

Objection No. 5

There was no testimony or evidence presented on objection No. 5.

FINDINGS OF FACT

4. There were no threats, intimidations, or acts of physical stoppage of vehicles to prevent employees from free entrance to the polling area.

5. There was insufficient evidence to sustain the Rhode Island public employees' objection that employees were influenced in the casting of their ballots.

6. The administrative rules of the State Labor Relations Board, per-

taining to distribution of literature at and around the polling place within the hours of voting, were not violated.

7. All electioneering by the unions stopped 200 feet from the voting area.

8. There were no complaints of the election to the Labor Relations Board by any of the parties.

9. There were no complaints made to the police by any of the parties or by any of the employees.

10. Members from both unions were intermingling outside the 200-foot mark throughout the polling hours.

11. There was no evidence to substantiate the charges of posting of large signs, urging the support and vote of Local 1033, throughout the polling area and on trees within the twenty-four hours prior to the election.

12. The board finds that the photographs were taken in an area beyond the 200-foot mark.

13. The gate was beyond the 200-foot mark from the entrance of the building where the election was being held and electioneering, near the entrance gate, was not in violation of the board's rules.

CONCLUSIONS

. . . The evidence and testimony presented before the State Labor Relations Board did not substantiate any of the five alleged violations to the election or election procedures as directed.

The evidence from the testimony submitted, with the exception of one witness, Mr. Barchi, was from rival members of both unions charging the other with threats and intimidations.

The only independent witness, Mr. Barchi, a city employee, testified to the effect that he was not intimidated or threatened in any manner by Local 1033.

The moving party should sustain its support by substantial evidence of its charges.

The evidence and testimony presented to the board did not substantiate any of the alleged violations to the elections or the election procedure as directed by the Labor Relations Board and the report upon secret ballot and fairness of election submitted by the State Labor Relations Board after the election were in due order.

The Labor Relations Board has overruled all of the Rhode Island Public Employees' objections to the election, and the Laborers International Union of North America has received a clear majority of the votes cast in the election, a certification will issue.

ORDER AND CERTIFICATION OF REPRESENTATIVE

. . . IT IS HEREBY ORDERED that the election objections filed herein by the Rhode Island Public Employees, Council 70, AFSCME, AFL-CIO on March 14, 1968, to the election conducted on March 8, 1968, be, and the same hereby are, overruled; and IT IS HEREBY CERTIFIED that the Laborers International Union of North America, AFL-CIO, has been designated and selected as representative for the purposes of collective bargaining by a majority of all employees employed by the city of Providence . . . and that pursuant to the provisions of 28–7–16(1) of the Rhode Island State Labor Relations Act, said union is the exclusive representative of all such employees. . . .

Dated: May 27, 1968   Rhode Island State Labor Relations Board
   Providence, R.I.

                Chairman

                Member

                Member

Discussion Questions

1. What was the purpose of the board rule banning all electioneering within 200 feet of the polling place?
2. If anything, what object lesson does this case contain for parties making specific allegations of wrongdoing?

In the Matter of

Army Materiel Command, Army Tank Automotive Command, Warren, Michigan (activity) *and* **American Federation of Government Employees, AFL-CIO, Local 1658 (petitioner)** *and* **National Association of Government Employees, Local R8–21 (intervenor)**

Case No. 52–2103 [4]

(United States Department of Labor before the Assistant Secretary for Labor–Management Relations)

DECISION ON OBJECTIONS AND DIRECTION OF SECOND ELECTION

On February 26, 1971, Hearing Examiner David London issued his report and recommendations in the above-entitled proceeding, finding that the American Federation of Government Employees, AFL-CIO, Local 1658, herein called AFGE, had engaged in a misrepresentation with regard to a leaflet which contained the statement that "NAGE national vice-president urges support of AFGE." The hearing examiner concluded that the voters' ability to evaluate the choices on the ballot was so impaired by the complained-of leaflet that they were unable to vote intelligently, and accordingly, he recommended that the election held on July 22, 1970, be set aside and a new election be directed under the terms of Executive Order 11491.

The Assistant Secretary has reviewed the rulings of the hearing examiner made at the hearing and finds that no prejudicial error was committed. The rulings are hereby affirmed. Upon consideration of the hearing examiner's report and recommendations and the entire record including the AFGE's request for review of the hearing examiner's report and recommendations and the parties' briefs, I adopt the findings and recommendations of the hearing examiner.

The NAGE filed numerous objections to the election in this case which can be separated into two categories: (1) objections to the conduct of the election because of alleged irregularities committed by the activity and representatives of the Department of Labor, and (2) objections concerning campaign literature prepared and distributed by the AFGE containing misrepresentations which allegedly affected the results of the election.

The alleged irregularities attributed to the activity and representatives of the Department of Labor include improper mailing of ballots, dual voting, improper management observers, unattended polling places, ineligible voters, incomplete eligibility lists, improper distribution of eligibility cards, and loss of a voting list from one of the polling places.

The hearing examiner noted that the NAGE's post-hearing brief contained no contentions or mention concerning any of these objections and restricted its contentions to two pieces of literature circulated on behalf of the AFGE as constituting a basis for setting aside the election.

In these circumstances, the hearing examiner concluded that the NAGE had apparently abandoned or withdrawn its objections in category 1 noted above. Nevertheless, the hearing examiner considered the entire record to determine whether these procedural objections had merit and he concluded that the NAGE had failed to establish that there was merit to any of these objections. He therefore recommended that they be overruled. The NAGE did not request review of the hearing examiner's report and recommendations in this respect. In all the circumstances and upon review of the record, I agree with the hearing examiner's recommendations overruling these objections.

The first campaign flyer prepared and distributed by the AFGE, in addition to containing propaganda derisive of the benefits received by the NAGE membership for dues paid to the NAGE national headquarters, includes a drawing of an airplane with the accompanying legend in broad type, "NAGE Raids Treasury! NAGE President Junkets High in the Sky —in Newly Bought $1,250,000 Lear Jet—Local Unions Demand Money and Representation!"

The record reveals that this leaflet was distributed to employees at the installation on the morning of July 17, 1970, five days prior to the election. The record reveals also that the NAGE had never owned a Lear jet and never purchased a Lear jet for $1,250,000.

The hearing examiner found that while the representation that NAGE owned and operated an expensive jet for its top officials was undoubtedly circulated to prejudice the voters against NAGE, the NAGE was partially to blame for causing this misrepresentation. The hearing examiner noted that the NAGE's newsletter, "The Fednews," on March 31, 1970, carried a picture showing NAGE officials standing in front of a plane. The caption beneath the picture reads "NAGE officials deplane from their Lear Jet 808." A similar picture appeared in the "Fednews" of June 10, 1970, with the caption reading "Shipyard local officials greet NAGE national officers as they enplane from the *Association's* Lear Jet 808." Moreover, the hearing examiner concluded that the NAGE had sufficient time in which to make an effective reply but failed to do so. Accordingly, he recommended that the NAGE objection based on the distribution of this circular be overruled.

In all the circumstances, I find that, taken in its entire context, the above-described leaflet distributed by the AFGE could be recognized by employees as campaign propaganda, and, properly evaluated, could not reasonably be expected to have a significant impact on the election.

Accordingly, the objection based upon this leaflet is hereby overruled.

The second leaflet complained of, distributed the day before the election, contained the statement, in bold type, "NAGE NATIONAL VICE PRESIDENT URGES SUPPORT OF AFGE," and attributed this statement to Andre E. La Croix, "National Vice President, Region 7, and President, NAGE Local R7–35." The reverse side of the leaflet was a verbatim copy of a letter from Andre E. La Croix. At the top of the reverse side of the leaflet was the following statement: "(The following letter was mailed Sunday, July 19, 1970, to the more than 400 members of NAGE Rock Island Arsenal, Local R7–35 by its President, Andre E. La Croix who is

National Vice President for NAGE Region Seven)." The body of the letter began as follows:

> Dear NAGE Members: The undersigned officers of the headquarters USAWECOM Local of NAGE at an executive board meeting have voted to support the American Federation of Government Employees in the August 4 election to select the bargaining agent for GS employees of the headquarters. . . .

The letter was signed by A. E. La Croix, President, and three other officers of the local. The record reveals the leaflet was distributed at the installation on July 21, 1970, the day before the election. The record also reveals that while La Croix is in fact the president of NAGE Local R7–35 in Rock Island, Illinois, he never was and is not now a national vice-president of the NAGE. Moreover, NAGE does not have now, or has it ever had, a national vice-president for NAGE Region 7.

The hearing examiner concluded with respect to the above misrepresentation that the voters' ability to evaluate the choices was so impaired by this "campaign trickery" that they were unable to vote intelligently. He also found that by distributing the leaflet on the day before the election, the NAGE was prevented from making an effective reply thereto.

The AFGE, in its request for review of the hearing examiner's report and recommendations, reiterates its contention that the above-mentioned leaflet was self-serving campaign literature and was the type that a voter would expect to see in an election campaign. It also argues that even if the leaflet contained a material misrepresentation, the NAGE could have prepared, published, and distributed an effective reply if it so desired. Finally, the AFGE argues that the hearing examiner's findings and recommendations on this objection were based on "subjective evidence."

In my view, the issue herein is not whether La Croix wrote the letter supporting the AFGE or whether he was president of the NAGE Local R7–35. Rather, it is the erroneous and deceptive characterization of La Croix as a national vice-president of the NAGE. I agree with the hearing examiner's conclusion that it is difficult to perceive a false representation more likely to create doubt, frustration, and dissension concerning the integrity of the NAGE's leadership than a plea by its own national vice-president to disavow its leadership and instead, support the AFGE. It is clear that the employees here had no independent knowledge as to persons holding national office in the NAGE and, consequently, were unable to recognize the leaflet as a misrepresentation of fact. In these circumstances, I find that the deception constituted campaign trickery involving a substantial misrepresentation of fact which impaired the employees' ability to vote intelligently on the issue. I find also that by distributing the leaflet on the day before the election the NAGE was prevented from making an effective reply thereto.

Accordingly, the election conducted on July 22, 1970 is hereby set aside and a second election will be conducted as directed below.

DIRECTION OF SECOND ELECTION

IT IS HEREBY DIRECTED that a second election be conducted as early as possible. . . .

Dated: June 15, 1971   /s/ W. J. Usery, Jr., Assistant Secretary of
        Washington, D.C.   Labor for Labor–Management Relations

Discussion Questions

1. Discuss the NAGE objections to the election proceedings. Why were they overruled?
2. What is the crucial determinant regarding liability for the distribution of questionable literature prior to an election?
3. Why was the election set aside?

Section 3. Requisite Employee Status for Voting Eligibility

In private employment, employees considered eligible to vote in representation elections will have been included on the firm payroll during the immediately preceding payroll period and also will be actively employed on the day that the election is to be held.

A challenged ballot situation develops when a vote is questioned by one of the parties to a representation election. The common procedure to resolve the challenges is to open and count the challenged ballots, but only if the number of challenged ballots is sufficient to affect the outcome of the election.

As the upcoming case demonstrates, a question as to voting eligibility may arise when an employee who had been laid off as a result of job-connected injuries for a protracted period of time votes in an election.

In the Matter of

General Services Administration, Memphis, Tennessee (activity) *and* **Local R5–66, National Association of Government Employees (petitioner)** *and* **Local 359, National Association of Post Office and General Service Maintenance Employees (intervenor)**

Case No. 41–1736(RO) [5]

(United States Department of Labor before the Assistant Secretary for Labor–Management Relations)

DECISION ON CHALLENGED BALLOTS

On March 11, 1971, Hearing Examiner Henry L. Segal issued his report and recommendations in the above-entitled proceeding. He recommended that the challenges to the ballots of Eva Cathcart, Louis Spry, and Charles McCormick be sustained and their ballots not be counted, and that the challenges to the ballots of Charles W. Sommers, Richard D. Holder, and Elsie Daniels be overruled and their ballots be opened and counted.

The Assistant Secretary has reviewed the rulings of the hearing examiner made at the hearing and finds that no prejudicial error was committed. The rulings are hereby affirmed. Upon consideration of the hearing examiner's report and recommendations and the entire record, I adopt the findings and recommendations of the hearing examiner except as modified herein.

Eva Cathcart. Miss Cathcart is classified as an occupational health nurse, GS–7. Local R5–66, National Association of Government Employees, herein called NAGE, challenged her ballot on the ground that she is a professional employee. The activity agrees that she is a professional employee but urges that her vote be counted because it was through lack of experience at the time of the execution of the consent election agreement that no provision was made for furnishing Miss Cathcart a self-determination professional employee ballot. The National Association of Post Office and General Service Maintenance Employees, herein called NAPOGSME, contends that she is an eligible voter.

Miss Cathcart's job description states that she serves as the nurse in charge of the health unit operated by the General Services Administration for employees of participating federal agencies in the Federal Building, Memphis, Tennessee. A requirement for appointment to this position is that the applicant be a registered nurse. The record establishes that Miss Cathcart is licensed as a registered nurse in the state of Tennessee.

I agree with the hearing examiner's conclusion that Miss Cathcart, as a registered nurse, is a "professional employee" within the meaning of the order and that therefore it would be contrary to the policy of Section 10 (b)(4) of the order to count Miss Cathcart's ballot where she cast a ballot identical to those provided for the nonprofessional employees. Accordingly, I hereby adopt the recommendation of the hearing examiner that the challenge to Miss Cathcart's ballot be sustained and that her ballot not be opened and counted.

Louis Spry. Mr. Spry was employed by the activity as a general mechanic in options of electrical and plumbing work. He suffered an injury on the job in 1967 and was placed in a leave without pay status (LWOP) on February 12, 1968. While in this status Mr. Spry received compensation under the Federal Employees Compensation Law from the Bureau of Employees Compensation, United States Department of Labor. He remained in this status until his retirement on January 29, 1971. Thus, at the time of the election on July 15, 1970, Mr. Spry was in an LWOP status. The NAPOGSME challenged his ballot since his name was not on the eligibility list.

The hearing examiner concluded that Mr. Spry was not eligible to vote since, at the time of the election, he had been absent from work for approximately three years and there was no reasonable expectancy that he would return to work. Under these circumstances, the hearing examiner concluded that Mr. Spry had no community of interest with the employees in the unit with respect to the terms and conditions of employment and recommended that the challenge to his ballot be sustained and his ballot not counted.

Record testimony indicates that the activity, acting pursuant to Federal Personnel Manual Letter 630–18, issued by the United States Civil Service Commission on May 1, 1969, believing that Mr. Spry would not be able to return to work, wrote to the Bureau of Employees Compensation on June 2, 1969, advising the bureau that the activity proposed to separate Mr. Spry unless he returned to work by August 11, 1969. As a result of this letter, Mr. Spry was examined by the United States Public Health Service which advised the activity on September 23, 1969, that Mr. Spry could not return to his former job but could perform light duty.

The evidence reveals that despite Mr. Spry's extended LWOP status because of health consideration, he, at all relevant times, was maintained on the activity's rolls as being in an employee status. As stated in the parties' agreement for consent election, eligible employees are those "*who were employed* during the payroll period indicated including employees who did not work during that period because they were out ill, or on vacation, or on furlough . . . who appear in person at the polls . . ." (emphasis added). In these circumstances, I conclude that Mr. Spry was employed by the activity during the payroll period indicated in the parties' agreement for consent election.

Accordingly, I find that Louis Spry was an employee who was eligible to vote in the election, and I hereby direct that his ballot be opened and counted.

Charles McCormick. Mr. McCormick is the area utilization officer and is concerned with the disposal of surplus personal property. He assists other agencies in complying with the reporting requirements for excess property. In this regard, he examines and verifies the condition of such property and, within guidelines, decides whether to offer such property for sale or transfer it to another federal agency or a state or local agency.

Mr. McCormick's vote was originally challenged by the NAGE on the ground that he was a supervisor. At the hearing, both the NAGE and the NAPOGSME took the position that Mr. McCormick was a supervisor, while the activity took the position that he was a management official. As a result, the parties stipulated that Mr. McCormick was either a supervisor or a management official and, therefore, was not eligible to vote. In view of such agreement by the parties and because there is no evidence to indicate that the parties' stipulation was improper, I hereby affirm the recommendation of the hearing examiner that the challenge to the ballot of Charles McCormick be sustained and his ballot not be opened and counted.

Charles W. Sommers. Mr. Sommers works in the Inter-Agency Motor Pool as an automotive equipment inspector, WG–11. It is his responsibility to inspect all the automobiles in the pool for preventive maintenance and, when automobiles come in for repairs, to insure that they need such repairs before referring them to a contractor. He also checks the automobiles after the repairs have been made. His ballot was challenged by the NAGE on the ground that he was a supervisor. After testimony was taken at the hearing concerning his duties, all parties stipulated that Mr. Sommers was not a supervisor within the meaning of the order and therefore was eligible to vote.

As there is no evidence to indicate that the parties' stipulation was improper, I hereby affirm the recommendation of the hearing examiner that the challenge to the ballot of Charles W. Sommers be overruled and his ballot be opened and counted.

Richard D. Holder. The ballot of Mr. Holder was challenged by the NAGE on the ground that he is a supervisor. Mr. Holder is employed as a transportation operations assistant (motor), GS–7, in the Inter-Agency Motor Pool. He reports to the chief of the pool, an acknowledged supervisor, and on those occasions when the chief is absent, he acts as pool chief.

The hearing examiner concluded that in the performance of his normal duties Mr. Holder met none of the supervisory criteria set forth in the order. He concluded also that the training he gave new employees consisted of no more than assistance from a more experienced employee to a less experienced employee, and that other employees within the proposed unit similarly assisted in training. In addition, the hearing examiner found that the fact that Mr. Holder substituted for the chief of the motor pool on a limited or sporadic basis was not a sufficient basis for finding that he was a supervisor.

The record establishes that Mr. Holder is concerned basically with making studies and recommendations concerning the use and care of vehicles in the pool. He advises other government agencies on the proper use of these vehicles to reduce operating and repair costs. Testimony indicates that while Mr. Holder assists in training new employees, no employees report to him and he makes no performance evaluations or effective recommendations concerning their retention. Testimony indicates also that Mr. Holder acted as chief for a total of two or three weeks in the course of a year.

Based on the foregoing, I adopt the conclusion of the hearing examiner that Richard D. Holder is not a "supervisor" within the meaning of the order, and I hereby affirm the recommendation of the hearing examiner that the challenge to the ballot of this individual be overruled and his ballot be opened and counted.

Elsie Daniels. The ballot of Mrs. Daniels was challenged by the NAGE on the ground that at the time of the election, July 15, 1970, she was a temporary employee and not eligible to vote.

The hearing examiner noted that Mrs. Daniels was given a career-conditional appointment under terms which made her eligible for employment only as required by the activity, which meant she might work any amount of time from one hour to forty hours per week. He reasoned that the controlling factor in determining whether Mrs. Daniels had a community of interest with the other employees in the unit should be the number of hours she worked and, more significantly, the regularity of her employment rather than the type of appointment she received. He noted that her attendance record indicates that she had worked during every week from the date she began work in May, 1970 up to the time that she was converted to a part-time employee in January, 1971, and that during that period she worked a substantial number of hours in each pay period. The hearing examiner noted also that she performed the same work as the other telephone operators before and after the election, and worked with such regularity that she had a sufficient community of interest with the other employees to render her eligible to vote.

The evidence demonstrates that in her first nine months of employment, Mrs. Daniels worked 70 percent or more of each eight-hour pay period, and while at work, performed the same functions as other telephone operators in the group. In these circumstances, I find that Mrs. Daniels was not a temporary employee as of the date of the election, and I hereby adopt the recommendation of the hearing examiner that the challenge to the ballot of Elsie Daniels be overruled and her ballot be opened and counted.

DIRECTION TO OPEN AND COUNT BALLOTS

IT IS HEREBY DIRECTED that the ballots of Louis Spry, Charles W. Sommers, Richard D. Holder, and Elsie Daniels be opened and counted at a time and place to be determined by the appropriate regional administrator. The regional administrator shall have a revised tally of ballots served on the parties, and take such additional action as required by the regulations of the Assistant Secretary.

Dated: October 19, 1971   /s/   W. J. Usery, Jr., Assistant Secretary of
       Washington, D.C.   Labor for Labor–Management Relations

Discussion Questions

1. The eligibility of several occupational categories to vote in representation elections is subject to challenge here. Discuss this fact.
2. Why, specifically, did the Assistant Secretary reverse the hearing examiner's ruling on the challenge to Louis Spry's vote?
3. Analyze the manner in which the "community of interest" standard is used in evaluating the validity of the challenges.

Section 4. Contract Bar to Representation Election

Contract bar rules refer to policies followed in determining when an existing agreement between an employer and a union will bar a representation election sought by a union attempting to unseat an incumbent employee representative. A question arises as to whether the bar remains in effect when a labor organization seeks to renegotiate an existing agreement. If so, the incumbent union is not required to defend its exclusive bargaining agent status in a new representation election. If the contract bar is deemed to have expired, then a rival labor organization can petition for an election.

However, a contract bar will not operate to prevent an election if a contract has been consummated during the period between the dismissal of the petition by an NLRB regional director and an appeal to the NLRB for the dismissal.

In the Matter of

National Center for Mental Health Services, Training and Research (activity) *and* **National Association of Government Employees (Ind.), Local R3–99 (petitioner)** *and* **Washington Area Metal Trades Council, AFL-CIO (intervenor)**

Case No. 22–2149 [6]

(United States Department of Labor before the Assistant Secretary for Labor–Management Relations)

DECISION AND DIRECTION OF ELECTION

. . . The hearing officer's rulings made at the hearing are free from prejudicial error and are hereby affirmed.

Upon the entire record of this case . . . the Assistant Secretary finds

1. The labor organizations involved claim to represent certain employees of the activity.

2. The petitioner, National Association of Government Employees (Ind.), Local R3–99, herein called NAGE, seeks an election in a unit of all nonsupervisory employees of the construction, electrical, mechanical, and garage sections of the maintenance branch of St. Elizabeth's Hospital, Washington, D.C., excluding supervisory and managerial employees, guards, professionals, and employees engaged in federal personnel work in other than a purely clerical nature within the meaning of Executive Order 11491.

The activity and the intervenor, Washington Area Metal Trades Council, AFL-CIO, herein called WAMTC, contend that the employees in the above-described unit are covered by a signed agreement which constitutes a bar to the processing of the petition in the subject case. This contract, approved by the Department of Health, Education, and Welfare on November 14, 1967, provides in Article XXIX entitled "Effective Date and Duration of Agreement":

1. This agreement shall be binding upon the employer and the council for a period of one year from the date of approval by the Department of Health, Education, and Welfare and from year to year thereafter unless either party shall notify the other party in writing at least sixty days, but not more than ninety days prior to such date or to any subsequent anniversary date, of its desire to modify or terminate this agreement, or a timely and valid request for redetermination of exclusive status has been received between the ninetieth and sixtieth day prior to the anniversary date of this agreement.

2. If either party gives notice to the other party as in Section 1 above, then between the sixtieth and forty-fifth day prior to the terminal date of this agreement, representatives of the employer and the council shall meet

and commence negotiations, provided a valid and timely request for re-determination of exclusive recognition has not been filed by another employee organization between the ninetieth and sixtieth day prior to the terminal date of this agreement.

In accordance with the above provisions, the WAMTC, by letter dated August 14, 1968, requested the activity to renegotiate the existing agreement, and the activity, by letter dated September 6, 1968, agreed to meet and suggested a meeting date of September 26, 1968, in its Administration Building. The record reveals that representatives of the activity appeared at the appointed time and place; however, no one representing the WAMTC appeared for the meeting, and therefore, no negotiations took place.

One year later, the WAMTC, by letter dated September 5, 1969, again advised the activity of its wish to renegotiate the agreement. Subsequently, on November 3, 1969, the WAMTC, in writing, requested that the agreement be extended until January 1, 1970, or until renegotiations were completed. The activity, by letter dated November 17, 1969, agreed to the proposed extension. However, no negotiations took place thereafter.

The record reveals that on occasions in 1968, 1969, and 1970, the activity and the WAMTC have processed grievances and have held meetings of safety committees apparently under what then was believed to be an existing agreement.

Based on the foregoing, the activity and the WAMTC take the position that the petition in the subject case was filed at a time when a negotiated agreement was in existence and that, therefore, the NAGE's petition in the subject case should not be processed.

As stated above, Section 1 of Article XXIX, the parties' 1967 agreement provides, with respect to duration, that the agreement automatically renews itself from year to year "*unless* either party shall notify the other party in writing at least sixty days, but not more than ninety days prior to such date or to any subsequent anniversary date, of its desire to modify or terminate this agreement . . ." (emphasis added). The evidence establishes that on September 5, 1969, the WAMTC *did* notify the activity of its desire to renegotiate the agreement. Therefore, by its terms, the agreement approved in 1967 terminated upon one of the parties thereto stating that it desired to renegotiate. Accordingly, after November, 1969, the agreement must be viewed as an oral agreement which would not serve as a bar to the filing of a representation petition.

Moreover, even assuming that the agreement continued in effect after the parties' above-mentioned communications in 1969, the exchange of letters between the parties in November, 1969 in effect resulted in the parties extending their agreement and setting a fixed termination date of

January 1, 1970, "or until renegotiations were completed." Consequently, after January 1, 1970, the agreement would be viewed as not having a fixed term or duration and could, therefore, not constitute a bar to an election.

Further, since no new agreement was negotiated thereafter, it is clear that there was no agreement of fixed term in effect at the time the petition in the subject case was filed on October 16, 1970 by the NAGE.

Based on all of the foregoing circumstances, I find that there was no bar to the processing of the petition in the subject case. Accordingly, I find that the following employees of the activity constitute a unit appropriate for the purpose of exclusive recognition under Executive Order 11491. . . .

DIRECTION OF ELECTION

An election by secret ballot shall be conducted among the employees in the unit found appropriate as early as possible, but not later than forty-five days from the date below. . . . Eligible to vote are all those in the unit who were employed during the payroll period immediately preceding the date below, including employees who did not work during that period because they were out ill, or on vacation or on furlough including those in the military service who appear in person at the polls. Ineligible to vote are employees who quit or were discharged for cause since the designated payroll period and who have not been rehired or reinstated before the election date. . . .

Dated: June 10, 1971   /s/ W. J. Usery, Jr., Assistant Secretary of
       Washington, D.C.   Labor for Labor–Management Relations

Discussion Questions

1. How did the notification on September 5, 1969 by the WAMTC of its desire to renegotiate the contract affect its contention that a contract bar existed?
2. Would the negotiation of a new contract have affected the validity of a petition for an election filed by a rival labor organization?
3. Assess the significance of a contract being of a fixed term or duration with regard to the contract bar concept.

Section 5. Timeliness of the Certification Petition

The NLRB has established a policy that prohibits the holding of representation elections when it is shown that a valid election has been held in the same bargaining unit within the preceding twelve months. Moreover, the board, in the absence of unusual circumstances, will not direct an election where it has issued a certification covering the same unit in the preceding twelve months.[7] In other words, a prior certification acts as a bar to another representation election. In any case, to obtain an election where an existing contract is in effect it must be shown that the union opposing the petition is not willing or able to carry out its obligation to fairly represent its members' interests. Once this has been demonstrated, the petitioner must file for certification within a period starting no more than thirty days before a reopening date and ending at the reopening or renewal date in order to insure the timeliness of the petition.

In the next decision, the New Jersey PERC must determine when the certification year becomes effective in order to evaluate the validity of a certification petition filed by a competing labor organization.

In the Matter of

City of Jersey City (public employer) *and* Local 1959, American Federation of State, County, and Municipal Employees, AFL-CIO (petitioner)

Docket No. RO–344

(State of New Jersey before the Public Employment Relations Commission)

DECISION

On September 14, 1971, petitioner filed with the commission a petition seeking certification in a unit of blue and white collar employees in the employer's Department of Public Works. Local 245, Jersey City Public Works Employees, Inc., opposes the petition and requests its dismissal on the ground it is barred by the commission's earlier certification of Local 245. The employer takes no position.

The pertinent history of proceedings involving this group of employees is as follows. The commission conducted an election in May, 1969 involving Locals 1959 and 245. That election was set aside based on meritorious objections by Local 245 and a rerun election was conducted in December, 1969 with Local 245 receiving a majority of the votes cast. Thereafter, Local 1959 filed objections to the rerun election, but the commission found them to be without merit and on July 27, 1970, certified Local 245 as the exclusive representative for purposes of collective negotiations. Shortly, thereafter, on August 10, 1970, Local 1959 obtained from the superior court, appellate division, a temporary order which stayed the commission's certification and restrained the employer and Local 245 from engaging in collective negotiations. Two weeks later, on August

25, 1970 the court dissolved the restraint on negotiations, but ordered that "Execution of a contract is stayed pending disposition of the appeal." According to Local 245, it commenced negotiations "a short time after August, 1970." The appellate division issued its decision on May 4, 1971, in which it rejected Local 1959's appeal and affirmed the commission's July, 1970 supplemental decision and certification of representative. No further appeal was taken. Local 245 states that an agreement with the employer was subsequently reached and a collective negotiations contract executed on October 8, 1971. That execution postdates the filing of the instant petition.

Petitioner asserts that the significant date in this history is August 25, 1970 when the court lifted the prohibition on negotiating an agreement. From that point forward, it argues, the employer and Local 245 were free to negotiate and from May 4, 1971 they have been free to execute a contract. No contract having been executed until October, the petition filed in September should be entertained. Local 245 contends that lifting the restraint against negotiations is not very meaningful when at the same time contract execution is restrained for the duration of the appeal. It urges that the date of certification is the date of the appellate division decision, as a result of which (no higher appeal having been taken) the parties were free of all restraint for the first time.

Section 19:11–15(b) of the commission's rules and regulations provides

(b) Where there is a certified or recognized representative, a petition will not be considered as timely filed if during the preceding twelve (12) months an employee organization has been certified by the executive director of the commission as the majority representative of employees in an appropriate unit or an employee organization has been granted recognition by a public employer pursuant to Section 19:11–14.

Traditionally, the purpose of such a provision, rooted in federal practice under the National Labor Relations Act, is said to be the creation of a reasonable period of protection after certification in which the certified representative can establish or reestablish a negotiating relationship with the employer and consummate an agreement without the disruption of competing claims for representation. The above rule contemplates that same kind of protection and for the same reasons. On the facts in this case it is evident that Local 245 did not receive the full benefit of the certification year when for the first nine months or so the parties were enjoined from executing an agreement. The fact that negotiations were permitted is not particularly beneficial when the final outcome of the appeal, and thus the negotiations, remains in doubt. Unless an appeal were patently frivolous, there may be a serious question that constructive negotiations could take place in the face of a challenge to a certification. The commission concludes that the "reasonable" period of freedom to contract intended by the rule was not available until the merits of the appeal were decided. By that time, however, the twelve (12) month period allowed under a literal reading of the rule, that is, beginning with commission certification, had for the most part been exhausted. Under these circumstances and in order to give effect to the rule, the commission finds that good cause exists and that fairness requires a liberal construction of the rule. The protected period will not be computed from the date of commission certification, but rather from May 4, 1971, the date of the court's decision. We conclude that the certification of Local 245 did not become fully effective until the final disposition of the challenge to it, that Section 19:11–15(b) is to be liberally construed as to the facts in this case to permit a reasonable period of protection, and that Local 1959's petition is filed at such time that, if entertained, it would deprive the certified representative of that reasonable period of protection intended by the rule. The petition is found to be untimely and is therefore dismissed.

By order of the commission.

Dated: December 2, 1971   /s/ William L. Kirchner, Jr.
      Trenton, N.J.   Acting Chairman

Discussion Questions

1. Trace the chronology of events in this case.
2. State the argument advanced by Local 1959 in support of its petition.
3. What position did Local 245 take?
4. Why did the commission rule against the petition submitted by Local 1959? Does this seem to be a fair interpretation?

Section 6. Decertification Following Consent Agreement Violations

A consent agreement preceding a consent election amounts to a stipulation by both parties as to the terms under which the election is to be held, including the date, the definition of the unit, the eligibility of employees to vote, and other details, where there is no need for hearings and decisions by NLRB officials to resolve disputes involving the items listed here. A consent agreement prior to a card check amounts to a similar stipulation by the parties prior to the actual counting procedure. The card check, which is the comparison of union authorization cards signed by employees against the employer's payroll to determine the extent of union support by the employees, will suffice as a substitute for an election if it is properly administered and, as will be shown, if there is an absence of wrongdoing.

In the Matter of

Aben, Inc. (employer) *and* **West Warwick Retail Clerks Association (petitioner)**

Case No. EE–1802

(State of Rhode Island before the State Labor Relations Board)

DECISION AND ORDER

On September 17, 1968, Local 328, Meat Cutters and Food Store Workers Union, Amalgamated Meat Cutters and Butcher Workmen of North America, AFL-CIO, filed with the Rhode Island State Labor Relations Board a motion to revoke certification of the West Warwick Retail Clerks Association as the collective bargaining agent for certain employees of Aben, Inc. Said motion alleged that the employees of Aben, Inc., and the West Warwick Retail Clerks Association failed to advise the Rhode Island State Labor Relations Board in their petition for certification of Local 328, Meat Cutters and Food Store Workers Union, Amalgamated Meat Cutters and Butcher Workmen of North America, AFL-CIO's interest in the organization of said employees. That the Rhode Island State Labor Relations Board conducted an improper card comparison of signatures on July 8, 1968.

On July 1, 1968, West Warwick Retail Clerks Association filed a petition for investigation and certification of representatives before the State Labor Relations Board to be the collective bargaining agent for certain employees of Aben, Inc. In its petition the West Warwick Retail Clerks Association stated that no other known individuals or labor organizations claimed, or may have claimed, to represent any of the employees in the collective bargaining unit. A consent agreement was signed by the parties authorizing the board to conduct a card comparison of signatures to determine whether or not the association had a majority. As a result of the card comparison of signatures, the West Warwick Retail Clerks Association was certified on July 15, 1968 as the collective bargaining agent for all employees of Aben, Inc.

Pursuant to notice, a hearing on the motion to revoke certification was held by the board . . . on October 22, 1968. At this hearing, testimony, including an affidavit by Prentice Witherspoon, secretary of Local

328, was introduced to establish that not all of the thirty-eight names of employees submitted by Aben, Inc., were eligible to participate in the election held on July 1, 1968. And further, that one Robert Souliare who was allowed to vote had never been employed by Aben, Inc. Mr. Witherspoon further testified that prior to the election employees of Aben, Inc., Mr. Collins, the vice-president of the West Warwick Retail Clerks Association and several other employees of the association were handed, or mailed, a pink pamphlet requesting that employees sign membership cards designating Local 328 as their collective bargaining agent. This pamphlet was introduced into evidence as Exhibit A. Aben, Inc., through its attorney, introduced Exhibits 1 and 2, commented on the exhibits, and contended that these exhibits were not for the purpose of organizing the employees but for informational picketing. . . .

CONCLUSIONS OF LAW

. . .

4. That the board finds Robert Souliare was never in fact an employee of Aben, Inc.

5. That Robert Souliare voted in the election held on July 8, 1968.

6. That several of the thirty-eight alleged employees who voted on July 8, 1968 were not in fact employees of Aben, Inc., nor had ever been employed by Aben, Inc.

7. That on July 1, 1968, there were less than thirty-eight employees eligible to participate in the election.

8. That the West Warwick Retail Clerks Association failed to notify the board of Local 328's interest in the collective bargaining unit of said employees of Aben, Inc. . . .

ORDER

Upon the basis of the foregoing . . . Conclusions of Law, the Rhode Island State Labor Relations Board hereby orders

That the Certification of Representatives be terminated as of November 8, 1968, and suggests that a new petition for certification be filed by any interested party.

Entered as Order of the
Rhode Island State Labor Relations Board
Dated: November 1, 1968
By _____
   Executive Secretary

Rhode Island State Labor Relations Board

/s/ Harry T. Brett
   Chairman

/s/ Armand E. Renzi
   Member

/s/ Samuel J. Azzinaro
   Member

Discussion Question

1. Discuss the violations that resulted in the revocation of the petitioner's certification.

In the Matter of

Illinois Air National Guard, 182nd Tactical Air Support Group *and* Illinois Air Chapter, Association of Civilian Technicians, Inc.

FLRC No. 71A–59 [8]

(United States Federal Labor Relations Council, Washington, D.C.)

DECISION ON APPEAL FROM ASSISTANT SECRETARY DECISION

BACKGROUND

This appeal arose from a decision of the Assistant Secretary which dismissed the unit clarification petition filed by the Illinois Air Chapter, Association of Civilian Technicians, Inc. (herein called the union); and which revoked the union's certification of representative in a bargaining unit composed of the activity's air national guard technicians employed at Peoria, Illinois. A brief statement of necessary facts is set forth below.

On June 25, 1970, a representation election was conducted among the activity's air national guard technicians. The election was conducted pursuant to a consent agreement entered into by the parties and approved by the Assistant Secretary's area administrator. The tally of ballots issued after the counting of the ballots disclosed that the election results were inconclusive since the votes cast for the union (46) did not constitute the required majority of the total of valid votes cast (282) plus challenged ballots (25).

Subsequently, on July 2, 1970, the union and the activity stipulated, in writing, that sixteen of the challenged voters were supervisors within the meaning of the order. The parties' stipulation resolving the status of fifteen of the aforementioned challenged voters stated

> It is hereby jointly stipulated by the parties concerned that the following named individuals are certified to be supervisors, as defined by Section 2 (c), "General Provisions," Executive Order 11491 and therefore excluded from representation by subject labor organization and also not eligible to vote in the instant certification of representatives. It is further stipulated as a result of the foregoing, the challenged ballots as cast by the below named individuals should be excluded from the tally of ballots. . . .

Based upon a revised tally of ballots which reflected these stipulations, the area administrator then determined that the union had received a majority of the valid votes cast and that the remaining unresolved challenged ballots were not determinative. On July 8, 1970, he certified the union as exclusive bargaining representative for the subject bargaining unit.

On September 25, 1970, the activity notified the union, by letter, that it considered twenty-nine named employees to be supervisors within the meaning of the order and thereby proposed to exclude them from the bargaining unit. This total was comprised of fourteen of the sixteen persons previously stipulated to be supervisors, seven of the nine unresolved challenged voters, and eight persons whose status previously had not been in issue.

The union thereupon filed the unit clarification petition here involved with the Assistant Secretary, on October 8, 1970, which sought clarification of the status of the twenty-nine persons claimed to be supervisors by the activity. Pursuant to the union's petition, a hearing was conducted by a hearing officer of the Assistant Secretary in which both the activity and the union presented evidence bearing upon the alleged supervisory status of the twenty-nine individuals named in the activity's letter of September 25, 1970.

The Assistant Secretary issued his decision on October 29, 1971, and found that the union had attempted to negate the stipulations by which it had obtained its certification of representative by filing the unit clarification petition. The Assistant Secretary concluded that the union had entered into "sham stipulations" for the sake of expediency and that its conduct constituted flagrant disregard of his established procedure for the resolution of determinative challenged ballots. Upon the foregoing basis, the Assistant Secretary dismissed the unit clarification petition, and, further, ordered that the union's certification of representative be revoked "because of the substantial doubt which has now been cast upon the validity of the prior certification of representative." (The Assistant Secretary made no determination as to the supervisory status of the disputed individuals.)

The union petitioned the council for review of the Assistant Secretary's decision. . . .

CONTENTIONS

The union argues that: (1) the filing of its unit clarification petition was proper under the Assistant Secretary's regulations; (2) it did not enter into sham stipulations or attempt to evade prescribed procedures of the Assistant Secretary; (3) the Assistant Secretary failed to note that "the activity was the initiating party in the setting aside of election stipulations"; (4) "The Assistant Secretary made a punitive decision depriving the union of exclusive certification . . . without cause, and in doing so deprived the employees of proper coverage of the order"; and (5) the Assistant Secretary's decision failed to provide a "ruling on the unit appropriateness and therefore did not establish reasons for setting aside the results of a secret ballot election as provided for in the order." The union requests that their certification be returned as of the date of revocation.

OPINION

The issue before the council is whether, in the circumstances of this case, the purposes and policies of the order have been effectuated by the Assistant Secretary's dismissal of the union's petition for unit clarification and revocation of its certification of representative. The Assistant Secretary, as detailed above, found that such action was warranted because of the improper conduct and motivation which he imputed to the union.

Although we sustain the Assistant Secretary's dismissal of the unit clarification petition, we disagree, for reasons indicated below, that the revocation of the union's certification of representative was warranted herein upon the grounds cited by the Assistant Secretary.

Section 6 of Executive Order 11491 provides, in pertinent part, that the Assistant Secretary shall "(1) decide questions as to the appropriate unit for the purpose of exclusive recognition and related issues submitted for his consideration; and (2) supervise elections to determine whether a labor organization is the choice of a majority of the employees in an appropriate unit as their exclusive representative, and certify the results. . . ." The Assistant Secretary must insure that, in the exercise of these responsibilities, the rights guaranteed the federal employees under Section 1(a) are preserved.

To assist in the carrying out of his functions under the order the Assistant Secretary has established by regulation procedures whereby questions as to appropriate unit and related issues can be resolved. This can be done in two ways. Where there is a dispute, the facts are determined through the hearing process with all the safeguards and opportunities for due process that accompany a hearing. The other method is through the use of consensual agreements between the parties. For example, consent election agreements as authorized by those regulations provide a useful and time-saving tool for permitting an election when it does not appear that the parties are in dispute over the appropriate unit and inclusions and exclusions in the unit. Similarly, throughout the processing of a representation petition there are occasions when stipulations are properly used to dispose of undisputed matters.

Regardless of the method used to establish the facts, the Assistant Secretary must insure that the interests of the employees are protected. Certainly since a stipulation replaces full litigation of an issue, the Assistant Secretary must obtain reasonable assurance prior to acceptance that the stipulation accurately represents the facts and does not operate to deny rights guaranteed by the order.

Further, where doubt concerning the appropriateness of an already accepted stipulation arises, the Assistant Secretary has the authority to vacate his approval of the stipulation so that a new determination can be made on the subject matter.

We view this as no less true even if a certification has already been issued. When the Assistant Secretary has sufficient reason to believe that a stipulation entered into by the parties is contrary to the interest of employees or otherwise inconsistent with the purposes of the order, he may revoke a certification which was premised on the stipulation.

In the instant case the filing of the clarification petition appears to have raised voter eligibility questions sufficient in number to affect the outcome of the election, notwithstanding the fact that the parties' stipulations purported to resolve the "determinative" challenged ballots. We agree that in such circumstances the Assistant Secretary may, if he should so decide, examine questions of voter eligibility by such means as administrative investigation or formal hearing for the purpose of determining whether the certification should be revoked. However, we view as inconsistent with the purposes of the order the punitive revocation of the certification solely because a party may have taken some action which casts doubt on the validity of the earlier stipulation.

Accordingly, while we leave to the discretion and judgment of the Assistant Secretary whether he will examine the merits of the challenged ballots and, if so, by what means he will conduct such examination, we overrule the revocation of the certification insofar as such action was taken because the union took actions inconsistent with its prior stipulation.

With respect to the dismissal of the clarification petition, the union does not challenge the authority of the Assistant Secretary to take such action, although it does not agree that it serves the purposes of the order or of determinative procedure. However, we see nothing arbitrary or capricious or inconsistent with the order in such an exercise of the Assistant Secretary's discretion.

For the foregoing reasons, and pursuant to Section 2411.17 of the council's rules of procedure we sustain the Assistant Secretary's dismissal of the unit clarification petition. We further find that the basis for the decision of the Assistant Secretary to revoke the union's certification of representative is inconsistent with the purposes of the order, and, therefore, it is set aside. The case is accordingly remanded to the Assistant Secretary for appropriate action consistent with this decision of the council.

By the council.

Dated: November 17, 1972. /s/ W. V. Gill
Washington, D.C. Executive Director

Discussion Questions

1. Of what significance was the filing of the clarification petition?
2. In what respects did the Federal Labor Relations Council agree with the Assistant Secretary's ruling? Where did they differ?

Section 7. Certification Without an Election

As already discussed here, an authorization card is a statement signed by an employee designating a union as authorized to act as his agent in collective bargaining. The employer can check the signatures authorizing union representation against employee signatures on the payroll to determine whether the union has majority support. He can, however, refuse to follow this procedure and insist on a representation election; this is done if the employer suspects that the employees have been pressured by the union into signing the cards. Documentation of this type would be spurious proof of the real wishes of the employees.

In the Matter of

County of Ulster and the Ulster County Sheriff's Office (employer) *and*
**CSEA Unit of the Ulster County Sheriff's Department, Ulster County
CSEA Chapter (petitioner)**

Case No. C–0382

(State of New York Public Employment Relations Board)

DECISION OF DIRECTOR

On January 26, 1970, this board issued a decision and order in this matter finding that the unit appropriate for purposes of collective negotiations consists of all deputy sheriffs excluding all other employees, and that the county of Ulster and the Ulster County Sheriff's Office are joint employers of the deputy sheriffs. In addition, the board ordered "that an election by secret ballot shall be held under the supervision of the director among the employees within the unit determined to be appropriate . . . unless the petitioner submits to the director . . . evidences sufficient to satisfy the requirements of Section 201.9(g)(1) of the rules of the board for certification without an election."

This determination of the board was subsequently reviewed by the courts upon the petition of the county of Ulster and the Ulster County Sheriff's Office. On August 4, 1970, the Supreme Court, Albany County, reversed the finding of the board with regard to the joint employer status of the petitioner.

On December 1, 1971, the Appellate Division of the Supreme Court, Third Judicial Department, reversed the decision of the Supreme Court and affirmed the prior decision and order of the board in its entirety. An appeal by the Ulster County Sheriff's Office to the Court of Appeals was dismissed "for want of prosecution" by the clerk of that court on April 20, 1972.

On December 24, 1971, the petitioner submitted to the board the evidences described below for possible certification without an election in the unit of deputy sheriffs previously designated as being appropriate for purposes of collective negotiations. On January 5, 1972, pursuant to a request by the assistant director, the Ulster County Sheriff's Office submitted an alphabetized list of the fifty-two employees in the unit who were employed on the payroll date immediately preceding the date of the decision of the Appellate Division.

The evidences submitted by the petitioner consist of cards executed by thirty-one of the employees within the negotiating unit during the months of November and December, 1971 which read, in relevant part, as follows:

> I hereby authorize the deduction from my salary of 50 cents weekly or $1 biweekly, or $1 semimonthly, or $2.16 monthly . . . for the payment of membership dues in the Civil Service Employees Association, Inc., to be my exclusive representative for collective negotiations under the Public Employees' Fair Employment Act and I hereby revoke any prior designations or authorizations.

Section 201.9(g)(1) of the rules provides that an employee organization will be certified without an election if

> a majority of the employees within the unit have indicated their choice by the execution of dues deduction authorization cards which are current, or by individual designation cards which have been executed within six months prior to the certification.

It is clear, and I find, that the evidences submitted by the petitioner are sufficient to satisfy the requirements for certification without an election. Accordingly, I conclude that the petitioner is entitled to be certified as the negotiating agent for the employees in the unit referred to above.

Dated: April 27, 1972
      Albany, N.Y.

/s/ Paul E. Klein
Director of Public Employment
Practices and Representation

Discussion Question

1. Describe the requirements in New York State that a petitioner must satisfy in order to be certified as an exclusive bargaining agent without the necessity for a representation election.

Section 8. An Unfair Labor Practice Charge As a Bar to Election

The attorney for one of the intervenors in the following case cited the *Schlacter Meat Company* case as authority for the position that a representation election could not be held pending the outcome of unfair labor practice charges involving one of the parties. *Schlacter Meat Co.* v. *NLRB,* 30 LRRM 1418 (1952),[9] indicated that the general NLRB policy is not to hold elections while unresolved unfair labor practice charges are pending unless the charging party files a request to proceed with the election despite the pending charges. "If the charging party requests, however, an exception can be made that then disallows later objections to the election results based on these charges of violations. But if the election be then lost by the union because of subsequent employer unfair labor practices or election interferences, the union may be allowed to reinstate the prior charges along with its subsequent objections as to employer conduct as the basis of showing bad faith continuously through the entire period of organizing." [10]

In the Matter of

City of Cranston (employer) *and* **Cranston Lodge No. 20, Fraternal Order of Police (intervenor)** *and* **Local 1, International Brotherhood of Police Officers (intervenor)**

Case No. EE–1769

(State of Rhode Island before the Rhode Island State Labor Relations Board)

DECISION AND ORDER

The city of Cranston, hereinafter called the petitioner, filed its petition pursuant to the *General Laws of Rhode Island, 1956, 28–7–16,* as amended.

. . . Upon consideration of the entire record, the board renders the following decision.

I. THE EMPLOYER

Testimony was presented on behalf of the city of Cranston by the City Solicitor . . . that on December 8, 1967 the city of Cranston through the Mayor, received a communication from Joseph A. Sisson, Jr., secretary-treasurer of Local 1, International Brotherhood of Police Officers, requesting that the city of Cranston begin negotiations with them.

On December 18, the Mayor was advised through a letter that the Fraternal Order of Police, Lodge No. 20, of the city of Cranston requested that the city meet with them and begin negotiations for a contract covering the years 1968–1969.

Having received those letters from both organizations, the city felt that they would be subject to unfair labor charges by either one of the groups if they commenced negotiations with the other one. For this reason, the city filed this petition with the board asking the board to make its determination.

The petition was filed pursuant to 28–7–16 of the State Labor Relations Act which provides for an election whenever there is a question or controversy and also pursuant to the regulations of the board that states that if the board determines that there is a question or controversy that an election shall be ordered by the board. The City Solicitor, Mr. Palumbo, further stated that whenever the board determined what organization represented the majority of employees of the Police Department, that they would begin negotiations within one week.

II. THE INTERVENORS

David F. Sweeney, Esq., presented the arguments for Local 1, International Brotherhood of Police Officers. He stated that Local 1 was certified by this board as a result of an election as the collective bargaining agent for the Police Department in Cranston in 1963 or in 1964. It has continued to act as collective bargaining agent since that time. As a result of activities of the municipal employer, charges were filed with this board alleging that the municipal corporation, through its executive officer, was guilty of committing an unfair labor practice by refusing to bargain in good faith with Local 1, International Brotherhood of Police Officers.

Mr. Sweeney cited paragraph 2733, of CCH, the citation being that when unfair labor practice charges have been filed and are still pending and more importantly when unfair labor practices are still unremedied such a situation will bar further proceedings on a representation petition unless the charging party waives its right to object.

This has not been done by the International Brotherhood of Police Officers. Mr. Sweeney further cited the case of *Schlacter Meat,* NLRB decision, 1952, reported at 30 LRRM 1418.

He further cited *General Electric Company* reported in 48 LRRM 1619, wherein the regional director dismissed the union representative's petition and also certain petitions filed by the employer in view of the issuance of an unfair labor practice complaint filed by the certified body unit.

It was further stated that another case, *Appleton Manufacturing Company,* reported in Volume 47, LRRM, "the NLRB will not conduct an election while unfair labor practice charges are pending unless the party filing the complaint waives the complaint and the bar."

Mr. Sweeney stated that the reason there is not a contract bar existing today is because the employer, through its chief officer, has refused to bargain with the certified bargaining agent.

Ronald H. Glantz, Esq., presented the arguments for the Fraternal Order of Police in which he contended that the board from its own rules and regulations adopted in 1963 must hold an election: "If the board is unable to secure voluntary compliance at an informal conference, this matter is set down for a formal hearing before the entire board. At this meeting, the respondent shall have the right to present evidence and cross-examine witnesses. Upon completion of testimony at such hearing, if the board determines that the petitioner has substantiated his claim that a controversy does exist, an election is ordered by the board."

III.

Harold W. Demopulos, attorney for the board, traced the history of the unfair labor charges against the city of Cranston now pending in the Superior Court of Providence County. Unfair labor practices charges were filed against the city of Cranston with the Rhode Island State Labor Relations Board by Local 1, International Brotherhood of Police Officers. At the time, Local 1 was the certified bargaining agent and had been the certified bargaining agent for the Cranston Police Department for approximately three years. These charges were filed on April 19 and on May 15, 1967.

Formal hearings were held before this board on July 13, 25, and August 8, 1967. A decision and order was entered by this board on October 27, 1967, with a finding that the city of Cranston did not bargain in good faith and the city of Cranston was ordered to bargain with the International Brotherhood of Police Officers, Local 1. The city refused to continue negotiations and took an appeal to the Superior Court, Providence County, State of Rhode Island, C.A. 67–4575; said appeal is presently pending in the superior court.

The Fraternal Order of Police represented by Mr. Glantz filed its petition EE–1762 on November 13, 1967 to be the certified bargaining agent for the Cranston Police Department. The Board found the Fraternal Order of Police's petition untimely and dismissed it without prejudice.

The Fraternal Order of Police, through its counsel, Mr. Glantz, petitioned the Superior Court, Providence County, for a writ of mandamus from the board's decision. Said petition is presently pending in the superior court. . . .

This present petition entitled, EE–1769, filed by the city of Cranston on December 15, 1967, requests assistance to determine which is the proper bargaining agent for the Cranston Police Department with Local 1 or the Fraternal Order of Police, Lodge No. 20, for the period of July 1, 1968 through June 30, 1969. The city has alleged that it has a doubt concerning the union with the majority status, and it does not want to be unfair to either of the aforesaid unions, and it requests the assistance of the State Labor Relations Board.

. . . It is a matter of general policy that the National Labor Relations Board will not conduct a representation election while unresolved unfair labor practices are pending against the employer involved unless there is a waiver of charges by the filing party or special circumstances to justify the conducting of an election.

Mr. Demopulos cited other cases, *Furr's Inc.* v. *NLRB,* 52 LC, *Brown & Root Caribe,* 123 NLRB 1817 (1956), *Pacemaker Corp.,* 120 NLRB 987 (1956). This is a general administrative policy that the courts have upheld on many occasions.

The National Labor Relations Board and the New York State Labor Relations Board have ruled for many years supported by the New York courts, the circuit courts of appeal, and the United States Supreme Court, that when there is a finding of a violation of Section 8, paragraph 5 of the National Labor Relations Act, in that the employer refused to bargain in good faith with the majority representative of its employees, the National Labor Relations Board in this case ruled the parties be given a reasonable amount of time without interference by any other labor organization to negotiate the terms and conditions of employment.

The National Labor Relations Board considers that a one-year period is a reasonable time if this is the same period which it gives a newly certified bargaining representative to bargain without interference by the election process of another labor organization.

. . . Mr. Demopulos further cited *National Labor Relations Board* v. *Great Southern Trucking Co.,* C.A. 4 (1944); 7 LC, paragraph 61, 955, 139 2d, 984: "Where an employer had not yet complied with court decree directing employer to remedy effect of previous refusal to bargain, board stated that policy of act would be thwarted by directing new election prior to compliance with court decree."

In view of the cases cited herein, Mr. Demopulos recommended that the board deny and dismiss the petition without prejudice.

Mr. Samuel J. Azzinaro, a member of the board, stated, "We (meaning the State Labor Relations Board) have ordered the city of Cranston to bargain with the respective union (Local 1, International Brotherhood of Police Officers) which had a contract, and my position is that the city of Cranston should bargain with this union that we have ordered it to bargain with."

FINDINGS OF FACT

. . . Local 1, International Brotherhood of Police Officers, is still the certified bargaining agent in that its certification has never been revoked.

The National Labor Relations Board would not entertain a petition for certification while there was an unfair labor practice charge pending.

There is presently pending an unfair labor charge against the Mayor of the city of Cranston, C.A. 67–4575, Providence County, Superior Court. . . .

ORDER

. . . IT IS HEREBY DIRECTED that, upon the basis of the fore-going Findings of Fact, the Rhode Island State Labor Relations Board hereby orders that the petition filed by the city of Cranston and the petitions to intervene filed by Local 1, International Brotherhood of Police Officers and Cranston Lodge No. 20, Fraternal Order of Police, are hereby denied and dismissed without prejudice.

Entered As Order of the
Rhode Island State Labor Relations Board
Dated: February 12, 1968
By _____
      Angelo E. Azzinaro
      Executive Secretary

Rhode Island State Labor Relations Board

_____
Chairman

_____
Member

_____
Member

Discussion Questions

1. What developments caused the city of Cranston to be unsure as to which labor organization was the certified bargaining agent?
2. How could the dispute over certification rights have been resolved at a much earlier date?
3. Cite certain private sector guidelines mentioned in this case.

Section 9. The Effect of Subsequent Trusteeship on Certification

Trusteeship provisions are permitted by most union constitutions and bylaws. They allow national or international unions to place local unions and other subordinate bodies under the supervision of the parent organization in the event that corruption or financial malpractice has resulted; democratic procedures have been perverted; normal collective bargaining duties have not been carried out; or other legitimate objectives of the local have been unfulfilled as a result of the local or subordinate organization running its own affairs. These provisions were contained in the Landrum-

Griffin Act of 1959 and can affect voting rights, according to a 1962 case, *Branch* v. *Vickers, Inc.,* USDC E. Mich., 51 LRRM 2275 (1962). The court there ruled that voting rights can be suspended during the period of the trusteeship because the Landrum-Griffin Act indicates that a trusteeship "suspends the autonomy" of the subordinate labor organization.[11] The final case in this chapter concerns the effect of a subsequent trusteeship on a prior election.

In the Matter of

Hudson County Board of Chosen Freeholders (public employer) *and* **Local 1959, American Federation of State, County, and Municipal Employees, AFL-CIO (petitioner)** *and* **Local 286, International Brotherhood of Teamsters (intervenor)**

Docket No. RO–315

(State of New Jersey before the Public Employment Relations Commission)

DECISION AND CERTIFICATION OF REPRESENTATIVE

Pursuant to a consent election agreement a secret ballot election was conducted under the commission's supervision on December 14, 1971. Eligible voters were given three choices on the question of representation: "Local 1959, AFSCME, AFL-CIO," "Teamsters Local 286," or "neither" organization. At the conclusion of the election, ballots were tallied as follows: 529 for Local 1959, AFSCME; 938 for Teamsters Local 286; 38 for neither organization; 216 ballots were challenged and 24 were declared void. Thereafter, objections to the election were timely filed by the American Federation of State, County and Municipal Employees, AFL-CIO. The Teamsters filed a reply denying the allegations so far as they related to Teamsters' conduct and asking that the objections be dismissed because they were not filed by a party to the proceeding; more specifically, the Teamsters contend that Local 1959 could properly object, but that AFSCME, the international organization and parent body of Local 1959, has no standing to file the objections.

The genesis of this case is as follows. Over an extended period of time seven petitions were filed, some by Local 1959, some by the Teamsters for various groupings of Hudson County employees. The petition for the largest unit of employees was that filed by Local 1959 for a unit of white collar clerical and blue collar employees employed by Hudson County in its hospitals and administration buildings. That petition bears the signature of

Robert Murphy, Local 1959's president, and it was that petition which finally emerged as the operative one. Teamsters Local 286 intervened on that petition and became a party. When the parties agreed to a unit and an election in November, 1971, Murphy signed the consent election agreement on behalf of "Local 1959, Council 61, AFSCME." That party was designated on the notices of election and on the ballot as "Local 1959, AFSCME, AFL-CIO." Following the election, no one filed objections in the name of Local 1959. As indicated, the parent body filed in its own name and the document was signed by Louis Kaplan, AFSCME's area director for New York and New Jersey.

After preliminary administrative investigation of the objections, a notice of hearing issued setting down certain objections for hearing. Notice was also given that the question of standing was within the scope of the hearing. Service of the notice of hearing and of other preliminary papers was made upon Local 1959 and also upon the parent body. The hearing commenced on March 9, 1972, but no one entered an appearance on behalf of Local 1959. An adjournment was taken to a fixed date, but prior to resumption the hearing was adjourned indefinitely because of restraints, imposed in connection with litigation between AFSCME and Local 1959.

The litigation referred to arose when, on January 12, 1972, AFSCME moved to impose a trusteeship on Local 1959

> because secession of the Local is threatened, dissipation or loss of the funds or assets of the Local is threatened, and the Local is acting in violation of the international constitution, lawful orders of the convention, the international executive board, and the international president.

AFSCME's Area Director, Louis Kaplan, was named trustee. Local 1959, its President Murphy, and others countered with an action against AFSCME in Superior Court Chancery Division, Hudson County, seeking restraint against alleged interference by the parent body and seeking other relief. The dispute was subsequently moved to United States District Court for the District of New Jersey, which court on February 1, 1972, entered orders of temporary restraint and show cause. The testimony phase of that suit has been completed, but no final determination on the merits has yet been reached. The restraint was vacated on appeal.

In an affidavit Kaplan asserts that Murphy refused to file objections to the election of December 14 and that Kaplan was "obliged to file objection myself, in the name of AFSCME and Local 1959." Kaplan also attached to that affidavit a copy of a letter which Kaplan states Murphy left with him. It is a letter dated December 20, 1971 from Murphy, as president of Local 1959, to the Hudson County Board of Chosen Freeholders, wherein he cites Local 1959's defeat in the representation election and gives notice that dues checkoffs cease: "Local 1959 feels, inasmuch as we are not in a position to represent these employees, it would be most unfair to continue to accept their dues."

Returning to the question of AFSCME's standing to file the objections, we take note of the following provisions. The beginning point is Section 19:11–19(f) of the commission's rules and regulations which provides that "any party may file objections. . . ." Section 19:11–16, referring to agreements for consent election, defines who are parties: "The parties to such proceeding shall be the public employer, the petitioner, and any intervenors who shall have complied with the requirements for intervention." The standard terms of the consent agreement reinforce the point by providing in paragraph 6 that objections may be filed ". . . by any of the undersigned parties. . . ." Elsewhere in the rules Section 19:10–5 provides

> The term "party," as used herein, shall mean any person, employee, group of employees, organization, or public employer filing a charge, petition, request, or application under these rules and regulations . . . or any other person, organization, or public employer whose intervention in a proceeding has been permitted or directed by the commission . . . but nothing herein shall be construed to prevent the commission, or any designated officer, from limiting any party's participation in the proceedings to the extent of his interest.

While the beginning elements of the last cited definition appear to be virtually all-encompassing, it is not particularly enlightening in view of the limitation placed at the end since the essential question here is what "interest," if any, does AFSCME demonstrate—which is another way of posing the question of standing. The other provisions cited above narrow the inquiry to whether or not AFSCME, the International Union, is a "petitioner" or an "undersigned party" by virtue of the fact that its subordinate body, Local 1959, petitioned and later executed the consent agreement.

Normally, it appears the issue would not arise because there is generally assumed to be a harmony of interest between an international and its local unions. But here it is abundantly clear that no such relationship existed. During the critical period, the five-day period following the election when objections must be filed, Local 1959 was so much at odds with its parent body that within a month the latter moved to impose a trusteeship. It is not necessary to determine the effect of that action on the question of standing had it occurred prior to that critical period since the facts are otherwise. Local 1959, a viable entity as demonstrated by its later suit, and the moving party in initiating this case, refused to contest the election in which it participated. We do not believe that the International, in obvious disagreement with the Local which theretofore had clearly been a party, and in reliance on the parent-subordinate relationship, should be permitted to act in derogation of the Local's right to refrain, to oust the Local as a party, and to substitute itself in the place of the dissenting Local. Given the peculiar circumstances in this case, we conclude that between AFSCME and Local 1959, the latter alone was a party entitled to file objections and that its failure to do so constituted a disclaimer which could not be circumvented. The issue here is wholly separate from the question of whether there existed sufficient basis for the trusteeship proceeding. That is an internal matter which the commission is not competent to judge and which, furthermore, is irrelevant to the matter decided here.

The objections filed by AFSCME are hereby dismissed. Having received a majority of the valid ballots, plus challenged ballots cast, Teamsters Local 286 will be certified.

CERTIFICATION OF REPRESENTATIVE

IT IS HEREBY CERTIFIED that Local 286, International Brotherhood of Teamsters has been designated and selected by a majority of the employees of the above-named public employer. . . .

By order of the commission.

Dated: April 25, 1972   /s/ Charles H. Parcells
      Trenton, N.J.   Acting Chairman

Discussion Questions

1. Was the trusteeship an important factor in this case? Why not?
2. Did Local 1959 contest the election results?
3. Why was the parent AFSCME organization ruled not a proper party to the proceeding?

CHAPTER 3

[1] Harry H. Wellington and Ralph K. Winter, Jr., *The Unions and the Cities* (Washington, D.C.: The Brookings Institution, 1971), pp. 87–88.

[2] Motorist Insurance Agency, Inc., 182 NLRB No. 142 (1970); Furnas Electric Co., 183 NLRB No. 1 (1970).

[3] 21 GERR 5003–5006 (RF–14) (Washington, D.C.: BNA, Inc., 1971).

[4] 21 GERR 5175–5176 (RF–27) (Washington, D.C.: BNA, Inc., 1971).

[5] 21 GERR 5287–5288 (RF–34) (Washington, D.C.: BNA, Inc., 1971).

[6] 21 GERR 5173–5174 (RF–27) (Washington, D.C.: BNA, Inc., 1971).

[7] LRX 441, sec. 14 (Washington, D.C.: BNA, Inc., 1968).

[8] 21 GERR 7027–7028 (RF–57) (Washington, D.C.: BNA, Inc., 1973).

[9] LRX 443, sec. 16 (Washington, D.C.: BNA, Inc., 1971).

[10] A. Howard Myers, *Labor Law and Legislation,* 4th ed. (Cincinnati, Ohio: Southwestern Publishing Company, 1968) p. 432.

[11] LRX 352(d), sec. 27, LRX 353, sec. 28, LRX 342(b), sec. 3 (Washington, D.C.: Bureau of National Affairs, Inc., 1963, 1966).

4 | The Collective Bargaining Process

THE RIGHT to negotiate a labor agreement is a key perquisite accompanying exclusive recognition status for a labor organization. The accumulated feelings and desires of employees represented by the union begin to take the shape of specific demands that will be presented to management. Through the negotiation process these demands will eventually become a new set of work rules that will supplement, or perhaps become a substitute for, those already in existence. The basic objective of negotiation is, therefore, to reach agreement on these procedures.

The 1972 report of the Committee on State Labor Law of the American Bar Association (ABA) summarized the inherent diversity in state public employee labor relations:

> [T]he fifty states and their political subdivisions display infinite variety with respect to collective bargaining among public employees. Some states still have no legislation whatever or legislation applying only to a limited class of employees . . . . In a growing number of states, however, legislation, frequently patterned after the National Labor Relations Act, contemplates the selection of an exclusive bargaining representative for all employees in an appropriate unit and imposes an affirmative obligation upon the public employer to negotiate in good faith with this representative concerning wages, hours, and working conditions. Between these extremes is a continuum of many differing systems not readily susceptible to generalization . . . .[1]

For example, twenty-five states have mandatory statutes providing for either "meet-and-confer" procedures or conventional collective bargaining processes. Fifteen other states have laws that are permissive in terms of collective bargaining or meet-and-confer activities, or provide a right only on the part of labor organizations to present proposals to the public employer.

The implementation of meet-and-confer laws usually results in discussions leading to the unilateral adoption of policy by a legislative body,

180

rather than by means of a written contract, and takes place with multiple employee representatives rather than with an exclusive bargaining agent. In California, for example, under the Meyers-Milias-Brown Act, the concept encompasses the mutual obligation to meet and confer personally in order to exchange freely information, opinions, and proposals and to endeavor to reach agreement on matters within the scope of representation. The only limit on the scope of representation is that it does not include consideration of the merits, necessity, or organization of any service or activity provided by law.

No such limitations are imposed in private employment where collective bargaining ordinarily refers to the performance by duly authorized management representatives and duly authorized representatives of a certified employee organization of their mutual obligation to meet at reasonable times and to confer in good faith with respect to wages, hours, and other terms and conditions of employment, and includes the mutual obligation to execute a written document incorporating any agreement reached. This obligation does not compel either party to agree to a proposal or to make a concession, however.

Derber views the objectives of public sector negotiations thus:

The objective of collective negotiations is to develop a set of mutually acceptable rules governing the conditions of employment and procedures by which employees and administrators jointly carry out the functions of a particular enterprise or agency . . . .[2]

In the federal government, Executive Order 11491 provides the basis for negotiating labor agreements. The principle of "good faith" bargaining is firmly established. The limitations of negotiations and retained management rights are specified. All else is negotiable "with respect to personnel policies and practices and matters affecting working conditions, so far as may be appropriate under applicable laws and regulations, including policies set forth in the federal personnel manual, published agency policies and regulations, a national or other controlling agreement at a higher level in the agency, and this order." It is clear that a wide range of negotiable areas exists.

From general experience, while the term *concession* is often used when management agrees to meet a union demand, it is an overworked term. To agree with a union proposal is not necessarily concession. Often it is simply an act of setting down a term in writing that the parties in any event would have accepted under normal conditions.

With regard to the mechanics of the bargaining process, once appointed, the management negotiator or committee becomes the focal point for an integrated management approach to relations with the union while negotiations are in process. In any case, the negotiating committee should be given full authority to negotiate. This means they are given the authority to bind the employer to agreement with the union. Any constraints that top management wishes to apply to the negotiators are usually clearly established for them prior to the formal negotiations. These constraints, however, should not be so broad as to render the negotiators impotent. One example of the delegation of negotiating authority in the federal service is the following provision in a Department of Defense regulation:

> Components are expected to delegate the broadest practicable authority to heads of activities in the areas of personnel policy and practices and matters affecting working conditions in order to maximize opportunities for meaningful and productive negotiations. Heads of Department of Defense activities will arrange for the full range of their authority on negotiable matters to be exercised by those persons designated to represent management in negotiations with labor organizations granted exclusive recognition.[3]

Similarly, the union negotiators have their final task to perform. They must submit the results of their negotiating efforts for approval. Generally, this means ratification by vote of the union membership. In most cases union negotiating committees obtain ratification of agreements, mainly because they have bargained in a competent fashion and have correctly assessed the "acceptability quotient" of the membership.

In the final analysis, an effective agreement is phrased in the most common terms so that it is understood by the entire work force. Although there may be a tendency to incorporate legally protective and qualifying clauses, such protection against later misinterpretation of meaning can usually be attained without highly technical legalistic language.

A major problem in government labor relations is determining the appropriate scope of bargaining in that a great many terms of employment are specified in Civil Service rules and regulations. Thus, the scope of bargaining will depend on the extent to which different government entities have concurrent or exclusive jurisdiction, as well as other factors: the level at which bargaining is conducted, the division of authority with management, the nature of the bargaining unit, and so on. Basically, most collective bargaining laws for government employees merely define the scope of bargaining to cover "wages, hours, and working conditions," which is similar to the private sector boundaries. Then, however, more precise definitions of the preceding bargainable topics are set out to impose restrictions or limitations on the parameters of bargaining. These are:

1. Items covered by legislation are deemed to be nonbargainable.
2. Protection of the civil service system, usually by a clause in the statute stating that civil service laws and authority of the Civil Service Commission shall supersede collective bargaining.

3. A specific list of items excluded from the scope of bargaining, reserving them for the sole prerogative of management.[4]

These and other problem areas surrounding the negotiation of collective bargaining agreements in the public sector will be investigated in this chapter.

Section 1. State Statute Barring Legally Enforceable Contracts with Public School Employee Organizations

California is one of the states in which various classifications of state employees are covered by separate labor relations statutes, each conferring different rights and obligations. The distinctions between the obligations under meet-and-confer legislation and obligations to bargain collectively are clearly demonstrated by that state's Winton Act. The act covers public school teachers where "meetings are often held with representatives of more than one labor organization, each purporting to speak for its own members. The public employer is under no obligation to negotiate in good faith concerning the proposals of any group." [5] The following case illustrates the limitations on bargaining rights placed on public education negotiations. By contrast, city employees in Los Angeles, covered by that municipality's employer-employee relations ordinance, enjoy the protection of binding arbitration of their grievances.

Placentia Unified Education Association v. Board of Education, Placentia Unified School District

Superior Court of the State of California for the County of Orange
No. 181943 Memorandum Decision[6]

The court finds against petitioner, denies the petition to confirm interim arbitration award and to compel arbitration, and grants respondent's petition to vacate interim arbitration award.

The award is vacated under the provisions of Code of Civil Procedure Section 1286.2(d).

The binding arbitration of grievances is a useful tool for resolving disputes between employers and employees. Its use has been increasing in the public sector and probably will continue to do so. There is every reason to believe that it would be a valuable tool in the public sector as it is in the private sector.

However, the public policy of the state, as expressed by legislation and judicial decision, is to circumscribe narrowly the powers of school districts, in the interests of state uniformity. In particular, the legislature has attempted by the Winton Act . . . to formulate . . . a regulation of the role of public employees and their employee organizations in the decision-making process. In light of its terms and legislative history and of the scope, nature, and legislative history of other legislation (particularly the Meyers-Milias-Brown Act . . .) dealing with employer-employee relations in the private and public sectors, the court concludes that the Winton Act does not authorize a school board, in the course of procedures therein outlined, to enter into legally enforceable contracts with employee organizations, whether relating to binding grievance arbitration or otherwise.

Without enumerating all considerations, the following features of the Winton Act are deemed to be significant aids to its construction:

1. Its preamble . . . which places emphasis upon the retention of rules and regulations that regulate tenure, merit, or civil service systems and other methods that administer employee-employer relations and the purpose of the act as the provision of "orderly methods of communications" between the employees and employers.

2. The absence of the typical collective bargaining provision for the constitution of a body or employee organization with legal authority to present "negotiating" demands on behalf of employees and to bind employees by its own concessions. The "certified employee council" . . . does not meet these specifications.

3. The absence of any provision for a written contract or written agreement as a culmination of the "meet-and-confer" sessions. Such a provision is typical in statutes authorizing collective bargaining.

4. The provision, instead, that the "agreement" that might result from the "meet-and-confer" sessions would be memorialized by "written resolution, regulation, or policy of the governing board. . . ."

5. The substitution . . . of the term "certified employee council" for "negotiating council" by the 1970 amendments. . . .

6. The absence from the act of the standard collective bargaining language: "in good faith" and the presence of the somewhat weaker word "conscientious" in Section 13081.

7. The provision (Section 13088) precluding application of Labor Code, Section 923, relating to collective bargaining, to public school employees.

8. The provision of Section 13088, apparently reserving the "final decision" to the public school employer, which construed with the language of Section 13081(d) adumbrates the legislative intent that the power of the school board to determine matters within its discretionary authority be not foreclosed by the outcome of the "meet-and-confer" sessions.

9. Lastly, the provision for resolution of "persistent disagreements"

by "nonbinding" recommendations or fact finding by a three-man committee. . . .

A further problem is presented by the unusual clause in Article XI of the document that was ratified by both parties. It provided that there would be no change, alteration, or modification thereof except by mutual agreement "except in the case where the Board of Education determines that an emergency exists," in which event the school board "shall notify the negotiating council of the nature of the emergency and of the anticipated changes that will be required to be made due to the emergency." The petitioner has questioned the power of the school board to invoke this provision, prior to the institution of the grievance proceeding, by amending the grievance procedure to provide that it be "advisory only." Both the arbitrator-chairman and the petitioner appear to believe that the power to modify was not exercisable because no emergency existed, or perhaps because the legal advice that the school board received could not reasonably in good faith have been considered by it to have created an emergency. The legal climate in which the document was negotiated and ratified was one of uncertainty as to whether the school board could bind itself contractually. Even nonlawyers know that "emergency" is an indefinite word. For the parties to use such a term, without definition or limitation, in a provision that the determination of whether an emergency existed was unilaterally reserved to the school board leads to the conclusion that they were content to enter into an illusory contract which, as a "gentlemen's agreement," may have been better in the circumstances than none at all.

Alternatively, they must have intended at least that the school board would not be held to strict standards of precision, objectivity, or restraint in making its determination of the existence of an emergency and of the modifications that the emergency required. In the court's opinion the legal advice, imprecise as it was, that the school board received sufficed to support its determination that an emergency existed and that the emergency required the abrogation of the provision for binding grievance arbitration.

The court concludes that the document ratified by the parties did not, at the time the arbitration procedure started, provide for binding arbitration of grievances, and that whether or not it so provided was never submitted to arbitration by the school board.

Dated: May 5, 1971   /s/ Wm S. Lee
                                      Judge of the Superior Court

Discussion Questions

1. Are the Winton Act restrictions on collective bargaining rights for teachers realistic in light of recent trends in public education labor relations?

2. Which problem common in public sector labor relations, which is virtually nonexistent in private employment, is present in this case?
3. Describe the problem of contract interpretation that the court was forced to decide.

Section 2. The Validity of a State Statute Allowing Private Preagreement Bargaining Sessions

In the private sector negotiations are almost always held in secret meetings between the respective negotiating teams. There is in fact, consensus that public disclosure of the bargaining positions and strategy of the parties would be detrimental in the sense that either side might be locked into an unrealistic bargaining posture by such publicity and would have difficulty retreating to a meaningful position as a result of the loss of prestige that would result. This resultant loss of flexibility and room for maneuver might then contribute toward a heightened incidence of industrial conflict. As will be indicated here, similar considerations seem to prevail in public employment, although the public clearly has a stronger claim to disclosure of certain relevant facts than exists in private industry.

Patricia K. Bassett et al. v. G. Holmes Braddock et al. v. Dade County Classroom Teachers Association, Inc. (a Florida corporation not for profit)
Circuit Court of the 11th Judicial Circuit in and for Dade County, Florida. Case No. 71–1462 (Judge Grossman)[7]

PARTIAL FINAL JUDGMENT

On the counterclaim of the intervenor, in this case, the court is required to enter a declaratory judgment on the following issues: Does F.S. 286.011 require governmental employers, when engaged in collective bargaining with their employees, to do so in public rather than in private?

The court is further required to determine whether the negotiations entered into by the school board in 1970–1971 were done so in a legal lawful manner.

The Supreme Court of Florida has declared, in *Dade County Classroom Teachers' Association, Inc. v. Ryan,* 225 So.2d 902 (1969) that Article 1, Section 6 of the Florida Constitution (1968 revision) imposes a mandate on all public employers to bargain collectively with their employees; that with the exception of the right to strike, public employees have the same rights of collective bargaining as those who work in private industry.

Collective bargaining is a process whereby representatives of management and labor, be they public or private, come together, negotiate in good faith, and generally agree on tentative proposals regarding salaries, working conditions, and rights and duties of one to the other.

The mechanics of the collective bargaining process for the governmental employer involve several steps.

First. The negotiating team must be chosen. This may consist of an independent negotiator, or all or part of the governmental employer or a committee thereof.

Second. The negotiator must be instructed with the facts and information necessary to meet his counterpart on the other side. Parameters of positions must be established. The final outcome will often depend on how much information a negotiator has about his limitations and authorizations and how he uses this information.

Third. The negotiating teams meet to discuss their proposals. If this is undertaken in good faith as the law requires, without posturing or improper demands, there is no reason why agreement cannot be reached on all issues. Even if an impasse is reached, there are many opportunities for resolution by mediation, fact finding, and arbitration. This is essential, since in the public sector there is no right to strike.

Fourth. When the negotiators reach tentative agreement on matters under discussion, the same is reduced to writing and is presented to employer and employees and the public for consideration, discussion, and eventual ratification or rejection.

Fifth. If approved or adopted, the tentative proposals become part of the code governing the relationship between employer-employee.

Until this time, certain parts of collective bargaining by Dade County governments and the school board have been conducted in private; that is, with the press and the general public excluded. Uncontradicted testimony by experts in the field of governmental collective bargaining (a) public sector employers; (b) employee groups; and (c) the neutral Michigan Employment Relations Commission establishes that if all portions of the collective bargaining process were conducted with the public present, the collective bargaining process itself would be destroyed. Each of the experts testifying indicated that publicized negotiations would inhibit any subsequent modifications. The question before the court is the validity of these practices.

The court has examined the several steps in the collective bargaining process and has construed the controlling provisions of both Article I, Section 6 of the Florida Constitution and F.S. 236.011 as they apply thereto. Clearly, some aspects of governmental collective bargaining must be completely open to public scrutiny at all times. Thus, on the first point above mentioned, the procedure for determining who shall negotiate and if an outside person, whoever he shall be, his qualifications, how much he shall be paid, and so on, are all matters which must be openly determined. The public is benefited, not harmed, by full disclosure. On the fourth point above mentioned, the presentation of the negotiators' tentatively agreed upon proposals for consideration by the government employer must be fully and openly done "in the sunshine." There must be the opportunity for the general public to know the terms of the tentative proposals as negotiated; to have the opportunity to express its views to the government employer, prior to its deliberations and decisions on such a package.

When one considers the second and third points as outlined above, a different conclusion must be reached: a government agency may, if it desires, privately instruct its negotiators on the limits of their authority to bargain. Moreover, good faith collective bargaining requires that the press and general public can also be excluded from negotiating sessions that take place *prior* to the time tentative agreement is reached on their positions.

To rule otherwise is to put the taxpayer at a gross disadvantage when *his* representatives are chosen and instructed and are negotiating. The "Government in Sunshine" law applied *only* to one side—the government employer. The employees' negotiator is, and will continue to be, instructed in secrecy. Since although these groups of state, county, and municipal employees do render a public function, nonetheless they do not fall within the purview of F.S. 286.011. His bargaining limits are known to his team alone. An obvious victim of such a procedure is the collective bargaining process itself and its capacity for maintaining peaceful relationships in the public sector. If this type of unilateral bargaining is required, the public board, in this case the school board, is hindered and seriously impaired in its ability to function as a bargaining representative, and thus the process of collective bargaining itself may be dispensed with since it would develop a pattern of conduct inconsistent with good faith bargaining. The purpose of collective bargaining is to promote the rational exchange of facts and arguments that will measurably increase the chance for amicable agreement. Public communication of the negotiations would virtually exclude genuine good faith negotiations and would, in effect, limit bargaining on all matters on which the public negotiator took a stand.

The temporary privacy of this portion of the collective bargaining process enables the government employer to bargain collectively, as he must under constitutional mandate, and to do so *on equal terms with his employees*. Since the word product of these negotiations is tentative and is binding on no one, and since the public will be given the opportunity to express itself on those proposals prior to their approval by the government employer, this temporary seclusion cannot be in violation of the letter, or purpose of the "Government in Sunshine" law.

Again to decide otherwise not only destroys the purpose and intent of F.S. 286.011 but also would permit this statute to assume precedence over the provisions of Article I, Section 6 of the Florida Constitution. This court finds, based on uncontroverted testimony, that meaningful collective bargaining will be destroyed if full publicity is accorded to each step. Two distinct evils derive from such publicity. First, publicity regarding firmness tends to make the public employer seal itself into its original position in such a way that, even if it wished to change that position at a later date, it cannot do so. Second, publicity regarding the employer's offer fixes in the minds of the employees the idea that the employer has set itself up as their representative and therefore the need for its own representatives and collective bargaining is superfluous. Since there is a constitutional mandate to engage in collective bargaining, statutory interference therewith would not be justified. To the extent that F.S. 286.011 would curtail collective bargaining, its provisions would be *pro tanto* unconstitutional. However, this court construes the provisions of F.S. 286.011 as not reaching into the collective bargaining session or the instructions given to the public negotiators. Such a construction saves the statute.

Applying these principles to the facts of this case, the court finds that, in 1970, pursuant to constitutional requirements, the school board and the intervenor, Dade County Classroom Teachers' Association, Inc., a Florida corporation not for profit, entered into a collective bargaining regarding salaries and conditions of employment. Each of the foregoing steps of the collective bargaining process was entered into. The court has examined these steps in light of the requirements of F.S. 286.011 and the constitutional requirements of collective bargaining.

First. The school board hired an independent negotiator as its representative pursuant to the rule 4135.3 of the school board. The record reflects that the school board retained its negotiator on April 1, 1970, at a meeting regularly scheduled and open to the press and to the public. There is no evidence that any discussion concerning the employment of the negotiator occurred prior to this time. After this date but before April 22, 1970, the school board members met socially with their negotiator, at a San Francisco convention of school board members. No school board business was discussed. On April 22, 1970, a vote was taken at an open and regularly scheduled board meeting to hire a different negotiator but this was defeated. The choice of the negotiator must be conducted in the open. There is no evidence in the record to the contrary. The question has arisen as whether the school board negotiator is an employee or agent. Having heard testimony presented, it is the finding of this court that the negotiator is the agent of the board and is governed by the provisions of F.S. 286.011 with the exceptions as hereinabove set forth.

Second. There is no testimony as to the manner in which the school board instructed or gave authority and limitations to its negotiator. Obviously, under these circumstances and under the court's ruling, no violation of the "Government in Sunshine" law exists, even if these instructions were in private. However, it is the duty of all the board members to meet with the negotiator and set out his guidelines and authority. During the 1970 negotiations, the record is void of specific authority given to the negotiator by the board members. This is due to the fact that the board attempted to work within the confines of F.S. 286.011.

Third. It has been conceded that the school board negotiator met in secret with representatives of the employees, reached tentative agreement, and subsequently presented these proposals to the school board. Under the principles announced this date, the school board's reliance on this practice was well placed. The public's interest does *not* lie requiring negotiators for public employers to come to the table stripped of strategy or tactics by premature exposure to the public and their adversaries.

Fourth. The tentatively agreed upon proposals as developed by the negotiators in private were presented to the school board on December 9, 1970, at an open and regularly scheduled meeting. The proposals were modified after debate as amended or modified, adopted on first reading.

The court finds that the entire procedure as above outlined clearly conforms to the interrelated requirements of Article I, Section 6 of the Constitution and F.S. 286.011. To the extent that the statute might prohibit a public employer from negotiating in private on the same terms as the public employee, it would deny equal protection and due process of law and would violate the good faith collective bargaining process required by Article I, Section 6 of the Florida Constitution. However, the court finds that F.S. 286.011 does not require so drastic a result and nothing therein prohibits collective bargaining to the extent herein detailed from being conducted in private.

Whereupon, it is adjudged as follows:

1. The relief prayed for in the counterclaim is granted.

2. The collective bargaining procedures as heretofore conducted by the Dade County School Board in 1970, and as described herein, are valid exercises of their authority and represent lawful activity on the part of the school board.

3. The school board's actions in considering and voting upon the negotiators' package at its meeting on December 9, 1970 was a lawful exercise of its authority; there is no bar to further action the school board may take with regard thereto.

4. Future negotiations between the school board and representatives of employees shall be conducted in a manner consistent herewith.

Done and ordered in chambers, at Miami, Dade County, Florida, this twenty-fifth day of March, 1971.

/s/ Rhea Pincus Grossman
Circuit Judge

Discussion Questions

1. Discuss the arguments supporting the privacy of negotiations in public sector bargaining situations.
2. In which aspects of public collective negotiations is the public entitled to full disclosure?
3. What specifically does the "Government in Sunshine" law encompass?
4. If the above statute were strictly construed, what constitutional impediments would result?

Section 3. The Good Faith Bargaining Concept

Under the Taft-Hartley Act an employer is required to negotiate with the union in good faith with an open mind in an attempt to reach an agreement if possible. This of necessity will require a subjective evaluation of the attitude of the negotiators evinced during the discussions. Because overt acts normally provide clues as to the intentions of individuals, the following types of employer conduct may justify a finding that good faith bargaining is absent: "(1) use of delaying tactics, (2) a refusal to discuss union proposals, (3) withdrawal of concessions previously granted," [8] "(4) failing to give negotiators sufficient authority to bind the employer, (5) refusing to sign an agreement already reached, (6) unilaterally granting wage increases or changing other benefits without consulting with the union." [9]

In the following instances, however, "good faith" is irrelevant, and the NLRB and the courts have ruled that there has been a prima facie violation of the bargaining obligation: (1) a refusal to discuss a subject within the area of so-called mandatory bargaining—"wages, hours, and other terms and conditions of employment"; (2) a refusal to meet a reasonable request for data necessary to an intelligent discussion of a mandatory bargaining topic; (3) insistence upon including in a contract a subject that is outside the scope of mandatory bargaining.[10] In this respect, the standards for the determination of genuine bargaining are quite similar in the public sector.

———————————

Typographical Pressmen's and Bindery Unions v. Personnel Division, Oregon State University, University of Oregon and State Printers
Oregon Public Employee Relations Board

FINDINGS OF FACT

The board accepts the stipulation of the parties as its findings herein.

COMMENTS

It was stipulated that negotiations began during May of 1970 and that the state printer, as administrative head of the state printing division, acted as representative of the employer. On or about June 9, 1970, these negotiations resulted in an agreement for a joint recommendation of a "proposed compensation adjustment to the respondent Personnel Division for implementation in modification of the compensation plan for classified service under Oregon Revised Statute 240.235." The Personnel Division rejected the adjustment, stating that the department's surveys indicated that the state's wage rates for the involved classifications would exceed rates paid by commercial shops in the localities in which the state shops were located and that, therefore, they could not justify acceptance of the recommended rates. In its response the Personnel Division stated,

(1) In matters of compensation, agreements made between state agencies and employee representatives are for the purpose of providing joint recommendations to the Personnel Division for implementation. The Personnel Division, utilizing these recommendations, will then exercise its responsibility in determining what wage rates will be incorporated in the compensation plan.

The Personnel Division has refused to enter a binding contract respecting compensation to be paid employees in the classifications . . . represented by the charging party. The issues were stipulated to be:

1. Are respondents obligated to negotiate a binding wage contract with charging parties respecting compensation to be paid employees represented by charging parties?
2. Do respondents have such authority?
3. Is the refusal of the Personnel Division to enter into such negotiations a violation of the obligation to bargain collectively in good faith under O.R.S. 243.745?

O.R.S. 243.711(1) defines "collective bargaining" as the "performance" of a duty stated to be "mutual" that being the duty to "confer in good faith" and "execute a written contract incorporating any agreement reached if requested." It is specifically noted that "this obligation does not compel either party to agree to a proposal or require the making of a concession."

Despite the use of the word "confer" the general context of this subsection, the fact that it is a definition of "collective bargaining," and its obvious patterning after the National Labor Relations Act compel us to the conclusion that the legislature intended to create an obligation essentially similar to that created by the federal act. However, the nature of government structure and the existence of other statutes also make it clear that the duties although similar are not identical.

The subject matter of this duty includes "direct or indirect monetary matters" as well as a wide area of other conditions of employment, all of which are included within the term "employment relations" [O.R.S. 243.711(2)]. Subsection 3 defines a labor organization as having as "one of its primary purposes representing . . . employees in their employment relationship with the public employer."

The foregoing seems to make it clear that the legislature intended public employers to bargain over wages, to do so in good faith, to hopefully reach agreement on the issue, and to be prepared to memorialize that agreement in the form of a contract.

Subsection 5 of O.R.S. 243.711 defines a public employer as "the state and any of its agencies and institutions." The statute used the conjunctive, not the disjunctive. Thus, even though as in the instant case, the institution, for example, the University of Oregon, is a public employer, so too is the state of Oregon. Thus the obligation to bargain in good faith extends to the state of Oregon as well as to the University of Oregon, Oregon State University, and the state printer.

O.R.S. provides that the Personnel Division

> shall adopt a compensation plan which shall include, for each class or position, a minimum and maximum rate, and such intermediate rates as are considered necessary or equitable. In establishing the rates the division shall consider the prevailing rates of pay for the services performed and for comparable services in public and private employment, living costs, maintenance, or other benefits received by employees, and the state's financial condition and policies.

This section further provides that: "Modifications of the plan may be adopted by the division and shall be effective only when approved by the Governor."

The position taken by the Personnel Division in the instant case would appear to be that the provisions of O.R.S. 240.235 exempt it from any duty to bargain collectively and impose upon it only a duty to consider the "recommendations" of the union and the state printer.

It must be assumed that the legislature in enacting O.R.S. 243.711 and the sections related therewith was aware of O.R.S. 240.235. We cannot conclude that the legislature intended to repeal the provisions of law relating to the Personnel Division's function in establishing compensation plans, particularly since that chapter was amended by the same session of the legislature which enacted O.R.S. 243.711, nor can we assume that the legislature intended to exempt the state from a duty to bargain in good faith as to classified employees. No such exemption is found in the statutes. Instead the board concludes that the legislature intended these statutes to be applied in a manner which harmonizes them.

The duty to bargain does not require either party to have present at the bargaining table the individual with final authority. Labor organizations are rarely able to do so since that final authority normally rests in the membership. On the other hand, the duty to bargain in good faith does place upon both parties the obligation to have at the bargaining table persons whose function is other than that of a messenger boy. The individuals engaged in the actual bargaining process must be persons empowered to present the facts and arguments in support of their own position and to weigh and evaluate the arguments and facts presented by their colleagues across the table.

Since the duty to bargain in good faith does not involve an obligation to agree, we see no merit in the contention that the state's duty as to classified service employees is somehow lessened by the fact that the Governor must approve a change in the classification rates. It is quite true that the bargainers cannot bind the Governor as it is equally true that the bargainers cannot bind the union membership. There is nothing to prevent the parties from negotiating to a point at which the Governor has neither accepted or not accepted a preferred agreement.

Neither the state printer nor the two universities nor the Personnel Division can be exclusively said to be the employer. Each is an employer and yet so is the state by definition as set forth in the act. The Personnel Division has the responsibility of establishing the rate structure. The statute sets out certain considerations which the Personnel Division must consider. These are not, however, exclusive considerations. These considerations are not in any sense inconsistent with the collective bargaining process. Indeed they are the considerations which are standard to collective bargaining in the private sector. It would be assumed that management representatives would be armed with this type of information and would make their judgments as to the acceptability or nonacceptability of union proposals in part, at least, in the light of these standards. There is no reason that the state may not do the same.

However, the fault here was not in the state's reliance on these standards but rather in its exclusive reliance on these standards and in the insistence of the Personnel Division that the union's role was that of a petitioner rather than a collective bargaining equal.

We find that under the facts of this case the state's obligation to bargain in good faith required that the Personnel Division should have been represented and involved in the collective bargaining process to the extent of entering into the good faith give and take of collective bargaining. We do not decide the precise nature by which its representation should have been effectuated, but it is the responsibility of the division to choose its own representatives who can give bona fide consideration to its arguments and its facts and who can supply the union with the reasons and facts relied upon by the Personnel Division and who can effectively give the union access to the Personnel Division in a collective bargaining sense.

It may well be that such collective bargaining would still have resulted in the division adhering to its position, but we are concerned here not with results but with the procedures.

The state has contended in this case that no binding agreement could be reached because neither the institutions nor agencies could bind the Governor nor could they bind the legislature. This, of course, does not prevent them from entering into a binding agreement, subject to the Governor's approval or after the Governor's approval, nor does it prevent them from entering into a binding agreement subject to the legislature's appropriating the necessary funds. In point of fact, this latter condition is so inherent in the structure of the government of this state that such a condition would be implied in any agreement even if not specifically set forth.

CONCLUSIONS OF LAW

As to the first issue "Are respondents obligated to negotiate a binding wage contract with charging parties respecting compensation to be paid employees represented by charging parties?" we answer that respondents are not obligated to negotiate a binding wage contract but they are obligated to make a good faith effort to do so. If such an agreement is reached and if the union requests that it be reduced to a written contract, the state is obligated to honor that request and such agreement may properly provide whatever caveats were included in the final settlement.

As to the second issue "Do respondents have such authority?" we answer that the named respondents have such authority subject to the agreement being conditioned upon approval by the Governor and subject to the legislature making it possible for the state to carry out the agreement.

In answer to issue three "Is the refusal of the Personnel Division to enter into such negotiations a violation of the obligation to bargain collectively in good faith under O.R.S. 243.745?" we find that the respondents' position as evidenced by the above quoted answer of the Personnel Division did constitute a violation of the obligation to bargain collectively in good faith.

ORDER

The respondents are ordered to bargain in good faith in accordance with the conclusions made herein.

Dated: March 31, 1971   Oregon Public Employee Relations Board
       Salem, Ore.

Discussion Questions

1. What are the basic issues in this case?
2. How does the Oregon statute define collective bargaining?
3. State the reasons offered by the Personnel Division to support the claim that it does not have to bargain collectively.
4. Were the statutes cited in conflict? If not, why not?
5. Discuss the extent of the authority with which the negotiators should be entrusted.
6. Private sector collective bargaining standards are mentioned in this case. How closely does the board rely on them as precedent?
7. In what respects was there a deviation from the board's interpretation of good faith bargaining?

Section 4. The Authority of an Individual Negotiator to Bind a Bargaining Committee

Collective bargaining would become an exercise in frustration if the negotiators were without authority to bind their organizations to the agreed-upon contract terms. The following statement summarizes the usual situation in private employment regarding the authority to execute and ratify agreements:

> The agreement reached by negotiators sometimes is not final and binding until ratification by the union membership and/or until final approval by the president or other executive functionary of the company. In the case of an employer association, approval may be required by individual employer members.[11]

Similar considerations obtain in public employment.

———

In the Matter of

Rhode Island State Labor Relations Board *and* **North Providence School Committee**

Case No. ULP–943

(State of Rhode Island before the State Labor Relations Board)

DECISION AND ORDER

On November 17, 1969, the North Providence Federation of Teachers, Local 920, AFL-CIO, filed with the Rhode Island State Labor Relations Board, hereinafter called the board, a charge alleging that the North Providence School Committee, hereinafter called the respondents, had engaged in, and were engaging in, certain unfair labor practices as set forth in the Rhode Island State Labor Relations Act, hereinafter called the act.

The board investigated said charge and an informal conference was held on December 2, 1969. A complaint then issued from the board on December 30, 1969, alleging in substance that the respondents, in their capacities, had refused to bargain with the complainant in violation of Sections 28–7 and 28–9 of the General Laws of Rhode Island, 1956, as amended. An answer by the respondents to this complaint was filed. A formal hearing was held by the board on January 19, 1970, at which time a motion to intervene by the North Providence Federation of Teachers, Local 920, AFL-CIO, hereinafter referred to as the union, was granted. All parties were represented by counsel, who participated in the proceedings, and were afforded full opportunity to be heard and to introduce evidence bearing upon the issues.

At this hearing the teachers presented testimony as to the circumstances surrounding the contract negotiations for the year 1969–1970. The pertinent part of this evidence showed that the parties had negotiated as to a proposed clause in the contract concerning detention duties by high school teachers. This proposal was initialed by the bargaining representatives of both sides. The bargaining representative of the school committee was Robert Cerisi, Esq., town solicitor of North Providence. On September 17, 1969 a document designated as the work agreement of the parties and containing the clause in question was signed by both the president of the union and the chairman of the school board. No one else signed this document although all, except one member, of the school committee and many members of the union's negotiating committee were present at this meeting.

The school committee chairman contended that it was not his intention to bind the school committee when he signed the above-mentioned work agreement. He testified that he was of the opinion that the final agreement had to be executed by the whole school committee before it was official. Members of the committee also testified that they believed any proposals initialed or approved by its negotiator must be resubmitted to them for final approval before it was official.

In October, 1969, a dispute arose as to whether the clause concerning detention duties of high school teachers was included in this contract. This dispute caused the filing of the complaint alleging the unfair labor charge and the hearings held thereon.

After reviewing the testimony and arguments presented by both parties, the board is of the opinion that there was a misunderstanding as to both the legal effect of the signing of the work agreement on September 17, 1969, and the designation of Mr. Cerisi as negotiator for the school committee. The committee thought that any final agreement would have to have their ultimate approval and that Mr. Cerisi had to bring all proposals back to them. The teachers thought Mr. Cerisi could bind the committee by initialing proposals and also that the chairman of the committee could bind it by signing the work agreement. The board feels that all the evidence presented shows that the committee entered into a legally enforceable agreement at least on September 17, when its chairman signed the work agreement. Because of the misunderstanding over the legal effect of this action, however, the board is not of the opinion that the committee intentionally committed an act which would make them guilty of an unfair labor practice. The committee indicated at the formal hearing that it would implement the disputed clause if it was determined that said clause was a part of the agreement. In light of this, the board finds that the respondents are not guilty of an unfair labor practice but does order them to implement all of the terms of the agreement signed on September 17, 1969.

For the reasons above-cited and upon consideration of the entire record the board makes the following

. . .

CONCLUSIONS OF LAW

. . .

4. The North Providence School Committee and the North Providence Federation of Teachers, Local 920, AFL-CIO did enter into a binding agreement on September 17, 1969.

5. That the North Providence School Committee failed to implement all of the terms of the agreement of September 17, 1969.

6. That the failure of the North Providence School Committee to

implement all of the terms of the agreement of September 17, 1969 was due to a misunderstanding as to the legal effect of this agreement.

7. That the North Providence School Committee is not guilty of an unfair labor practice as charged in the complaint.

ORDER

Upon the basis of the foregoing Findings of Fact and Conclusions of Law, and pursuant to the power vested in the Rhode Island State Labor Relations Board by the Rhode Island State Labor Relations Act, it is hereby ordered, that the North Providence School Committee is not guilty of an unfair labor practice as charged in the complaint but that said North Providence School Committee must implement all of the terms of the agreement entered into by it and the North Providence Federation of Teachers on September 17, 1969.

Dated: March 31, 1970   Rhode Island State Labor Relations Board

---

Chairman

Member

Member

Discussion Question

1. There was an obvious misunderstanding as to the degree of authority vested in certain individuals to make binding commitments in negotiations in this case. How might this unfortunate situation have been avoided?

Section 5. Precedence of a Collective Bargaining Agreement Over Prior Individual Contract

When a collective bargaining relationship has been established, the normal rule is that neither the union nor the employer may unilaterally change the terms and conditions of employment already in existence. Such action would constitute a breach of the mutual bargaining obligation. However, there are instances where the employer may negotiate individual contracts with employees despite the presence of a collective agreement with a labor organization. In the private sector the *J. I. Case Co.* decision [*J. I. Case Co.* v. *NLRB*, 321 U.S. 332, 14 L.R.R.M. 501 (1944)], is the leading case. It describes the circumstances under which individual agreements may be negotiated, indicating that they will be permitted if:

1. The individual contract pertains only to matters outside the scope of the collective agreement.
2. It is not inconsistent with the collective agreement.
3. It does not constitute an attempt by the company to interfere with the employees' right to organize and bargain collectively through a union.
4. It does not diminish in any way the company's obligations to the employees under the collective agreement; in other words, it does not undercut the agreement in any manner.
5. It does not bind the employee to do anything he is not required to do under the collective agreement.[12]

In the Matter of

Bullock Creek School District of Midland County (respondent) *and* **Bullock Creek Education Association (charging party)**

Case No. C68 C–16

(Bullock Creek School District of Midland County)

DECISION AND ORDER

On November 1, 1968, James R. McCormick, trial examiner, issued his decision and recommended order in the above-entitled matter, finding that respondent public employer had engaged in unfair labor practices within the meaning of the Public Employment Relations Act, Act 336 of the Public Acts of 1947, hereinafter referred to as PERA, and recommending that the Michigan Employment Relations Commission order respondent to cease and desist from such practices and to take such other affirmative action as set forth in the recommended order.

The trial examiner's decision and recommended order were issued and served upon the interested parties in accordance with Section 16(d) of the act. The parties had an opportunity to review said decision and recommended order for a period of at least twenty (20) days from the date of service thereof on them, and exceptions were filed by respondent.

In addition to the charges under review here, the trial examiner had before him respondent's refusal to rehire one of its teachers and a member of the charging party, Kenneth Galloway, which refusal charging party alleged violated Section 10 of PERA. By stipulation of the parties, that issue was decided without the submission of briefs and separately from the issues here on review. The trial examiner issued his decision and recommended order on that aspect of the charges on May 19, 1968, and, no exceptions having been filed, the Michigan Employment Relations Commission, on July 19, 1968, by its order, adopted the trial examiner's decision and recommended order.

The respondent filed eight exceptions to the trial examiner's decision and recommended order of November 1, 1968. They are here considered and discussed in the numerical order of the exceptions.

1. This decision nullifies the contract provisions and terms of the current agreement negotiated and binding on the parties.

At the time this matter was heard (April 4, 1968), there was no "current agreement." The prior agreement had expired March 1, 1968, and the parties were in the process of negotiating a new agreement. We find no merit to this exception.

2. The impracticability of this decision results in that now no Michigan school district can possibly continue public school under these rules.

The record contains no evidence to support this claim.

We note respondent's preference for "a separate agency handling only the problems of public employment." Wisconsin is cited as an example. If respondent examines the Wisconsin statutes, it will discover that the Wisconsin Employment Relations Commission has jurisdiction of *both* private employers and their employees and public employers and their employees, including the state of Wisconsin and its employees. The Michigan Employment Relations Commission may not be vested with jurisdiction over the state of Michigan and its employees because of Article XI, Section 5, and Article IV, Section 48, of the Michigan Constitution.

3. Exceptions three to eight are concerned with the issue of whether issuance of individual contracts violates an employer's bargaining obligation under the Public Employment Relations Act.

The decision and recommended order of the trial examiner would prohibit the respondent from submitting to teacher members of the bargaining unit an individual contract and requiring the individual teacher to execute and return the contract to the board within a specified time—before a collective bargaining agreement has been consummated.

Respondent contends that if no agreement is reached, respondent will never, under the trial examiner's decision and recommended order, be in a position to legally enter into individual contracts with its teachers and, therefore, bind them to teach for the coming year. The respondent alleges that it will be *forced* to enter into a collective bargaining agreement with the representative of the teachers in violation of Section 15 of PERA.

Respondent overstates the events which would result from the trial examiner's decision and recommended order. It is not correct that respondent would "never" be in a position to legally enter into an individual contract with its teachers. Under the trial examiner's rationale, individual contracts would await the execution of a collective bargaining agreement or, if no agreement were reached, await an impasse between respondent and the labor organization representing the teachers. Neither the School Code of 1965, as amended, nor the Public Employment Relations Act requires such a procedure.

We find no inconsistency between the requirement for individual contracts as specified in Section 569 of the School Code (Mich. Stat. Ann. 15.3569; C.L. 48, para. 340.569) and the Public Employment Relations Act. Any possible inconsistency was eliminated by enactment of Section 569(b) [Public Acts, 1966, No. 82; Mich. Stat. Ann. 15.3569(2); C.L. 48, para. 340.569(b)], which authorizes a Board of Education, by agreement with a teacher or by agreement between the board and any organization representing the teacher, to "terminate an existing contract for the services of the teacher and substitute a new contract which provides an increased benefit to the teacher." The statute provides that the new contract "shall be binding without regard to any preexisting duties or obligations of either the school board or the teacher under the first contract."

Section 569(b), which became effective March 10, 1967, is a statutory recognition of individual contracts between a school board and a teacher. The section is consistent with the intent of the Public Employment Relations Act. In the event a collective bargaining agreement providing increased benefits for a teacher should be entered into after an individual contract has been signed, the collective bargaining agreement prevails and modifies the individual contract to the extent that the two documents vary. In the event, however, that there should be no collective bargaining agreement, as may occur under Section 15 of the Public Employment Relations Act, the individual contract remains in effect.

Individual teacher contracts have a valid status within the schools' legal framework. We disagree with the trial examiner's interpretation of the interrelationship of PERA Section 15 and School Code Section 569. The enactment of PERA did *not,* in our opinion, effect a merger of the two sections. If it should be held that a merger does take place, it would only occur upon the consummation of a collective bargaining agreement.

The Attorney General's opinion, cited by respondent, does not hold that Section 569 requires individual contracts of all teachers. Rather, the opinion states,

> This is a strong and persuasive indication that the legislature did not contemplate a collective bargaining agreement as being sufficient to establish contractual relations between the school boards and an individual teacher. . . .

Respondent, citing four decisions from other states, urges that the Michigan Attorney General's opinions are binding on school boards. Three of these decisions found Attorney General opinions binding on public officials because of a specific statute so providing. *Commonwealth ex rel.* v. *Woodruff,* 282 P.A. 306, 197 A. 828 (1925); *Eelkema* v. *Board of Education of City of Duluth,* 215 Minn. 590, 11 N.W.2d 76 (1943); *State ex rel. Johnson, Attorney General* v. *Baker,* 74 N.D. 244, 21 N.W.2d 355 (1945). The other decision held that a public official *could act* in reliance on an Attorney General's opinion. *State ex rel. Englert* v. *Meir,* 115 N.W.2d 574 (1962).

No Michigan statute binds school boards, courts, or this board to follow the Attorney General's opinions relating to the powers vested in the school board, courts, or the Labor Mediation Board. The Attorney General is a legal advisor; and his opinions are expressions of his expert judgment, but still are less than positive determinations.

A long-standing principle in private employment is that a collective bargaining contract governs only the employment relations; and, absent specific language to the contrary, is not an employment contract or guarantee of employment. This concept is well stated in *J. I. Case Co.* v. *NLRB,* 321 U.S. 332, 14 L.R.R.M. 501, 503 (1944):

> The result (of collective bargaining) is not, however, a contract of employment except in rare cases; no one has a job by reason of it and no obligation to any individual ordinarily comes into existence from it alone. The negotiations between union and management result in what often has been called a trade agreement, rather than a contract of employment. Without pushing the analogy too far, the agreement may be likened to the tariffs established by a carrier, to standard provisions prescribed by supervising authorities for insurance policies, or to utility schedules of rates and rules for service, which do not of themselves establish any relationships but which do govern the terms of the shipper or insurer or customer relationships whenever and with whomever it may be established.

However, neither private nor public employer may use individual employment contracts to frustrate the employees' right to bargain collectively. As the National Labor Relations Board held in *General Electric Co.,* 150 NLRB No. 36, 57 L.R.R.M. 1491 (1964), an employer's statutory obligation is to deal *with* its employees *through* the exclusive bargaining agent; not to deal with the agent through the employees.

The case at hand involves two issues: (1) are individual contracts in violation of the duty to bargain with a majority representative; and (2) are individual contracts in derogation of the employees' right to bargain collectively. Our answer is negative to both of these issues.

Teachers on continuing tenure are employees, as defined in Section 2 of the Public Employment Relations Act, whether or not they are parties to individual or collective contracts. *Garden City* v. *Michigan Labor Mediation Board,* 358 Mich. 258 (1959); *School District for the City of*

Holland v. *Holland Education Association,* 380 Mich. 314 (1968); *Lester* v. *Weiss,* Wayne Cir. Ct. No. 122–970 (1969). School boards may count on tenure teachers being in their classrooms at the opening of school unless they resign prior to July 1, or are excused from reporting or discharged pursuant to statute. Charging party's position—that Section 9 gives teachers the right to evaluate the collective bargaining contract before deciding whether they wish to teach—is erroneous as related to post July 1, and argumentative before that date. We decline the apparent invitation to transgress the tenure act as well as the mandate of the Supreme Court.

J. I. Case held that collective bargaining contracts were not employment contracts. Section 569, *Garden City, Holland,* and *Lester* support the same rule for teachers and their dual system of contracts.

There is an interpretive problem with respect to Section 569 which states, "The board of every district *shall hire and contract* with such duly qualified teachers as may be required." (Emphasis supplied.) PERA provides that public employers shall bargain with certified representatives of their employees, and reduce any agreements to writing (contract, ordinance or resolution).

When two statutes are in apparent conflict, they should be read together to maintain the integrity of each. *People* v. *Buckley,* 302 Mich. 12 (1942); *Rathburn* v. *State of Michigan,* 284 Mich. 521 (1938). See *Smigel* v. *Southgate Community Schools,* 70 L.R.R.M. 2042 (Cir. Ct. 1968); *Clampitt* v. *Warren Consolidated Schools,* 68 L.R.R.M. 2996 (Cir. Ct. 1968).

The blanket principles of employee status as enunciated in *Garden City, Holland,* and *Lester* are restricted to teachers on continuing tenure. The *Lester* decision apparently does away with the necessity of individual contracts where there is a duly designated collective bargaining agent. This decision must, however, be viewed in the light of the factual framework from which it evolved. The Gibraltar School Board was seeking an injunction requiring striking teachers to sign individual contracts before returning to the classroom. Judge Ryan found that the purpose of the suit was to avoid dealing with the collective bargaining representative and to side step the PERA bargaining obligation.

We are of opinion that Section 569 requires a written contract between a school board and the teachers it employs. Section 569 contemplates an employment contract for the services of a teacher.

The salary for such services and the conditions under which they are performed, however, have been subject to collective bargaining since the enactment of the Public Employment Relations Act. This is the only justification for the addition of Section 569(b) to the Teachers' Tenure Act after July, 1965. The effect of Section 569(b) is to recognize the severance of salary and working conditions determination from the Teachers Code and the transfer of such determination to PERA, wherever there is a collective bargaining agent for the teachers.

We conclude that the issuance of individual employment contracts is not a refusal to bargain or interference with employee rights. There is nothing in PERA indicating legislative intent to dissolve the concept of individual employment contracts. Employment contracts are not mandatory subjects of bargaining, since a school board may not bargain away its statutory obligations.

The issuance and return dates on individual employment contracts *are* voluntary subjects of bargaining. Neither party may insist to impasse on its position, but a provision relating to issuance and return dates of individual contracts may properly be included in a collective contract. Both parties should be interested in recruiting new and transfer teachers of ability, and thus wish to ascertain which teachers will continue to teach in the system.

School boards may determine to issue employment contracts without a specific salary figure included, but rather, include a notation that the salary will be established by a collective contract resulting from negotiations. If an impasse occurs, or no contract has been reached, the school board may institute and operate under the last offer made to the teachers' representative without commission of an unfair labor practice.

Returning to the factual situation of the case at hand, the charging party alleges that it is coercive to require teachers to sign employment contracts before they know what the terms and conditions of employment will be. This argument is a *nonsequitur*. The right to negotiate has been delegated to the bargaining agent, which should keep the employees it represents apprised of the terms and conditions being negotiated. The members have final approval of what has been negotiated. Once a bargaining agent has been selected, the right to individual bargaining is lost. *National Labor Relations Board* v. *Allis-Chalmers,* 388 U. S. 175 (1967).

It is true that many collective bargaining agreements have not been completed until fall. Once the July 1 deadline has passed, a teacher has no privilege to say, "The terms and conditions are not good enough; I quit."

We find no coercion or threats in the case at hand regarding the issuance of contracts. The evidence discloses that some teachers were upset with, or misunderstood, the amount of the salary. However, the letter accompanying the individual contracts plainly stated that if there is an error or a question, a teacher could see Mr. Coe. The letter mentioned notification of intent to leave, as well as *appreciation* of the return by the date specified. There was no veiled threat or coercive language in the letter *requiring* the return of the contracts.

The superintendent verbally stated that the contracts would be void if not returned in April. Continuing tenure teachers have until July 1 to notify of their intent to leave. The deadline was a nullity as to them.

The teachers knew of the policy regarding return of contracts. Merely because their representative disagreed with the policy and was seeking to bargain about it does not establish that the policy was interference or coercion.

Finally, the contract provided that it was "subject to amendment or revision to correspond with any contract that may be negotiated with the Bullock Creek Teachers Club." There were at least two bargaining sessions after issuance of the contracts and before the deadline for their return.

The record is devoid of any evidence of respondent's acts which were in derogation of their PERA bargaining obligation, or coercive of employee rights.

IT IS HEREBY ORDERED that the charges be dismissed.

Dated: August 20, 1969   Michigan Employment Relations Commission
                              (formerly Labor Mediation Board)

                              /s/ Robert G. Howlett, Chairman
                              /s/ Leo W. Walsh, Commission Member
                              /s/ Morris Milmet, Commission Member

Discussion Questions

1. What is the legal status of opinions of the Michigan Attorney General?
2. According to the Michigan law, did the issuance of individual employment contracts, requesting their return prior to the sixty days tenure notification date, constitute coercion?
3. Did the issuance by the school district of individual employment contracts constitute individual bargaining in violation of the collective bargaining obligation?
4. Were the issuance of, and return dates on, individual employment contracts mandatory subjects of bargaining?

Section 6. Unilateral Management Action During an Impasse Period

In the private sector, the Taft-Hartley Act establishes a mandatory sixty-day bargaining period prior to the expiration date of a contract, during which time the parties are required to make good faith efforts to reach a new agreement. If they are unable to do so, a so-called impasse has been reached and they are free to exercise economic force in the form of a strike or lockout in most situations if the breakdown in negotiations continues after the contract has expired. As the following case indicates, the situation is somewhat different in the public sector in that an impasse period can be established by joint consent. During that period an impasse panel attempts to produce a satisfactory settlement. However, if one or the other side attempts to unilaterally change a term or condition that existed in the old contract, the question then becomes one of whether this action, which occurred during the impasse period, amounts to a breach of a contract that is still in full force and effect.

In the Matter of

District No. 1—Pacific Coast District, Marine Engineers Beneficial Association, AFL-CIO *and* the City of New York and the Department of Marine and Aviation

Decision No. B–1–72

Docket No. BCB–91–71

(Board of Collective Bargaining)

DECISION AND ORDER

By petition filed with the Office of Collective Bargaining on May 10, 1971, District No. 1—Pacific Coast District, Marine Engineers Beneficial Association, AFL-CIO (hereinafter referred to as the union) seeks a finding that the city has violated Section 1173–7.0c(3)(d) by eliminating certain permanent civil service lines resulting in the dismissal of ten ferryboat officers represented by petitioner at a time when an impasse panel was holding hearings in connection with contract negotiations between the parties.

In substance, the petition makes the following allegations:

1. The union had a contract with the city which covered the period July 1, 1967 to June 30, 1970.

2. On May 1, 1970, the union filed a bargaining notice demanding the commencement of bargaining for a new contract to take effect July 1, 1970.

3. Negotiations for a new contract commenced August 26, 1970.

4. On January 11, 1971, the union filed a request with this office for the appointment of an impasse panel and the city having consented, a panel was appointed and commenced hearings in the matter on April 23, 1971.

A second hearing was held on April 30, 1971, subsequent to the filing of the petition herein.

5. On May 4, 1971, the employer advised the union that it proposed to reduce ferry service in connection with budget cutbacks and that certain civil service lines would be eliminated resulting in the layoff of some ferryboat officers represented by the union.

The answer of the city concedes all of the facts set forth above except those stated in item 5 which the city maintains are ill-pleaded and not susceptible to any response which would fairly and fully state the position of the city. However, in doing so the city's pleading consists, in effect, of a general denial of item 5 of the union's petition.

The union, by its reply, denies the foregoing allegation of the answer, affirmatively setting forth the existence of a job security clause in the collective agreement; the city's action to implement its decision to curtail ferryboat service and laying off union members in violation of the status quo provision of the NYCCBL; and the institution of court action in the New York County Supreme Court to enjoin the city from laying off union members.

The union's motion for an injunction was denied by Justice Lane in a decision dated June 14, 1971. In the Article 78 proceeding, Mr. Justice Lane determined solely that the status quo provision did not, per se, enlarge any rights with respect to the city's authority to terminate employment. The factual issue of *good faith* in terminating employment, which is our responsibility under the New York City Collective Bargaining Law, was not involved.

On June 8, 1971, the city filed with this office a motion to dismiss the petition and the reply of the union. The motion is based on technical grounds relating to the sufficiency of the pleadings to which it is addressed. Read together, however, the pleadings, the city's motion to dismiss, and the union's answering affidavit clearly present a justiciable issue; we will therefore deny the motion to dismiss and consider the substantive issues presented.

The city's motion argues: (1) that, if the reply is dismissed, leaving the record void of any detailed pleading of specific language of the contract dealing with job security and layoffs, then the petition must be dismissed because it complains of unilateral action by the city in an area where the city has an absolute right to act unilaterally under the management prerogative provisions of Section 5(c) of Executive Order 52; and (2) that if the reply is not dismissed and if the contract between the parties is thus pleaded in detail, then all provisions of the contract apply, including Article XIV thereof which reads as follows:

All disputes relating to the interpretation or application of any of the provisions of this contract which may arise between the parties hereto, shall be governed and controlled by, and in accordance with, the grievance procedures set forth in Mayoral Executive Order No. 52, dated September 29, 1967, Section 8, Grievance Procedures, Subsections a, c, d, and e, or any amendment thereto.

The city contends, therefore, that the appropriate manner of dealing with the controversy between the parties is to submit it to arbitration and that the instant proceeding should be dismissed.

In its answering affidavit the union argues with regard to item 1, above, that the matter of layoffs may initially have been within the exclusive control of the city but that the city bargained away that exclusive control when it entered into the last contract with the union which included, in Article II, a job security provision which reads as follows:

Article II—Job Security. During the term of this agreement the employer will attempt to retain all licensed officers who hold positions by permanent appointment. If curtailment, because of a reduced number of runs becomes necessary, the employer will make every effort to reemploy such officers in vacancies or to replace persons who have provisional appointments to positions for which such licensed officers are eligible, at the rates and working conditions prevailing in the department in which such licensed officers are reemployed. However, no such curtailment shall become effective without prior discussions with the association.

In response to item 2, above, however, the union maintains that the arbitration provisions of the contract do not apply because the contract terminated on June 30, 1970, and its provisions are no longer in effect. This latter argument is offered by the union with direct reference to the city's citation of *Matter of Allied Building Inspectors Local 211,* Decision No. B–6–70. In that case the expired contract between the parties provided for discussion prior to changes in work schedules. The union there maintained that the city had violated the status quo provisions of NYCCBL Section 1173–7.0c(3)(d) by making unilateral changes in work schedules during the period of negotiation for a new contract. The board held that since the contract contained not only the provisions cited by the union with regard to changes in work schedules but also an arbitration clause which provided for the arbitration of disputes relating to the terms and conditions of the contract, the matter should have been submitted to arbitration and that the petition for a finding that the city had violated the status quo provisions of Section 1173–7.0c(3)(d) was inappropriate. The decision in that case, the union here points out, included the following language which distinguishes it from the instant matter:

Both parties concede and allege that their contract is still in full force and effect. . . .

Although negotiations for a new contract have been conducted, and an impasse panel appointed, the contract between the parties concededly still is in effect and governs the present rights and obligations of the parties.

The union thus seeks to invoke the issue of job security on the basis that by its inclusion in the prior contract, job security has come within the area of wages, hours, and working conditions contemplated by Section 1173–7.0c(3)(d); and to reject the contention that controversies relating to the terms and conditions of the contract must be submitted to arbitration on the basis that the contract terminated on June 30, 1970 and is no longer in force or effect.

Clearly the matter pivots upon the interpretation of the scope and effect of the status quo provisions of Section 1173–7.0c(3)(d) which reads, in pertinent part, as follows:

(d) Preservation of status quo. During the period of negotiations between a public employer and a public employee organization concerning a collective bargaining agreement, and if an impasse panel is appointed during the period commencing on the date on which such panel is appointed and ending thirty days after it submits its report . . . the public employer shall refrain from unilateral changes in wages, hours, or working conditions. . . . For purpose of this subdivision the term "period of negotiations" shall mean the period commencing on the date on which a bargaining notice is filed and ending on the date on which a collective bargaining agreement is concluded or an impasse panel is appointed.

A labor relations statute and the policy with which it is implemented are intended to promote collective bargaining and provide appropriate means of dispute resolution. All labor relations acts have certain characteristics in common but each such act has unique qualities which relate to the particular needs which it is intended to serve. Thus the National Labor Relations Act creates certain restraints upon the actions of both labor and management which are specifically aimed at fostering and protecting negotiations during the period between the expiration of contracts and the execution of new ones. In *Carpenters District Council* v. *Rocky Mountain Prestress, Inc.,* 68 L.R.R.M. 1325, the board discussed at length the rationale and legislative history of Section 8(d) of the National Labor Relations Act which provides for the sixty-day notice to terminate or modify a labor contract.

The NLRA deals with a milieu in which it is contemplated that all forms of self-help, including the strike, may ultimately be resorted to. An employer, in the private sector, is guilty of an unfair labor practice in violation of Section 8(a)5 of the NLRA where it unilaterally changes wages or other conditions of employment which are mandatory subjects of bargaining (*NLRB* v. *American National Insurance Co.,* 343 U.S. 395, 30 L.R.R.M. 2147); but this limitation does not apply after impasse has been reached (*NLRB* v. *Katz,* 396 U.S. 736, 50 L.R.R.M. 2177).

The Railway Labor Act deals with a sensitive and vital area of the economy; the act is consequently more far-reaching than the NLRA in the matter of delaying, if not preventing, resort to self-help. In *Detroit and Toledo Shore Line R.R. Co.* v. *United Transportation Union,* 396 U.S. 142, 72 L.R.R.M. 2838, the court analyzed not only the act, itself, but its under-lying purposes.

That decision makes clear that even the RLA is not intended to pre-vent ultimate resorts to various forms of self-help, but only to delay them for the purpose of advancing the prospects of peaceful settlement. It con-templates the fact that in certain circumstances strikes may occur despite all the procedures and waiting periods which must be gone through first. In short, the Railway Labor Act goes even further than the National Labor Relations Act in the effort to prevent strikes but does not prohibit the strike as a force in labor management relations.

In the public sector, in most jurisdictions including our own, there is in operation an additional factor which does not exist in the private sector generally nor in the railroad industry. This unique factor is that public employees are not given the right to strike. The law under which we operate specifically prohibits strikes (Section 210 Subheads 1 and 2 of the Taylor Law, which, under the provisions of Section 212, is applicable to the city of New York as well as all other jurisdictions of the state, forbids any kind of work stoppage by public employees). The framers of the New York City Collective Bargaining Law recognized that a law intended to maintain a bargaining relationship in a system in which the respective pressures and strengths of the parties were so extensively realigned, as would be the case where labor was denied the power of the strike, would have to seek to redress the resultant imbalance. They acknowledged this fact in the *State-ment of Public Members of Tripartite Panel to Improve Municipal Bar-gaining Procedures,* dated March 31, 1966 and approved and signed by representatives of the city and of the city employee organizations. This document which outlines the New York City Collective Bargaining Law, including the status quo provision, states, at p. 3:

> Because the rights normally enjoyed by employees in private employment are not available by law to employees in public employment, there is the greater need to ensure that collective bargaining takes place, and that provision be made for effective procedures for the peaceful resolution of differences when bargaining results in an impasse. The procedures set forth herein are designed to meet this greater need. These procedures offer posi-tive assurance: (a) that employees will be treated fairly; (b) that the city

will be able faithfully to discharge its obligations as employer, without interruption to the public services it furnishes; and (c) that the people of the city will be protected, as they have a legal and moral right to be, in their access to essential public services.

We are of the opinion that the meaning and purpose of the status quo provision of the NYCCBL is to maintain the respective positions of the parties and the relationship between them essentially unchanged during periods of negotiation, during impasse panel proceedings and for thirty days after issuance of panel reports. This end is obtained, in part, by prohibiting the change of any condition created by a prior contract during the period prescribed by the status quo provision. This interpretation of the status quo provision is consistent with the policy enunciated in the report of the tri-partite committee of March 31, 1966. The "rights normally enjoyed by em-ployees in private employment [but] not available by law to employees in public employment" are, in our view, intended to be replaced by the as-surance that upon termination of a prior contract the terms and conditions of their employment cannot be reduced or otherwise changed except by negotiation during the statutory period. The denial of the power to strike is balanced by the maintenance of the status quo.

A similar concept is read into the Railway Labor Act by the Supreme Court in *Shore Line R.R.* v. *Transportation Union, supra,* where it says

> when one party wants to change the status quo without undue delay, the power which the act gives the other party to preserve the status quo for a prolonged period will frequently make it worthwhile for the moving party to compromise with the interests of the other side and thus reach agreement. . . .

Even in the private sector and in areas not covered by the Railway Labor Act there are circumstances in which the right to strike, though not entirely eliminated, may be suspended; when this happens the very type of readjustment of the balance of power between the parties which we are making here is found in the applicable law. Thus, where a strike in the private sector imperils the national health or safety it may be enjoined, un-der Section 208 of the Labor Management Relations Act, for a period of eighty days. Where this emergency measure is employed, however, man-agement's powers are also curtailed in order to maintain balance in the relationship between the parties. In *U.S.* v. *Longshoremen (ILA)*, 50 L.C. 19, 278, the U. S. District Court, Southern District of New York, held that its injunction against a strike by the union therein should include a provi-sion continuing in full force and effect the provisions of the expired collec-tive bargaining agreement between the parties. Reasoning that such a provi-sion served to maintain the status quo and to preserve the relationship between the parties, the court said, in pertinent part:

Equity requires that if union members are to be restrained from striking during the eighty-day cooling-off period, employers be prevented also from reducing work gangs or taking any of the steps they had sought to persuade the unions to accept in prestrike negotiations. The prior collective bargaining agreement provides ready reference to the respective rights and duties of the parties.

We hold, therefore, that in this case, the status quo includes the terms and conditions established by the prior contract between the parties and that all such terms and conditions are continued, by operation of the statute, in full force and effect during the period of negotiations, during impasse panel proceedings and for thirty days after issuance of impasse panel reports. In our view, the collective bargaining agreement including the grievance and arbitration procedure, is the best guide as to the "wages, hours or working conditions" which are not to be unilaterally changed during the status quo period. The rights and duties of the parties during the status quo period are statutory in nature.

In the instant matter the parties have raised the issue as to whether or not the underlying controversy should be dealt with in accordance with the grievance and arbitration provisions of the prior contract between them or treated as an alleged failure of full faith compliance with the statute. In this and in all cases such as this arising under the status quo provisions of the New York City Collective Bargaining Law this board has and will exercise primary jurisdiction in determining, on a case-by-case basis, the means to be employed in dealing with the specific controversies presented. Since each such case arises out of an alleged violation of the law which it is the duty of this board to administer, the board has exclusive power and discretion to determine whether a given matter should be dealt with as such or whether it is appropriate in a given case to direct that the matter be referred to an arbitrator following the arbitration provisions and procedures of the prior contract between the parties, if such provisions were included and, if not, in accordance with the arbitration provision of Executive Order No. 52. We find that in a case such as this, where the underlying controversy derives solely from the statutory extension of the provisions of a prior contract, the arbitration provisions—either contractual or statutory—which applied during the term of the contract provide the most appropriate means of dealing with such a controversy arising during the period covered by the status quo provisions of the New York City Collective Bargaining Law.

ORDER

Pursuant to the powers vested in the Board of Collective Bargaining by the New York City Collective Bargaining Law, IT IS HEREBY ORDERED that the city's motion to dismiss herein be, and the same hereby is, denied; ordered, that in accordance with the decision herein, the union's petition herein be, and the same hereby is, denied without prejudice to the union's right to request arbitration of the controversy presented herein in accordance with this decision.

Dated: January 7, 1972 /s/ Arvid Anderson   /s/ Timothy W. Costello
       New York, N.Y.   Chairman   Member

                      /s/ Walter L. Eisenberg /s/ William Michelson
                          Member   Member

                      /s/ Eric J. Schmertz   /s/ Harry Van Arsdale
                          Member   Member

Discussion Questions

1. Did the reduction in force during the impasse period constitute a breach of the statutory status quo provisions?
2. Why did the board rule that arbitration was the proper form of settlement for the controversy?

Section 7. Mandatory Bargaining Subjects

The Taft-Hartley Act, in Section 8(d) indicates that employers and employee representatives are obligated to bargain in good faith with respect to "wages, hours, and other conditions of employment."

Specifically, bargaining is required on the following topics: "Piece rates or other incentive pay rates; individual merit increases; health and accident insurance plans; pension plans; profit-sharing retirement plans; stock-purchase plans; vacations, holidays; discounts on company products; safety rules; rest and lunch periods; union security arrangements." This is, it should be noted, by no means an exhaustive list. These are mandatory topics and the parties are required to bargain to impasse, if necessary, in an effort to resolve differences.[13] However, because no two cases are exactly alike, the NLRB has encountered difficulties in defining what "other terms and conditions of employment" means in specific instances. Therefore, it can be predicted that similar problems of interpretation will arise in public employment with regard to a delineation of mandatory topics. Kilberg has pointed out an important difference between public and private bargaining over required topics:

> In the private sector, when a subject is declared "mandatory," negotiation over that subject may be pushed to impasse; and the use of economic weapons—strike or lockout—are permissible. . . . In the public sphere, where there is no right to strike or lockout, pushing a subject to impasse would, presumably, merely result in the implementation of impasse pro-

cedures such as mediation, fact finding, or some form of arbitration, none of which constitutes the ultimate economic conflict presented by a strike or a lockout.[14]

Yet, a similarity between the two realms that has become apparent is that failure of either side to bargain when a mandatory topic is involved would undoubtedly invite an unfair labor practice charge—refusal to bargain in good faith.

In the Matter of

Sanilac County Road Commission (respondent) *and* **Teamsters Local No. 339, An Affiliate of the International Brotherhood of Teamsters, Chauffeurs, Warehousemen, and Helpers of America (charging party)**

Case No. C69 B–17

DECISION AND ORDER

On July 22, 1969, Trial Examiner Joseph B. Bixler issued his decision and recommended order in the above-entitled matter, finding that the respondent, Sanilac County Road Commission, has not engaged in, and was not engaging in, certain unfair labor practices and recommended that the charges in the above-entitled matter be dismissed as being without merit.

The trial examiner's decision and recommended order were issued and served upon the interested parties in accordance with Section 16(b) of Act 336 of the Public Acts of 1947, as amended. The parties have had an opportunity to review said decision and recommended order for a period of at least twenty days from date of service thereof on the parties, and no exceptions have been filed by any of the parties to the proceedings.

ORDER

Pursuant to Section 16(b) of the act, the recommended order by the trial examiner shall become the order of the commission and the charges and complaint are hereby dismissed.

Michigan Employment Relations Commission
(formerly Labor Mediation Board)

/s/ Robert G. Howlett, Chairman
/s/ Leo W. Walsh, Commission Member
/s/ Morris Milmet, Commission Member

TRIAL EXAMINER'S DECISION AND
RECOMMENDED ORDER

Appearances: for the employer, Riley & Roumell by George T. Toumell, Jr., Attorney; for the charging party, Walter Sacharczyk, president.

The above-captioned matter came on for hearing before the undersigned trial examiner of the Labor Mediation Board on February 25, 1969, at Sandusky, Michigan. On the basis of testimony of the witnesses, exhibits, closing arguments of counsel, and posthearing briefs filed by council on July 8, 1969, the undersigned makes the following findings of fact, conclusions of law, and recommended order:

FINDINGS OF FACT AND CONCLUSIONS OF LAW

Sanilac County Road Commission, hereinafter referred to as the employer, is a public employer within the meaning of Act 336 of the Public Acts of 1947, as amended (Public Employment Relations Act, hereinafter referred to as PERA).

Teamsters Local No. 339, as affiliate of the International Brotherhood of Teamsters, Chauffeurs, Warehousemen and Helpers of America, hereinafter referred to as the Teamsters, is an employee organization representing public employees within the meaning of PERA.

The unfair labor practice charges in this case, which were filed on February 7, 1969, allege that the employer had refused to bargain collectively with the representatives of its public employees. Specifically, the charge alleges that the employer has refused to negotiate and refuses to put into effect a pension plan for its employees after they previously agreed in the contract to do so.

At the hearing, the charging party, the Teamsters, contended that the employer has refused to negotiate on a pension plan, and that they refused to put a pension plan into effect, because they claim it is illegal.

BACKGROUND

The Teamsters have been the unquestioned exclusive bargaining agent of the employees of the employer for several years of a unit described as: "All hourly rated employees of the Sanilac County Road Commission." A collective bargaining agreement had been entered into on May 1, 1966, between the parties which expired on December 31, 1968. This expired contract provided in regard to pension in Article 14 as follows:

> The present Sanilac County Road Commission Pension Plan shall be in effect until the opinion of the Attorney General is handed down as to the

legality of the commission to negotiate and put into effect the Teamsters Pension Plan.

The negotiations for the 1969 to 1972 contract began in October of 1968. On October 21, 1968, Walter Sacharczyk, president of the Teamsters Local, wrote a letter to Mr. Fred Elwood, the managing engineer of the employer, setting forth certain proposals to be included in the new contract relative to pension; these proposals indicated certain contributions that the Teamsters wished the employer to make for 1969, 1970, and 1971.

Subsequent to the submission of these proposals by the Teamsters, there were various collective bargaining meetings between the employer and the Teamsters. Just how many meetings there were, the record does not reflect. However, the next meeting of any significance, was on December 24, 1968.

Just what occurred at the December 24, 1968 meeting is not revealed by the record. However, subsequent to that meeting, Sacharczyk wrote up a draft of a tentative agreement reached between the parties, and submitted this to the employer and the employer's negotiatior, Elwood, on December 31, 1968. This tentative agreement at Article 14, entitled "Pensions," provides as follows:

> The present Sanilac County Road Commission pension plan shall be in effect until the opinion of the Attorney General is handed down as to the legality of the commission to negotiate and put into effect the Teamsters pension plan.

At the meeting on December 31, 1968, the road commission contended that certain aspects of the agreement as submitted by Sacharczyk, were not according to the agreements reached on December 24, 1968.

The next meeting was held on January 9, 1969, in the presence of a mediator of the state Labor Board. At this meeting, the matter of pension again came up. According to Sacharczyk, at the January 9, 1969 meeting, it was agreed to ask the state mediator to request the Labor Mediation Board to ask the Attorney General about the legality of the pension plan proposed by the Teamsters.

On January 14, 1969, Sacharczyk wrote up a memorandum of the agreement and understanding resulting from the meeting of January 9, 1969. Relative to pension, this memorandum provides at Article 14 as follows:

> Memorandum of understanding by and between the Sanilac County Road Commission and Teamsters, Local No. 339, the state Labor Board Mediator, Mr. Dan Gallagher, and Mr. George Roumell, attorney for the commission, as follows: The state Labor Mediation Board is to secure an opinion from the Attorney General on the amended section of Public Act

No. 211 regarding pension participation of the Sanilac County Road Commission for its employees who have entered into a collective bargaining agreement through the Teamsters Local No. 339, prior to January 1, 1969, and for whom the Sanilac County Road Commission agreed to put into effect in May, 1966, pending the opinion of the Attorney General.

The employer, after the January 9, 1969 meeting, prepared a draft of the agreements as reached between the parties on January 9. This draft states at Article 14 in regard to pension as follows:

The present Sanilac County Road Commission pension plan shall be in effect until the opinion of the Attorney General is handed down as to the legality of the commission to negotiate and put into effect the Teamsters pension plan.

Sacharczyk admits that this was agreed upon, and that this language would be the new contractual language. The Teamsters, however, despite the fact that the draft, submitted after the January 9 meeting, reflects the agreement reached between the parties refused to sign the contract.

On January 22, 1969, Sacharczyk sent a telegram to the employer stating as follows:

Gentlemen: Pursuant to most recent Attorney General's opinion this is to advise that Teamsters Local Union No. 339 requests meeting immediately to negotiate Teamsters pension plan for the employees of Sanilac County Road Commission. Anticipating your cooperation and your immediate reply, I remain truly yours.

On February 5, 1969, in reply to the foregoing telegram, Elwood wrote to Sacharczyk as follows:

Dear Mr. Sacharczyk:
We cannot negotiate the Teamsters pension plan for the following reasons:

1. Act 211 of 1968 restricts county road commissions to the plan the County Board of Supervisors has provided for all county employees, except where the road commission had its own plan prior to the supervisors plan. However, the road commission can only improve the present plan (Mutual of New York) or switch to the supervisors plan. We cannot adopt a third entirely different plan such as the Teamsters pension plan.
2. Section 12(a) of Act 156 of the Public Acts of 1851, as amended, specifically states that the employee must have attained the age of 60 years. An employee 57 years of age could not legally retire and draw a pension under the present law.
3. Section 12(a) further limits the amount of pension to a maximum of $100 per month. Therefore, an employee could not receive $300 per month as the Teamster's plan provides until the age of 62.

4. Section 12(a) further restricts the pension benefits to 2 percent of the average monthly earnings of the employee times the years of service of the employee. This sum cannot exceed the $100 per month limitation.

5. Act 211, Section 5(b) again refers to the age limit of 60 and the $100 per month maximum benefit allowed. Section(b) reads "provide benefits within the dollar limitation of this section," and (c) reads "provide benefits in accordance with the conditions of eligibility of this section."

6. Our agreement reached with Mr. Gallagher, the state labor mediator, provided that Walter Sacharczyk would send a letter to Mr. Gallagher requesting an Attorney General's opinion on Act 211 of 1968. Mr. Gallagher stated he would then request the state Labor Mediation Board to ask the Attorney General's office for an opinion. As of this date no Attorney General's opinion has been given on Act 211 of 1968.

In addition to all of the above, Mr. Earl Rogers of the County Road Association has advised this office that it would be illegal for the Sanilac County Road Commission to negotiate and adopt the Teamsters pension plan.

I have talked with Mr. Lawrence Ferrell, director of the Michigan State Employee Retirement System and his assistant Mrs. Florence Blumley regarding Section 12(a) of the supervisor's act, Act 211 of 1968, and the Teamsters pension plan. They advise that they would have to rule on the Teamsters pension plan before we could put it into effect. Also, they pointed out several areas that the plan differs from Section 12(a) and Act 211 and therefore the plan would not qualify. Their telephone number is 517–373–0001.

In addition to all of the above, I have talked with Mr. Solomon Bienfeld of the Attorney General's opinion board and he advises me that no Attorney General's opinion has been given on Act 211 of 1968. Therefore, your telegram is not correct as you refer to a most recent Attorney General's opinion. His telephone number is 517–373–1178.

We have done everything possible to check into the legality of the Teamsters pension plan if it were accepted by the board. Everywhere we turn the answer is the same that it cannot be done legally. Until we could do so legally we really cannot even negotiate the matter. We have confronted you with this information previously and you have ignored it. It is time that you brought forth evidence that will show our information to be incorrect. Until you do so there is no reason to expect us to negotiate the Teamsters pension plan.

Very truly yours,

/s/ Fred Elwood

Fred Elwood, P. E.
Engineer-Manager
Sanilac County Road Commission

The Employer's Position

1. That because the Teamster pension plan does not comply with statutes of the state of Michigan, it need not negotiate on that plan.
2. That the employer is not required by PERA to agree to any particular proposal.
3. That the parties to this matter did negotiate on the Teamster pension plan and incorporated this agreement in a contract (not at present signed).

The first of the three contentions of the employer is based upon Public Act 156 of 1851 as amended [MSA 5.333(1)].

These acts provide that county road commissions and county boards of supervisors can institute pension, hospitalization, and life insurance plans for their employees.

Relative to the pension plans, the two acts contain certain restrictions such as retirement age, length of service required, and maximum benefits. The record does not reflect the terms and conditions of the Teamsters pension plan. It does, however, establish that what the Teamsters were requesting was negotiation on the inclusion of the Teamsters pension plan into the contract.

This aspect of the contention of the employer therefore raises a question of whether a belief that a particular contract proposal is illegal would excuse a refusal to discuss the matter, or secondly whether such a belief of illegality would justify a refusal to agree to the item of questioned legality.

The undersigned is of the opinion that the answer to the first aspect of the question stated above is no. The board has determined that, despite an opinion of the Attorney General of the state, compulsory arbitration was not justified by any statutory authority for school boards; it was a mandatory subject for collective bargaining, and a county board of supervisors and the county sheriff could lawfully enter into an agreement providing for compulsory and binding arbitration. *Oakland County Sheriff,* 1968 Labor Opinions 1. The board's determination in the *Oakland* case entailed a finding by the board that binding arbitration was legal. It would appear, therefore, that a public employer when refusing to bargain on a *subject matter* because of an honest belief that it is illegal acts at risk of an unfair labor practice should the board find the subject matter to be one that is legal and a mandatory subject of collective bargaining. The sincerity of the belief of illegality does not excuse the breach of the duty to bargain.

A refusal to agree to a particular proposal, however, based upon a belief of illegality of the subject matter would not be a refusal to bargain.

PERA provides at Section 15 that the collective bargaining duty does "not compel either party to agree to a proposal or require the making of a concession." It would appear that the motive for rejection of a proposal is not important unless it can be shown that the rejection was for the purpose of frustrating bargaining and to prevent the culmination of bargaining in a collective bargaining agreement or to undermine the employee representative. Such determinations in this area that have been made by the National Labor Relations Board on the basis of the whole course of conduct of the bargaining, rather than the rejection of one proposal.

In the case at hand, the real issue is not one of whether a pension plan or retirement benefits is a proper subject for bargaining; the parties concede, properly, that pensions must be bargained upon. The question is whether the statutes [P.A. 156 of 1851, as amended, MSA 9.110(1) and P.A. 185 of 195, MSA 9.111(5)] are in conflict.

The board in the *Oakland County Sheriff* case, 1968 Labor Opinions 1, found that PERA prevailed, to the extent it was in conflict with the so-called sheriff's act (MSA 5.861 *et seq.*) on the ground that PERA was specific legislation.

In this case, P.A. 185 of 1965, MSA 9.111(5) specifically refers to PERA and provides that pension plans negotiated by a county board of road commissioners prior to January 1, 1968, covering a bargaining unit determined pursuant to PERA, could be continued in spite of the fact that the pension plan did not conform to P.A. 185 of 1965. I would conclude that Public Act 185 of 1965 is the more specific statute, passed after PERA, and intended by the legislature to limit the terms of pension plans county road commissions may agree to pursuant to collective bargaining.

CONCLUSION AND RECOMMENDATION

Under the circumstances presented by this record, the undersigned concludes that the Sanilac County has fulfilled its duty to bargain as imposed by Section 10 of PERA. The parties did discuss the pension plan proposed by the Teamsters union during the negotiations for the earlier collective bargaining agreement and the one presently pending. In both the differences over the legality of the Teamsters pension plan was resolved in contract terms by the agreement to hold the matter in abeyance until the Attorney General passed upon its legality. While I do not believe, as indicated above, that the opinion of the Attorney General would be an excuse for a refusal to bargain if this board disagreed with the opinion, the matter was resolved in collective bargaining and it is recommended that the charges be found to be without merit.

RECOMMENDATION

It is recommended the charges be dismissed.

Dated: July 22, 1969   Michigan Labor Mediation Board
                                         /s/ Joseph B. Bixler
                                         Trial Examiner

Discussion Questions

1. Are pension plans a mandatory bargaining topic?
2. What risk does a public employer face who refuses to discuss a mandatory subject of bargaining?
3. In this case was the obligation to bargain fulfilled by the public employer?

Section 8. Prohibited or Permissive Bargaining Subjects

Certain subjects, such as the closed shop or compulsory dues checkoff, are not considered to be proper bargaining demands because they are prohibited by existing federal law. Consequently, a refusal to negotiate would not constitute an unfair labor practice. Moreover, if such demands are presented, the initiating party would be liable to an unfair labor practice charge for refusing to bargain in good faith because the demands are illegal. On the other hand, voluntary or permissive topics are defined as those that are not included within the categories of "wages, hours, and other conditions of employment," which are mandatory subjects. Examples are union demands that the company bargain over health benefits for retired workers; that there be negotiations over strike insurance that the employer has purchased; or that the union should be able to influence the firm's price policy.

They may be presented for discussion but a party may not insist that they be bargained to impasse; such a demand could bring on an unfair labor practice complaint alleging bad faith bargaining. In fact, "the other party may not be required either to bargain on them or to agree to their inclusion in the contract." [15] Another important consideration in the public sector is the fact that the public employer may face constraints on the permissible scope of negotiations if wages, pensions, and benefits are established by state or local laws and work rules are determined by civil service regulations.

In the Matter of

Communications Workers of America, AFL-CIO (petitioner) *and* the City of New York (respondent)

Decision No. B–7–72

Docket No. BCB–89–71

(Office of Collective Bargaining, Board of Collective Bargaining)

DECISION, ORDER, AND DETERMINATIONS

On April 14, 1971, Communications Workers of America filed a petition pursuant to Rule 7.3 of the Consolidated Rules of the Office of Collective Bargaining alleging that during its contract negotiations with the city for a unit of administrative, titled personnel a disagreement had arisen over the negotiability of two demands advanced by the union: a training fund, and a prohibition against the lateral transfer of nonadministrative-titled employees into the bargaining unit. The city declined to bargain on these subjects, contending that they were not mandatory subjects of collective bargaining. The union, therefore, requests that the Board of Collective Bargaining make a final determination as to whether these matters are mandatorily within the scope of bargaining, and whether they must be submitted to an impasse panel as have other mandatory items in dispute. An impasse panel was designated on March 5, 1971 and made its report on July 6, 1971 on all issues save those of the training fund and lateral transfers, which had been held in abeyance pending the board's determination of the negotiability of these subjects.

The union's prior contract, which ran from January 1, 1969 to December 31, 1970, contained clauses covering both a training fund (Article 12) and a prohibition of lateral transfers (Section 6 of Appendix B, Supplemental Agreement covering certain employees in the Department of Social Services, dated April 25, 1969).

The city's answer to the union's petition denies that the union's demands are mandatory subjects of bargaining, and asserts that there is no obligation on its part to bargain on either of these demands because the matter of a training fund is a permissive or voluntary subject of bargaining, and the matter of a lateral transfer is a prohibited—or at least a permissive—subject of bargaining.

In a letter dated June 24, 1971, the union added the further contention that the city, by refusing to negotiate on the two subjects which had been part of the prior, expired contract, had violated Section 1173–7.0c (3)(d) of the New York City Collective Bargaining Law (preservation of status quo). It also requested that it be permitted to present oral argument to the board. The cited section of the status quo provision of the NYCCBL provides as follows:

> During the period of negotiations between a public employer and a public employee organization concerning a collective bargaining agreement, and, if an impasse panel is appointed during the period commencing on the date on which such panel is appointed and ending thirty days after it submits its report, the public employee organization party to the negotiations, and the public employees it represents, shall not induce or engage in any strikes, slowdowns, work stoppages, or mass absenteeism, nor shall such public employee organization induce any mass resignations, and the public employer shall refrain from unilateral changes in wages, hours, or working conditions. This subdivision shall not be construed to limit the rights of public employers other than their right to make such unilateral changes, or the rights and duties of public employees and employee organizations under state law. For the purpose of this subdivision the term "period of negotiations" shall mean the period commencing on the date on which a bargaining notice is filed and ending on the date on which a collective bargaining agreement is concluded or an impasse panel is appointed.

The parties submitted briefs and further clarified their positions at a conference on August 25, 1971. The union initially contended that the city contravened the status quo provision by refusing to negotiate on the two subjects contained in the expired contract but later contended that the city's cessation of training fund programs during the negotiation period and the suspension of the prohibition against lateral transfers during that period had violated Section 1173–7.0c(3)(d) of the NYCCBL.

The union's contentions and the city's responses raise three principal issues:

1. Is a training fund demand by the union to provide additional training and education beyond those provided by the Department of Personnel, and to provide preparation for advancement and upgrading, within the scope of bargaining?
2. Is a demand by the union for a prohibition against lateral transfers into unit titles within the scope of bargaining?
3. Did the city violate the "preservation of status quo" provision by unilaterally changing wages and working conditions during the status quo period?

THE TRAINING FUND DEMAND

The training fund provision in the expired contract sought by the union to be continued and included in the new agreement reads as follows:

For the term of this contract, the city agrees to allocate a fund equal to $20 for each employee covered by this contract.

The fund shall be used to provide additional training and educational opportunities beyond those presently provided by the Department of Personnel, designed to increase the effectiveness and efficiency of employees covered by this contract, and to prepare them for advancement and upgrading.

The city Department of Personnel will develop, conduct, administer, coordinate, and evaluate all training programs initiated pursuant to this contract. The Department of Personnel shall consult on a regular and continuing basis with the union on its plans for all such programs, and the union will participate in the selection and recruitment of employees receiving such training.

The board, in Decision No. B–4–71 (*Matter of the Association of Building Inspectors and Housing and Development Administration*), determined that a demand for a training fund to provide tuition and released time "manifestly falls within the areas reserved to management" and, "therefore, involves a voluntary or permissible, not a mandatory, subject of collective bargaining." The board further declared,

> As such, it may not be submitted to the impasse panel without the consent of the city or proof of a "practical impact" on the employees, not here claimed or established. . . . The voluntary nature of the subject is not altered by the fact that training funds are provided in collective bargaining agreements with other unions and that general provisions concerning such funds are contained in the citywide contract covering matters which must be uniform for all career and salary employees. As stated in Decision B–11–68 (*Matter of Social Service Employees Union*), "The fact that such agreement (on a voluntary subject) has been reached and included in a contract cannot transform a voluntary subject into a mandatory subject . . . for the latter is fixed and determined by law."

In the instant case the union seeks to distinguish its demand for a training fund from that involved in Decision No. B–4–71. It asserts, *inter alia,* that its proposal calls for training on employee time only; that, unlike the building inspectors, CWA did have a training fund in its preceding contract; that the city, during the bargaining for a training fund in the earlier contract negotiations, had not indicated that it was bargaining on the issue voluntarily, and hence should now be estopped from so maintaining; and that the rescission of the training fund program would disadvantage its members who must compete in promotional examinations against members of other unions who receive free preparatory courses under existing contractual training funds.

We adhere to our holding in Decision No. B–4–71 that training funds, per se, are a permissive matter of bargaining, and find no weight in the circumstances advanced by the union for modifying that holding in the instant case. A training fund demand impinges upon the management right of the city to "determine standards of service to be offered by its agencies; . . . maintain the efficiency of governmental operations; . . . determine the methods, means, and personnel by which government operations are to be conducted; . . . and to exercise complete control and discretion over the technology of performing its work." Section 5(c), Executive Order 52. The city has the management right to determine the quantity and quality of the services to be delivered to the public, and, therefore, also the quantity and quality of the training required to achieve that service. Whether the training is on employee time or released time, and whether or not the city explicitly states during negotiations that it considers a subject a voluntary one, cannot alter the nature of the subject matter if, as a matter of law, it is an exercise of a management prerogative. Moreover, if a subject is a permissive or voluntary subject of bargaining, the city may properly elect to bargain on it with one union and not with another. The exercise of such discretion in the absence of discriminatory motivation designed to interfere with the rights of employees under the NYCCBL or to discredit the union does not, in our view, make the city's conduct inherently discriminatory so as to constitute a per se violation of the NYCCBL.

THE DEMAND FOR A BAN AGAINST LATERAL TRANSFERS

The lateral transfer clause in the expired contract which the union sought to include in the new agreement reads as follows:

> The city agrees that employees in nonadministrative titles shall not be laterally transferred to titles covered by this agreement.

The reason for this demand in 1969 was the union's fear that the reorganization of the Department of Social Services would result in wholesale layoffs of case workers and supervisors (represented by another union) who could then be laterally transferred, pursuant to Rule 6.1.9 of the Civil Service Commission's rules and regulations, to administrative-titled positions represented by CWA, thus creating "a severe threat to the security and career advancement of the administrative-titled employees."

Rule 6.1.9, which was adopted by the Civil Service Commission in 1969, and which is described as "a landmark change in the administration of the civil service," provides for an exception to the rule (Rule 6.1.1) which forbids transfers to a different title without a competitive examination. It permits a permanent employee in a competitive position to request a transfer to another title if he personally meets all the requirements for a competitive examination in the other title. Then, if no preferred or promotion lists for the other title exist, and the basic salary range is not appreciably higher than his present title, and if the releasing and receiving city agencies join in the employee's request for the transfer, and if the Civil Service Commission ascertains that other employees will not be adversely affected to a degree outweighing the benefits gained, the employee requesting the lateral transfer will be given a noncompetitive examination for the other title. The clause in CWA's expired contract, and its present demand, would prohibit such lateral transfers of non-administrative employees into administrative titles represented by CWA.

The union maintains that the subject of prohibiting lateral transfers into the bargaining unit is a mandatory one because it was included in the expired contract and because the city did not indicate in the prior bargaining that it regarded the subject to be a permissive one. It alleges that a similar clause is included in a contract with another union.

The city takes the position that the subject of banning lateral transfers is a prohibited subject, or, at the very least, a voluntary or permissive subject of collective bargaining. It maintains that the clause prohibiting lateral transfers was included in the earlier contract because the city then believed it to be a voluntary subject, but that this erroneous belief cannot transform a prohibited subject into a voluntary or a mandatory one. The city further contends that the subject is in fact a prohibited or unlawful matter because any agreement by the city not to make lateral transfers into the unit would violate the civil service rule authorizing such transfers; would restrict the rights of individual employees (not necessarily in the bargaining unit) to obtain lateral transfers; and would restrict the powers delegated to city agency heads to request lateral transfers.

We find the subject of a ban on lateral transfers not a mandatory subject as the union maintains, nor a prohibited subject as the city urges, but a voluntary or permissive subject of collective bargaining.

To bargain on this subject would not involve the breach of "an obligation or duty fixed by law" and therefore is not a prohibited subject. (*City of New York and Social Service Employees Union,* Decision B–11–68.) The ban on lateral transfers sought by the union does not abridge the authority of the Civil Service Commission (which does not initiate lateral transfers) by compelling either approval or disapproval of such a transfer; it merely obligates the city not to request such a transfer of the commission, which, in the absence of such request, has nothing to act upon. The city's agreement not to seek lateral transfers into unit titles is no more than a waiver by the city of its managerial discretion to request such transfers. Nor does Rule 6.1.9 confer on an employee an enforceable right to demand a lateral transfer; it merely gives a competitive class employee an "eligibility" for such transfer, which becomes realized only when the city, in its discretion, requests the transfer, and only after the Civil Service Commission, having approved the request, gives the employee a noncompetitive examination.

But if the subject of prohibition of lateral transfers is not a prohibited subject, neither is it a mandatory subject, for it clearly encroaches on the city's managerial right to "determine standards of selection for employment, maintain the efficiency of government operation, determine the methods, means, and personnel by which government operations are to be conducted, and exercise complete control and discretion over the organization and the technology of performing its work." Accordingly, we determine that the subject of a prohibition of lateral transfers is a voluntary subject of bargaining which may be negotiated only on mutual consent, and, likewise, may be submitted to an impasse panel only on mutual consent.

THE VIOLATION OF THE STATUS QUO PROVISION

In a recent decision (*District Council No. 1—Pacific Coast District Marine Engineers' Beneficial Association, AFL-CIO*, Decision No. B–1–72), the board, interpreting the meaning and purpose of the status quo provision of the NYCCBL, concluded that during the period prescribed by the section the parties to an expired contract are prohibited from unilaterally changing any condition created by the prior contract. Our holding underscored the realistic view that, in the field of public employment relations, "the denial of the power to strike is balanced by the maintenance of the status quo." The board, however, realizing that different factual circumstances necessarily require different results, reserved the right "to determine in future cases, based upon the clear intent of the parties and the special nature of the circumstances involved, that a particular term or condition of employment expired with the term of the contract."

In the instant case we find that the training fund provision and the ban-on-lateral-transfers provision of the expired contract, although voluntary subjects of bargaining, nevertheless continued, by operation of the statute, in full force and effect during the status quo period.

The question then remains whether the city, by its actions during the status quo period, unilaterally altered the surviving conditions and thus violated Section 1173.7.0c(3)(d) of the NYCCBL.

The union does not charge that the city took any steps to make lateral transfers into administrative positions during the status quo period. Indeed, it concedes that the city did not in fact seek to make any such lateral transfers despite its refusal to negotiate a ban on lateral transfers in the new contract. Accordingly, we shall dismiss the union's charge in this respect.

As to the training fund provision which survived the expiration of the contract, we find that the material set forth in the pleadings is insufficient to permit a finding that the city violated the status quo provision of the NYCCBL. An analysis of the expired contractual provision warrants no definite conclusion at what intervals and in what amounts funds were to be allocated by the city to the training fund. Nor has the union satisfactorily shown what training programs, if any, the city declined to set up or implement during the status quo period. Accordingly, though we find that the training fund provision was in force and effect during the status quo period by operation of statute, the board, nevertheless, denies the union's petition, with leave to the union, however, if it claims that the training fund condition was in fact violated, to file an application to the board, with notice thereof to the city, for the appointment of a trial examiner to hear, report, and make recommendations to the board with respect to these matters, including an appropriate remedy.

DETERMINATIONS AND ORDER

Pursuant to the powers vested in the Board of Collective Bargaining by the New York City Collective Bargaining Law, IT IS HEREBY DETERMINED that the union's demand for a training fund is a voluntary subject of collective bargaining; and IT IS FURTHER DETERMINED that the union's proposal for a prohibition against lateral transfers is neither a prohibited subject nor a mandatory subject, but rather a voluntary subject of bargaining; and IT IS FURTHER ORDERED that the union's petition charging that the city violated Section 1173–7.0c(3)(d) of the NYCCBL by discontinuing the ban on lateral transfers during the status quo period be, and the same hereby is, denied; and IT IS FURTHER ORDERED that the union's petition charging that the city violated Section 1173–7.0c(3)(d) of the NYCCBL by suspending the training program during the status quo period be, and the same hereby is, denied, without prejudice, however, to the union filing a petition, if so desired, with this board, with notice thereof to the city, for the designation of a trial examiner to hear and report to this board all of the relevant facts and circumstances regarding the alleged breach of the city's obligation with respect to the training fund program during the status quo period and to recommend to the board an appropriate remedy, and IT IS FURTHER ORDERED that the union's request for oral argument before the board be, and the same hereby is, denied.

Dated: March 15, 1972 /s/ Arvid Anderson   /s/ Eric J. Schmertz
       New York, N.Y.   Chairman   Member

                /s/ Walter L. Eisenberg /s/ Edward Silver
                Member   Member

Discussion Questions

1. Which two union demands created an issue of negotiability?
2. List the three principal issues that arose as a result of the union's demands and the city's responses.
3. Discuss how each of these issues was resolved.

In the Matter of

Veterans Administration Independent Service Employees Union *and* Veterans Administration Research Hospital, Chicago, Ill.

FLRC No. 71A–31

(United States Federal Labor Relations Council, Washington, D.C.)

DECISION ON NEGOTIABILITY ISSUE

BACKGROUND

The Veterans Administration Independent Service Employees Union holds exclusive recognition in a unit which consists of all service employees, with the usual exclusions, at the Veterans Administration Research Hospital, Chicago, Illinois. The activity has had in effect, since July 1969, a merit promotion plan covering the employees involved. The plan establishes certain procedures for selecting employees for promotion. However, the employees have been concerned that "preselection" decisions were being made by supervisors in violation of this plan, and that adequate review of complaints about such practice was not available.

To remedy this concern, the local parties agreed, during negotiations, to a union proposal on promotions which required that, upon request of the union, a management official who had not participated in the selection would review the promotion decision and render a final decision thereon. More specifically, the provision reads as follows:

> Positions will normally be filled from within the hospital structure when there are three highly qualified candidates available. Prior to notifying the Personnel Division of a proposed selection the selecting official shall advise the VAISEU steward of the proposed selection. If the steward desires, the selecting official shall provide him with information concerning the reasons for the proposed selection and the written materials used in making said selection (written materials concerning an employee shall only be provided with his consent). Notification to the Personnel Division shall not be made until the steward has had until the end of the steward's

second tour of duty following receipt of notice of the proposed selection from the selecting officer to request review by the next highest level supervisor who has not participated in the proposed selection under review. The decision by this supervisor will be final and not subject to further review. If the steward has decided not to seek review of the decision he shall immediately notify the selecting officer so that the Personnel Division may receive notice of the decision.

The VA central office directed that the proposal be deleted from the final agreement, apparently because of a question as to its permissibility. The union then appealed to the agency head for a negotiability determination. The agency head determined that the proposal was non-negotiable. The union appealed to the council from such determination, and the council accepted the union's petition for review pursuant to Section 11(c)(4) of the order.

OPINION

The agency takes the position, contrary to the union, that the union's proposal is non-negotiable because it would violate certain provisions of (1) Executive Order 11491, (2) Civil Service Commission requirements, and (3) Veterans Administration regulations. We will review each of these grounds below.

1. *Executive Order 11491.* The agency asserts that the union's proposal conflicts with management's right to "promote" under Section 12(b)(2) of the order. That section provides in context as follows:

Section 12. *Basic provisions of agreements:* Each agreement between an agency and a labor organization is subject to the following requirements . . . :

(b) management officials of the agency retain the right, in accordance with applicable laws and regulations . . .

(2) to hire, *promote,* transfer, assign, and retain employees in positions within the agency, and to suspend, demote, discharge, or take other disciplinary action against employees. . . .

The requirements of this section shall be expressly stated in the initial or basic agreement and apply to all supplemental, implementing, subsidiary, or informal agreements between the agency and the organization. (Emphasis in body supplied.)

In support of its position, the agency argues that the union's proposal seeks to permit a union steward to participate in the selection of an employee for promotion, in violation of 12(b)(2), by establishing the levels of review of a selection decision and enabling the union steward to substitute his judgment for that of the selecting official. However, the union denies that its proposal interferes with management's right to promote, pointing out that only higher level management review of a lower level management action is involved, and that the final decision as to who would be promoted remains exclusively with management.

The union's proposal, as previously set forth, would (a) require that the first-line selecting official notify the union of a promotion selection and, if requested, furnish supporting reasons and materials; and (b) permit the union, upon timely request, to obtain review by the next higher, nonparticipating supervisor, whose decision would be final. Such provision, in our opinion, is not violative of Section 12(b)(2) of the order.

Section 12(b)(2) dictates that in every labor agreement management officials retain their existing authority to take certain personnel actions, that is, to hire, promote, and so on. The emphasis is on the reservation of management authority to decide and act on these matters, and the clear import is that no right accorded to unions under the order may be permitted to interfere with that authority. However, there is no implication that such reservation of decision making and action authority is intended to bar negotiations of procedures, to the extent consonant with law and regulations, which management will observe in reaching the decision or taking the action involved, provided that such procedures do not have the effect of negating the authority reserved.

Here, the union's proposal would establish procedures whereby higher level management review of a selection for promotion may be obtained before the promotion is consummated. The proposal does not require management to negotiate a promotion selection or to secure union consent to the decision. Nor does it appear that the procedure proposed would unreasonably delay or impede promotion selections so as to, in effect, deny the right to promote reserved to management by Section 12(b)(2).

Under these circumstances, we find that the union's proposal is not rendered non-negotiable by Section 12(b)(2) of the order.

2. *Civil Service Commission regulations.* The agency head further determined that the union's proposal is non-negotiable because it violates Section 771.302 of CSC regulations and FPM Chapter 335, subchapter 3, paragraph 7 (b) and (c), and subchapter 5, paragraph 1(d). The union disagrees.

Since the Civil Service Commission has the primary responsibility for the issuance and interpretation of its own directives, the council, in accordance with usual council practice, requested the commission for an interpretation of its directives as they pertain to the questions raised in the present case. The commission replied as follows:

> You specifically ask whether a union proposal with respect to promotions violates Section 771.302 of the commission's regulations, which is concerned with agency grievance procedures. However, FPM Chapter 771, which contains the commission's instructions on implementing Part 771

of the regulations, provides, in Section 3–6(d)(1), that "grievances . . . may not be initiated by labor organizations." Therefore, Section 771.302 is not pertinent to the union's proposal since by definition the proposed procedure is not a grievance.

The commission's regulations clearly make the actual selection of a candidate for promotion non-negotiable. Section 3–7(c) of FPM Chapter 335 provides that the selecting official is entitled to choose any of the candidates on a promotion certificate. Section 5–1(d) of that chapter identifies the decision on which candidate among the best qualified to select for promotion as a reserved management right and, consequently, not appropriate for negotiation.

On the other hand, *none of the regulations cited in your letter or any other regulation of the commission puts any mandatory requirement on the level at which the selecting authority should rest. We view this as a matter that is subject to management discretion.* (Emphasis supplied.)

Based on the above interpretation by the Civil Service Commission, we find that the union's proposal, which relates to the level at which final selection will be made, is not violative of CSC requirements. Accordingly, the contrary determination that was made by the agency head in the present case is improper.

3. *Veterans Administration regulations.* Finally, the agency head determined that the union's proposal is non-negotiable by reason of VA regulation MP–5, Part I, Chapter 335, Section B, paragraph 3(g)(2). This regulation, which is part of an issuance by VA to supplement FPM Chapter 335, reads as follows:

(g) *Selection.* . . .
(2) The responsibility of selection must be vested in a selecting official who possesses the experience and knowledge to best determine the attributes necessary in the candidates to be selected. Since the selecting official is responsible for the efficiency of his operations, he is responsible for selecting the type of employee who can best assist him carrying out the functions of his organization. Panels or committees will not make final selections. The official personnel folders and all other pertinent records will be made available to the selecting official during the selection process.

In determining that the union's proposal violates this regulation, the agency head stated,

Your proposal is also in violation of . . . MP–5, Part I, Chapter 335, Section B, paragraph 3(g)(2) states that: "The responsibility of selection must be vested in a selecting official." To require a review and justification of a promotion selection to a union steward or higher level supervisor before the selection is final infringes on the designated selecting official's responsibility under VA regulations.

As provided in Section 11(c)(3) of the order, an agency head's determination as to the interpretation of the agency's regulations with respect to a proposal is final. However, the union in effect contends, among other things, that the agency head misinterpreted the union's proposal and therefore that the VA regulation, as interpreted by the agency head, is not a bar to negotiations under Section 11(a) of the order. We agree with the union's contention in the circumstances of this case.

In his determination, as quoted above, the agency head referred to the union's proposal as requiring "a review and justification of a promotion selection to a union steward or higher level supervisor before the selection is final." This characterization of the proposal is more fully discussed in the agency's opposition to the union's appeal. There the agency states at the outset:

> In its petition the union has attempted to obscure the simple fact that the administrator determined that the VA regulation [MP–5, Part I, Chapter 335, Section B, paragraph 3(g)(2)] means that a promotion decision shall be made solely by a selecting official and concluded that *this interpretation did not permit sharing this management prerogative with a union official, which is really what the union is seeking.* (Emphasis added.)

Further, the agency explained in summarizing its opposition:

> Thus, reduced to simple terms, *this proposal seeks to permit a union steward to participate in the selection process. It would permit the steward to substitute his judgment for that of the selecting official.*

Therefore, there can be no doubt that the proposal under consideration is non-negotiable under the provisions of Executive Order 11491 *and appropriate VA regulations.* Otherwise, management has lost its right to promote employees. (Emphasis added.)

It is clear from the foregoing that in making his determination the agency head relied on a characterization of the union's proposal which would require "justification of a promotion selection to a union steward or higher level supervisor," and "sharing this management prerogative with a union official," and would "permit the steward to substitute his judgment for that of the selecting official." However, we find none of these characteristics present in the proposal. On the contrary, the record establishes that the proposal merely would permit the union, upon timely request, to obtain review of a first-line official's promotion selection by a higher level supervisor whose decision would be final.

Accordingly, in view of the erroneous characterization of the union's proposal by the agency, and under the particular circumstances of this case, the agency has failed in our opinion to establish that its regulation is applicable so as to preclude negotiation of the proposal under Section 11(a) of the order.

CONCLUSION

Based on the foregoing reasons, we find the union's proposal is negotiable under Section 11(a) of the order. We do not, of course, decide that the proposal is desirable, or that it must be accepted by the agency. We decide only that the proposal is negotiable.

Therefore, pursuant to Section 2411.27 of the council's rules of procedure, we find that the determination by the Veterans Administration that the union's proposal is non-negotiable is improper, and the determination is set aside.

By the council.

Issued: November 22, 1972

/s/ W. V. Gill
Executive Director

Discussion Questions

1. Describe the negotiability issue in this case.
2. Why does the agency claim that the union's proposal is non-negotiable?
3. Discuss the ruling in favor of negotiability.

Section 9. Parameters of Managerial Prerogatives

While the term *concession* is often used when management agrees to meet a union demand, it is an overworked term. To agree with a union proposal is not necessarily concession. Often it is simply the act of writing down terms that the parties would have lived by anyway. As an example, it would not necessarily be a good idea to reject a union proposal on the grounds that it does not change anything and will simply cost money to publish. To agree to such provisions is not truly a concession and there is some advantage in having given something in a cooperative spirit.

However, there are areas known as managerial "prerogatives" or management rights where the employer adamantly resists union negotiating incursions and insists on unilateral authority in order to carry out certain basic, managerial functions. For instance, a recent study of 400 representative union contracts in effect indicated that management rights provisions were included in 68 percent of the documents. Oft-mentioned prerogatives were "(1) the right to direct the work force, (2) the right to manage company business, and (3) the right to control production methods." [16]

The above-mentioned study involved contracts in private industry. In the public sector, specifically the federal service, the scope of management rights is expressed in the following language in Section 11(b) of Executive Order 11491:

> [T]he obligation to meet and confer does not include matters with respect to the mission of an agency; its budget; its organization; the number of employees; and the numbers, types, and grades of positions or employees assigned to an organizational unit, work project, or tour of duty; the technology of performing its work; or its internal security practices.

Kilberg, in the following comparison, points out in lucid fashion what is probably the most significant distinction between management powers in the public and private sectors:[17]

> When management in the public sector gives up some of its "prerogatives," therefore, it foregoes the right to make decisions in the name of all the people. When management in the private sector loses its unilateral power to act, however, the public loses little or nothing because the decision-making process is merely transferred from one private group to another, rather than from public to private. The loss of the power to manage unilaterally in the public service is, therefore, more serious than the same phenomenon in the private sector.

Of course, if a subject that a union believes should be susceptible to joint determination is in reality within management sovereignty, the employer can refuse to negotiate with impunity.

The Pennsylvania Labor Relations Board v. State College Area School District, The Board of School Directors
Commonwealth of Pennsylvania, The Pennsylvania Labor Relations Board, Case No. PERA–C–929–C

NISI DECISION AND ORDER

A charge of unfair practices was filed with the Pennsylvania Labor Relations Board, herein called the board, on February 26, 1971, by the State College Area Education Association, herein called the complainant, alleging that the Board of School Directors of State College Area School District, herein called the respondent, has engaged in unfair practices contrary to the provisions of the Public Employee Relations Act, herein called the act, and more particularly of clause (5) of subsection (a) of Section 1201 of Article XII thereof.

The respondent in its answer to said charge denied refusal to negotiate item 19 and admitted refusal to bargain the other items on the grounds that they were matters of inherent managerial policy over which it was not required to bargain by virtue of the provisions of Section 702 of the act.

In its charge of unfair practices the complainant specified twenty-three items which it alleged the respondent refused to negotiate, as follows:

1. The availability of proper and adequate classroom instructional printed material;

2. The provision for time during the school day for team planning of required innovative programs;

3. The timely notice of teaching assignment for the coming year;

4. Providing separate desks and lockable drawer space for each teacher in the district;

5. Providing a cafeteria for teachers in the senior high school;

6. Eliminating the requirement that teachers perform nonteaching duties such as but not limited to hall duty, bus duty, lunch duty, study hall, and parking lot duties;

7. Eliminating the requirement that teachers teach or supervise two consecutive periods in two different buildings;

8. Eliminating the requirement that teachers substitute for other teachers during planning periods and teaching in noncertificated subject areas;

9. Eliminating the requirement that teachers chaperone athletic activities;

10. Eliminating the requirement that teachers unpack, store, check, or otherwise handle supplies;

11. Providing that there shall be one night each week free for association meetings;

12. Providing that a teacher will, without prior notice, have free access to his personnel file;

13. Permitting a teacher to leave the building any time during the school day unless he has a teaching assignment;

14. Providing special teachers with preparation time equal to that provided for other staff members;

15. Provision for maximum class sizes;

16. Provision that the association will be consulted in determining the school calendar;

17. Provision that school will officially close at noon of the last day of classes for Thanksgiving, Christmas, Spring, and Summer vacation;

18. Provision that at least one-half of the time requested for staff meetings be held during the school day;

19. A provision that school teachers not be required to be in the school more than ten minutes prior to the time students are required to be in attendance and not more than ten minutes after students are dismissed (withdrawn);

20. A provision that the present Tuesday afternoon conference with

parents be abolished and teachers hold conferences with parents by appointment at a mutually convenient time;

21. Provision that secondary teachers not be required to teach more than twenty-five periods per week and have at least one planning period each day;

22. A provision that elementary teachers shall have one period or fifteen minutes per day for planning purposes; and

23. Provision for released time for the president of the association for association business (withdrawn).

The board issued a complaint and notice of hearing and set April 26, 1971, at State College, Pennsylvania as the time and place thereof.

The aforesaid hearing was held before Alan R. Krier, Esq., a duly designated hearing examiner of the board, at which hearing a full opportunity to examine and cross examine witnesses and to present testimony and introduce evidence was afforded to all parties in interest.

FINDINGS OF FACT

The board, on the basis of the testimony and evidence presented at the hearing, and from all other matters and documents of record, finds the following facts:

· · ·

3. That the complainant proposed to negotiate with the respondent, the twenty-three items specified in its charge of unfair practices, which items are hereinbefore set forth.

4. That the respondent refused to negotiate the twenty-three items hereinbefore set forth as being matters excluded from negotiation by the provisions of Section 702 of the act.

5. That both complainant and respondent have negotiated in good faith on numerous other items.

6. That item No. 19 of the twenty-three items hereinbefore set forth is not in issue having been withdrawn by stipulation of the parties at the hearing.

7. That respondent has proposed to meet and discuss with complainant the remaining twenty-one items (19 and 23 having been withdrawn) hereinbefore set forth.

8. That complainant has refused to "meet and discuss" with respondent as to said twenty-two items.

DISCUSSION

The real question before the board in this case is what is the scope of bargaining under the act, with specific reference as to whether or not the twenty-two items hereinbefore set forth, if any, are

(a) bargainable items;

(b) not bargainable items; or,

(c) meet-and-discuss items pursuant to the provisions of Sections 701 and 702 of the act.

The act in Article I, Section 101 declares *inter alia,* "it is the public policy of this Commonwealth and the purpose of this act to promote orderly and constructive relationships between all public employers and their employees subject, however, to the paramount right of the citizens of this Commonwealth to keep inviolate the guarantees for their health, safety, and welfare. . . . Within the limitations imposed upon the governmental processes by these rights of the public at large . . . the General Assembly has determined that the over-all policy may best be accomplished by . . . (2) requiring public employers to negotiate and bargain with employee organizations representing public employees and to enter into written agreements, evidencing the result of such bargaining; and (3) establishing procedures to provide for the protection of the rights of the public employee, the public employer, and the public at large."

With this declaration of public policy in mind the assembly included in the act Article VII, titled, "Scope of Bargaining," in which Sections 701, 702, and 703 thereof provide as follows:

Section 701. Collective bargaining is the performance of the mutual obligation of the public employer and the representative of the public employees to meet at reasonable times and confer in good faith with respect to wages, hours, and other terms and conditions of employment, or the negotiation of an agreement or any question arising thereunder and the execution of a written contract incorporating any agreement reached, but such obligation does not compel either party to agree to a proposal or require the making of a concession.

Section 702. Public employers shall not be required to bargain over matters of inherent managerial policy, which shall include but shall not be limited to such areas of discretion or policy as the functions and programs of the public employer, standards of services, its overall budget, utilization of technology, the organizational structure, and selection and direction of personnel. Public employers, however, shall be required to meet and discuss on policy matters affecting wages, hours, and terms and conditions of employment as well as the impact thereon upon request by public employee representatives.

Section 703. The parties to the collective bargaining process shall not effect or implement a provision in a collective bargaining agreement if the implementation of that provision would be in violation of, or inconsistent with, or in conflict with any statute or statutes enacted by the General Assembly of the Commonwealth of Pennsylvania or the provisions of municipal home rule charters.

It appears to the board that to arrive at a sound and logical decision in this case, the members of the complainant, being teachers, be considered as having a dual status: one as employees, which they clearly are, having an employment relationship with their employer; and the other as professionals, having a relationship as such with their clients, the students.

If teachers are viewed in such contexts it appears quite clear that the act intended to speak to their employee status with consideration being given to their professional status by the use of their professional expertise in meet-and-discuss matters.

Albeit that teachers are professionals and the board respects their status as such, they are nevertheless employees with the four corners of the act and are to be considered as such in its application to them.

A microscopic reading of the act supports this view. Witness phrases in Section 101: "it is the public policy . . ."; and "the purpose of this act is to promote orderly and constructive relationships between all public employers and their employees"; "recognizing that harmonious relationships are required between the public employer and its employees"; . . . that the overall policy may best be accomplished by "(1) granting public employees the right to organize and choose freely their representatives; (2) requiring public employers to negotiate and bargain with employee organizations representing public employees . . . ; and (3) establishing procedures to provide for the protection of the right of the public employee. . . ." In Section 301(2) the definition of "public employee" or "employee" means any individual employed by a public employer . . . excluding certain named persons. Professional employees are not named in the excluded group.

Granted Section 301(7) defines professional employees, but solely for the purpose of distinguishing them from nonprofessional employees in the determination of the kinds of employees composing an appropriate unit in accordance with the provisions of Section 604 of the act.

From the foregoing, it appears to this board that in disposing of the issues in this case the teachers must be viewed in the context of an employee status rather than in their status as professionals.

An employee, according to *Webster's New International Dictionary, Second Edition,* is "One who works for wages or salary in the service of an employer." Hence, upon the execution of the contract of employment with the respondent, teachers assume the status of employees subjecting themselves to the authority and supervision of their employer, who is the agency created by the Public School Code in the case of school districts in this Commonwealth created by the legislature, to administer the public school system pursuant to the constitutional mandate to the General Assembly to "provide for the maintenance and support of a thorough and efficient system of public education to serve the needs of the Commonwealth of Pennsylvania."

The purpose of the act, hereinbefore quoted, is to promote orderly and constructive relationships between all public employers and their employees, subject to the paramount right of the citizens of the Commonwealth to keep inviolate the guarantees for their health, safety, and welfare.

In fulfillment of this purpose the act in Section 701 thereof, hereinbefore quoted, places a mutual obligation upon the public employer and the representative of the public employees to bargain in good faith with respect to wages, hours, and other terms and conditions of employment, but excludes from the scope of such bargaining by the provisions of Section 702 of the act, hereinbefore quoted, *matters of inherent managerial policy such as, but not limited to, the functions and programs of the public employer, standards of service, its overall budget, utilization of technology, the organizational structure and selection* and direction of personnel, with the admonition to the public employers that they are required to meet and discuss on policy matters affecting wages, hours and terms and conditions of employment as well as the *impact* thereon upon request by public employee representatives. (Emphasis supplied.)

Additionally, the scope of bargaining is further limited by the provisions of Section 703 of the act, hereinbefore quoted, which provides that matters in violation of, or inconsistent with, or in conflict with any statute or statutes of the Commonweath of Pennsylvania shall not be effected or implemented in collective bargaining.

Matters of "inherent managerial policy" over which public employers are not obligated to bargain are such matters that are firmly fixed and belong to the employer as a right or permanent and inseparable element, quality, or attribute involved in the constitution or essential character of the employer, and incapable of being surrendered or transferred where specifically prohibited by statute.

Note the Hickman report's recommendations as to what the act should contain by its statement that "The new law should recognize the right of all public employees . . . to bargain collectively, subject to enumerated safeguards," and included as one of said safeguards that "Bargaining should be permitted with respect to wages, hours, and conditions of employment, appropriately qualified by a recognition of existing laws dealing with aspects of the same subject matter and by a carefully defined reservation of managerial rights."

The policy-making function belongs solely to the school district and its Board of School Directors and their duly authorized agents by virtue of the powers conferred upon them by statute, specifically or by necessary implication. . . .

Broad discretionary powers have been given school authorities to enable them in exercising their policy-making function to ensure a thorough, efficient, effective, and better education for the children of this Commonwealth and any erosion of these powers should be strictly constructed on the basis that the public interest is paramount.

It has long been recognized that school officials are trustees of the powers vested in them and cannot divest themselves of the powers which have been conferred upon them for a public purpose. . . .

Policy matters are thought of as rules of conduct and to the extent they *affect* (influence, impinge, encroach, bear upon, or concern) wages, hours, and terms and conditions of employment as well as their *impact* (used metaphorically to mean the result, effect, or consequence) thereon become mandatory meet-and-discuss items by the public employer upon request of the public employee representative.

In light of the foregoing the respondent is not required by the act to bargain over matters which are the responsibility and prerogative of management, but is required to meet and discuss policy matters *affecting wages, hours, and terms and conditions of employment* as well as the impact thereon upon request of employee representatives. (Emphasis supplied.)

Turning now to the twenty-two requests, hereinbefore set forth, for bargaining that were proposed by the employee representatives to the respondent, this board sets forth its observations as gleaned from the testimony and evidence presented at the hearing, the comments expressed by parties that presented their views at the "scope of bargaining" meeting held by this board on September 9, 1971 . . . decisions of the Pennsylvania courts, articles published on the scope of bargaining, the provisions of the act, as follows:

Items 1, 3, 4, and 5 are not bargainable matters because they are within the scope of matters of inherent managerial policy specifically in the areas of standards of services, functions, programs, and the overall budget of the respondent.

Items 2, 14, 18, 21, and 22 are not bargainable matters because they are within the scope of inherent managerial policy specifically in the areas of functions and prógrams of the respondent and the direction of its personnel.

Items 6, 7, 8, 9, 10, and 13 are not bargainable matters because they are within the scope of inherent managerial prerogatives, specifically in the areas of standard of services, functions, and programs of the respondent and direction of its personnel.

Item 11 is not a bargainable matter because it is within the scope of inherent managerial policy in the areas of functions and programs and standard of services.

Item 12 is not a bargainable matter because it is within the scope of inherent managerial policy and is further regulated by the Public School Code.

Item 15 is not a bargainable matter because it is within the scope of inherent managerial policy, specifically within the areas of standards of services, functions and programs, and the overall budget of the respondent.

Items 16 and 17 are not bargainable matters because they are within the scope of inherent managerial policy and further regulated by the Public School Code.

Item 20 is not a bargainable matter because it is within the scope of inherent managerial prerogatives, specifically the areas of functions and programs, and standard of services of the respondent and the direction of its personnel.

The board notes from the testimony that even though the act does not require the public employer to meet and discuss on policy matters except upon request by the public employee representative it did offer to meet and discuss many of the foregoing items but the complainant refused.

CONCLUSIONS OF LAW

. . .

4. That the respondent has not committed an unfair practice in refusing to bargain in violation of Section 1201(a)5 of the act.

ORDER

The Pennsylvania Labor Relations Board, therefore, after due consideration of the foregoing and the record as a whole, hereby orders and directs that the charge of unfair practices filed on February 26, 1971, by the State College Area Education Association, be and the same is hereby dismissed, and the complaint thereon is rescinded. . . .

Signed, sealed, and dated at Harrisburg, Pennsylvania, this fourteenth day of October, 1971.

Pennsylvania Labor Relations Board
/s/ Malcolm B. Petrikin, Chairman
/s/ George B. Stuart, Member

Discussion Questions

1. Describe the real issue in this case.
2. How did the Pennsylvania statute limit the scope of managerial prerogatives?
3. What does the phrase "inherent managerial policy" refer to and how is it defined by the board?
4. In the final analysis, how many of the complainant's bargaining requests were approved?
5. Outline the public policy toward public sector labor relations in Pennsylvania.
6. Were teachers as professionals given preferential treatment vis-à-vis collective bargaining rights over regular state employees?
7. Can a public employer voluntarily bargain away his prerogatives in all cases?
8. Distinguish between meet-and-discuss and full-fledged collective bargaining requirements.

In the Matter of

Local Union No. 2219, International Brotherhood of Electrical Workers, AFL-CIO *and* Department of the Army Corps of Engineers, Little Rock District, Little Rock, Ark.

FLRC No. 71A–46 [18]

(United States Federal Labor Relations Council, Washington, D.C.)

DECISION ON NEGOTIABILITY ISSUE

BACKGROUND

The activity (Little Rock District, Corps of Engineers) is headquartered at Little Rock, Arkansas. Among its responsibilities, the activity operates five hydroelectric power plants, located in Arkansas and Missouri, called Bull Shoals, Dardaneele, Greers Ferry, Norfolk, and Table Rock.

In October, 1966, the union was granted exclusive recognition for a bargaining unit consisting of approximately ninety operating and maintenance personnel employed by the activity. Negotiations for an agreement ensued. All issues were ultimately resolved except one concerning the rotating shift work schedules of power plant operators or, more specifically, the activity's practice of assigning "swing" operators in such a way as to avoid overtime and holiday pay. That issue is the subject of the instant proceeding, and the pertinent circumstances surrounding the dispute are as follows:

1. *Method of work scheduling at activity.* The five power plants operate on a continuous, twenty-four-hour day, seven-day-week basis, and each is manned by at least one full-time operator at all times. In order to cover the twenty-one eight-hour shifts per week, and accommodate normal absences for annual leave, sick leave, holidays, and usual days off, each plant has a complement of five operators, working on rotating shifts. In any one week four employees occupy the classification of regular operator and one employee that of "swing" operator (the nature of "swing" assignments is described below). All five employees take turns working in each classification and the change is made weekly. Thus, a given employee will be a regular operator on each of the four regular operator shifts for four weeks and swing operator in the fifth week, and then the cycle repeats. In this manner the week's twenty-one shifts are covered.

At the beginning of each calendar year, the activity draws up and posts at each power plant a tentative work schedule which lists each operator's scheduled workdays, off days, and insofar as known at that time, annual leave hours for the coming year. From this annual schedule, thirty-five-day (five-week) final work schedules are posted two weeks prior to their effective dates showing any changes from the tentative schedule for the coming five-week period. The administrative workweek is Sunday through Saturday.

In practice, when none of the operators at a plant is to be absent during an entire week it is necessary for two operators to work on a single shift, as four employees working forty hours each week cover twenty shifts. In such circumstances, "doubling up" is necessary on four shifts during that week and is scheduled on the first shift (8 A.M. to 4 P.M.) on Monday through Thursday. The second man on the doubled-up shifts is the so-called "swing" operator. The swing operator returns as the sole operator on the day shift on Friday and is then scheduled for nonwork-days on the Saturday and Sunday immediately following. (This is the only time an operator is scheduled for consecutive Saturday and Sunday days off during the five-week cycle.)

However, in the case of absence of a regular operator on a Saturday or Sunday which has not been accounted for in the posted five-week schedule, it has been the practice of the activity, in order to avoid paying overtime to one of the other regular operators, to relieve that week's swing operator of work on a scheduled workday and require that he work instead on the uncovered Saturday or Sunday which was scheduled as his off day.

Likewise, it appears that when a holiday occurs on a day on which the regular operator and swing operator are scheduled to work the day shift together, the activity, in order to avoid the payment of holiday pay to both operators, often cancels the scheduled day off of the swing operator (that is, Saturday or Sunday) and relieves him of his scheduled workday which falls on the holidays.

2. *Disputed proposals.* The union has not objected to the activity's practice of changing the shifts for which the swing operator is scheduled within his regular workdays, that is, moving a swing operator from the first to the second or third shifts on his scheduled workdays. It has objected to the changing of the swing operator's off days as specified in the annual schedule, to avoid the payment of overtime and holiday pay, on the ground that this creates a situation where the swing employee can neither make advance personal plans for the use of his off time nor be compensated for his inconvenience by receiving premium pay. To remedy this situation, the union submitted the following proposals during the course of negotiations:

> *Article 4, Section D(2)(d).* No operator's nonworkdays shall be changed unless he receives overtime pay for said change.

> *Article 6, Section D.* Schedule will provide for tours which will allow holidays off to all operators to the maximum extent possible; and which will use the swing operator to avoid the unnecessary payment of holiday pay, except that the swing operator will not be scheduled to return to duty with less than sixteen (16) hours off, when the purpose of the return is to avoid payment of unnecessary holiday pay to another operator. The swing operator's nonworkday(s) will not be changed for the sole purpose of avoiding the payment of holiday pay.

The activity refused to accept the union's proposals and an impasse resulted. The dispute was thereafter submitted by the union to the Federal Service Impasses Panel; however, in the course of the panel's proceedings the agency claimed that the proposals were in fact violative of applicable law and regulations, and the negotiability issue was referred to the procedures of Section 11(c) of the order. . . .

The union then appealed to the council, which accepted the union's petition for review. Both the union and the agency have filed briefs in this proceeding.

3. *Positions of the parties.* The agency in effect determined and asserts before the council that both of the union's proposals violate management's right under Section 12(b)(4) of the order "to maintain the efficiency of government operations entrusted to them" and management's

responsibilities under 5 U.S.C. Sections 301, 302, and 305 to maintain and improve "efficiency and economy in the operation of the agency's activities, functions, or organization units." The agency further contends, as to the overtime proposal [Article 4, Section D(2)(d)], that such proposal is unlawful since it would entitle an employee to overtime pay regardless of whether he has satisfied the requirement of an eight-hour workday or a forty-hour workweek under 5 U.S.C. Section 5544(a).

The union argues that its proposals concern matters affecting working conditions upon which an agency has an obligation to bargain under Section 11(a) of the order. Also, the union denies that its proposals are violative of any statutory requirements.

OPINION

The questions presented for council decision are whether the union's proposals are negotiable under Section 11(a) of the order as matters affecting working conditions, or non-negotiable, as contended by the agency, because (1) they interfere with management's right under 5 U.S.C. Sections 301, 302, and 305 and under Section 12(b)(4) of the order, to run its operation efficiently and economically; and (2) with particular reference to the union's proposed Article 4, Section D(2)(d), such proposal violates 5 U.S.C. Section 5544(a).

Section 11(a) of the order, which relates to the negotiation of agreements, provides that the parties shall meet and confer in good faith regarding "personnel policies and practices and matters affecting working conditions, so far as may be appropriate under applicable laws and regulations, including . . . this order."

Plainly, management policies and procedures concerning the assignment of employees to particular shifts or the assignment of overtime or holiday work directly affect the jobs of employees and are "matters affecting working conditions." They have traditionally been so recognized. Without more, the union's proposals, which are directed to such management actions, would be negotiable under Section 11(a).

1. *5 U.S.C. Sections 301, 302, and 305 and Section 12(b)(4) of order.* As already mentioned, the agency contends that the union's proposals are nevertheless excepted from the obligation to negotiate, on the grounds that they would violate applicable law (5 U.S.C. Sections 301, 302, and 305 and Section 12(b)(4) of the order).

Section 12(b) of the order establishes rights expressly reserved to management officials under any bargaining agreement, including "the right, in accordance with applicable laws and regulation . . . (4) to maintain the efficiency of the government operations entrusted to them." Section 305 of Title 5, along with the general agency authority in Sections 301 and 302, indirectly requires management to maintain "efficiency and economy in the operation of the agency's activities, functions, or organization units." . . .

The agency argues principally that "the *raison d'être* for the swing shift is the minimizing of overtime and other premium costs to the employer"; and that the proposals would thwart "management's efforts to use the 'swing' operator effectively and attack the very purpose for establishing a 'swing' shift, by imposing prohibitions and limitations on the use of the fifth operator to reduce premium pay costs." In essence, therefore, it is the agency's position that, since the union's proposals would constrain the agency in reducing premium pay costs, the proposals of necessity would impair the agency's ability to maintain efficiency and economy in its operations.

In our opinion, the agency position equating reduced premium pay costs with efficient and economical operations improperly ignores the total complex of factors encompassed within the concept of "efficiency and economy." It fails to take into account, for example, the adverse effects of employee dissatisfaction with existing assignment practices, and the very real possibility that revised practices along the lines proposed, by reason of their actual impact on the employees, might well increase rather than reduce overall efficiency and economy of operations.

In general, agency determinations as to negotiability made in relation to the concept of efficiency and economy in Section 12(b)(4) of the order and similar language in the statutes require consideration and balancing of all the factors involved, including the well-being of employees, rather than an arbitrary determination based only on the anticipation of increased costs. Other factors such as the potential for improved performance, increased productivity, responsiveness to direction, reduced turnover, fewer grievances, contribution of money-saving ideas, improved health and safety, and the like, are valid considerations. We believe that where otherwise negotiable proposals are involved the management rights in Section 12(b)(4) may not properly be invoked to deny negotiations unless there is a substantial demonstration by the agency that increased costs or reduced effectiveness in operations are inescapable and significant and are not offset by compensating benefits.

Applied to the instant case, the agency has asserted that increased premium pay costs would derive from the union's proposals. However, it has not established in the record before us that such costs would be significant in nature, nor that offsetting factors such as adverted to above would fail to overcome those increased costs. On the other hand, the union has shown that its proposals are limited in scope to certain aspects of swing operator scheduling and assignment, and that its proposals seek to reduce what the employees feel are unusual hardships in the working conditions of the unit.

In these circumstances, we find that the agency's determination of non-negotiability under Section 12(b)(4) of the order and similar language in related statutes is insufficiently supported and must be set aside.

2. *5 U.S.C. Section 5544(a)*. The agency also in effect determined, as previously stated, that the union's overtime proposal [Article 4, Section D(2)(d)] is non-negotiable because it would entitle an employee to premium pay whenever he is called to work on his scheduled day off, regardless of whether he has satisfied the overtime requirements in Section 5544 (a) of Title 5. That section of the code reads in pertinent part that: "An employee whose basic rate of pay is fixed and adjusted from time to time in accordance with prevailing rates by a wage board or similar administrative authority serving the same purpose is entitled to overtime pay for overtime work in excess of eight hours a day or forty hours a week."

The agency's position is without merit. The union's proposal reads, "No operator's nonworkdays shall be changed unless he receives overtime pay for said change." Nothing in the language of this proposal would require the payment of overtime *before* the statutory minimums have been met. Moreover, in its petition the union expressly states that its "proposal inherently contemplates that when the employer cancels the 'swing' operator's nonworkdays and requires him to work on those days, it will *not* relieve the operator from any scheduled work."

Accordingly, we find that the agency erred in its determination that the union's proposal on overtime is non-negotiable under 5 U.S.C. Section 5544(a) and this determination must also be set aside.

CONCLUSION

For the reasons discussed above, we find that the union's proposals are negotiable under Section 11(a) of the order. We do not, of course, pass upon the wisdom of the proposals, nor indicate in any manner that they should be accepted by the agency. We merely hold that the proposals are subject to negotiation by the parties under the order.

Therefore, pursuant to Section 2411.27 of the council's rules of procedure, we find that the determination by the agency that the union's proposals are non-negotiable is improper, and the determination is set aside.

By the council.

Issued: November 20, 1972   /s/ W. V. Gill
                                     Executive Director

Discussion Questions

1. Which managerial prerogatives does the agency assert are being infringed on by the union demand?

2. How does the union respond to these alleged violations?
3. Analyze the council's ruling concerning the negotiability issue.
4. In what respect does the council limit its determination as to the merits of the case?

Section 10. Requirements for a Valid Labor Contract

The determination as to whether a proper collective bargaining agreement has been consummated is important in deciding "whether the agreement will bar a rival union from obtaining an election to determine the bargaining agent while the agreement remains in effect. It may also be of importance in determining whether the purported contract is enforceable by the courts. . . ." [19]

The decision of the NLRB in the *Appalachian Shale Products Co.* case, which is cited in the decision that follows, indicated that additional requirements for a valid agreement are that it "must contain terms and conditions of employment sufficient to stabilize the bargaining relationship; otherwise it won't serve to bar an election. An agreement limited to wages only or to a few provisions the board doesn't regard as 'substantial' won't make the grade." [20]

In the Matter of

Zambarano Memorial Hospital, Pascoag, Rhode Island (employer) *and* **Rhode Island General Council, AFL-CIO on Behalf of Local Union 1134, Affiliate of the Laborers International Union of North America (petitioner)** *and* **Rhode Island State Employees Association (intervenor)**

Case No. EE–1801

(State of Rhode Island and Providence Plantations, Providence, Sc. before the State Labor Relations Board, Rhode Island State)

DECISION AND DIRECTION OF ELECTION

STATEMENT OF THE CASE

On June 25, 1968, the Rhode Island General Council, AFL-CIO, on behalf of Local 1134, Affiliate of the Laborers International Union of North America, hereinafter called the petitioner, filed a petition with the Rhode Island State Labor Relations Board, hereinafter called the board, pursuant to Section 28–7–16, General Laws of Rhode Island, 1956, as amended, requesting certification of all hospital employees excluding . . . those employed by Zambarano Memorial Hospital.

On July 17, 1968, a hearing was duly held before the Rhode Island

State Labor Relations Board. At the hearing, the Rhode Island State Employees Association, hereinafter called the intervenor, moved for leave to intervene. The motion to intervene was granted by the board. . . .

Full opportunity to be heard, to examine and cross-examine witnesses, and to introduce evidence bearing upon issues was afforded all parties.

A copy of an agreement signed on May 28, 1968 between the state of Rhode Island, through the director of administration, and the Rhode Island State Employees Association was introduced as Exhibit A on behalf of the Rhode Island State Employees Association.

There was a dispute on whether or not the document, subsequently marked Exhibit A, introduced on behalf of the intervenor, is a valid labor contract, and therefore, should be a bar to any petition for election and subsequent certification.

The petitioner contended that this petition was filed beyond the one year protection provision contained in Chapter 28–7–18 of the Rhode Island State Labor Relations Act which provides that any certification of a bargaining representative made pursuant to an election . . . shall be effective for one year from the date of such election.

The intervenor, who claimed to be the certified bargaining agent for the Zambarano Memorial Hospital's employee unit, contended that the petition submitted by the petitioner should be dismissed as being imperfect, improper, and barred by a labor contract signed by the state of Rhode Island and the intervenor on May 28, 1968.

The intervenor attempted to establish that the document introduced and marked Exhibit A dated May 28, 1968 constituted a valid binding labor contract.

Peter Clare, the representative of the state of Rhode Island at the hearing, took the position that the document signed by the state and the intervenor was not, in his opinion, a labor contract per se, but an agreement setting up the ground rules for the state and the intervenor to continue their negotiations to reach a valid labor contract. In other words, he felt that Exhibit A is nothing more than an understanding on behalf of both parties to commence and continue negotiations until an executed agreement is entered into and finalized. . . .

The petitioner contended that the agreement on May 28, 1968, marked Exhibit A, was not a labor contract specific enough to bar an election in that the *Appalachian Shale Products Co.* case, 1958, 121 NLRB 1160, states . . . "that a contract must be adequate as to form, scope, and employee coverage. The document must contain substantial terms and conditions of employment." Also, according to the *Industrial Raw Materials* case, 1954, 109 NLRB 1295, it must be wide enough in scope to guide adequately the day-to-day bargaining relationship.

It was felt that this labor contract, if at all a labor contract, was only a partial contract, not a fully completed contract.

CONCLUSIONS

The board concludes

. . .

4. That the certification date had elapsed on June 23, 1968.

5. That the document dated May 28, 1968 and marked Exhibit A is not a labor contract, but an agreement to proceed with future negotiations.

6. That the Rhode Island State Employees Association prior to the expiration of the certification date failed to request an extension of time on its certification from the Rhode Island State Labor Relations Board. . . .

THE ELECTION

By virtue and pursuant to the power vested in the Rhode Island State Labor Relations Board by the Rhode Island State Labor Relations Act, IT IS HEREBY DIRECTED that an election by secret ballot shall be conducted within a reasonable date hereof . . . among all hospital employees excluding . . . employed by Zambarano Memorial Hospital, employed during the payroll period ending August 17, 1968, to determine whether they desire to be represented, for the purposes of collective bargaining, as provided for in the act, by the Rhode Island General Council, AFL-CIO on behalf of Local Union 1134, Affiliate of the Laborers International Union of North America or the Rhode Island State Employees Association or by no organization.

Entered as order of the
Rhode Island State Labor Relations Board
Dated: August 16, 1968

Rhode Island State Labor Relations Board

/s/ Harry T. Brett
Chairman

/s/ Armand E. Renzi
Member

/s/ Samuel J. Azzinaro
Member

Discussion Questions

1. Cite the requirements that must be satisfied in the private sector before a valid contract is completed. Did the board closely adhere to these conditions?
2. Why did the agreement in this case fail to meet the prerequisites for a finalized document?
3. What effect does the incompleteness of an agreement have on its capacity to constitute a bar to a representation election?

Section 11. Requirement to Reduce Negotiated Items to Writing

An oral contract can be negotiated by the parties that will be enforceable in court if neither side has requested that the terms be in written form. However, if the union and employer have reached an agreement on the substance of the contract and a request is made that it be reduced to writing, that condition must be satisfied or the reneging party will not have met its duty to bargain as defined by the Labor Management Relations Act.[21]

In the Matter of

Rhode Island State Labor Relations Board *and* West Warwick School Committee

Case No. ULP–996

(State of Rhode Island before the State Labor Relations Board)

DECISION AND ORDER

On April 19, 1971 the West Warwick Teachers Alliance, Local 1017, AFT (AFL-CIO) filed with the Rhode Island State Labor Relations Board, hereinafter called the board, a charge alleging that the West Warwick School Committee, herein called the respondents, had engaged in, and were engaging in, certain unfair labor practices as set forth in the Rhode Island State Labor Relations Act, hereinafter called the act.

The board investigated said charge and a complaint was then issued on April 21, 1971 alleging in substance that the respondents, in their capacities, had refused to bargain with the complainant in violation of Sections 28–7 and 28–9 of the General Laws of Rhode Island, 1956, as amended. An answer by the respondents to this complaint was filed. At the formal hearing held by the board on May 7, 1971, a motion to intervene by the West Warwick Teachers Alliance, Local 1017, AFT (AFL-

CIO), hereinafter referred to as the union, was granted. This union was the certified bargaining representative for the teachers of the West Warwick school system. All parties were represented by counsel, who participated in the proceedings, and were afforded full opportunity to be heard, and to introduce evidence bearing upon the issues.

At this hearing, the facts as presented by the union were mostly undisputed. In substance, the union and the respondents engaged in the collective bargaining process pursuant to Section 28–9.3 of the Rhode Island General Laws, 1956, as amended, the *Michaelson Act* so-called. These negotiations resulted in a collective bargaining agreement for the 1971–1972 school year. This agreement was not reduced to writing, however, pending the outcome of the annual financial Town Meeting of the town of West Warwick. At the financial Town Meeting, the appropriation for the school budget as presented and recommended by the respondents was greatly reduced. As a result of the reduction, the respondents refused to reduce the agreement to writing on the basis that sufficient funds were not appropriated to satisfy its terms.

Section 28–9.3–4 of the Michaelson Act provides as follows: The board is of the opinion that any question as to the relationship of the financial Town Meeting and the provisions of the Michaelson Act is not properly before it; the only question presently before the board is whether the respondents have complied with the terms and provisions of the Michaelson Act; it is the opinion of the board that the above-cited language of Section 28–9.3–4 clearly imposes a duty on the respondents to reduce any agreement reached to a written contract and the evidence shows that this has not been done.

Accordingly, it is the opinion of the board that the Michaelson Act imposes an obligation upon the respondents to reduce any agreement that they may have reached with the union to a written contract. Therefore, the board directs the respondents to comply with the provisions of the act and to execute a written contract.

The board is of the further opinion that the conduct complained of in this matter is not of the intentional type that would justify finding the respondents guilty of an unfair labor practice. They were acting in good faith at all times in their relationships with the union.

CONCLUSIONS

4. The West Warwick School Committee and the West Warwick Teachers Alliance reached a collective bargaining agreement through negotiations pursuant to Section 28–9.3 of the Rhode Island General Laws, 1956, as amended.

5. The West Warwick School Committee failed to reduce the above-

mentioned agreement to writing as required by Section 28–9.3–4 of the
Rhode Island General Laws, 1956, as amended.

ORDER

Pursuant to the power vested in the Rhode Island State Labor Relations Board by the Rhode Island State Labor Relations Act, IT IS
HEREBY ORDERED that the West Warwick School Committee execute
a written contract embodying the terms of the collective bargaining agreement for the 1971–1972 school year.

Entered as order of the
Rhode Island State Labor Relations Board
Dated: May 17, 1971

Rhode Island State Labor Relations Board

/s/ Armand E. Renzi
Member

/s/ Samuel J. Azzinaro
Member

Discussion Questions

1. Why did the respondent refuse to reduce the agreement to writing?
2. Did the board consider the merits of the financial Town Meeting appropriation of funds decision and its subsequent effect on contractual commitments?
3. Of what significance was the Michaelson Act in this proceeding?

In the Matter of

The City of White Plains (respondent) *and* **Professional Fire Fighters
Association of White Plains, Inc., Local 274, IAFF, AFL-CIO
(charging party)**

Case No. U–0382

Board Decision

(State of New York Public Employment Relations Board)

BACKGROUND

The Professional Fire Fighters Association of White Plains, Inc., Local
274, International Association of Fire Fighters, AFL-CIO, filed a charge

on October 12, 1971 alleging that the city of White Plains violated Section 209-a.1(d) of the Public Employee's Fair Employment Act by refusing to reduce to writing an agreement reached on June 21, 1971 and, in a supplemental charge filed on October 29, 1971, by refusing to negotiate in good faith.

The record indicates the following:

(1) The charging party proposed in 1970 a reduction in hours and a two-platoon "tour of duty."

(2) The charging party and respondent agreed upon a reduction of hours from forty-eight to forty-six.

(3) Though no express agreement was reached by the parties on the subject of tours of duty, respondent did, in January 1971, put in effect the work schedule sought by charging party and has continued the two-platoon tour of duty in effect to the date of the hearing.

(4) The position of the employer was that the two-platoon system would be continued for the life of the contract, and this position would be confirmed in writing but that it would not be included in the contract setting forth the negotiated terms and conditions of employment.

Admittedly, as pointed out by the hearing officer, a public employer may not be requested to reduce to writing the negotiated terms and conditions of employment until there has been complete agreement upon all issues in dispute.

However, we do not find this to be the position of the employer here. Rather, it appears to be the position of the employer that, while it has put into effect the two-platoon system sought by the employee organization and it is willing to assure the employee organization that it will be maintained for duration of the negotiated contract, it will not include a provision for the two-platoon system in the negotiated contract.

We deem this posture of the employer to be a violation of Section 209-a.1(d). It clearly would frustrate the purposes of the act to permit an employer to adopt a posture that it may refuse to incorporate in the written agreement an agreed-upon term and condition of employment.

As noted above, the obligation to reduce negotiated terms and conditions of employment to writing does not arise until there is complete agreement, but it is a violation of the obligation to negotiate in good faith to take the position in the negotiating process that under no circumstances will an agreed-upon term and condition of employment be included in the written contract embodying the negotiated terms and conditions of employment.

Therefore, IT IS ORDERED that

1. With regard to the negotiation dealt with in this decision, the employer include in any written agreement resultant therefrom a clause providing for tours of duty in accordance with the agreement reached by the parties on this item.

2. The employer cease and desist from adopting a posture during collective negotiations that it will refuse to incorporate in the written agreement an agreed-upon term and condition of employment.

Dated: April 28, 1972   /s/ Robert D. Helsby, Chairman
　　　　Albany, New York

Discussion Questions

1. State the prerequisite to a request to a public employer that negotiated terms and conditions of employment be reduced to writing.
2. Distinguish this case from the West Warwick decision that was immediately preceding.
3. Why did the board rule that the employer's conduct was in violation of the state law?

Section 12. The Duty of Municipal Employers to Appropriate Sufficient Funds to Pay Negotiated Employee Benefits

Valid contractual commitments in the areas of wage compensation and other monetary benefits are negotiated items subject to court enforcement in the event of default or breach of contract in the private sector. In public employment, however, the management negotiator may be without authority to implement monetary commitments already made because of a lack of appropriated tax revenues to satisfy the obligation. This situation may arise because a third party not privy to the negotiations— be it a board, council, or budget director—has the unilateral authority to provide the funds and may refuse to take such action. However, the next case to be discussed indicates that judicial determinations in the public sector may result in the same type of binding contractual commitment regarding monetary benefits.

In the Matter of

James H. J. Tate, Mayor of Philadelphia, et al. (Appellants) v. Louis Antosh et al. (Appellees)

No. 77 C.C. 1971 [22]

(In the Commonwealth Court of Pennsylvania)

Honorable James H. J. Tate, Mayor of Philadelphia, et al.(Appellants) v. Mario Monacello et al. (Appellees)

No. 78 C.D. 1971

(In the Commonwealth Court of Pennsylvania)

City of Philadelphia, etc., Honorable James H. J. Tate et al. (Appellants) v. District Council 33 of the American Federation of State, County and Municipal Employees, AFL-CIO by its President and Trustee, ad litem (Appellees)

No. 80 C.D. 1971

(In the Commonwealth Court of Pennsylvania)

BACKGROUND

Opinion by Presiding Judge Bowman filed August 30, 1971.

Although not so posed by the parties to these consolidated appeals, the fundamental issue is whether the judiciary—to enforce an admitted obligation of the city of Philadelphia to certain of its employees—may direct the legislative branch of the government of that city to appropriate funds to meet such obligations.

Prior decisional law makes solution of the issue difficult. Compounding the difficulty is the impact, if any, of recent legislation on the subject of labor relations between public employees and their government employer.

The essential facts are not in dispute and, for the most part, have been stipulated. For the fiscal year July 1, 1970 to June 30, 1971, the city had appropriated $2,725,000 for disability payments to city employees who were or became eligible therefor as a result of service connected injury as prescribed by Civil Service Regulation 32.

In substance, this regulation provides that employees totally and permanently disabled shall receive full salary for three years; those permanently and partially disabled shall be placed in secondary positions and shall receive as supplemental pay the difference between the salary of the secondary position and that of their prior regular pay. Failure to cooperate fully with the job placement program or failure to accept or to continue in the employment offered shall limit the employee's receipt of benefits to a period of one year.

On January 15, 1971, when it became apparent that budgeted funds for payment of Regulation 32 benefits would soon become exhausted, eligible city employees were so notified in writing by the city personnel director based upon advice given to him by the finance director. The letter concluded that no payments would be made after the fund was exhausted.

This advice precipitated the suits in question which were filed on January 22, 1971. By complaint in equity the nonuniformed employees, through their union, sought judicial relief directing continuation of payments to those eligible and the appropriation of the necessary funds to meet such payments. Similar complaints in equity were filed by the policemen and firemen and their unions. The policemen also filed a complaint in mandamus. In all actions, the Mayor of the city, sundry fiscal officers, and the members of the City Council are named defendants.

After hearing, the lower court entered orders enjoining defendants from discontinuing payments to eligible employees and directing them to appropriate funds for the purpose of financing such payments. These appeals followed, incident to which this court superseded the orders of the lower court.

Before the lower court and here, the city maintains a single position which it contends insulates the city against an action of any kind being asserted against it for the payment of Regulation 32 benefits to eligible city employees.

Citing *O'Donnell* v. *Philadelphia,* 385 Pa. 189, 122 A.2d 690 (1956) and *Baxter* v. *Philadelphia,* 385 Pa. 424, 123 A.2d 634 (1956) as controlling, it argues that the exhaustion of the appropriated funds for these purposes bars judicial remedy.

O'Donnell involved a declaratory judgment proceeding by a labor union and several city employees as a class suit to recover wages for work performed in excess of forty hours each week during the year 1952; their claim rested partly on an ordinance and partly on a labor agreement, both of which reduced the work week from forty-eight to forty hours with provision for overtime payment. However, upon adoption of the Home Rule Charter effective January 7, 1952, the Civil Service Commission, acting under authority of the charter, reinstated the hours of work as those in force during 1951. The reduced work week, as provided by ordinance and the labor agreement, was in effect for only a five day interval and it was the overtime payments for this period which were the subject of the litigation. After concluding that the particular plaintiffs were not parties to the labor agreement in question, the court proceeded to state:

There is another and conclusive reason why the order of the lower court must be affirmed, this reason being that council never made any appropriation to provide for overtime pay on the basis of a forty-hour week in pursuance of either the agreement or the ordinance, except partially for the union members employed in the Department of Public Works. That there can be no recovery of the city in the absence of such an appropriation is so fundamental and so well established as to preclude the necessity of discussion. All the statutes relating to Philadelphia, such as the act of April 21, 1858, P.L. 385, the act of June 1, 1885, P.L. 37, and the act of June 25, 1919, P.L. 581, provided, in varying phraseology, that "no debt or contract shall be binding upon the city of Philadelphia unless . . . an appropriation sufficient to pay the same be previously made by the councils"; or that "no liability shall be enforceable against the city by any action at law in equity or otherwise, upon any contract not supported by a previous appropriation of council." The home rule charter contains numerous sections—for example, 6–104, 6–106, 6–400(a), and 8–200(3)—to like effect. As for the decisional law on the subject, case after case has laid down the same rule, which was called by Judge Thayer "the palladium of Philadelphia taxpayers" (*Bladen* v. *The City,* 9 Phila. 586, 589). In *Thiel* v. *Philadelphia,* 245 Pa. 406, 408, 91 A. 490, 491, the court stated, "Without an appropriation there can be no payment of salaries. This is too well settled to admit of argument." In *Gamble* v. *City of Philadelphia,* 14 Phila. 223, the court said, in a statement quoted with emphatic approval in *Leary* v. *Philadelphia,* 314 Pa. 458, 472, 473, 172 A. 459, 465, that "It has been repeatedly determined both by the courts of this county and by the Supreme Court that this provision (that no debt or contract shall be binding upon the city of Philadelphia unless an appropriation sufficient to pay the same be previously made by councils) is not merely directory, but that it is in the highest degree mandatory, and binding upon all who deal with the city departments, officers, or agents. The words are words of positive prohibition and constitute a perfect and unanswerable defense to the claim of every contractor which is not brought within the specified conditions. . . . In order to make the city liable, not only must there be an appropriation, but a sufficient appropriation. Its responsibility cannot be made to extend beyond the amount actually appropriated.

To overcome this formidable pronouncement supported by a host of precedent, appellees advance two independent arguments: (a) that the administration of justice and the public interest require a contrary result and (b) that the instant claims are based upon negotiated labor contracts under new statutory law which make the pronouncement of *O'Donnell* obsolete. They also emphasize that the claims in question are for *benefits* and not for *wages,* urging that this fact distinguishes the instant cases from *O'Donnell* and its predecessor decisions, all of which were concerned with wage claims or third party contract claims.

The lower court, in ordering continuation of payment of Regulation 32 benefits and the appropriation of the necessary funds to do so, based its decision essentially upon appellees' second contention.

We note in passing that appellees' first argument suggests that the denial of the benefits in question may provoke widespread strikes, albeit unauthorized, by police, firemen, and other city employees with calamitous results to the city and its citizens, thus seriously affecting the "administration of justice" and the public interest generally. Appellees say *Commonwealth ex rel. Carroll* v. *Tate,* 442 Pa. 45, 274 A.2d 193 (1971) supports judicial enforcement of appellees' rights under such circumstances.

In our opinion, *Carroll* cannot be so extended. It declared that the judiciary as a co-equal and independent branch of government possesses the power to compel the executive and legislative branches of government to provide the reasonably necessary funds for the functioning and administration of the judicial branch. As a necessary exception to the separation of powers doctrine, we can find no support for appellees' contention in the *Carroll* holding. While police officers particularly are certainly involved in and essential to the enforcement of the law, they are not of the judicial system in the "administration of justice." Nor can potential threat of strike by those opposing the action taken by the city afford a basis for the creation of a right which does not otherwise exist. Redress of such grievance is not properly sought before the judicial branch of government. While sympathetic to the potential disruption to the functioning of the city of Philadelphia caused by a public employees strike, we are without power to direct the city to pay disability benefits on the basis of such a threat standing alone.

Although we cannot accept appellees' first argument, we are persuaded by their second argument that the circumstances of these cases render the *O'Donnell* holding inapplicable.

In these appeals we are confronted with the question of whether the city of Philadelphia may avoid payment of Regulation 32 benefits which it agreed to pay to its employees by mere failure of its legislative branch, the City Council, to appropriate sufficient funds to cover its liabilities under the regulation for fiscal 1970–1971. Clearly we are dealing with a "bargained for" benefit on the part of the public employees bringing these suits and we must examine the origin and nature of the employer-employee agreements creating these benefits and the resulting legally enforceable duty of the city of Philadelphia to provide such benefits. . . .

The powers of the city of Philadelphia are contained in its *Home Rule Charter.* This charter was enacted pursuant to the enabling legislation pertaining to cities of the first class contained in the act of April 21, 1949, P.L. 665, 53 P.S. Section 13101, *et seq.* Section 11 of that act delegated to the city of Philadelphia the power to regulate its own affairs and directed that the *Home Rule Charter*

> shall supersede any existing charter and all acts or parts of acts, local, special, or general, affecting the organization, government, and powers of such city, to the extent that they are inconsistent or in conflict therewith. All existing acts or parts of acts and ordinances affecting the organization, government, and powers of the city, not inconsistent or in conflict with the organic law so adopted, shall remain in full force.

However, Section 18 of the same act provides:

> Notwithstanding the grant of powers contained in this act, no city shall exercise powers contrary to, or in limitation or enlargement of, powers granted by acts of the General Assembly which are—
> (b) Applicable in every part of the Commonwealth.
> (c) Applicable to all the cities of the Commonwealth.

The grievance procedures set forth in Article III, Section 31 of the Pennsylvania Constitution and the 1968 implementing legislation are within the ambit of Section 18 of the 1949 enabling act. Therefore, the city of Philadelphia may not act in derogation of any of the rights guaranteed to policemen and firemen by the constitution and its implementing legislation applicable to all political subdivisions of the Commonwealth.

The city of Philadelphia and all political subdivisions were mandated by the constitution to carry into effect any arbitration award issued by a board "selected and acting in accordance with law. . . ." It is undisputed that both the policemen and firemen here involved were parties to binding arbitration awards as to their labor agreements with the city. These arbitration awards constitute the "findings of panels and commissions" contemplated by Article III, Section 31, *supra.* These awards include all the terms either resolved by the arbitration panel and specifically set forth or previously agreed upon by amicable negotiation and incorporated by reference.

Regulation 32 was a previously agreed-upon term which was not altered or adjusted by the specific resolutions in each award and was fully within the contemplation of the parties to the award during negotiation and arbitration. Because Regulation 32 was part of the labor agreement and therefore a necessary condition precedent to compliance by the parties to the award, the city of Philadelphia is bound by the award to continue Regulation 32 payments.

Simply because City Council refuses to appropriate sufficient funds to effectuate payment, the city as a public employer is not relieved of its duty to follow the mandate of the arbitration panel. The appropriation of funds does not involve the performance of any illegal act on the part of the city. Unquestionably the city has the power to make appropriations for all lawful purposes as defined in its *Home Rule Charter.* The city can lawfully make the necessary appropriation and, where it has a mandatory duty to do so pursuant to a valid arbitration award, a court may order that duty to be performed.

In the *Washington Arbitration Case,* 436 Pa. 168, 177, 259 A.2d 437, 442 (1969), our Supreme Court has stated,

> The essence of our decision is that an arbitration award may only require a public employer to do that which it could do voluntarily. We emphasize that this does not mean that a public employer may hide behind self-imposed legal restrictions. An arbitration award which deals only with proper terms and conditions of employment serves as a mandate to the legislative branch of the public employer, and if the terms of the award require affirmative action on the part of the legislature, they must take such action, if it is within their power to do so.

In that case, the Supreme Court concluded that the local government had no duty to pay hospital insurance premiums for members of public employees' families because such payment would be contrary to the provisions of the act of May 22, 1933, P.L. 927, 53 P.S. Sections 37403–53, regulating the conduct of third class cities, and therefore illegal. In the instant case, the city of Philadelphia is specifically vested with the power to make emergency appropriations to perform a legal duty.

The issue of what additional duties would be imposed upon the City government by a judicial order directing the appropriation of requisite funds is not before this court. We note, however, that our Supreme Court has spoken by way of dicta that the powers of the courts are broad enough to require a local government to raise taxes to provide the funds necessary for complete performance under the directives of an arbitration award benefiting policemen and firemen.

> Furthermore, if we do hear a case in which the tax millage, as a matter of record, cannot permissibly be raised so as to provide sufficient funds to pay the required benefits to the employees, it will still be open to this court to rule that the act of June 24, 1968, impliedly authorizes a court-approved millage ceiling increase to pay the arbitration award where necessary, or to hold that the municipal budget must be adjusted in other places in order to provide resources for policemen's or firemen's salaries. [*Harvey* v. *Russo,* 435 Pa. 183, 193, 255 A.2d 560, 565 (1969).]

. . .

The uniformed employees of the city of Philadelphia represented in these proceedings by District Council No. 33 of the American Federation of State, County, and Municipal Employees, AFL-CIO, are protected by no constitutional provision comparable to Article III, Section 31. The rights and duties of these employees and their public employer are contained in a collective bargaining agreement which became effective on February 20, 1968. Upon expiration this labor agreement was twice continued for an additional period through June 30, 1971 with several additional terms and conditions not here relevant. Therefore, the nonuniformed employees' relations with the city were governed by this agreement when the unilateral decision was made to terminate Regulation 32 benefits.

Two provisions of the negotiated agreement are essential to a full examination of appellees' rights. A section entitled "Service Incurred Disability" specifically includes the benefit provisions for permanent and total disability and permanent and partial disability contained in Regulation 32.

The second provision of the labor agreement which affects the rights and duties here contested is the "savings clause."

> In the event that any provisions are found to be inconsistent with, altered, or conditioned by provisions of the Civil Service regulations, the *Home Rule Charter,* or other statutes, then the provisions of such regulations, charter, or other statutes shall prevail.

The nonuniformed employees have on the one hand acquired a legally enforceable contract right against the city in terms of specific disability benefits. On the other hand, the enforcement of such benefits may not necessitate illegal or unauthorized action on the part of the city.

The *Home Rule Charter* is explicit in its prohibition of any payment of city funds due under an otherwise legal contract absent a previous appropriation for the purpose: Section 8–200(3), *Philadelphia Home Rule Charter.* If the employer were a private contractor, there is no question that the courts of Pennsylvania could enforce the terms and conditions of a binding collective bargaining agreement. See *Shaw Electric Company, Inc.* v. *International Brotherhood Electrical Workers Local Union No. 98,* 418 Pa. 1, 208 A.2d 769 (1965); *Building Service Employees International Union, Local 252* v. *Schlesinger, et al.,* 449 Pa. 448, 451 n.2, 269 A.2d 894, 895 n.2 (1970). But, because we are involved with a public employer, such enforcement is not so easily imposed by the courts.

The enforceability of contract rights for wages by public employees has been proscribed by the *O'Donnell* and *Baxter* decisions cited above.

However, we are of the considered opinion that both the logic and the underlying rationale of those decisions are clearly inappropriate to the instant facts and circumstances.

We are not here concerned with the payment of wages to public employees under a contract for which no appropriation has been made as was the case in *O'Donnell*. "Bargained for" benefits are the subject of this controversy which must represent a continuing obligation of the city even though such obligation is not susceptible to exact calculation and projection for any fiscal period. The emergency appropriation provision of the *Home Rule Charter* contemplates and provides for a method of funding unforeseen financial contingencies. No city employee can be expected to undertake the colossal task of examining a proposed city budget cast only in general terms and lump-sum appropriations to assure himself that there will be sufficient funds to pay his potential disability benefits. He is not an individual making a contract with the city for his unique services but rather a part of a large and complex collective bargaining process which renders former case law on the subject of public employee labor contracts inapposite, at least as to benefits of the kind with which we are here concerned.

The realities of modern urban life in the city of Philadelphia compel us to recognize that the government itself is not the only representative of the public interest but that equal modicums of public interest and benefit may be discovered in both the duties and responsibilities of the public employer and the public employees as a group. Certainly the public interest is best served by having a viable and active force of public service employees protected against unilateral disregard for their rights by the public employer. This awareness has been formalized in the new Public Employee Relations Act, *supra:*

> Section 101. The General Assembly of the Commonwealth of Pennsylvania declares that it is the public policy of this Commonwealth and the purpose of this act to promote orderly and constructive relationships between all public employers and their employees subject, however, to the paramount right of the citizens of this Commonwealth to keep inviolate the guarantees for their health, safety, and welfare.

We thus conclude that the city of Philadelphia has a judicially enforceable duty to its uniformed and nonuniformed employees to pay to those employees the Regulation 32 disability benefits to which they became entitled during the fiscal year 1970–1971, for which benefits they have not been paid, and that it must appropriate sufficient funds to perform this duty notwithstanding the exhaustion of the appropriation for such purpose in its 1970–1971 budget. However, until such an appropriation is made by the legislative branch of the government of the city of Philadelphia, there was and is no duty upon its executive officers, named as defendants in these suits, to continue payment of disability benefits upon exhaustion of the funds appropriated therefor. To compel them to do so would require them to perform an illegal act. We must, therefore, reverse the various orders of the lower court directing continuation of payment of such benefits by the named defendants absent funds appropriated for this purpose.

The orders of the lower court are otherwise affirmed.

Discussion Questions

1. What official action brought on the court actions in this case?
2. Describe the rulings in the *O'Donnell* and *Baxter* cases.
3. Why were *O'Donnell* and *Baxter* found to be inapplicable in the present proceeding?
4. Discuss the gist of the Washington arbitration case and its applicability in the instant fact situation.
5. Is the city in any way limited in its obligation to implement the terms of the collective bargaining agreements with municipal employees?

Section 13. Precedence of Seniority Clause Over Religious Preference

In prohibiting religious discrimination in employment in the private sector, Section 703(a)(1) of the Civil Rights Act of 1964 obligates employers to attempt to accommodate reasonably the religious needs of employees and potential employees if the adjustments can be achieved without adversely affecting the firm's business operations.

In *McCann L. Reid* v. *Memphis Publishing Co.,* 468 F.2d 346 (6th Cir. 1972) the plaintiff, a Seventh Day Adventist, applied for a copyreader position with the *Memphis Press-Scimitar,* demonstrated his qualifications during a day's trial period, and was offered a position by the editor. When he informed the editor that his religious beliefs would preclude Saturday employment the job offer was withdrawn with the condition that he could secure work if he decided that it would be possible for him to accept Saturday job assignments. In denying relief, the trial court indicated that the defendant was under no obligation "to accommodate an employee's or potential employee's religious belief contrary to the employer's established and required work schedule." [23] The court further indicated that new workers were assigned to Saturday work "to give preference of other work days to employees with more seniority. . . ." [24]

The following public sector decision has a quite similar fact situation and also involves a conflict between a negotiated seniority arrangement and an individual employee's religious preference.

Richard M. Dawson v. J. G. Mizell
United States District Court for the Eastern District of Virginia, Richmond Division, Civil Action No. 528–70–R[25]

MEMORANDUM

. . .

Plaintiff, a member of the Seventh Day Adventist Church whose tenets preclude labor on their Sabbath Day, which is from sundown Friday until sundown Saturday, is an employee of the United States Post Office Department in the capacity of a regular carrier.

Defendant Mizell, is the postmaster of the post office in Richmond, Virginia, wherein plaintiff is employed.

From the pleadings, stipulations, and evidence introduced before the court, the court finds that the plaintiff commenced his employment with the post office in June of 1966 as a temporary substitute carrier. Subsequently his employment was converted to a career appointment as a regular city carrier. The post office operates under an agreement between the United States Post Office Department and certain organizations of employees of the Post Office Department, which agreement calls for bidding for work assignments on the basis of seniority. As a practical result, when a vacancy in a position occurs, same is posted, mail carriers submit their applications for same, and award of the position is made on the basis of seniority.

At the time of plaintiff's initial employment, he was not a member of the Seventh Day Adventist Church but became so on May 9, 1970, although he had for some time prior thereto been observing the tenets of the church. There is no doubt of the plaintiff's conscientious and sincere belief in the teachings of his church.

By reason of his lack of seniority, plaintiff now finds himself assigned to a position which requires that he work on Saturday. In an effort to maintain his position consistent with his religious beliefs, plaintiff instead of working on the Saturdays on which he was scheduled to work took those days off and they were charged against accrued annual leave or charged as leave without pay.

On May 4, 1970, plaintiff was advised that he would be discharged from the postal service by reason of his excessive absences, to wit: five Saturdays during the months of February, March, and April of that year.

On October 2, 1970, a temporary restraining order was entered enjoining the defendant from removing the plaintiff from his position in the Post Office Department, Richmond, Virginia, for failure to perform work on Saturdays by reason of his religious convictions. This order was subsequently thereto elevated to a preliminary injunction pending the outcome of this litigation.

The court finds that plaintiff attempted to secure relief through the local union, but was unsuccessful. Under the agreement between the post office and the unions, any deviation of the same is a violation, except that the postmaster may make temporary assignments.

The defendant herein, in an effort to cooperate with the plaintiff, investigated and was advised that any temporary assignment of this plaintiff would be objected to by the union.

There are 1,865 employees in the post office system in Richmond. Of these employees, 381 are regular letter carriers, of whom 304 are assigned to work on Saturdays. A little more than a third of the employees in the system work on Saturdays.

There is available to the plaintiff the opportunity to transfer from a regular carrier to a substitute carrier, which would render to him the same amount of money that he is now paid, but would result in the loss of certain of his seniority privileges, which the plaintiff is understandably reluctant to do.

The court finds that the work of the post office requires that mail be processed on a seven day a week basis.

The court finds that the seniority provisions of the agreement between the post office and the unions are some of its more valued aspects. The agreements under which the post office works affect approximately 700,000 employees throughout the United States.

The plaintiff seeks relief from the defendant's intention to discharge him by reason of his inability to work on Saturdays.

The court finds that the assignment by defendant Mizell of the plaintiff to a position resulting in his having Saturdays off would be violative of the spirit as well as the substance of the agreement under which the post office employees work.

Plaintiff contends that defendant's contemplated removal of the plaintiff from the postal service by reason of his declining to work from sundown on Fridays until sundown on Saturdays would impose, under the circumstances of this case, a burden of the free exercise of his religion.

The court concludes that there is no constitutional prohibition against the defendant insisting that plaintiff either agree to perform the duties assigned to him or suffer the consequences. This court cannot agree with the suggestion of counsel that there would be little, if any, adverse effect on the federal interest in the operation of the Post Office Department and the delivery of the United States mail at Richmond, Virginia, resulting from the assignment of plaintiff to a six day work week with Saturday as a day off. True, the mere granting to plaintiff Saturdays off would not, in and of itself, affect the operation of the post office; but the court cannot overlook the fact that approximately 700,000 people are governed by the agreement which plaintiff suggests the defendant violate.

There can be no doubt from the evidence before this court, indeed from the plaintiff's own testimony, that the seniority rights contained in the agreement are of the utmost importance to the employees.

The court finds no infringement of plaintiff's rights concerning his religious beliefs. Religious discrimination should not be equated with failure to accommodate.

Since 1878 it has been recognized that the First Amendment cannot be interpreted as an absolute prohibition on the part of the government from interfering with the exercise of religion. The religious freedom guaranteed under our Constitution was that one could be assured that the legislature would make no law respecting the establishment of religion or prohibiting the free exercise thereof. See *Reynolds* v. *United States,* 98 U.S. 145 (1878). Since the *Reynolds* case it has been recognized that religious practices are subject to reasonable government interference under certain conditions and circumstances.

The First Amendment provides that "Congress shall make no law respecting an establishment of religion, or prohibiting the free exercise thereof. . . ." As a consequence, simply stated we have two religious clauses, one pertaining to "free exercise" and the other pertaining to the "establishment" of religion. The free exercise clause undoubtedly bars regulation of religious beliefs or interference with the dissemination of religious ideas. Its purpose is to prohibit misuse of secular governmental programs "to impede the observance of one or all religions or . . . to discriminate invidiously between religions . . . even though the burden may be characterized as being only indirect." *Gillette* v. *United States,* 39 U.S.L.W. 4305, decided March 8, 1971, quoting from *Braunfeld* v. *Brown,* 366 U.S. 599, 607.

Undoubtedly, any burden on First Amendment values must be justifiable in terms of a government's valid aims. Having concluded that in order to accommodate plaintiff's request to select his day off would require a violation on the part of defendant of a binding contract affecting 700,000 people, it is obvious that any incidental burden felt by the plaintiff is certainly justified when one considers that it would be literally impossible to accommodate the religious preference of every employee of the Post Office Department. As stated by Mr. Chief Justice Warren in *Braunfeld, supra,* ours is a cosmopolitan nation "made up of people of almost every conceivable religious preference. These denominations number almost three hundred. . . . Consequently it cannot be expected, much less required, that legislators enact any law regulating conduct that may in some way result in an economic disadvantage to some religious sects and not to others because of the special practices of the various religions." In *Braun-*

feld, supra, the court upheld the validity of a statute forbidding the retail sale on Sundays of certain commodities.

In addition, it should be noted that the central purpose of the establishment clause is to insure government neutrality in matters of religion. The rule of seniority as called for under the post office's agreement cannot, by any stretch of the imagination, be deemed to discriminate on the basis of religious affiliation or belief. All that the establishment clause requires is that when government activities touch on the religious sphere "they must be secular in purpose, evenhanded in operation, and neutral in primary impact." *Gillette* v. *United States, supra.*

Plaintiff contends that the court is bound by the rule laid out in *Sherbert* v. *Verner,* 374 U.S. 398. In that case appellant was a member of the Seventh Day Adventist Church who lost her position with a private employer by reason of her refusal to work on the Sabbath day of her faith. Unable to obtain other employment because from conscientious scruples she would not take said work, she filed a claim for unemployment compensation benefits under the South Carolina Unemployment Compensation Act. That act provided that to be eligible for benefits, a claimant must be "able to work and . . . available to work," and further that a claimant is ineligible for benefits if he has failed, without good cause, to accept available suitable work when offered him by the employment office or the employer. The South Carolina administrators held the appellant to be ineligible for benefits. Appellant's argument before the respective courts was to the effect that the provisions of the South Carolina law abridged her right to the free exercise of her religion secured under the free exercise clause of the First Amendment through the Fourteenth Amendment. The United States Supreme Court, speaking through Mr. Justice Brennan, stated that for appellant's constitutional challenge to be withstood, it must rest either because her disqualification as a beneficiary represented no infringement by the state of her constitutional right of free exercise, or because any incidental burden on the free exercise of appellant's religion may be justified by "compelling state interest in the regulation of a subject within the state's constitutional power to regulate. *NAACP* v. *Button,* 371 U.S. 415, 438. See also *Bates* v. *Little Rock,* 361 U.S. 516, 524.

It should be noted that in the *Sherbert* case it was pointed out that the law of South Carolina expressly saved the Sunday worshiper from having to make the kind of choice which was imposed upon the appellant in that case. Not so in our instant case. There is no evidence of any blanket permission to those who believe Sunday to be the Sabbath to be relieved from work. The holding in *Sherbert* was limited to a finding that a state "may not constitutionally apply the eligibility provisions so as to constrain a worker to abandon his religious convictions respecting the day of rest." That holding, paraphrasing the words of Justice Brennan, merely reaffirmed the principle to the effect that no state may exclude members of any faith, or lack of it, from receiving the benefits of public welfare legislation.

There is nothing in the instant case which suffers the plaintiff to be excluded from any rights because of his faith. The court finds no action on the part of the Post Office Department which interferes with plaintiff's right to exercise his religion as he sees fit. The fact that no regular mail deliveries are scheduled on Sunday, the court finds, is attributable to the fact that the business community dictates the workload. The court does not find *Sherbert* v. *Verner, supra,* to be apropos in the instant case. In that case the individual was discriminated against in allowance of a public benefit, as distinguished from the instant case.

It is true that there is, to a certain extent, a burden imposed on the plaintiff Dawson in reference to the exercise of his religious belief, to the extent that as a result of the defendant not accommodating the post office work schedule to coincide with plaintiff's exercise of his religion, the instant unfortunate situation is created. But as heretofore stated, accommodation cannot be equated with discrimination.

While the court does not find that any burden imposed upon the plaintiff Dawson is constitutionally prohibited, even were the court to find that the free exercise and establishment clauses were brought into play in the instant case, it can hardly be argued that there is not a compelling governmental interest in the post office entering into an agreement providing for seniority rights; for as a corollary to those rights the post office is assured of adequate personnel in the movement of the mail. The burden on this agency of the government to accommodate its pattern of work to the special requirements of each individual's religion would result in a chaotic and impossible situation.

Plaintiff's contention that the actions of the defendant are prohibited by the 1964 Civil Rights Act by virtue of Executive Order 11478, August 8, 1969, has no validity in the instant case.

As sympathetic as the court may be with plaintiff's predicament, the court finds no violation on the part of the defendant of any constitutional right of the plaintiff, and the injunction heretofore entered must be dissolved.

An order consistent with these findings will be entered.

Dated: March 24, 1971 /s/ Robert R. Merhige, Jr.
United States District Judge

Discussion Questions

1. Could the plaintiff have made an adjustment in his work schedule that would have resolved the basic difficulty?

2. What potential consequences might ensue if the employer granted the request for nonSabbath employment?
3. Discuss the basic conflict that resulted from the request for religious preference.
4. Analyze the constitutional aspects of religious freedom and their relevance to the facts in this case.
5. Did the plaintiff's local union play a significant role in this case?
6. Why did the appellate court disagree with the trial court's ruling?
7. Contrast this case with the *Sherbert* decision.

Section 14. Interpretation of a Sabbatical Leave Clause in a Contract

In private employment, both parties have access to the courts for suits alleging contract violations. In the last case in this chapter, although the term *breach* is not used, the plaintiffs are in fact claiming that a negotiated clause was not properly implemented by the defendant and are relying on a court action to determine whose interpretation was proper.

Betty Eagle, Robert Covyeau, Oliver Vogel, and the Englewood Cliffs Education Association (a nonprofit corporation of the state of New Jersey) v. Board of Education of the Borough of Englewood Cliffs, Bergen County
Superior Court of New Jersey, Law Division: Bergen County, Docket No. L–15025–71, Oral Decision[26]

THE COURT

On January 20, 1971, the three individual plaintiffs, teachers in the Englewood school system, and the corporate plaintiff, their association, brought this action. . . . Proceeding by an order to show cause the plaintiffs sought to restrain defendant from adopting any budget for the ensuing year until the dispute before the court was resolved. In brief, plaintiffs sought to compel defendant to include sufficient funds in its budget to finance three sabbatical leaves. Plaintiffs contended that defendant intended to provide funds for only two such leaves. By order of this court the public hearing on the budget proceeded but no vote could be taken on its adoption. On January 27, the return day of the order to show cause, defendant moved to dissolve the preliminary restraint issued and this motion was granted. The court could find no authority, nor could plaintiffs cite any, that would permit the court to interfere with the legislative function of the board as mandated by N.J.S.A. 18(a): 22–7. In support of its motion to dissolve, defendant submitted the affidavit of Harold

Klotz, president of defendant board. The affidavit revealed the existence of a "Current Operating Appropriations Budget" or surplus with funds clearly sufficient to finance the additional sabbatical if plaintiffs were to prevail here. The court then ordered defendant to set aside or earmark the sum of $5,200, which sum represents the cost of one sabbatical, pending final disposition of this matter. It should be noted that the court in no way interfered with the budget per se, and it is assumed that appropriate action has taken place pursuant to law.

Now plaintiffs seek to obtain relief in the form of an adjudication that plaintiffs are entitled to three sabbaticals. On the other hand, defendant moves to dismiss the complaint on several grounds. At this point the court will elaborate on the facts underlying this controversy and briefly touched upon previously.

On January 22, 1970, plaintiff association and defendant entered into an employment agreement of one year's duration, effective July 1, 1970 through July 31, 1971, and encompassing some twenty-three articles. It is Article 19, entitled "Sabbatical Leaves," which has given rise to the dispute at bar. It provides:

A. A sabbatical leave shall be granted to a teacher for study, including study in another area of specialization, for travel, or for other reasons of value to the school system as approved by the board upon recommendation of the superintendent.

B. Sabbatical leaves shall be granted, subject to the following conditions:

1. If there are sufficient qualified applications, sabbatical leaves shall be granted to a maximum of 4 percent of teachers at any one time.
2. Requests for sabbatical leave must be received by the superintendent in writing in such form as may be mutually agreed upon by the association and the superintendent, no later than December 15, and action must be taken on all such requests no later than the first public board meeting in March of the school year for which the sabbatical leave is requested.
3. The teacher has completed at least seven full school years of service in the district.
4. A teacher on sabbatical leave shall be paid by the board at two-thirds of the salary rate which he would have received if he had remained on active duty, based on a ten months' salary schedule.
5. The period of sabbatical program shall be ten months between July 1 and the beginning of school in the subsequent year.
6. No full time employment shall be undertaken by a person on sabbatical leave. Part time employment must be approved by the superintendent of schools.
7. As a condition of eligibility for sabbatical leave, the teacher shall promise to return to service in Englewood Cliffs for at least one year following such leave.

8. No tuition stipends shall be granted during the sabbatical leave year.
9. On returning to classroom service after sabbatical leave, the teacher shall obtain all salary and fringe benefits as would have been obtained had he been active in his regular position for one year.

Pursuant to Article 19 the three individual plaintiffs applied for sabbatical leaves. The superintendent of schools has advised the plaintiffs that all three qualified, but he could only choose two as per instructions from defendant board. Thereafter the plaintiffs brought the matter to this court.

Construction of Language in Agreement

We now reach the merits of the controversy before the court. Once again, the pertinent language in Article 19 reads:

A. Sabbatical leaves shall be granted, subject to the following conditions:

1. If there are sufficient qualified applicants, sabbatical leaves shall be granted to a maximum of 4 percent of teachers at any one time.

It is defendant's contention that the word "teachers" means only those actually in the classroom and not what are termed teacher aides. The affidavits of the superintendent of schools and the president of the Board of Education state that the staff consists of 72.4 teachers, the fraction accounting for two teachers not employed on a full time basis. The superintendent does not consider eleven teacher aides in arriving at his figure. In effect, defendant disputes the definition of "teachers" in the agreement which bears defendant's signature. Article I of the agreement states:

Unless otherwise indicated, the term "teachers," when used hereinafter in this agreement, shall refer to all professional employees represented by the association in the negotiating unit as above defined.

When checking the appropriate definition, it is found that the association represents "regular and special teachers, librarians, nurses, psychologist, guidance counselor, teacher aides, and coordinators." Plaintiff's verified complaint states that there are eighty-five teachers within this definition. By a process of simple arithmetic, 4 percent of eighty-five would be 3.4 or 3 teachers. Defendant cannot now complain that the meaning of "teachers" was dependent on its context in a particular provision. The language is clear and the court has no duty other than to carry its meaning into effect. *Korb* v. *Spray Beach Hotel Co.*, 24 N.J. Super, 151 App. Div. (1953). It is obvious that defendant's argument in this regard must fail. Moreover, even if the court were to accept defendant's figure of 72.4, then 2.89 teachers would be involved. Obviously the court would consider this as 3 teachers in the same manner that 3.4 would be 3 and not 4. Defendant must remember that the sabbatical leave is of value to the teacher, student, and school system, to all parties involved. Therefore, it behooves the court to attempt to give full meaning to the language of the agreement.

The crux of the problem lies in the language "Sabbatical leaves shall be granted to a maximum of 4 percent of teachers." It is defendant's position that the inclusion of the word "maximum" empowers defendant in its discretion to grant sabbaticals to less than 4 percent of the qualified applicants. Apparently defendant believes that 4 percent would be clearly entitled only in the absence of the word "maximum." Plaintiffs first note the use of the word "shall" and its connotation of a mandatory, not discretionary action. . . .

Plaintiffs thus read the word *maximum* as provision for the "situation where there may be applications by qualified persons in excess of 4 percent of the teachers."

It cannot be said that the language is clear and unambiguous. Under the circumstances the court must resort to the rules of construction. . . . Professor Williston states, "The fundamental object of all rules of interpretation, whether primary or secondary, is to ascertain and give effect to the intention of the parties. . . ."

If the defendant is correct then the corollary of its position must be that it can grant no sabbatical leaves if it sees fit. For if defendant can grant leaves to less than 4 percent of the teachers, what is to prevent defendants from allowing only one or even none as opposed to the two it opts for here. The effect of this would be to render meaningless a right bargained for by plaintiffs. In *Russell* v. *Princeton Laboratories Inc.,* 50 N.J. 30, 38 (1967), although the court was speaking about a possible forfeiture in an employees' profit sharing trust, some of its language is pertinent: "A contract should not be read to vest a party or his nominee with the power virtually to make his promise illusory." The same principle should apply to a contractual provision. Moreover, Professor Corbin states it thusly:

> If, therefore, the words of a contract have more than one possible meaning and one of these includes or would produce a legal effect that the court believes the parties intended to produce, while another one would not, the court should unhesitatingly adopt the first meaning. On the other hand, a specific provision in an otherwise valid contract should not be given a meaning that would have a legal effect that the court is convinced the parties did not intend, even though any alternative meaning will cause the provision to have no legal effect whatever. 3 *Corbin on Contracts* Section 546 at 169.

Certainly here the court cannot say that it at all convinced the parties intended the interpretation that defendant asserts. . . . It is certainly in the public interest that teachers who comprise the staff of public schools should receive what is rightfully theirs through collective bargaining. Equally it is in the public interest that guardians of the public trust, such as defendant, should protect the public's tax dollars while simultaneously providing for the best possible in public education. . . .

Finally, a perusal of defendant's first draft of its budget on December 16, 1970 . . . shows that defendant appropriated an amount sufficient to finance three such sabbaticals. Clearly, while this is not dispositive of the matter, it bears mention. Professor Williston in his treatise states:

> An important aid in the interpretation of contracts is the practical construction placed on the agreement by the parties themselves. The process of practical interpretation and application is a further indication of the meaning which they have placed upon the terms of the contract they have made. Courts give great weight to these expressions, be they acts or declarations.

For the reasons given, the court is convinced that plaintiffs' interpretation of the language is the correct one. It is this interpretation that best fulfills the rights and equities of the parties.

Discussion Questions

1. What did the court do to ensure that sufficient funds would be available to fund the sabbaticals?
2. Which contract terminology was disputed as to its meaning? Were there ambiguities?
3. Why did the court find for the plaintiffs?
4. Is the definition of "teachers" important? Why?
5. Describe the rules of construction the court resorts to in order to clarify the ambiguous contract language.

CHAPTER 4

1 61 GERR 201 (RF–51) (Washington, D.C.: BNA, Inc., 1972).

2 Milton Derber, "Who Negotiates for the Public Employer?" Institute of Labor and Industrial Relations, University of Illinois Bulletin (July 2, 1969), p. 53.

3 Defense Supply Agency Regulation No. 1426 (July 9, 1970), p. 15.

4 Collective Bargaining in Public Employment and the Merit System, U.S. Department of Labor (Washington, D.C.: United States Government Printing Office, April, 1972), pp. 66–67.

5 61 GERR 201 loc. cit.

6 GERR (No. 402) (F1–2) (Washington, D.C.: BNA, Inc., 5–24–71).

7 GERR (No. 396) (E1–2) (Washington, D.C.: BNA, Inc., 4–12–71).

8 LRX 73, sec. 26 (Washington, D.C.: BNA, Inc., 1971).

9 LRX 58a, sec. 4 (Washington, D.C.: BNA, Inc., 1965).

10 *Ibid.*

11 LRX 87, sec. 3 (Washington, D.C.: BNA, Inc., 1971).

12 LRX 95, sec. 23 (Washington, D.C.: BNA, Inc., 1971).

13 LRX 58a, sec. 3; 58b, sec. 5; 59, sec. 7; 60, secs. 8, 9 (Washington, D.C.: BNA, Inc., 1971).

14 William J. Kilberg, "Appropriate Subjects for Bargaining in Local Government Labor Relations," *Maryland Law Review,* Vol. XXX, No. 3 (Summer, 1970), pp. 188–189.

15 LRX 58a, *loc. cit.*

16 21 GERR 7029–7031 (RF–57) (Washington, D.C.: BNA, Inc., 1973).

17 Kilberg, *op. cit.,* p. 193.

18 GERR (No. 426) (F1–3) 11–8–71.

19 LRX 92, sec. 15 (Washington, D.C.: BNA, Inc., 1971).

20 LRX 87, sec. 2 (Washington, D.C.: BNA, Inc., 1971).

21 LRX 129, sec. 19 (Washington, D.C.: BNA, Inc., 1969).

22 21 GERR 7023–7025 (RF–56) (Washington, D.C.: BNA, Inc., 1972).

23 5 *Employment Practices Decisions* 6725 (Chicago, Ill.: Commerce Clearing House, Inc., 1972).

24 *Ibid.,* p. 6728.

25 GERR (No. 417) (E1–4) (Washington, D.C.: BNA, Inc., Sept. 6, 1971).

26 GERR (No. 396) (F1–3) (Washington, D.C.: BNA, Inc., April 12, 1971).

5 | Unfair Labor Practices

IN the book thus far the reader will have noted that unfair labor practice charges have been brought in a number of cases: that is, improper election conduct, refusal to bargain in good faith, failure to meet contract obligations, and the like, where other aspects of the fact situations were investigated to the exclusion of the key elements involved in a determination of improper practices. In this chapter the variety of unfair labor practices that have constituted the basis for complaint charges in the public sector will be discussed in greater detail. Space limitations preclude an exhaustive treatment of this topic, but an effort will be made to include representative case materials.

In private employment, the NLRA, as amended, sets out in detail a list of both unfair employer and unfair union practices. Management is not to interfere with the organizational rights of employees; dominate or interfere with the formation or administration of a labor organization or make financial contributions or other support to it; discriminate in regard to hire or tenure of employment to encourage or discourage membership in any labor organization; discharge or otherwise discriminate against an employee because he has filed charges or given testimony under the act; or refuse to bargain collectively with representatives designated or selected by the majority of employees in a bargaining unit. Unions are not to "coerce employees who do not want to join a union; force employers to pressure workers into joining a union; force an employer to discriminate against an employee whom the union refuses to admit to membership; refuse to bargain collectively with the employer; engage in certain types of secondary boycotts; charge excessive initiation fees when union membership is compulsory because of a union shop agreement; and . . . force an employer to pay for services not performed." [1]

Executive Order 11491 governing labor-management relations in the federal government, the various state statutes, and municipal ordinances controlling the same subject matter are closely patterned after the private sector legislation. Section 19 of the order prohibits the federal government as an employer and labor organizations representing its employees from interfering with, restraining, or coercing employees in their exercise of their organizational rights, and from encouraging or discouraging membership

278

by discrimination in regard to hiring, tenure, promotion, or other conditions of employment. Other prohibited conduct includes the sponsoring, controlling, or assisting of any labor organization, or the disciplining of any employee who has filed a complaint or offered testimony under the program. The federal government and its agencies are also prohibited from refusing to grant appropriate recognition or from refusing to consult, confer, or negotiate with a union as required by the order. Similarly, unions are not to coerce their members through punishment or reprisal with the intent of hindering or impeding their performance as federal employees. Labor organizations are also prohibited from initiating strikes, work stoppages, or slowdowns; engaging in related picketing against the government; or discriminating against an individual employee with regard to terms and conditions of membership because of race, creed, color, or national origin.

The various state laws and a number of city ordinances define unfair labor practices in substantially the same way.

Section 1. Preelection Conduct as an Infringement on Organizational Rights

Experience has demonstrated that employers and unions are generally able to agree on appropriate election details so that all eligible voters are provided an opportunity to cast a free and secret ballot during appropriate times. However, the conduct of the parties in the campaign preceding the actual balloting may be such that improper influences will prevent the employee from making a rational choice. As to the election itself, no electioneering can be allowed in or near polling places. Election campaign literature should be removed from polling places and nearby areas. The parties are encouraged to agree on a neutral zone around a poll to minimize the possibility of objections. In many cases labor organizations agree that there will be no distribution of any election campaign literature on election day. Despite these precautions, numerous types of wrongdoing occur, and in fact, as will be shown, a variety of improper activities may actually characterize one fact situation.

Pennsylvania Labor Relations Board v. Conemaugh Valley Memorial Hospital

Commonwealth of Pennsylvania, Pennsylvania Labor Relations Board
Case Nos. PERA–C–1262–C, PERA–C–1271–C

NISI DECISION AND ORDER

A charge of unfair practices was filed with the Pennsylvania Labor Relations Board, hereinafter referred to as the board, on September 8,

1971, and supplemented on September 15, 1971 by Local 1199P, National Union of Hospital and Nursing Home Employees, hereinafter referred to as complainant. The charges allege that the Conemaugh Valley Memorial Hospital, hereinafter referred to as respondent, had engaged in unfair practices contrary to the provisions of the Public Employee Relations Act, hereinafter referred to as the act, and more particularly contrary to Section 803, and clauses (1) and (5) of Section 1201, subsection (a).

Specifically the complainant charged that respondent made repeated telephone calls to its employees, threatened to reduce wages, held captive audience meetings, granted a unilateral wage increase, failed to post the sample ballot and eligibility list along with the order and notice of election, granted Blue Cross and Blue Shield coverage to its employees, and issued refund checks to the employees two days before the election.

The complaint and supplemental complaint were consolidated for the purpose of hearing. Said hearing was held on October 5, 1971, pursuant to the complaints and notices of hearing issued by the board on September 16 and 22, 1971. The hearing was continued from October 5, 1971 to Novem-23 and 24, 1971, and concluded on February 1, 1972, with testimony being reported in four separate volumes.

At the hearing held before Alan H. Krier, Esq., the duly designated hearing examiner of the board, a full opportunity to examine and cross-examine witnesses, present testimony, and introduce evidence was afforded to all parties in interest.

The board, on the basis of the testimony and evidence presented at the hearing and from all other matters and documents of record, makes the following:

FINDINGS OF FACT

1. That the Conemaugh Valley Memorial Hospital is a nonprofit institution operating in the Commonwealth of Pennsylvania.

2. That Local 1199P, National Union of Hospital and Nursing Home Employees, affiliated with the AFL-CIO, is an employee organization which exists for the purpose, in whole or in part, of dealing with employers concerning grievances, wages, rates of pay, hours of employment, and terms and conditions of employment.

3. That organizational activity on the part of the complainant came to the attention of respondent in March, 1971 (N.T. Vol. 1, p. 20).

4. That a petition for representation was filed by complainant on April 1, 1971, and an election was scheduled as a result thereof on September 9, 1971, by order and notice of election, PERA–R–1028–C, issued August 23, 1971.

5. That on April 27, August 10, August 25, August 27, and Septem-

ber 7, respondent held meetings with its employees to put forth its views about petitioner and the coming election (N.T. Vol. 2, pp. 55–58, 103–104).

6. That several months prior to the election, respondent promulgated a broad no-solicitation rule, but approved the wearing of antiunion buttons in work areas while the rule was in effect (N.T. Vol. 4, pp. 93–94, 96–97).

7. That at least one employee was told to remove his union button by his supervisor pursuant to the no-solicitation rule, at the direction of respondent's public relations director (N.T. Vol. 3, pp. 61–67; Vol. 4, pp. 4–7, 63–66).

8. That respondent approved the extension of Blue Cross and Blue Shield coverage to its employees on July 22, 1971, but waited until July 30, 1971 before instructing the assistant credit manager to start working up the necessary information for the refund of the employee July payments (N.T. Vol. 1, pp. 49–52; Vol. 4, pp. 83–84).

9. That the information necessary for the issuance of the refund checks was ready August 15, but the checks were not issued until September 7 (N.T. Vol. 4, pp. 83–84, 86; Vol. 1, p. 55).

10. That one of the items of campaign literature distributed by respondent was a poster made up of excerpts from newspaper articles concerning the strike at Ingleside Hospital in Ohio; with said poster being distributed on the hospital premises September 8, the day before the election (N.T. Vol. 2, p. 70).

11. That the Ingleside poster had deleted from it the name of the union involved in the strike at that hospital, and was authorized to be posted in that manner by the hospital administrator with the knowledge that the union involved was not Local 1199 (N.T. Vol. 2, pp. 70–72).

12. That the same day the Ingleside poster was distributed, a letter which dealt with petitioner's alleged propensity for protracted strikes was hand delivered to employees (N.T. Vol. 3, pp. 69–70, 82).

13. That respondent failed to post the sample ballot and eligibility list as directed by the board's order and notice of election (N.T. Vol. 1, pp. 12–16).

DISCUSSION

At the hearing petitioner withdrew the specification charging respondent with making repeated telephone calls to its employees and amended paragraph (2) of Charge 1262–C to include "threatening loss of jobs and/or employment at captive audience meetings." After the hearing petitioner withdrew the charges concerning the respondent's granting a unilateral wage increase and Blue Cross and Blue Shield coverage shortly before the election.

The specifications in the complaints may now be summarized as charging respondent with holding captive audience meetings; allowing employees to wear antiunion buttons, while forbidding them to wear prounion buttons; issuing refund checks for the employees' Blue Cross and Blue Shield coverage on September 7, 1971; failing to post the eligibility list and sample ballot as directed by the board's order and notice of election, PERA–R–1028–C issued August 23, 1971; and issuing campaign literature containing material misrepresentations at such a time as to render impossible the holding of a valid election. Each of these specifications will be discussed separately below.

CAPTIVE AUDIENCE MEETINGS

Under the rule laid down in *Livingston Shirt Corp.*, 107 NLRB 400, 409 (1953), "in the absence of either an unlawfully broad no-solicitation rule (prohibiting union access to company premises on other than working time) or a privileged no-solicitation rule (broad, but not unlawful because of the character of the business), an employer does not commit an unfair labor practice if he makes a preelection speech on company time and premises to his employees and denies the union's request for an opportunity to reply." This general statement may be taken as the rule in Pennsylvania, subject to the board's determination that other channels of communication were available to the union for the purpose of reaching the employees.

In the instant case there was testimony that it was understood that the no-solicitation rule was to apply only to working hours, and thus was lawful (N.T. Vol. 4, pp. 94–95). It further appears from the volume of prounion literature and the number of union meetings held that at least these lines of communication were open to the complainants.

In view of the above, it cannot be said that the captive audience speeches made by respondent in this case, were, of themselves, an unfair practice.

PROHIBITING THE WEARING
OF PROUNION BUTTONS

Complainant contends that by approving the wearing of antiunion buttons, while forbidding the wearing of prounion buttons, respondent committed an unfair practice. Respondent, on the other hand, contends that the antiunion buttons were presented for approval to the hospital administrator as required by the no solicitation rule, while the prounion buttons were not so presented. Respondent, however, overlooks the fact that wearing union insignia has long been held to be a reasonable form of union activity, and as such is protected by Article IV of the act, and can be forbidden only where some valid business reason is put forth to justify the prohibition. By attempting to call button wearing solicitation, respondent fails to change its true nature; and by relying on the no-solicitation rule to justify its prohibition, respondent has committed an unfair practice in violation of Section 1201, subsection (a), clause (1). *Floridan Hotel of Tampa, Inc.,* 137 NLRB 1484, 50 L.R.R.M. 1433 (1962).

ISSUANCE OF BLUE CROSS AND BLUE SHIELD REFUND CHECKS

Complainant also charges respondent with attempting to influence the election by issuing checks to a large number of its employees on September 7, 1971, two days before the election. The check represented respondent's decision to extend Blue Cross and Blue Shield coverage to its employees, and was a refund of the employees' August payments which were made in July.

The recommendation to grant such coverage to the employees of the hospital was made by the Hospital Council of Western Pennsylvania, as part of its annual recommendation of wage and benefit increases. Respondent first informed its employees that it was considering the Hospital Council's recommendations on April 20, 1971, one month after the union's organizing campaign had begun, with the plan finally being adopted by the hospital on July 22, 1971 (N.T. Vol. I, pp. 49–52). Although the timing of the plan's adoption by respondent was fortuitous to say the least, it was recommended and adopted in the same manner as such increases in prior years, and cannot be said to be unlawful interference in the election. *Sheboygan Sausage Co.,* 156 NLRB No. 130, 61 L.R.R.M. 1299 (1966).

Issuing the Blue Cross and Blue Shield refund checks two days before the election however, presents a different situation. There was testimony by the person charged with preparing the information for the checks that the processing of them was merely "extra work" for the assistant credit manager, and that the information necessary for their issuance was done by August 15, 1971 (N.T. Vol. 4, pp. 83–84). This is in direct conflict with the hospital administrator's testimony that "We worked on it continually until we could finally make the rebate on September 7, 1971" and "we wanted to get rid of it as soon as we could" (N.T. Vol. 1, p. 55).

From the foregoing it is apparent that while the timing of the increase in employee benefits may have been fortuitous, the issuance of the refund check two days before the election was not, but was rather an attempt to illegally influence the outcome of the election. *NLRB* v. *Tennessee Packers, Inc., Frosty Morn Division,* CA6, 65 L.R.R.M. 2619 (1967) enf'g 154 NLRB 819 (1965).

RESPONDENT'S CAMPAIGN LITERATURE

There was vigorous preelection campaigning by both the union and respondent, with at least 100 different pieces of antiunion literature distributed by the employer alone. Complainant contends that several pieces of this antiunion literature were materially misleading and issued at such a time so as to prevent an effective reply by the union.

Perhaps the most devastating example of complainant's charge is Exhibit C–42, referred to as the "Ingleside poster," which was posted September 8, 1971, the day before the election. This poster consisted of a series of excerpts from newspaper articles describing a tragic situation which occurred at Ingleside, Ohio. One of the articles begins as follows: "Blaming threats of bombing, arson, and future strike violence, Ingleside Hospital has closed its doors and will be put up for sale. . . ."

The article goes on to describe how strikers prevented essential services from reaching the hospital, how nonstrikers and administrators were threatened, and how patients had to be moved to other hospitals for their safety. The articles were introduced with the caption, "Don't Let This Happen Here." The name of the union involved in this strike was deleted in such a manner that it appeared as a defect in copying or typing rather than a complete and intentional obliteration.

The same day that Exhibit C–42 was posted, a letter was distributed to employees (Exhibit C–15, 16). The letter dealt with 1199's strike record inferring that this union was given to protracted strikes. The deletion on the Ingleside poster, together with the letter, makes it clear that it was intended that the employees would think that Local 1199 was involved at Ingleside.

By taking the letter and poster together with the public relations director's statement at a captive audience meeting on September 7, 1971 that a union had stopped medical supplies and oxygen from getting into a hospital and that he would kill the first person that tried to stop him from getting into the hospital (N.T. Vol. 2, pp. 103–104; Vol. 3, p. 29), the tone which the hospital was trying to set for the election, by its misrepresentations, becomes apparent.

Although the board does not wish to interject itself into preelection campaigns and sit as a judge of permissible propaganda, it must in this case hold that such campaign tactics are unacceptable. This in no way is meant to limit or penalize hard electioneering by either party. To the contrary, vigorous campaigns are to be encouraged, for it is in this way that the employees can best be informed of and evaluate the position of the employer and the union. However, the board cannot permit material misrepresentations to be foisted upon employees at the eleventh hour so that effective reply by the other party is prevented and an informed choice by the employees is precluded. *Hollywood Ceramics Co.,* 140 NLRB 221 51 L.R.R.M. 1600 (1962); *Walgren Co.,* 140 NLRB, 1141, 52 L.R.R.M. 1193 (1963).

FAILURE TO POST SAMPLE BALLOT AND ELIGIBILITY LIST

Complainant's final charge concerns respondent's failure to post the sample ballot and eligibility list as required by the order and notice of election, PERA–R–1028–C, August 23, 1971, and by Rule 6.1 of the Public Employee Relations Act Rules.

The purpose of including a sample ballot with the notice of election is obvious. It gives the employees an advanced look as to the set-up in the ballot and prevents confusion at the polls with the attendant possibility that the vote of the employees may be incorrectly registered. For this reason it is mandatory that the sample ballot be included in the posting.

The hospital attempted to excuse its failure to follow the order of the board by asserting that a telephone call was made to an employee of the board, who informed it that the sample ballot and eligibility list need not be posted. Whatever may be the truth of this testimony, the fact remains that posting of these items is required by the rules and was clearly stated in the order and notice of election.

The foregoing events must be considered in the context in which they occurred, for as was said by the national board in *General Shoe Corp.,* 77 NLRB 124, 127, 21 L.R.R.M. 1337, 1341 (1948), "In election proceedings, it is the board's function to provide a laboratory in which an experiment may be conducted, under conditions as nearly ideal as possible, to determine the uninhibited desires of the employees."

As a result of the respondent's timing of the issuance of the employees' refund checks, the content and timing of the campaign literature, and the prohibition on the wearing of union buttons such laboratory conditions were not present here, and the experiment must be conducted again.

CONCLUSIONS OF LAW

The board, therefore, after due consideration of the foregoing and the record as a whole, concludes and finds

1. That the Conemaugh Valley Hospital is a "public employer" within the meaning of Section 301, subsection (1) of the act.

2. That Local 1199P of the National Union of Hospital and Nursing Home Employees, is an employee organization within the meaning of Section 301, subsection (3) of the act.

3. That the Pennsylvania Labor Relations Board has jurisdiction over the parties hereto.

4. That respondent failed to post properly the notice of election as required by Rule 6.1 of the Public Employee Relations Act Rules.

5. That respondent attempted to influence the outcome of the election by making material misrepresentations regarding the involvement of complainant in the Ingleside strike, in violation of Section 1201, subsection (a), clause (1) of the act.

6. That respondent attempted to influence the outcome of the election by issuing a refund check two days before the election, in violation of Section 1201, subsection (a), clause (1).

7. That respondent attempted to influence the outcome of the election by prohibiting the wearing of union buttons, in violation of Section 1201, subsection (a), clause (1) of the act.

8. That respondent's actions listed in conclusions 4 to 7 did interfere with the employees in the exercise of the rights guaranteed to them in Article IV of the act, and to such an extent that the employees' freedom of choice in the election of September 9, 1971 was impaired.

9. That respondent has not committed any unfair practice in violation of Section 803 of the act.

10. That respondent has not committed any unfair practice in violation of Section 1201, subsection (a), clause (5) of the act.

ORDER

The Pennsylvania Labor Relations Board, therefore, after due consideration of the foregoing and the record as a whole, hereby orders and directs that Conemaugh Valley Memorial Hospital shall

1. Cease and desist from in any manner interfering with, restraining, or coercing its employees in the exercise of their rights to organize, form, join, or assist in employee organizations or to engage in lawful concerted activities for the purpose of collective bargaining or other mutual aid and protection within the meaning of Section 1201(a)(1) of the act.

2. Cease and desist from in any manner refusing to obey the orders and directives of the board and specifically in failing to post properly notices of election or other material ordered posted by the board within the meaning of Section 1201(a)(7) of the act.

3. Take the following affirmative corrective action which the board finds necessary pursuant to Section 605(6) of the Public Employee Relations Act:

> (a) Post the notice of second election to be ordered by the board as required by Rule 6.1 of the Public Employee Relations Act rules.

(b) Do not attempt to influence the outcome of the second election by making any material misrepresentations regarding the involvement of Local 1199P, National Union of Hospital and Nursing Home Employees in the Ingleside strike or otherwise.

(c) Do not attempt to influence the outcome of the second election by taking any unilateral action by issuing refund checks or otherwise.

(d) Do not attempt to influence the outcome of the second election by prohibiting the wearing of union buttons or otherwise.

(e) Post a copy of this order within five (5) days from the effective date hereof in a conspicuous place readily accessible to the employees and have the same so posted for a period of ten (10) consecutive days.

(f) Furnish satisfactory evidence to the Pennsylvania Labor Relations Board by affidavit or affidavit of compliance with this order within twenty (20) days from the effective date hereof.

It is hereby further ordered and directed that in the absence of any exceptions filed pursuant to Rule 15.1 of the rules and regulations of the Pennsylvania Labor Relations Board, approved October 9, 1970, as amended, within ten (10) days of the date hereof, this decision and order shall become and be absolute and final; that a copy of this order shall be posted within five (5) days from the effective date hereof in a conspicuous place readily accessible to the employees and have the same so posted for a period of ten (10) consecutive days.

Signed, sealed and dated at Harrisburg, Pennsylvania, this 27th day of July, 1972.

Pennsylvania Labor Relations Board

/s/ Raymond L. Scheib
Chairman

/s/ Joseph J. Licastro
Member

Discussion Questions

1. List and discuss the types of improper activities in which the respondent engaged prior to the election.
2. What is the *Livingston Shirt Corp.* rule? Did the respondent violate it?
3. Can an employer prohibit the wearing of prounion buttons during a preelection campaign?

4. Distinguish between the issuance by the respondent of Blue Cross and Blue Shield refund checks and the facts in the *Sheboygan Sausage Co.* case.
5. Did the respondent make material misrepresentations in its campaign literature?
6. Why is it important for the employer to post a sample ballot and eligibility list prior to the election?

Section 2. The Distribution of Antiunion Statements by an Employee

Situations arise in which a small number of promanagement workers actively participate in a preelection campaign in an attempt to persuade their fellow employees to vote against the presence of a labor organization in the affairs of the firm. A question then arises as to whether these individuals were acting on their own or as agents of the employer in the dissemination of antiunion propaganda. In private employment the U.S. Supreme Court ruled in the *International Association of Machinists* v. *NLRB*, 7 L.R.R.M. 282 (1940), "that rank-and-file employees may be held to be employer agents when the other employees have reasonable cause for believing that the employees are acting on the employer's behalf." [2] There must, in other words, be grounds for believing that the persons distributing the literature are authorized to speak for the employer. For example, the NLRB will hold an employer responsible for representations made by supervisors unless the employer "effectively repudiates them." [3] Of course, a determination must be made that the individuals were acting in a supervisory capacity in the first place.

In the Matter of

California Army National Guard, 1st Battalion, 250th Artillery Air Defense (respondent) *and* National Association of Government Employees, Local R12–35 (Ind.) (complainant)

Case No. 70–1532 [4]

(United States Department of Labor before the Assistant Secretary for Labor–Management Relations)

DECISION AND ORDER

On March 23, 1971, Hearing Examiner Henry L. Segal issued his report and recommendations in the above-entitled proceeding, finding that the complainant had not met the burden of proof with respect to the 19 (a)(1) and (2) allegations contained in the complaint and recommending that the complaint be dismissed in its entirety. Therefore, the complainant filed exceptions with respect to certain specific recommendations contained in the hearing examiner's report and recommendations.

The Assistant Secretary has reviewed the rulings of the hearing examiner made at the hearing and finds that no prejudicial error was committed. The rulings are hereby affirmed. Upon consideration of the hearing examiner report and recommendations and the entire record in subject case, including the exceptions and statement of position filed by the complainant, I hereby adopt the findings, conclusions, and recommendations of the hearing examiner.

The complainant did not except to the hearing examiner's conclusions and recommendations that unit employee William E. Dilena did not possess any supervisory authority in his capacity as a civilian employee in the unit and that the respondent had in no way assisted or encouraged Dilena in the dissemination of antiunion propaganda. After careful review of the evidence in this respect, I adopt these recommendations of the hearing examiner.

The exceptions filed by the complainant relate solely to the conclusions and recommendation of the hearing examiner that the respondent is not responsible for Dilena's conduct by virtue of the fact that in Dilena's "military capacity" as a noncommissioned officer in the National Guard he possesses certain "supervisory authority." In its exceptions, the complainant contends that the respondent must be held responsible for Dilena's conduct because as a noncommissioned officer in the National Guard he could effectively influence and coerce unit employees by exercising "supervisory" authority while functioning in his military status. After careful review of the evidence and the contentions made in the complainant's exceptions, I adopt the recommendation of the hearing examiner that Dilena's military "supervisory" status, in this case, is not sufficient to make him part of agency management or a supervisor within the unit or render the respondent responsible for his antiunion activities. Accordingly, there was no basis for finding that the respondent violated Section 19(a)(1) of the order.

The complainant did not except to the recommendation of the hearing examiner that no evidence was presented which could conceivably constitute discrimination in regard to hiring, tenure, promotion, or other conditions of employment. After careful review of the evidence, I adopt the finding of the hearing examiner that, in the circumstances, there is no basis for finding a violation of Section 19(a)(2) of the executive order.

ORDER

Pursuant to Section 6(a)(4) of Executive Order 11491 and Section 203.25(b) of the regulations, the Assistant Secretary of Labor for Labor-Management Relations hereby orders that the complaint be, and it hereby is, dismissed.

Dated: June 1, 1971   /s/ W. J. Usery, Jr.
      Washington, D.C.   Assistant Secretary of Labor
                          for Labor-Management Relations

Discussion Question

1. Discuss the principal issue in this case and its determination by the Assistant Secretary.

Section 3. Discrimination as a Result of Participation in Union Activities

As indicated earlier, employers are prohibited from discriminating against employees who engage in organizational activity that contributes to the certification of a labor organization. Section 8(a)(1) of the Labor–Management Relations Act provides that an employer will be guilty of an unfair labor practice if his conduct tends "to interfere with, restrain, or coerce employees in the exercise of the rights guaranteed in Section 7." Section 8(a)(3) also shields the individual's organizational rights by forbidding an employer to discharge or otherwise discriminate against a worker's job status because of his union activity. "In literally hundreds of decisions, the NLRB has repeated a U.S. court's conclusion that a discriminatory discharge of an employee because of his union affiliations goes to the very heart of the Wagner Act." [5]

Management may also encounter legal difficulties if an employee's union activities influence decisions to offer or withhold promotions or carry out or postpone demotions or transfers.

Public sector experience thus far indicates that the above-mentioned type of employer interference is not uncommon and is being challenged frequently by labor organizations that do not hesitate to challenge such infringements.

In the Matter of

Fashion Institute of Technology (respondent) *and* **United Federation of College Teachers, Local 1460, AFL-CIO (charging party)**

Opinion of Member Crowley and Order of Board

Case No. U–0262

(State of New York Public Employment Relations Board)

BACKGROUND

United Federation of College Teachers, Local 1460, AFL-CIO (UFCT) filed, on April 29, 1971, an improper practice charge against the Fashion Institute of Technology (respondent) alleging a violation of Sections 209–a.1(a) and (c) of the Public Employees' Fair Employment Act (act) in that Mrs. Sarason, a part-time teacher, was not reappointed to her position as lecturer in the spring term of the 1970–1971 academic year because of her activities on behalf of UFCT.

Respondent denied all the material allegations of the charge.

The hearing officer concluded that the UFCT did not sustain its burden of proving that the denial of reappointment was unlawfully motivated and, therefore, recommended that the charge be dismissed in its entirety.

The basic contention of the UFCT is that Mrs. Sarason, a member of the part-time faculty of respondent, was denied reappointment because of her activities as a member of the negotiating committee acting on behalf of the part-time faculty.

Respondent contends that Mrs. Sarason was not given a teaching assignment in the spring term of 1971 because there were no assignments available due to the fact that full-time faculty members volunteered to teach in the evening session as part of an effort to upgrade the quality of instruction in the evening session.

POSITION OF CHARGING PARTY

Mrs. Sarason was first employed by respondent in September, 1958, as a member of the full-time faculty. After one semester she was offered a position on the part-time faculty and continued as a member of the part-time faculty until February, 1971. During the twelve-year period as a member of the part-time faculty, she regularly taught courses in the evening session of respondent's school.

Prior to 1967 neither the full-time faculty nor the part-time faculty was organized for the purpose of collective negotiations. However, in 1967 the UFCT was certified as the negotiating agent for the full-time faculty of respondent and thereafter agreements between respondent and UFCT were concluded setting terms and conditions of employment for the full-time faculty.

In March, 1970, the UFCT was certified as the representative of the part-time faculty employed by respondent. Negotiations between UFCT and respondent as to the terms and conditions of employment of part-time faculty did not commence until February, 1971. However, during the period March, 1970 to February, 1971, the negotiating committee of the UFCT was preparing and drafting demands to be presented to respondent covering the terms and conditions of employment of the part-time faculty.

Mrs. Sarason was active in organizing the part-time faculty. In fact, she was described by the president of the UFCT as one of the persons who inspired the union to organize the part-time faculty. After UFCT had been certified as the negotiating agent of the part-time faculty, Mrs. Sarason became a member of the negotiating committee and participated in the formulation of the demands to be presented to respondent. In particular, she was an outspoken advocate for the proposal that the part-time faculty be given some form of job security. Her organizational activities were quite open, both in the distribution of union literature and in the solicitation of union membership, as was her membership on the negotiating committee.

The UFCT contends that the full-time faculty members in the fashion illustration department, wherein Mrs. Sarason was employed, strongly opposed the granting of job security to part-time faculty and that they, together with the chairman of the department, decided to deny reappointment to Mrs. Sarason because of her advocacy of job security for part-time faculty.

POSITION OF THE EMPLOYER

Respondent initiated courses in fashion illustration in the fall of 1958. Mrs. Sarason was offered a position on the full-time faculty to teach fashion illustration. Her work, according to Professor Shapiro, who was then chairman of the fashion illustration department, was rather poor and he recommended to the dean at that time that Mrs. Sarason not be retained. The dean, however, determined that Mrs. Sarason would continue to teach as a member of the part-time faculty in the evening session, where she remained until the spring term, 1971.

In the fall of 1969, Professor Dwan became the chairman of the fashion illustration department and, during the academic year 1969–1970, she and other full-time members of the fashion illustration department held several meetings to consider measures to be taken to upgrade the fashion illustration program in the evening school. In the fall of 1970, it was decided by the fashion illustration department, as part of the effort to upgrade the evening program, to hold a mid-term review of the work of evening students. Such a review was held in November, or early December, 1970. The review dealt with the work of students taught by Mrs. Sarason and by Miss Cavanaugh, who also taught fashion illustration as a member of the part-time faculty in the evening session.

It was the testimony of respondent's witnesses that this mid-term review indicated of about 17 or 18 of Mrs. Sarason's students, only 3 were doing passing work, and that of Miss Cavanaugh's students, only one of 17 or 18 was doing passing work. Respondent contends that this midterm review did provide an opportunity to evaluate the teaching ability of both Mrs. Sarason and Miss Cavanaugh.

In view of all of the above, Department Chairman Dwan and three other members of the full-time faculty of that department, decided in mid-January, 1971, that the quality of instruction in the evening program would be enhanced if the courses in fashion illustration were taught by members of the full-time day faculty. Accordingly, the three members of the full-time faculty volunteered to teach in the evening session in the spring term, 1971. It was understood at the time this decision was made that the necessary result of the decision would be that, in the absence of an unusually large registration for the spring term, there would not be classes available for either Mrs. Sarason or Miss Cavanaugh. Mrs. Sarason was advised upon the close of registration, on February 4, 1971, that there would not be classes available for her in the spring term. Miss Cavanaugh was also similarly advised. In fact, the registration for the spring term was below expectations, so that the services of only two of the three full-time faculty volunteers were required for the evening school.

It is the contention of respondent that Professor Dwan, the chairman of the fashion illustration department, and the other three full-time faculty members who participated in the decision were, at the time the decision was made, unaware of Mrs. Sarason's organizational activities on behalf of the part-time faculty, and unaware of her membership on the negotiating committee and, *a fortiari,* were unaware that she was an advocate of the proposal for job security for part-time faculty members.

DISCUSSION

The issue thus raised is a quite familiar one in the law of labor relations. The employee claims to be a victim of discrimination by the employer because of employee organizational activities, and the response of the employer is that the decision or action complained of was based on good and sufficient cause completely unrelated to organizational activities of the employee. In order for the charging party to sustain its charge, it must show that the alleged discriminatee was engaged in protected activity; that the employer knew of such participation; and that the alleged act of discrimination was motivated in whole or in part by such participation.

There is no question but that Mrs. Sarason's organizational activities on behalf of the part-time faculty and her activities as a member of the negotiating committee are protected activities within the meaning of Sections 202 and 203 of the act. There is, however, a very substantial question raised here as to the knowledge on the part of Chairman Dwan and the other three full-time faculty members who made the decision as to Mrs. Sarason's membership on the negotiating committee and as to her advocacy of job security for part-time faculty. While Professor Dwan and the other three were members of the UFCT, they were not on the negotiating committee. Professor Dwan, however, was a member of the executive committee of the UFCT. The record does indicate that the subject of negotiating for part-time faculty was discussed at the October meeting of the executive board and that Chairman Dwan was present at this meeting. Chairman Dwan, however, testified that she usually arrived late at such meetings and that she had no recollection of hearing or participating in any discussion of part-time faculty negotiations of the executive committee prior to February, 1971. Chairman Dwan did testify that sometime in late November or December she became concerned that the negotiations for part-time faculty might affect the right of full-time faculty to appoint or reappoint part-time faculty. She was unable, however, to state the source of her knowledge that the question of job security or tenure for part-time faculty had been proposed. The only explanation she could offer as to the source of her knowledge was that it was "in the air" or that she heard rumors.

UFCT contends that Professor Dwan's testimony is not credible and that she must have learned of this from Professor Heilemen, a fellow departmental chairman, who knew Mrs. Sarason was on the negotiating committee and knew that she was advocating job protection for part-time faculty. However, there is no evidence in the record which supports this contention of the UFCT. The facts in the record establish that sometime in the fall of 1970 Professor Dwan learned of the proposal for job security for part-time faculty; that she was strongly opposed to it; that she voiced her concern to the chapter chairman of the UFCT. When she expressed her concern to the chapter chairman, however, she testified that she was unaware of Mrs. Sarason's participation on the negotiating committee. The other three full-time faculty members who participated in the decision testified that they did not know either of Mrs. Sarason's organizational activities or her participation in the negotiations for part-time faculty until after Mrs. Sarason had not been reappointed.

The hearing officer found the testimony of Professor Dwan and the other three faculty members to be credible. The hearing officer had the opportunity to observe the demeanor of those four witnesses as they testified. I find no basis to overrule his conclusion as to their credibility.

The charging party was unable to submit any direct evidence showing that Professor Dwan or the other three full-time faculty members had knowledge of Mrs. Sarason's protected activities, particularly those relating to negotiations, prior to or at the time of the decision not to reappoint her. However, UFCT contends that the facts and circumstances present in this case are sufficient to establish with reasonable certainty the inference that the respondent had such knowledge and, thus, the unlawful motivation for her nonreappointment. In substance, the UFCT contends that the timing of the alleged discriminatory act supports such an inference. Mrs. Sarason had been employed for about a thirteen-year period without interruption and she was given no adverse criticism of her teaching ability during that period, except after her first semester of teaching. Further, while all of the four participants in the decision not to reappoint her testified that for a long period of time they thought poorly of Mrs. Sarason's teaching ability, no action was taken until the time that Mrs. Sarason was engaged in protected activities.

After reviewing all the evidence herein, I find that (a) the full-time faculty of the fashion illustration department had been concerned, at least since the fall of 1969, about the standards of the evening school and the quality and performance of the students therein; (b) the chairman of the department knew in December, 1970 of the proposal concerning job security or tenure for part-time faculty; (c) the chairman and other full-time faculty in the department were strongly opposed to a grant of job security or tenure to part-time faculty; and (d) said chairman and full-time faculty had regarded Mrs. Sarason and Miss Cavanaugh as poor teachers.

The inference I do draw from all of the above facts is that the chairman and other full-time faculty in the fashion illustration department, concerned that some form of job security would be accorded to part-time faculty as the result of collective negotiations and that it would encompass members of the part-time faculty whom the chairman and other full-time faculty deemed to be unsatisfactory, decided to take action against Mrs. Sarason and Miss Cavanaugh prior to the establishment of tenure or some other form of job security.

Thus, I conclude that UFCT has not established that Mrs. Sarason was denied reappointment because she was engaged in organizational activities or because she was an advocate for job security for part-time faculty. This conclusion is buttressed by the fact that Miss Cavanaugh was also denied reappointment at the same time and there is no claim here that such action was taken against her because of any activity in behalf of an employee organization. Indeed, there is no evidence in the record that she was a participant in such activities. However, this conclusion is not dispositive of the instant charge; rather, my findings herein raise a further question.

As stated previously, I have concluded (1) that the chairman of the department knew that the employee organization representing the part-time faculty was seeking job security or tenure; (2) that the chairman and other full-time faculty (who participated in the decision not to reappoint) were strongly opposed to such proposal; and (3) that the chairman and the other full-time faculty denied reappointment to Mrs. Sarason and Miss Cavanaugh to prevent their obtaining such job security or tenure. Does this action violate Section 209–a.1(c) of the act? I conclude that it does. The act guarantees to public employees in this state the right to participate in an employee organization and to be represented by an employee organization in the negotiation of their terms and conditions of employment. Conduct of an employer or one acting in his behalf which has a predictably chilling effect on such employee organization's activities clearly discourages membership in or participation in the activities of an employee organization. Thus, conduct of an employer which is inherently destructive of such employee rights is a violation of Section 209–a.1(c) even in the absence of proof of any intention to weaken the employee organization. This is particularly so when the conduct is intended to subvert the negotiations demands of the employee organization. In the instant case, it seems clear that respondent employer, acting through its department chairman, took action against employees because of a pending negotiation proposal and to avoid the implementation thereof as to such employees. This conduct of respondent is inherently destructive of important employee rights. It inhibits to a serious degree an employee's participation in the activities of an employee organization in the negotiating process when such a participation can result in the loss of employment.

The position of respondent that such action was taken because the two employees were, in the opinion of respondent's department chairman, unsatisfactory employees, does not cure this violation. The simple fact is that these two employees would not have been denied employment in February, 1971 but for the fact that part-time faculty might have been granted tenure or some other form of job security as a result of negotiations. I would point out that the facts here establish a rather unique situation. Normally, an employer could, in the course of negotiations, establish procedures to obviate the grant of tenure to an unsatisfactory teacher. However, in the instant case, the department chairman and three other full-time faculty members who participated in the decision were not part of management's negotiating team. Indeed, they were members of another negotiating unit. Thus, the action herein complained of was taken by them to circumvent the negotiating process. The respondent is responsible for their action because the respondent cloaked the department chairman with the authority and power to deny reappointment. I, therefore, conclude that respondent has violated Section 209–a.1(c).

It is therefore ordered that

1. Respondent offer reinstatement to her former position to Mrs. Sarason.

2. Respondent compensate Mrs. Sarason for wages lost as a result of the violation we have found herein, plus interest at the rate of 6 percent.

3. Respondent cease and desist from any further similar discriminatory acts toward employees because of the exercise by employees of their protected rights under the act.

Dated: April 28, 1972 /s/ Joseph R. Crowley, Member
Albany, N.Y.

CONCURRING OPINION OF MEMBER FOWLER

I concur in the result reached by Member Crowley and in the order at the conclusion of his opinion, but I reach my conclusion on different grounds. I think that Member Crowley and Chairman Helsby misread the evidence.

I agree with the UFCT contention that the testimony of Professor Dwan is not creditable; I find merit in the UFCT argument that the facts and circumstances present in the case are sufficient to establish with reasonable certainty the inference that Professor Dwan had knowledge that Mrs. Sarason was the protagonist for job security for part-time faculty. The very timing of the action taken against Mrs. Sarason supports such an inference. Mrs. Sarason had been employed for about thirteen years without interruption. During this period she received no adverse criticism of her teaching ability except after her first semester of teaching. Further, while all of the four participants in the decision not to reappoint Mrs. Sarason testified that they had long deemed Mrs. Sarason to be a poor teacher, the fact is, no action was taken by them until the time Mrs. Sarason advocated job security for the part-time faculty. The opposition of the four decision makers to job security for the part-time faculty is manifest in the record. Simply put, they were jealous of the power and control that they had exercised over the appointment and reappointment of part-time faculty.

The reason offered by respondent for the nonreappointment of Mrs. Sarason appears from the record to be pretextual. Admittedly, the full-time faculty did have a concern about the standards in the evening school. However, the evidence indicates that this concern was about the open admissions policy in the evening school and the overall quality of the students. The concern of the full-time faculty as to the teaching quality of the part-time faculty did not arise until Mrs. Sarason advocated job security for the part-time faculty. Other departmental chairmen in the same division as Chairman Dwan knew that Mrs. Sarason was on the negotiating committee; they knew that she was an advocate for job protection for part-time faculty. Professor Dwan claims that this was never discussed in her presence. Nevertheless, she concedes that she knew that there was a possibility that negotiations for the part-time faculty might affect the right of the full-time to appoint or reappoint part-time teachers. She explains that she received the knowledge from "the air." It appears clear to me that if Mrs. Sarason had not, as a member of the negotiating committee, proposed job security for part-time faculty, she would have continued as a member of the part-time faculty. I, therefore, conclude the charging party has sustained its burden and that, in the denial of the appointment to Mrs. Sarason, respondent violated Section 209–a.1(c).

Dated: April 28, 1972   /s/ George H. Fowler, Member
       Albany, N.Y.

DISSENTING OPINION OF CHAIRMAN HELSBY

The record supports the factual analysis of Member Crowley, but I believe that he has reached the wrong result. As explained in Member Crowley's opinion, Mrs. Sarason was discharged at the time she was because it was found that if she were retained longer she would gain tenure by virtue of union negotiations. This was resisted by Professor Dwan and her associates, not because of any general intention to frustrate the union —indeed, they were all members of the union and Professor Dwan was on its executive committee—but because they believed that Mrs. Sarason was inadequate as a teacher. The significance of the UFCT negotiations' posture was that it triggered the decision to dismiss Mrs. Sarason, but the decision was made for educational reasons. In my judgment, this does not constitute a violation of CSL Section 209–a.1(c).

Dated: April 28, 1972   /s/ Robert D. Helsby, Chairman
       Albany, N.Y.

Discussion Questions

1. What alleged unfair labor practice was committed by the respondent?
2. State the reason offered by the respondent for not reappointing Mrs. Sarason.

3. Which elements of proof must be satisfied by the charging party in this type of case?
4. Was the respondent found guilty of any prohibited activity?
5. What factors do the concurring and dissenting opinions stress?

In the Matter of

The Haldane Board of Education, School District No. 1, for the Towns of Phillipstown, Putnam Valley, Putnam County, and the Town of Fishkill, Dutchess County (respondent) *and* **Haldane Faculty Association (charging party)**

Case No. U–0350

(State of New York Public Employment Relations Board)

HEARING OFFICER'S DECISION

On September 2, 1971, the Haldane Faculty Association (herein referred to as the charging party) filed, pursuant to Part 204 of the rules of procedure (herein referred to as the rules) of the New York State Public Employment Relations Board (herein referred to as the board), an improper practice charge alleging that the Haldane Board of Education, School District No. 1, for the towns of Phillipstown, Putnam Valley, Putnam County, and the town of Fishkill, Dutchess County (herein referred to as the respondent) violated Sections 209–a.1(a) and (c) of the Public Employees' Fair Employment Act (herein referred to as the act) by terminating the coaching position of one Frank Milkovich because of his activities on behalf of the charging party.

On September 22, 1971, the respondent interposed its answer denying the material allegations of the charge and asserting in an amended answer the affirmative defense that the improper practice charge was filed more than four months after the occurrence of the alleged act of reprisal and thus is barred by Section 204.1 of the rules.

On October 7, and November 22, 1971 a formal hearing was held before the undersigned at which all parties were present and represented by counsel.

The respondent is a small school district employing approximately sixty faculty members. Its athletic program is conducted by members of its teaching staff who double as coaches and are paid an extra stipend for their coaching duties in addition to their regular teacher's salary. The coaching positions are nontenured and require reappointment on an annual basis.

Prior to the start of the 1971–1972 school year, the coaching staff was headed by an athletic director who was responsible for overall coordination of the respondent's athletic program. Assisting him were head coaches for the four major sports of football, basketball, baseball, and track. In addition, there were assistant coaches for football and basketball and coaches for various other sports such as wrestling, tennis, and winter track.

Milkovich was the respondent's head football coach. He was also an active member of the charging party, the recognized negotiating representative for the respondent's teachers, being its president during the 1967–1968 school year and a member of its negotiating team since 1967. The other head coaches of the major sports were also active in the affairs of the charging party. Patrick Shields, head track coach, was chairman of the charging party's negotiating team for the 1970–1971 school year. John Kiefer, head baseball coach, was president of the charging party during the 1970–1971 school year and a member of its negotiating team since 1968. John Rath, head basketball coach, was president of the charging party during the 1969–1970 school year and a member of its negotiating team since 1967.

On February 1, 1971, the respondent posted a new job announcement advising the faculty that it was seeking a candidate for the position of athletic director and coach of major sports to start the beginning of the 1971–1972 school year. The former athletic director had submitted his resignation two years earlier to become effective the beginning of the 1971–1972 school year. The duties of this new position were to include all the responsibilities of the former athletic director and also the additional obligation to act as head coach for football, basketball, and baseball. The respondent thereafter interviewed several candidates for this new position, including one of its own physical education teachers. On April 14, 1971, Ralph Paonessa was hired to fill the new position.

Sometime shortly thereafter, the job duties of the new athletic director were modified so that he would no longer be required to coach basketball and baseball. As a result of this modification, John Rath, the former head basketball coach, and John Kiefer, the former head baseball coach, were reappointed to fill their former coaching positions for the 1971–1972 school year.

On May 21, 1971, Milkovich received the following letter from the supervising principal:

> At a special meeting of the Board of Education, which took place last evening, I was instructed to inform you that our new athletic director for 1971–1972 has been assigned as head coach of football for the 1971 season. This action must of necessity terminate your services as head coach of football.

I should like to express for the board, and for myself, sincere thanks for your effort in this position over the past years.

The charging party contends that Milkovich's coaching position was abolished as an act of reprisal because he engaged in protected activities on behalf of the charging party. In support of this contention, it refers back one year to the period of negotiations for the 1970–1971 contract. After an extensive period of negotiations and mediation, the parties met in early March, 1970 to conclude the final contract. At that meeting a misunderstanding arose as to the amount of compensation to be paid the coaches. Each side apparently believed that there was agreement on this issue when in fact there was not. The respondent's negotiating team adjourned for a short caucus and upon their return indicated that they accepted the charging party's demand regarding the coaches' compensation. John Perpetua, president of the school board and its chief negotiator, then angrily told the charging party's coach-negotiators: "We've had to eat crow this time. Of course you realize these positions don't have to be filled. [You'll] be hearing more about this next year."

As further evidence of the respondent's alleged animus, one of the charging party's negotiators testified that dealings in the past with the respondent were "hard nosed." In addition, one of the candidates for the job of athletic director testified on behalf of the charging party that during the job interview he was told by the superintendent of schools that there was a coaches' "clique" which was detrimental to the school.

The respondent does not dispute any of the above testimony, but rather argues first that the charge is barred by the statute of limitations and second that the job duties assigned to the new athletic director were determined on the basis of a new philosophy designed to correlate the physical education and athletic programs rather than because of any desire to terminate Milkovich as head football coach.

With regard to the respondent's first contention that the charge is barred by the four month rule, I disagree. The instant cause of action arose on May 21, 1971 when the respondent notified Milkovich that his services would not be needed for the following school year. The substance of the charging party's complaint herein is not the hiring of Paonessa on April 14, but rather, the termination by respondent of Milkovich's coaching duties. Milkovich was notified of the respondent's intention not to reappoint him as a coach on May 21, 1971, and it is from this date that the four month statute of limitations commences to run. Accordingly, I find that the instant charge is not barred by the four month rule.

I now turn to the merits of the charge. It is well established that absent an unlawful motive, the act permits an employer to terminate the services of an employee for a good reason, a poor reason, or no reason at all.

Accordingly, the charging party, in order to prove its case of reprisal, must establish by a preponderance of the credible evidence that the respondent knew prior to its refusal to reappoint Milkovich that he was a member or active supporter of an employee organization; second, that the respondent's agents responsible for its refusal to reappoint Milkovich had an anti-employee organization animus; and, third, that the refusal to reappoint Milkovich would not have occurred when it did *but for* the employee's protected activities.

In order to support its charge, the charging party relies upon an isolated statement made by the president of the respondent's school board during the heat of negotiations. However, for more than a year no action was taken by the respondent that can at all be deemed to have been pursuant to its president's indication of malevolence toward the coaches. Thus, Milkovich and his fellow coach-negotiators were routinely rehired for the 1970–1971 school year. Further, all four head coaches were apparently equally active in the affairs of the charging party but only Milkovich was ultimately terminated. One head coach was not affected at all by the employer's actions and the other two were rehired after a brief period of time.

Moreover, there is nothing to indicate that the president's ire was directed more to Milkovich than the other coaches; indeed, Kiefer, the head baseball coach, was the charging party's president during the 1970–1971 negotiations and Shields, the head track coach, was its chief negotiator during that period. In addition, the charging party's testimony that the negotiations were "hard nosed" and that the coaches' clique was detrimental to the school is not evidence that the respondent would restructure its entire athletic program merely to get rid of one of its four head coaches. The respondent's decision to consolidate the duties of the athletic director and football coach does not appear to be so unreasonable that I can conclude that it was a fiction to disguise the real intent of the respondent to discharge Milkovich as a reprisal for his protected activities.

Therefore, for the reasons set forth above, the charge should be, and hereby is, dismissed in its entirety.

Dated at Albany, N.Y., /s/ Howard A. Rubenstein
this twenty-ninth day of February, 1972 Hearing Officer

Discussion Questions

1. What was the basis for the unfair labor practice charge in this case?
2. Why did the hearing officer rule in favor of the respondent?

In the Matter of

Rhode Island State Labor Relations Board *and* Pete A. Pakey, in his capacity as city manager of the city of East Providence and Michael J. Fox, in his capacity of fire chief of the city of East Providence

Case No. ULP–927

(State of Rhode Island before the State Labor Relations Board)

DECISION AND ORDER

STATEMENT OF THE CASE

On February 21, 1969, Local No. 850, International Association of Fire Fighters, AFL-CIO, filed with the Rhode Island State Labor Relations Board, hereinafter called the board, a charge alleging that Pete A. Pakey in his capacity as city manager of the city of East Providence and Michael J. Fox in his capacity of fire chief of the city of East Providence, hereinafter called the respondents, had engaged in, and were engaging in, certain unfair labor practices as set forth in the Rhode Island State Labor Relations Act, hereinafter called the act.

The board investigated this charge and held an informal conference on February 28, 1969. A complaint was then issued by the board on March 17, 1969. The complaint alleged in substance that the respondents, in their respective capacities, had discriminated against a captain in the East Providence Fire Department solely because of his involvement in union activities in violation of the provisions of Section 28–7–13 of the act and had violated the provisions of the collective bargaining agreement in existence between the parties in violation of Section 28–7–13 of said act.

On April 22, 1969, a formal hearing was held by the board. The parties were represented by counsel, who participated in the proceedings, and were afforded full opportunity to be heard, to examine, and cross-examine witnesses and to introduce evidence bearing upon the issues. Paragraphs (1) and (2) of the complaint were admitted by the respondents.

At this hearing, Captain George Kent testified that he had been a member of the East Providence Fire Department for over twenty years and that the performance of his duties was always well accepted by the city. He further testified that he spent considerable time fulfilling the duties of an assistant chief of said fire department and that he ranked second in seniority among the captains of said fire department. It was admitted by the respondents that because of retirements from the rank of assistant chief sometime after October of 1968 two vacancies in that position had to be filled. These vacancies were filled by making provisional appointments of Captains Harold J. Carey and Robert D. Connelly to these posts. Captain Kent testified that he was passed over for one of these provisional appointments solely because of his activities on behalf of Local No. 850, International Association of Fire Fighters, AFL-CIO. He testified that for several years prior to these provisional appointments he was one of the primary spokesmen for the union in contract negotiations and grievances hearings. Captain Kent testified that the respondent Fire Chief Michael J. Fox did not approve of his union activities and that on several occasions had complained to him about the same. As a result of these provisional appointments, Captain Kent attended a meeting with the respondent Pete A. Pakey, city manager of East Providence, at which Mr. Pakey allegedly made statements concerning Captain Kent's union activities. The statement primarily mentioned by Captain Kent as having been made by Mr. Pakey was in substance that Mr. Pakey would not promote a labor-oriented employee to the position of assistant chief even if he was more qualified. This testimony of Captain Kent was corroborated by William Bowen, president of Local No. 850, who was present at this meeting with Mr. Pakey. Mr. Bowen also corroborated the fact that Chief Fox had made some complaints to Captain Kent about his union activities.

Chief Fox testified that although Captain Kent was well qualified to fill the position of assistant chief that it was within his discretion to promote the man he wanted in that post. Chief Fox further testified that seniority in rank was not the sole criterion for promotion. It must be noted, however, that provisional appointments made to captains at the same time or shortly thereafter were based primarily on seniority and rank. It must also be pointed out that Chief Fox was very evasive in his testimony. He stated that he did not recall ever telling Captain Kent that he did not approve of his union activities. His reason for not recommending Captain Kent for promotion was a question of his loyalty. This question of loyalty was based upon statements or remarks made to Chief Fox but the chief did not recall who made any such statements or what they concerned. The chief also denied discussing this promotion with anyone before January 9, 1969, but Captain Kent testified that he had learned of it on the evening of January 8. Chief Fox could not remember whether or not he may have told Captain Kent on January 8.

Mr. Pakey testified that he could not recall making any remarks to Captain Kent about his union activities. Mr. Pakey testified that he made the promotion solely upon the recommendation of Chief Fox. Mr. Pakey's testimony was also somewhat evasive in that he could not recall the substance of conversations between himself and Captain Kent. He did testify that he discussed these provisional appointments with the personnel director of the city of East Providence before January 9, 1969. Mr. Rendine, said personnel director, testified that he never discussed these provisional appointments with Mr. Pakey until after Chief Fox had made his recommendations on January 9.

In short, the testimony of Mr. Pakey, Chief Fox, and Mr. Rendine was completely inconsistent and did not corroborate itself. Reviewing this testimony, it does appear to the board that the only reason for not making the provisional promotion of Captain Kent to assistant chief was his engagement in union activities. No other credible reason was advanced by the respondents.

Upon the entire record of this proceeding, the board makes the following findings of fact and conclusions of law:

FINDINGS OF FACT

1. The city of East Providence is a municipal corporation duly organized under the laws of Rhode Island. The city of East Providence conducts no interstate business and makes no sales to points outside of Rhode Island. Said city qualifies as an employer and has its offices and principal place of business at City Hall, East Providence, Rhode Island.

2. Local No. 850, International Association of Fire Fighters, AFL-CIO is a labor organization within the meaning of the provisions of the State Labor Relations Act, as amended.

3. That Pete A. Pakey in his capacity as city manager of the city of East Providence and Michael J. Fox in his capacity of fire chief of the city of East Providence are guilty of unfair labor practices in that they have discriminated against George Kent, a captain in the East Providence Fire Department, solely because of his involvement in union activities in violation of the provisions of Section 28–7–13 of the General Laws of Rhode Island, 1956, as amended.

4. That Pete A. Pakey and Michael J. Fox are guilty of an unfair labor practice in that they have failed to promote provisionally George Kent to the position of assistant chief solely because of his involvement in union activities in violation of the provisions.

CONCLUSIONS OF LAW

1. The city of East Providence is a municipal corporation duly organized under the laws of Rhode Island. The city of East Providence conducts no interstate business and makes no sales to points outside of Rhode Island. Said city qualifies as an employer and has its offices and principal place of business at City Hall, East Providence, Rhode Island.

2. Local No. 850, International Association of Fire Fighters, AFL-CIO is a labor organization within the meaning of the provisions of the State Labor Relations Act, as amended.

3. That Pete A. Pakey in his capacity as city manager of the city of

East Providence and Michael J. Fox in his capacity of fire chief of the city of East Providence are guilty of unfair labor practices in that they have discriminated against George Kent, a captain in the East Providence Fire Department, solely because of his involvement in union activities in violation of the provisions of Section 28–7–13 of the General Laws of Rhode Island, 1956, as amended.

4. That Pete A. Pakey and Michael J. Fox are guilty of an unfair labor practice in that they have failed to promote provisionally George Kent to the position of assistant chief solely because of his involvement in union activities in violation of the provisions.

ORDER

Upon the basis of the foregoing Findings of Fact and Conclusions of Law, the Rhode Island State Labor Relations Board pursuant to Section 28–7–22 of the Rhode Island State Labor Relations Act, IT IS HEREBY ORDERED:

1. That Pete A. Pakey in his capacity as city manager of the city of East Providence and Michael J. Fox in his capacity of fire chief of the city of East Providence cease and desist discriminating against members of Local No. 850, International Association of Fire Fighters, AFL-CIO, solely because of their union activities.

2. That said Pete A. Pakey and Michael J. Fox in their respective capacities cease and desist making any statements regarding the union activities of any members of Local No. 850.

Entered as order of the Rhode Island State Labor Relations Board
Dated: May 28, 1969
By _____
     Angelo E. Azzinaro
     Executive Secretary

Rhode Island State Labor Relations Board

_____
Chairman

_____
Member

_____
Member

Discussion Questions

1. What was the nature of the unfair labor practice charge brought against the city manager and the fire chief?

2. Discuss the reasons offered by the defendants for turning down Kent's promotion.

3. Why did the board decide that Kent was discriminated against as a result of his organizational activities?

Section 4. The Agency Shop Clause in Contravention of a Maintenance-of-Membership Requirement

In an agency shop an employee is not required to join a union but must pay a fee equal to the union dues assessment to compensate the union for the benefits accruing him from the union's bargaining activities. This relationship allows an employee with a strong philosophical bias against mandatory union membership to retain his freedom of association. Another type of union security, which developed during World War II as a compromise between supporters of the open shop (no union) and advocates of the closed shop (compulsory union affiliation as a prerequisite for employment), was the so-called maintenance of membership. In maintenance of membership no employee could be forced to become a union member, but those individuals who belonged to the union when a contract took effect or who voluntarily became members during the duration of a contract were obligated to remain members until the contract expired. Employees could exercise the choice of joining or remaining nonunion during a ten- or fifteen-day period at the beginning of the contract term, known as an "escape" period. If they decided against membership they would not be required to pay dues for the duration of the contract. A similar decision would be made with each subsequent contract.

The union shop has replaced maintenance of membership as the most prevalent form of union security in private industry in the post-World War II period. In fact, the latter arrangement has all but disappeared. However, as the following case demonstrates, it is utilized in the public sector in those states where the agency shop is considered to contravene public policy.

The Pennsylvania Labor Relations Board v. Teamsters Local Union No. 8 and The Pennsylvania State University

Commonwealth of Pennsylvania, the Pennsylvania Labor Relations Board, Case No. PERA–C–1075–C [6]

NISI DECISION AND ORDER

A charge of unfair practices under the Public Employee Relations Act, Section 1201, was filed on April 29, 1971, with the Pennsylvania Labor Relations Board by the complainant, Erika S. M. Zelem, against The Pennsylvania State University hereinafter called university, and Teamsters Local Union No. 8, hereinafter called union. Answers were filed by both respondents and replies to new matter were filed at the hearing by complainant over objection of respondent union. . . .

A hearing was held on June 16, 1971, at State College, Pennsylvania before Alan R. Keier, Esq., a duly designated hearing examiner of the board.

The specifications charged that complainant was threatened with discharge from employment if she failed to pay amounts equal to regular union dues and initiation fees of the respondent union pursuant to the existing collective bargaining agreement between the university and the union.

The university denied any unfair practices and averred that the union security provisions contained in the agreement of July 1, 1970 were "agency shop" and not illegal under the Pennsylvania Labor Relations Act. The answer of the union denied unfair practices and set forth that the provisions of the agreement of July 1, 1970 were merely an extension of the modified agency shop provided in the previous agreement. The answer further interposed an issue as to the statute of limitations.

The basic issues presented are whether the union security provisions in the current agreement are valid under the provisions of Act 195.

FINDINGS OF FACT

The board, on the basis of the testimony and evidence presented at the hearing, and from all other matters and documents of record, finds the following facts:

.   .   .

4. That the university and the union negotiated a collective bargaining agreement effective for the period October 1, 1967 through May 31, 1970 which contained the following union security provision:

Article III, Union Security. Section 1. All employees in the bargaining unit on October 1, 1967 who within the previous fifteen-month period designated in writing the union as their exclusive collective bargaining representative shall during the term of this agreement be required to pay to the union as a condition of employment amounts equal to the union's regular initiation fees and periodic dues commencing on October 1, 1967. *Section 2.* All employees in the bargaining unit on October 1, 1967, who during the term of this agreement designate in writing the union as their exclusive collective bargaining representative shall during the term of the agreement be required to pay to the union as a condition of employment amounts equal to the union's regular initiation fees and periodic dues commencing after the dates of such authorizations. *Section 3.* All persons who become members of the bargaining unit as newly hired employees on or subsequent to October 1, 1967 shall during the term of this agreement be required to pay to the union as condition of employment amounts equal to the union's regular initiation fees and periodic dues commencing at the conclusion of the probationary period of forty-five workdays.

Section 4. All persons who became members of the bargaining unit as newly hired employees and completed the probationary period of forty-five workdays on or subsequent to September 1, 1967 shall during the term of this agreement be required to pay to the union as a condition of employment amounts equal to the union's regular initiation fees and periodic dues commencing after the conclusion of the probationary period or October 1, 1967, whichever date is later.

5. That another collective bargaining agreement was negotiated between the union and university effective for the period of July 1, 1970 through May 31, 1973, which agreement contains the following provisions with respect to union security:

Article II, Security. 2.1 Membership in the union is not compulsory. Employees have a right to join, not join, maintain, or drop their membership in the local union as they see fit. Neither party shall exert any pressure on or discriminate against an employee as regards such matter.

2.2 Membership in the local union is separate, apart, and distinct from the assumption by one of his equal obligation to the extent that he receives equal benefits. The local union is required under this agreement to represent all of the employees in the bargaining unit fairly and equally without regard to whether or not an employee is a member of the local union. The terms of this agreement have been made for all employees in the bargaining unit and not only for members in the local union. Accordingly, it is fair that each employee in the bargaining unit pay his own way and assume his fair share of the obligation along with the grant of equal benefit contained in this agreement.

2.3 In accordance with the policy set forth above, it is agreed that:

(a) All employees in the bargaining unit on the effective date of this agreement who are members of the union or who prior to the effective date of this agreement were required to pay to the union as a condition of employment amounts equal to the union's periodic dues, shall, during the term of this agreement, be required to pay to the union as a condition of employment amounts equal to the union's regular periodic dues commencing on the effective date of this agreement.

(b) All employees who become members of the bargaining unit on or subsequent to the effective date of this agreement shall during the term of this agreement be required to pay to the union as a condition of employment amounts equal to the union's regular initiation fees and periodic dues. The obligation to make such payment shall commence the first of the month following the sixtieth calendar day of regular employment status.

(c) All employees in the bargaining unit who prior to the effective date of this agreement were not required to pay to the union amounts equal to union dues and regular initiation fees, shall, effective January 1, 1971, be required to pay to the union as a condition of employment amounts equal to the union's regular initiation fees and periodic dues.

2.4 The university shall inform all employees at the time of hire of the existence of this agreement and the obligation of such employee to pay to the union as a condition of employment amounts equal to the union's regular initiation fees and periodic dues. The university shall notify the union after sixty (60) calendar days from the date of hire of the name and address of each employee so hired.

6. That the university and the union mutually agreed to extend the contract identified as joint Exhibit 1 beyond its expiration date of May 31, 1970 until the signing of a new agreement.

7. That on or about December 10, 1970 a meeting was held for non-union members of the bargaining unit represented by the union, which meeting was attended, *inter alia,* by complainant and Adam Condo, an official of the personnel department of the university.

8. That at the meeting aforesaid, complainant was informed by Mr. Condo that by January 1, 1971, complainant and other nonunion members of the bargaining unit similarly situated would be required to pay, as a condition of employment, amounts equal to the dues and initiation fees of the union.

9. That prior to January 1, 1971 complainant had not been a member of nor contributed financially to the union.

10. That complainant wrote various letters to university officials of state government protesting the payment of the aforesaid sums to the union.

11. That on January, 1971 complainant paid to the union an amount equal to the union's dues and initiation fees, which payment was made "under protest" in order to retain employment.

12. That on or about March 9, 1971 complainant was informed by LeRoy Burd, secretary-treasurer of the union, that if she did not continue to pay the sums required under the agreement the union would request her discharge.

13. That on or about March 10, 1971 complainant was informed by counsel for the university that if discharge was requested by the union, they would comply with the collective bargaining agreement and discharge her.

14. That complainant continued to pay the sums equivalent to union dues through March, 1971 under protest to retain her employment, and so indicated by letter.

15. That had said sums equivalent to dues not been paid, had no

charges been filed, and had the request been made by the union, the university would have discharged complainant.

16. That complainant was also informed by various other union and university personnel on divers occasions that she may be subject to discharge if she failed to pay the sums equivalent to union dues and initiation fees, including Rodney Knepp, union steward, Ray T. Fortunato, assistant vice-president of union, and Robert Eberhart, assistant professor and direct supervisor of complainant.

17. That there is no evidence of any formal request ever being made by the union to the university that Miss Zelem be discharged.

DISCUSSION

Section 401 of the Public Employee Relations Act makes it clear that employees may not be required to join or assist in employee organizations except as may be required pursuant to a maintenance of membership provision in a collective bargaining agreement. Assisting an employee organization would fairly seem to include financial assistance.

Section 301(18) defines the term of maintenance of membership as follows:

> Maintenance of membership means that all employees who have joined an employee organization or who join the employee organization in the future must remain members for the duration of a collective bargaining agreement so providing with the proviso that any such employee or employees may resign from such employee organization during a period of fifteen days prior to the expiration of any such agreement.

This definition is in keeping with the accepted meaning of "maintenance of membership" in the labor field. *Rothberg on Labor Relations,* Chapter VII, Section 6. Section 705 of the Public Employees Relations Act contains the following:

> Membership dues deductions and maintenance of membership are proper subjects of bargaining with the proviso that as to the latter, the payment of dues and assessments, while members, may be the only requisite employment condition.

When Section 705 is read together with Section 401, it indicates an intent by the legislature that maintenance of membership is to be the most extensive form of union security permitted under the act. Moreover, Section 705 does not permit a broad form maintenance-of-membership clause as is sometimes found in private sector contracts, requiring continuance of "membership in good standing," which may require participation beyond mere payment of dues. Under Section 705, payment of dues "while members" may be the only requisite employment condition.

Hence, a union security provision contained in a contract negotiated after January 1, 1970, which goes beyond the narrow maintenance-of-membership clause permitted by the act is void, unless saved by the provision of Section 904.

Section 904 provides that any provision of any collective bargaining agreement in existence on January 1, 1970, which is inconsistent with any provision of Act 195 but not otherwise illegal, shall continue valid until the expiration of the contract. Section 904 further states, "The parties to such agreement may continue voluntarily to bargain on any such items after the expiration date of any such agreement and for so long as these items remain in any future agreement."

Herein lies the crux of the dispute. The respondents advance the argument that if, in the first instance, union security beyond the act's "maintenance of membership" is prohibited under the Public Employee Relations Act, nevertheless, the second sentence of Section 904 means that a provision inconsistent with the act contained in a prior agreement may be bargained upon and extended so long as the inconsistent provision remains in future agreements. If this is so, then the current union security clause would be valid since the agreement in existence on January 1, 1970 contained a union security provision which exceeded that permitted by the act. By negotiation, resulting in the agreement of July 1, 1970, the union security clause, while modified, required the same payments to the union.

On the other hand, complainant argues that the second sentence of Section 904 means that the parties may continue to bargain for the inclusion of the inconsistent term or terms in succeeding contracts but the provision may not provide for a more severe union security clause than existed in the prior contract.

Section 101 of the act recites, inter alia, that the purpose of the act is "to promote orderly and constructive relationships between all public employers and their employees. . . ." One of the purposes of Section 904 is to ensure that such relationships established prior to its enactment not be undermined. However, Section 904 must be read as part of the entire statute; it is presumed that the legislature intends the entire statute to be effective and certain. . . . It must also be considered in the light of the circumstances under which the act was enacted and the contemporaneous legislative history. . . .

The Hickman Commission, which was established for the purpose of studying the "whole area" of public employee relations and recommending legislation governing those relations recommended that "the right to collect dues from the members of the bargaining unit who are not members of the employee organization should be recognized as a bargainable issue under appropriate safeguards." That this recommendation was rejected by the legislature is clear from the language of Section 401. The exception set forth in Section 904 is a legal necessity by virtue of the constitutional prohibition against impairment of contract, but there can be no doubt of the intention of the legislature to limit such nonmember assessments by employee organizations to those already embodied in contracts valid immediately prior to the enactment of the Public Employee Relations Act.

The legislature intended that a union security provision more extensive than that provided in the act may be saved if it is within the provisions of Section 904. However, the parties may not by collective bargaining, entered into after January 1, 1970, change the effect of that provision. This is precisely what the parties have done, in derogation of complainant's rights as a pre-October 1, 1967 employee, and as evidenced by a comparison of Section 2.3(c) of the agreement of July 1, 1970 with the provisions of Article III of the agreement effective from October 1, 1967 through May 31, 1970. Under the prior agreement the complainant, unless she had designated the union as her representative, did not have to pay initiation fee and dues. Under the new agreement she must. Therefore, the effect upon her is more severe and in violation of Act 195.

A claim has been made in this case that complainant's charge is barred by the limitations provision in Section 1505 of the act. The charge of unfair practices was filed on April 29, 1971, thus commencing the proceeding. The effective date of the particular provision of the labor agreement, to which complainant has objected, was January 1, 1971. Obviously, therefore, complainant commenced her action within four months of the time her right of action accrued.

We wish to note that our decision applies only to the particular circumstances here established, and that future claims of this nature will be disposed of on the individual merits of each case.

CONCLUSIONS

The board, therefore, after due consideration of the foregoing and the record as a whole, concludes and finds

. . .

4. That the agreement of July 1, 1970, between the university and the union, is inconsistent with the provisions of Act 195 and is therefore unenforceable as to the complainant, a pre-October 1, 1967 employee, to either join the union or to pay to the union amounts equal to what would be paid if such person joined the union, something the prior agreement did not require.

5. That the charge in the instant matter was timely filed.

6. That the university and the union did interfere with complainant in her exercise of the rights guaranteed in Article IV of the act, and are guilty of an unfair practice within the meaning of Sections 1201(a)(1) and 1201(b)(1) of the act.

ORDER

The Pennsylvania Labor Relations Board, therefore, after due consideration of the foregoing and the record as a whole, hereby orders and decrees that the charge of unfair practices filed in this case by Erika S. M. Zelem is sustained and that Pennsylvania State University and Teamsters Local Union No. 8 have both committed unfair practices within the meaning of Section 1201(a)(1) and Section 1201(b)(1) of the act, respectively; and that Teamsters Local Union No. 8 shall immediately cease and desist from continuing to collect from Erika S. M. Zelem any amounts of money which are in lieu of union dues, assessments, initiation fees, or other like payments, and that all of such amounts heretofore paid by Erika S. M. Zelem to Teamsters Local Union No. 8, between January 1, 1971 and the present time shall immediately be reimbursed to Erika S. M. Zelem. . . .

Signed, sealed and dated at Harrisburg, Pennsylvania, this twentieth day of December, 1971.

Pennsylvania Labor Relations Board
/s/ Malcolm B. Petrikin
/s/ George B. Stuart

DISSENTING OPINION

I do not agree with the majority's holding that an enlargement of the scope of an agency shop clause which is specifically protected by Act 195 constitutes a violation of that act. My reasons are based in both law and equity.

Section 904 of the act expressly preserves the validity of "any provision of any collective bargaining agreement in existence on January 1, 1970 which is inconsistent with any provision of this act but not otherwise illegal . . . until the expiration of such contract." There is no contention that the agency shop provisions of the contract between the respondents as of January 1, 1970 were illegal, although it is conceded that they do not meet the requirements of Act 195. If Section 904 contained this language and no more, I should be forced to concede the validity of the majority's reasoning, inasmuch as the contract which bound the parties on

January 1, 1970 expired May 31, 1970. However, the legislature added a further sentence to the section: "The parties . . . may continue voluntarily to bargain on any such items after the expiration date of any such agreement and for so long as these items remain in any future agreement." As the majority points out, the Statutory Construction Act requires that the entire statute must be given effect, and thus we are bound to pay at least as much attention to the second sentence of Section 904 as the first.

The key word is "bargain." Section 33 of the Statutory Construction Act provides that words must be given their meaning "according to their common and approved usage" or, if they "have acquired a peculiar and appropriate meaning," that meaning shall be applied. Both dictionary and case law apply a definition involving give-and-take to the word "bargain." *Webster's Seventh New Collegiate Dictionary* cites as a synonym, in its definition of bargain, "haggle." Common sense, as well as the legal and etymological history of the word, clearly indicates that bargaining is a two-way street, not an activity in which one party merely tries to retain what he has while the other attempts to diminish it; this is what the majority would read into the second sentence of Section 904. By using a word which is commonly understood to imply that the union will try to increase its protection and benefits, and an employer to diminish them, the legislature must be presumed to have intended Section 904 to permit the enlargement of contract items which retained their binding force after the passage of the act despite admitted inconsistency with the act.

Even were this not the case, I do not believe that justice is served by requiring the union to refund to the complainant all of the monies paid by her pursuant to the July 1, 1970 contract. Complainant, like all members of the bargaining unit, has benefited from the representation of a union and the contract it negotiated with the university. Certainly, some portion of the dues and initiation fee she has paid under that contract is attributable to the cost of negotiating and administering it. I consider the approach of the Michigan Court of Appeals in *Smigel* v. *Southgate Community School District* (No. 7298, 1970) is the proper one to be followed here, even though it was decided under Michigan's public employee statute, which does permit the agency shop.

In *Smigel* the court remanded the case for the taking of testimony to establish the relationship between the amount payable by nonmembers as dues and the nonmembers' share of the cost of negotiating and administering the contract which protected them. As the nonmembers have not protested receipt of benefits under the union contract, they should have no basis for protesting liability for their share of the cost of obtaining those benefits on a *quantum meruit* basis.

/s/ Joseph J. Licastro, Member

Discussion Questions

1. Discuss the significance of Section 904 of the Public Employee Relations Act.
2. Which type of union security is permitted by PERA?
3. In what respect does the dissenting opinion differ from the majority ruling?
4. What are the basic issues in this case?
5. Distinguish between "broad" and "narrow" maintenance-of-membership provisions.

Section 5. Refusal to Bargain in Good Faith

In private employment the union and the employer are required to make a serious effort to negotiate a written contract concerning "wages, hours, and other terms and conditions of employment." The existence of a written document is prima facie evidence that such an obligation was carried out. Neither side is required to make concessions, however, and if agreement is not forthcoming on disputed issues, they may reach an impasse, after which a strike or lockout is permitted. Because overt acts generally indicate intent, the actions of the parties in the negotiation process furnish credible evidence as to whether a genuine effort has been mutually made to reach an acceptable agreement. Cases in public employment indicate that the private sector good faith bargaining criteria are being closely adhered to.

In the Matter of

Combined Hebrew/Yiddish Cultural Schools, An Affiliate of the Jewish Welfare Federation of Metropolitan Detroit (respondent) *and* **Combined Hebrew/Yiddish Cultural Schools Teachers Association, An Affiliate of the Hebrew Teachers of Metropolitan Detroit, MFT/AFT (charging party)**

Case No. C69 E–57

DECISION AND ORDER

On August 13, 1969, Trial Examiner Joseph B. Bixler issued his decision and recommended order in the above-entitled matter, finding that respondent, Combined Hebrew/Yiddish Cultural Schools, an affiliate of the Jewish Welfare Federation of Metropolitan Detroit, had engaged in, and was engaging in, certain unfair labor practices and recommended that it cease and desist therefrom and take certain affirmative action as set forth in the trial examiner's decision and recommended order attached hereto.

The trial examiner's decision and recommended order were issued and served upon the interested parties in accordance with Section 23(c) of Act 176 of the Public Acts of 1939, as amended. The parties have had an opportunity to review said decision and recommended order for a period of at least twenty days from date of service thereof on the parties, and no exceptions have been filed by any of the parties to the proceedings.

ORDER

Pursuant to Section 23 of the act, the commission hereby adopts as its order, the order recommended by the trial examiner.

Dated: September 8, 1969   Michigan Employment Relations Commission
(formerly Labor Mediation Board)
/s/ Robert G. Howlett, Chairman
/s/ Leo W. Walsh, Commission Member
/s/ Morris Milmet, Commission Member

TRIAL EXAMINER'S DECISION AND RECOMMENDED ORDER

Appearances: for the employer, Herbert Oushinsky, chairman of the board of directors of the Combined Hebrew/Yiddish Cultural Schools; for the charging party, Bernard Fieger, Esq.

Pursuant to the provisions of the Labor Mediation Act (Act 176 of the Public Acts of 1939 as amended), hereinafter referred to as the act, a hearing was held on June 24, 1969, at Detroit, Michigan, before Joseph B. Bixler, a trial examiner of the Michigan Labor Mediation Board, hereinafter referred to as the board, on charges filed by Combined Hebrew/Yiddish Cultural Schools Teachers Association, an affiliate of Hebrew Teachers of Metropolitan Detroit, MFT/AFT, hereinafter referred to as the charging party.

The charge alleges that Combined Hebrew/Yiddish Cultural Schools, an affiliate of the Jewish Welfare Federation of Metropolitan Detroit, hereinafter referred to as the employer, violated Section 10(e) of the act as follows:

> The employer has failed and refused to bargain in good faith by refusing to execute an agreement reached between the parties and by making demands for changes in said agreement which would make benefits in said agreement inapplicable to the employees covered by said agreement.

THE FACTS

The Combined Hebrew/Yiddish Cultural Schools, is a private school, existing for the purpose of providing Jewish cultural education. The school is run by a board of education that makes all decisions in reference to teachers, with the advice of another private school named the United Hebrew Schools. The United Hebrew Schools, in addition to extending advice relative to teachers, also supervises the employer in its administration; it also handles the monetary affairs of this employer, and makes out the paychecks for the teachers and other expenses. This record does not disclose that the employer is an affiliate of the Jewish Welfare Federation of Metropolitan Detroit, but rather that the employer is a beneficiary of that organization as well as various other organizations in the Jewish community in the metropolitan Detroit area.

Sometime about September 30, 1968, the employer recognized the charging party as the collective bargaining agent for all of its classroom teachers. Thereafter, bargaining commenced between the employer and the charging party. The employer was represented at the bargaining table by a team made up of members of the board of education of the employer. On or about March 12, 1969, the employer demanded that the agreement be changed to conform to the contract between the United Hebrew Schools and the representative of its teachers.

After May 12, on May 27, a mediation session was held and no resolution of the differences of the parties was arrived at at that meeting.

CONCLUSIONS AND RECOMMENDATIONS

The parties in the tentative agreement reached on or about March 12, 1969, did provide at Article 16 as follows: "The terms of this agreement will become effective with the approval by the Board of Governors of the Jewish Welfare Federation of metropolitan Detroit."

The record does not reflect however, that this tentative agreement was ever submitted to the Jewish Welfare Federation of metropolitan Detroit. The only testimony relative to this matter is that it was not submitted. It would appear, therefore, that the rejection of the tentative agreement by the school board of the employer, through the assistant superintendent of the United Hebrew Schools, did not take place pursuant to the contractual provision of the tentative agreement. Under these circumstances, the undersigned is of the opinion that the employer herein has failed to bargain in good faith. The employer met with the union by a committee made up of its school board members, and held out to the charging party that they had authority to reach an agreement with the representative of its teaching employees. The employer then, after negotiations and the culmination of those negotiations in a tentative agreement, cannot then submit the tentative agreement reached to a third party and allow that third party, who is a stranger to the negotiations, to exercise a veto over the whole agreement. Further, the position adopted by the representatives of the employer, after extensive negotiations, that the tentative agreement could not be agreed to because it did not conform to an agreement governing employees of another employer, would also constitute a failure to bargain as required by the act.

There is a difference between bargaining under the Public Employment Relations Act and the Labor Mediation Act. A public employer cannot delegate full authority to bind the public employer to an agent who engages in collective bargaining for a public employer without delegating its legislative function, an act that is prohibited. *City of Saginaw,* 1967 Labor Opinions 465. A private employer may give its bargaining representative authority to reach binding agreement. In fact, a private employer is bound to give its representative authority to reach agreements with the lawful representative of its employees. *Lock Nut Corporation of America,* 77 NLRB 600; *Alameda Bus Lines Inc.,* 142 NLRB 445.

In the case at hand, the negotiators for the employer were members of the school board of the employer. It is my opinion that the tentative agreement reached by the negotiators does embody the agreement between the parties and that the employer is bound thereby when and if the agreement is approved by the Board of Governors of the Jewish Welfare Federation of Metropolitan Detroit, as provided for in Article XVI of the March 12, 1969, agreement.

RECOMMENDED ORDER

It is recommended that the board order Combined Hebrew/Yiddish Cultural Schools of Metropolitan Detroit to:

(a) Cease and desist from refusing and failing to fulfill its obligation to bargain under Section 16(b) of the Labor Mediation Act.

(b) Submit the agreement reached on or about March 12, 1969, by said Combined Hebrew/Yiddish Cultural Schools of Metropolitan Detroit and the Combined Hebrew/Yiddish Cultural Schools Teachers Association an affiliate of Hebrew Teachers of Metropolitan Detroit, MFT/AFT, to the Board of Governors of the Jewish Welfare Federation of Metropolitan Detroit for approval. If said agreement is approved by the Board of Governors of the Jewish Welfare Federation, put the terms and provisions of said agreement into effect.

(c) Post a signed copy of the attached notice for a period of thirty (30) days.

It is further recommended that the charges be dismissed as to the Jewish Welfare Federation of Metropolitan, as there is no basis for determining that organization to be an employer of the employees represented by the charging party.

Dated: August 13, 1969
Michigan Labor Mediation Board
/s/ Joseph B. Bixler
Trial Examiner

Discussion Questions

1. Who constituted the bargaining team for the employer in this case?
2. Was the bargaining team for the employer authorized to make binding commitments without the approval of the employer?
3. Can an employer submit a contract reached with the bargaining agent for its employees to a third party for approval and allow that third party to disapprove the agreement reached?

In the Matter of

City of Elizabeth (respondent) *and* Elizabeth Fire Officers Association (complainant)

Docket No. CE–9

(State of New Jersey before the Public Employment Relations Commission)

DECISION AND ORDER

Pursuant to a notice of hearing to resolve a question concerning a charge alleging violations of the act, a hearing was held before Hearing Officer Theodore A. Winard on December 8, 1969. The hearing officer's report and recommendation were served on the parties February 6, 1970. The employer has filed exceptions to the report and recommendation. The commission has considered the record, the hearing officer's report and recommendation, and the exceptions and, on the facts in this case, finds

1. The city of Elizabeth is a public employer within the meaning of the act and is subject to the provisions of the act.

2. The Elizabeth Fire Officers Association is an employee representative within the meaning of the act.

3. A charge has been filed with the commission alleging violations of

the act by the public employer; a question concerning alleged violations of Section 7 of the act exists and this matter is appropriately before the commission for determination and order.

4. The hearing officer found that the employer had refused to negotiate with the certified representative for a unit of fire officers including the chief, deputy chiefs, and battalion chiefs. The employer does not dispute its refusal but contends it was justified because the unit includes the chief, deputy chiefs, and battalion chiefs, who, it claims, are managerial executives within the meaning of the act and thus excluded from the act's coverage. The hearing officer concluded that the composition of the unit was determined in a prior proceeding, PERC No. 4, to which the employer was a party, that no compelling reason exists, such as newly discovered or previously unavailable evidence or special circumstances, which requires reconsideration of that determination, and that the commission's decision and subsequent certification are therefore conclusive. Although the hearing officer permitted evidence on the question of the managerial status of the three (3) classifications in question, he declined to make a recommendation on that issue.

The employer excepts to this disposition essentially on the following grounds: (1) it did not participate in the prior proceeding because it mistakenly understood that the only issue to be resolved was which of several competing organizations would represent its rank and file firemen; it was not aware that the proceeding would involve an officer's unit; (2) its failure to participate should not prejudice its right to question the unit's composition now; (3) the disputed job titles alone indicate managerial executives and the evidence supports the inference. The hearing officer observed with respect to the prior proceeding that the employer was served with notice that a hearing was scheduled to resolve the question concerning representation of fire department personnel, that such notice indicated the complainant here was a party, and that the employer's attorney appeared but only long enough to indicate that the employer took no position and would abide by the commission's decision. Thereafter Hearing Officer Kleeb issued his report and recommendations. In his preliminary remarks the hearing officer stated, "if [the parties] do not agree with the facts and recommendations set forth herein they may file exceptions with the commission. . . ." Thereupon the hearing officer recited certain facts agreed upon by the three (3) participating employee organizations, including the following:

> Fire officers (chiefs, deputy chiefs, battalion chiefs, and captains) are supervisory employees but may be appropriately grouped with the uniformed firemen. . . .
>
> Elizabeth Fire Officers Association was formed on July 11, 1968. . . . EFOA is interested only in representing "line" officers which includes the classifications chief, deputy chief, battalion chiefs, and captains. Since its

inception, EFOA has represented fire officers before the Mayor and City Council in discussing wages, hours, and working conditions and has also handled grievances for fire officers. . . .

Hearing Officer Kleeb found, *inter alia,* that a unit limited to fire officers and probationary fire officers was appropriate and recommended that an election be conducted giving such officers the option of separate representation by Elizabeth Fire Officers Association. The employer did not file exceptions to the hearing officer's report and recommendation. The commission adopted the report and recommendation with certain modifications not pertinent here. The employer did not challenge the commission's decision and direction of election. In the election which followed each of the disputed employees voted; the employer did not challenge any of these ballots.

In spite of the fact the employer previously dealt with the complainant for those in question and was notified that the complainant was a party to the representation case, it may be that, initially, the employer misunderstood the scope and significance of that earlier proceeding. But it is difficult to perceive how such misunderstanding could continue after the hearing officer's report was issued. At the very least the commission, as well as other interested parties, is entitled to expect that an aggrieved party will exercise due diligence in protecting its interest and will assert its claim at the appropriate time. Lack of due diligence is not sufficient cause to reexamine the earlier determination. We therefore affirm the hearing officer's conclusion in the instant case that the prior certification is conclusive and that the unit may not be challenged in this proceeding.

As part of the remedy for the violation found, the hearing officer recommended that the employer post a notice for the benefit of its employees. The commission affirms the finding of a violation but, because of the nature of that violation, concludes that notice posting is not appropriate. Otherwise, the commission adopts the hearing officer's recommended remedy.

ORDER

Pursuant to the act, the commission hereby orders that the respondent, city of Elizabeth, its officers and agents shall

1. Cease and desist from:

(a) Refusing to negotiate collectively with the Elizabeth Fire Officers Association as the exclusive collective negotiating representative of the employees in the following unit: All fire officers and probationary fire officers excluding uniformed firemen, probationary firemen, linemen, the supervisor in the Bureau of Communications, mechanics, the supervisor in the Bureau of Repair, and all clerical employees.

(b) Interfering with the efforts of said employee organization to negotiate for or represent employees as such exclusive collective negotiating representative.

2. Take the following affirmative action, which will effectuate the policies of the act: Upon request negotiate collectively with the Elizabeth Fire Officers Association as the exclusive representative of all employees in the unit with respect to grievances and terms and conditions of employment.

By order of the commission

Dated: April 2, 1970
Trenton, N.J.

/s/ Walter F. Pease
Chairman

Discussion Questions

1. How did the employer attempt to justify its refusal to negotiate with the certified bargaining representative of the fire officers?
2. Did the commission allow the employer's challenge to the appropriateness of the bargaining unit in question?

Section 6. Failure to Implement an Executed Contract

The NLRB has held, and been upheld by the courts, "that an employer who unlawfully refused to execute an agreed-upon contract should be required to execute the contract. . . ." [7] This problem arises in those instances where the negotiators have reached a written agreement on certain contract provisions, signed the document, and subsequently seen a delay in implementation. In another private sector case management reneged on a contract a week after signing it; the NLRB directed the employer to "honor" the contract. An appellate court upheld this award and stated that such a decision by the board was justified in that "it had the limited role of putting the parties back in the position they occupied prior to the unlawful repudiation." [8]

In the Matter of

Los Angeles Building and Construction Trades Council (charging party) *and* **County of Los Angeles (respondent)**

No. UFC 2.1
Opinion Supplementing Order
Dated: March 26, 1971 [9]

(Los Angeles County Employee Relations Commission)

BACKGROUND

The question for decision in this case is whether the county of Los Angeles has violated Section 12(a)(3) of the Los Angeles County Employee Relations Ordinance. That section provides that it shall be an unfair employee relations practice for the county of Los Angeles to "refuse to negotiate with representatives of certified employee organizations on negotiable matters." The certified employee organization in this case, the Los Angeles Building and Construction Trades Council, filed an unfair employee relations charge with this commission on January 22, 1971, alleging a violation of Section 12(a)(3) of the ordinance. Following investigation of the charge by the commission's executive secretary, the commission, on February 10, 1971, issued a charge and notice of hearing alleging that the county of Los Angeles violated Section 12(a)(3) of the ordinance in that county management reneged on an agreement to recommend that the County Board of Supervisors implement a signed memorandum of understanding which county management and Local 45 of the International Brotherhood of Electrical Workers had negotiated. The County Board of Supervisors was not named in the charge.

On due notice to all of the parties, the commission on February 19 and 26, 1971 held a hearing on the allegation set out in the charge. Both Local 45 and the county were represented by counsel at the hearing. On the basis of the evidence presented at the hearing, we issued a brief written order on March 26, 1971, deciding this case in favor of the charging party. This decision and opinion supplements the findings in our order dated March 26, 1971, that the management of Los Angeles County has committed an unfair employee relations practice.

FACTS AND DECISION, I

The material facts in this case are essentially undisputed. Acting pursuant to the County Employee Relations Ordinance (hereinafter referred to as ordinance), this commission held hearings in April and May 1969 to determine the appropriate employee representation unit for a class of communications employees involved in the present dispute. Following those hearings and an election supervised by this commission, Los Angeles Building and Construction Trades Council (BCTC) was certified as the majority representative for the employees involved in this dispute as well as other employees. Thereafter, International Brotherhood of Electrical Workers Local Union 45 (herein referred to as Local 45) was duly designated by BCTC to negotiate with the county on behalf of the communications classes.

Negotiations between Local 45 and county management commenced. They were unsuccessful. This commission appointed a mediator; and his efforts were unsuccessful. Then, at the joint request of the parties, this commission appointed a fact finder mutually selected by the negotiating parties. The fact finder conducted a hearing during which he heard and considered evidence and argument from both sides. On December 8, 1970, the fact finder filed findings of the fact and recommendations which favored granting substantial benefits to the employees. These recommendations were not accepted by county management. It requested Local 45 to negotiate a settlement in substitution for the provisions recommended by the fact finder. The union reluctantly accepted the county's request to negotiate a substitute settlement, and further negotiations resulted in an agreement dated December 30, 1970.

Local 45's leadership then recommended to the employees involved that they accept the compromise settlement. This recommendation was based in part upon the County Personnel Department's written promise of December 30, 1970 that it would "move swiftly to present a joint recommendation to the Board of Supervisors for effectivity the legally required thirty (30) days following board approval." Affected employees accepted their union leader's recommendations and voted to ratify the agreement. The Director of Personnel, Mr. Gordon T. Nesvig, then recommended to the Board of Supervisors that the agreement be approved and implemented and that agreed salary increases be enacted. His letter to the board was dated January 6, 1971. The director of personnel's letter noted that this agreement was not a midyear increase. He described it as "the terminal point of a negotiating process that started prior to July 1, 1970." He noted further in his letter of January 6, 1971 that money to fund these increases was included in the 1970–1971 budget and that the total cost of the increase amounted to $30,249.

On January 21, 1971, the recently appointed Chief Administrative Officer, Mr. Arthur G. Will, recommended to the board that Mr. Nesvig's letter of January 6, 1971 be tabled. The Director of Personnel, Mr. Nesvig, concurred in that recommendation and the board accepted the joint recommendation to table the letter and the negotiated agreement.

The object of the tabling motion, as described at the hearing by the county administrative officer, was to delay indefinitely the implementation of the agreement by the Board of Supervisors. It was the county administrative officer's intention to recommend implementation of the agreement at an indefinite time in the future when the county's financial condition improved. When asked at the hearing whether the tabling action meant that the implementation of the agreement would be given retroactive effect when implemented in the future, the county administrative officer replied that he could not answer that question. On the same subject, the county director of personnel was emphatic. He said that the agreement, if and when implemented, would not be given retroactive effect. It was this joint recommendation to table, offered by the county administrative officer and the county director of personnel, which led to the unfair employee relations charge in this case.

II

It is the county's position that the existence of a $59 million county deficit, the exact nature and size of which was not discovered until shortly before the memorandum of understanding was signed, made it incumbent upon county management to recommend to the Board of Supervisors that implementation of the agreement be tabled indefinitely. The county administrative officer testified that shortly after taking office on December 12, 1970 he received instructions from the Board of Supervisors to ascertain the county's financial condition. The county administrative officer immediately undertook this task and by Christmas weekend, 1970, he had projected a county deficit of between $8 and $30 million. By the following weekend he had projected a county deficit of $50 million. The following Monday, January 3, 1971, study of other projected budget items added $9 million to the deficit.

While Mr. Will was determining the size of the county's deficit, the county's personnel director worked closely with him and was party to all information concerning the size and scope of the deficit. Thus, when the memorandum of understanding was signed by county management on December 30, 1970, both the county administrative officer and the county director of personnel knew that the county had a sizeable deficit. When the director of personnel wrote the Board of Supervisors on January 6, 1971 recommending that the Board of Supervisors put the memorandum of understanding into effect, the nature of the deficit and its full implications were known to him and to the county administrative officer. At no time on or prior to January 6, 1971 was it made known to Local 45 that county management would not take steps to recommend approval of the agreement. Failure to so recommend, it has been charged, was a breach of that obligation. We agree.

We infer from the county administrative officer's testimony that he believed that he was not bound by the commitment of the director of personnel to seek the board's approval of the settlement. He had the right and the obligation, as he saw it, to use his own judgment whether or not to support the commitment of Mr. Nesvig. That view is not our view. We think that the director of personnel did purport to bind, and did indeed bind, all of county management, including the chief administrative officer, when he executed the memorandum of understanding. It is clear then that county management was committed to seek the board's approval of the agreement. County counsel concedes that there was at least an implied obligation to take certain action to implement the memorandum of understanding. We believe that on the basis of the facts presented to us there was both an implied obligation and an express obligation on management's part to seek the board's approval. All of county management, including Mr. Will, was bound by that obligation.

In the context of this case, we think tabling and rejection of the negotiated agreement are almost synonymous. Tabling is not as final as rejection but it is almost as final. Tabling has had the effect of denying approval of this agreement and of denying the benefits provided for; that is the equivalent up to this point of rejection. Outright disapproval by the board may seem to be, without actually being, more nearly final. The director of personnel's testimony that there will be no retroactivity if and when this agreement is ever approved means that there has been a permanent rejection of at least part of the negotiated benefits.

III

The Los Angeles County Employee Relations ordinance was enacted by the Board of Supervisors on September 3, 1968, following receipt of a report by a distinguished panel of consultants who drafted the ordinance and recommended its adoption by the Board of Supervisors. Section 12 (a)(3) of the ordinance provides that it shall be an unfair employee relations practice for the county "to refuse to negotiate with representatives of certified employee organizations on negotiable matters." A similar duty is imposed upon employee organizations by Section 12(b)(2) of the ordinance, which makes it an unfair employee relations practice for a certified employee organization or their representatives or members to "refuse to negotiate with county officials on negotiable matters." Section 3(o) of the ordinance defined negotiation as follows:

"Negotiation" means performance by duly authorized management representatives and duly authorized representatives of a certified employee organization of their mutual obligation to meet at reasonable times and to confer in good faith with respect to wages, hours, and other terms and conditions of employment, *and includes the mutual obligation to execute a written document incorporating any agreement reached.* (Emphasis added.)

The ordinance is careful to protect both bargaining parties from any duty to make a concession to the other party. If the parties in good faith are unable to resolve their differences after a good faith attempt to do so, no negotiated agreement comes into existence and the ordinance, under those circumstances, does not compel them to reach an agreement.

The obvious purpose of these provisions is to assure that county management and the employee organizations authorized to represent county employees make a good faith effort to reach a negotiated agreement which is to their mutual satisfaction. Needless to say, the obligation of negotiating parties to make a good faith effort to iron out their differences and to reach accommodation, if possible, is the very heart and essence of the collective negotiations process.

In this case, Section 12(a)(3) of the ordinance required that the agreement reached by county management and Local 45 be reduced to writing and signed by the parties. By signing the agreement, county management necessarily became obligated to make every effort to seek implementation of the agreement by recommending to the Board of Supervisors that it be implemented. If signing a negotiated agreement does not so obligate county management, then signing a negotiated agreement is a meaningless act on the part of county management.

If signing a negotiated agreement is a meaningless act, then that portion of the ordinance requiring that negotiated agreements be reduced to writing and signed is a meaningless provision, of no use to employee organizations or the county of Los Angeles. If negotiated agreements need not be reduced to writing and signed, it follows that no attempts need be made by county management or a certified employee organization to negotiate an agreement. In that event, the entire ordinance would consist of a mere collection of words on paper, without meaning and without purpose.

We assume, as we must, that the Los Angeles County Employee Relations ordinance was not enacted with the understanding that it would have no meaning. It follows that an interpretation of the ordinance which would effectively render it meaningless must be rejected. We accordingly find that county management is in violation of Section 12(a)(3) of the ordinance by virtue of its failure to recommend approval of the memorandum of understanding which it reached with Local 45. We reject county management's defense that a fiscal crisis precluded it from recommending that the memorandum of understanding be approved. The county's financial condition was known when the memorandum of understanding was signed; the county's financial condition was known when the county's director of personnel recommended that the Board of Supervisors implement the memorandum of understanding. Plainly, this defense is without merit.

We do not suggest that there was malice or evil intent on the part of county management. On the contrary, it is argued that Mr. Will felt bound by a more pressing obligation—as the board's chief staff adviser—to recommend tabling of their settlement (and freezing of other county obligations and capital expenditures unless they were "already legally committed") because of the county's large fiscal deficit. Certainly Mr. Nesvig was not motivated by any malice or intention to do an injustice. But, good intentions, such as those described to us, have limited weight in the commission's determination whether the ordinance has been violated. We have found that county management, not including the board, did violate the ordinance, as charged.

Having found that county management violated the ordinance in this case, the ordinance requires that we fashion a remedy for the charging party. In this case, we withhold fashioning a remedy at this time, as the principal parties to this dispute, having been made aware of our decision by means of our written order of March 26, 1971, have agreed to attempt to fashion a remedy consistent with our decision in this case. If the parties are unable to agree upon an acceptable remedy this commission will fashion a remedy in accordance with its obligations as set out in Section 12(e) of the ordinance. At our meeting scheduled for April 16, 1971, we will consider what progress the parties have made to this end.

Though we are holding the description of a remedy in abeyance, we feel compelled at this time to describe the nature of the commission's remedial powers under the ordinance. Section 12(e) of the ordinance provides that when the commission decides that the county has engaged in an unfair employee relations practice or has otherwise violated the ordinance, "the commission shall direct the county to take appropriate corrective action." That section further provides that if compliance with the commission's decision is not obtained within the time specified by the commission, it shall so "notify the other party, which may then resort to its legal remedies." Thus, this commission has no legal authority to bind county management with an order in favor of an employee or an employee organization, even though employee organizations and employees are effectively bound by the commission's orders in favor of the county. Concerning this aspect of our obligations under the ordinance, we quote from the report of the consultants' committee, which drafted and recommended adoption of the ordinance:

> The commission would lack authority to compel the county to obey its orders, although it would presumably advise the Board of Supervisors of any refusal by a county agency to comply. Thus, ultimately, the issue would become whether the Board of Supervisors intended to support the commission. Refusal by the board to do so would of course endanger the continued existence of the commission.

> We feel compelled to emphasize that if the recommended ordinance were simply to provide the basis for more litigation in the courts, it would fail utterly to achieve its intended purpose.

We agree with the sense of that statement. Further, we think the absence of a meaningful remedy in this case would have an adverse effect on the stability of employee relations in county government. Employee organizations would not know whether a signed agreement meant an agreement which county management would support before the Board of Supervisors. We make these observations in the context of this case. For the county administrative officer admitted that this was an unusual situation;

that only the projected deficit prevented county management from recommending to the Board of Supervisors that the memorandum of understanding be implemented by the board. This being an unusual case, it follows that compliance with our decision may not be regarded as having set an unfavorable precedent for the county.

Accordingly, this decision, supplementing our order of March 26, 1971, finding county management in violation of Section 12(a)(3) of the Los Angeles County Employee Relations ordinance will be further supplemented at a future date with a description of an appropriate remedy consistent with our findings and decision in this case, unless the parties advise us that they have mutually fashioned a remedy which will make further action by this commission unnecessary.

Dated: April 9, 1971   Employee Relations Commission
/s/ Melvin Lennard, Chairman
/s/ Ben Nathanson, Commissioner
/s/ Reginald H. Alleyne, Jr., Commissioner

Discussion Questions

1. Did the director of personnel have authority to make binding commitments during the negotiations?
2. What effect did tabling the negotiated agreement have?
3. If retroactivity were denied, what effect would this have had on contractual commitments once the agreement was implemented?
4. Describe the negotiating obligations incumbent upon the parties.
5. Which specific act on the part of management required it to seek implementation of the agreement?
6. Discuss the probable consequences for the bargaining process if the contract was not put into effect.
7. Why is the county's financial condition an unacceptable excuse for nonobservance of the contract?

Section 7. Breach of Contract Obligation

It is an accepted fact in private employment, with rare exceptions, a collective bargaining agreement is not a contract of employment guaranteeing that a certain number of workers will be provided with jobs. If however, "the collective agreement provides for continuing the employment of existing employees for the term of the contract and guarantees the pay of each employee for the life of the contract, the 'rare' case is presented of a collective agreement being also a contract of employment. In such a case, employees who lost their jobs . . . during the term of the contract were permitted to recover damages. *Hudak* v. *Hornell Industries,* N.Y. Ct. App., 30 L.R.R.M. 2317 (1952)." [10] The following decision indicates that under similar facts, in the public sector, private industry precedent will be determinative.

In the Matter of

National Realty Company, d/b/a Strand Theatre (employer) *and* IATSE, Local No. 23

Case No. ULP–894

(State of Rhode Island and Providence Plantations, Providence, Sc. before the State Labor Relations Board, Rhode Island State)

DECISION AND ORDER

IATSE, Local No. 23, through its business agent, filed an unfair labor charge against the National Realty Company, d/b/a Strand Theatre, on May 17, 1968.

After investigation, a complaint was issued by the Rhode Island State Labor Relations Board, in which unfair labor charges were brought against the National Realty Company. Answer of respondent, amended answer of respondent and motion to clarify complaint, and motion for bill of particulars were filed. Two hearings were held—one on December 27, 1968, and the other on January 31, 1969. At these hearings oral testimony was taken from witnesses. Admitted into evidence were the following documents: (a) a contract dated the nineteenth day of July, 1966, herein called operation contract; (b) agreement dated October 27, 1966, *re* Maintenance Stagehand Contract-Strand Theatre; (c) lease between the National Realty Company and the Providence Cinema Company by an accompanying letter correcting the name of the lessee to the Strand Theatre instead of Providence Cinema Company; (d) a letter of termination dated July 5, 1966, effective July 1, 1967, from the National Realty Company to John E. Rafferty.

At the above-mentioned hearings, testimony was presented and the parties agreed that a contract was entered into between National Realty Company and the union dated October 27, 1966, and which incorporated by reference certain provisions of the operations contract already in effect. This contract provided in part that the company would employ one stagehand. At the time the contract between the parties was executed and until July 1, 1967, John E. Rafferty, a stagehand-maintenance man and a member of the union, was employed by the company. Mr. Rafferty was given a notice of termination dated July 5, 1967. He had been so advised of his termination some time in June, 1967, with reason being that the National Realty Company had leased the premises to the Esquires Theatre, Inc. Mr. Rafferty, the stagehand, was employed by Esquires Theatre, Inc., for two to three months when Esquires terminated his employment. Subsequently thereto, the union took an appeal to the National Labor Relations Board, which found that Esquires Theatre was not bound by the contract between the National Realty Company and the union. Some time in April or May of 1968, the Esquires Theatre ceased doing business at the Strand Theatre and the National Realty Company assumed the operation of said theatre. The union requested in the first week of May, 1968 that the National Realty Company rehire a stagehand according to their original agreement of October 27, 1966. The company refused to do so, and the union filed this unfair labor charge.

FINDINGS OF FACT

Upon the entire record of this proceeding, the board makes the following findings of fact:

1. The National Realty Company, d/b/a Strand Theatre, is a duly constituted employer within the city of Providence. Said company qualifies as an employer and has its offices and principal place of business at 77 Washington Street, Providence, Rhode Island.

2. International Alliance of Theatrical Stage Employees, Local 23, is a labor organization within the meaning of the provisions of the State Labor Relations Act, as amended.

3. That the company and the union entered into a written agreement on or about October 27, 1966, that would terminate in October of 1969.

4. That the National Realty Company did lease the Strand Theatre to Esquires Theatre, Inc., as of July 1, 1967.

5. That the Esquires Theatre, Inc., did some time in April or May cease doing business at the Strand Theatre.

6. That the National Realty Company resumed its operation of the Strand Theatre and that the union attempted to place an employee under the terms of its agreement.

7. That the National Realty Company refused to hire a stagehand-maintenance employee or honor or negotiate concerning the conditions of the agreement with the union.

8. That the union attempted to bargain with the National Realty Company as to the hiring of an employee and was unable to do so due to the negative attitude of the employer.

9. That the National Realty Company has failed to bargain with the union.

10. That the National Realty Company failed to honor the agreement.

CONCLUSIONS OF LAW

1. The National Realty Company, d/b/a Strand Theatre, is a duly constituted employer within the city of Providence. Said company qualifies as an employer and has its offices and principal place of business at 77 Washington Street, Providence, Rhode Island.

2. International Alliance of Theatrical Stage Employees, Local 23, is a labor organization within the meaning of the provisions of the State Labor Relations Act, as amended.

3. That the contract dated October 27, 1966 constituted an agreement covering the wages, hours, and working conditions for stagehand-maintenance work.

4. That the National Realty Company refused to hire a stagehand-maintenance employee or negotiate concerning the conditions of the contract with the union.

5. That the union attempted to bargain with the National Realty Company as to the hiring of an employee and was unable to do so due to the negative attitude of the employer.

6. That the National Realty Company has failed to bargain with the union.

7. That the National Realty Company failed to honor the agreement set forth in the contract.

8. That the agreement entered into by the parties on or about October 27, 1966, although suspended by the act of subletting the theatre to Providence Cinema Company, was never in effect terminated.

9. That the failure of the employer to honor the conditions of the contract in not employing a stagehand-maintenance employee has eliminated the union as a collective bargaining agent.

THE REMEDY

We find that the respondent has engaged in unfair labor practices by refusing to honor the agreement entered into by and between the National Realty Company and the union. In accordance with the mandate of the act, we will order that the respondent cease and desist from such unfair labor practices.

For affirmative action, our order will direct the respondent to reinstate John E. Rafferty to his former position, discharging, if necessary, the person or persons who may have taken his place.

We will also order back pay to John E. Rafferty from the date of the respondent's refusal to honor the agreement, April or May, less deductions, if any, for sums earned by him during said period.

ORDER

Upon the basis of the foregoing Findings of Fact and Conclusions of Law, pursuant to 28–7–22 of the Rhode Island State Labor Relations Act, IT IS HEREBY ORDERED that the respondent, National Realty Company, d/b/a Strand Theatre, its officers, agent, successors, and assigns, shall

1. Cease and desist from
   (a) Refusing to honor an agreement entered into by and between the National Realty Company, d/b/a Strand Theatre, and the union.

2. Take the following affirmative action, which the board finds is necessary to effectuate the policies of the act:
   (a) Offer to John E. Rafferty immediate and full reinstatement to his former position with respondent without prejudice to any right or privilege previously enjoyed by him; discharge, if necessary, any person or persons employed in his place.
   (b) Make whole said John E. Rafferty, by paying to the Rhode Island State Labor Relations Board, for and on behalf of him, a sum of money equal to that which the said John E. Rafferty would have earned with the respondent at 77 Washington Street, Providence, Rhode Island, from the date of such refusal to hire to the date of said offer of reinstatement, less the amount, if any, actually earned by him in other employment during said period.

Entered as order of the Rhode Island State Labor Relations Board
Dated: March 7, 1969
By _____
      Angelo E. Azzinaro
      Executive Secretary

                      Rhode Island State Labor Relations Board

                      /s/ Harry T. Brett
                            Chairman

                      /s/ Armand E. Renzi
                            Member

                      /s/ Samuel J. Azzinaro
                            Member

Discussion Questions

1. What effect did the leasing of the theater by the National Realty Company have on Rafferty's employment rights?
2. How were Rafferty's rights affected by the reassumption of control over the theater by National Realty?
3. Describe the remedy in this case.

Section 8. Attempt to Bypass a Negotiated Grievance Procedure

The rationale for negotiated grievance procedures is aptly summarized in the following statement:

> Most collective bargaining agreements set up some sort of grievance machinery to settle differences which may arise between management and the union as to the interpretation or application of the agreement and to pass on disputes arising in day-to-day working relations. This grievance machinery represents an extension of the collective bargaining process to call attention to contract violations or individual injustices or to meet situations not specifically covered in the contract itself. . . .[11]

Once a contract is consummated, an employer who refuses to process a grievance brought by an individual employee under the grievance procedure established in the agreement may be found guilty of refusing to bargain in good faith. In fact, "where an employer refuses to abide by the grievance-arbitration provisions of a contract, the union can sue to compel specific performance." [12] Moreover, if an employer attempts to bypass the union and goes directly to an employee who has grieved with an offer for unilateral settlement, such action constitutes an unfair practice in that it undermines the union's role as exclusive bargaining agent (which includes the processing of grievances on behalf of bargaining unit members).

In the Matter of

United States Army School/Training Center, Fort McClellan, Ala. (respondent) *and* American Federation of Government Employees, AFL-CIO, Local 1941 (complainant)

Case No. 40–2190(CA)[13]

(United States Department of Labor before the Assistant Secretary for Labor–Management Relations)

DECISION AND ORDER

This matter is before the Assistant Secretary pursuant to Regional Administrator J. Y. Chennault's December 7, 1970 order transferring the case to the Assistant Secretary of Labor pursuant to Section 205.5(a) of the regulations. Upon consideration of the entire record in the subject case, which includes the parties, bilateral stipulation of facts and accompanying exhibits, I find as follows:

The parties' stipulation of facts reflects the following:

In a letter dated April 24, the complainant filed an unfair labor practice charge pursuant to Section 203.2 of the rules and regulations wherein it was contended that the respondent had violated Executive Order 11491 by letters of March 23 to the complainant's president and to one of respondent's employees, Mrs. Annie H. Boatman. As an informal satisfactory resolution of the charge, the complainant sought letters of apology. The commanding officer of the respondent rejected the charge and stated his agreement to submitting the allegations to the Assistant Secretary of Labor for review by way of stipulation.

On June 25, a complaint was filed against the respondent alleging violations of Sections 19(a)(1), (5), and (6) of Executive Order 11491 in that by the March 23 letters to the complainant's president and to Mrs. Boatman the respondent had (1) disparaged the ability and integrity of a complainant official; (2) hinted to a grieving employee that she would have been better advised to present her grievance directly to management without the participation of the complainant; (3) refused to accord appropriate recognition to the complainant; and (4) failed to have a meaningful meeting to resolve a grievance. The complaint was properly served on the respondent.

In the parties' stipulation of facts it is requested that the Assistant Secretary of Labor render a decision with regard to the respondent's above-mentioned letters to the complainant's president and to employee Mrs. Annie Boatman.

The complainant has exclusive recognition for a unit of the respondent's employees. The parties executed a collective bargaining agreement on March 17, 1969 which had an expiration date of March 17, 1971.

On January 12, the complainant's president filed a grievance with the respondent, pursuant to the negotiated grievance procedure, on behalf of employee Mrs. Annie Boatman objecting to a written reprimand that had been given Mrs. Boatman on October 31, 1969. On March 2, a meeting was held in accordance with the negotiated grievance procedure. In attendance were Mrs. Boatman, the complainant's president, acting as Mrs. Boatman's representative, and the respondent's deputy commander.

During the course of the grievance meeting a dispute developed between the complainant's president and the deputy commander when the former made certain allegations concerning employee treatment at the activity. The deputy commander repeatedly asked the complainant's president to either support the contention with details or withdraw the criticism. The grievance meeting ended without a resolution of either the grievance or the "side dispute" that had developed between the complainant's president and the deputy commander.

By letter sent to Mrs. Boatman on March 23, the respondent's commanding officer informed her that the written reprimand which had given rise to the above-described grievance was being withdrawn inasmuch as, "I feel that the reprimand has served its intended purpose and because of your otherwise good work record. . . ." The letter concludes,

> My decision to remove the reprimand is in no way based on the information presented by your representative . . . in the meeting on 2 March, 1970. As you will recall, the comments offered . . . related mostly to the unsupported allegations of unsatisfactory working conditions at the Noble Army Hospital. I believe that had you approached Wither (chief, nursing service) . . . or me reasonably soon after the incident and receipt of the reprimand with an attitude of contriteness, that all of the efforts and time involved in your grievance could have been avoided.

Also on March 23, the commanding officer forwarded a copy of the above-mentioned letter to the complainant's president and the commanding officer of the Noble Army Hospital. Accompanying the letter to Mrs. Boatman the respondent, on March 23, sent a separate letter addressed directly to the complainant's president which stated in part:

> The action that I am taking is *not* as a result of the (grievance) meeting, as I consider that your presentation in that meeting did more to jeopardize Mrs. Boatman's position than help it. My action is based upon an independent evaluation of her conduct on the date in question and her long time record of good service. It is my desire that there be open communication between supervisors and employees. I am personally interested in the welfare of all of my civilian employees and will listen to their complaints after they have made honest efforts to resolve any differences with their supervisors. I am also interested in and aware of your rights to represent employees either informally or formally.

This letter stated with respect to the complainant president's conduct at the grievance meeting:

> [Y]ou made broad allegations concerning the treatment of civilians assigned to nursing service in the hospital with particular emphasis on reluctance of civilians to work on the surgical ward, you were requested either to present a formal grievance signed by disgruntled civilians or submit a written retraction of your broad allegations. You have not, as yet, responded to the request. As president of Lodge 1941, you have considerable responsibility to your members and to the office to which you have been elected. Included in your leadership role is your responsibility to confine your testimony in a formal grievance to the issue at hand rather than to

rely upon vague, generalized statements. In short, you have to act responsibly. In the aforementioned grievance meeting you were more inclined to make open condemnation of management of the hospital than to confine your testimony to the simple issue in Mrs. Boatman's grievance.

In the interest of performing my command responsibility relative to the morale and welfare of civilians at Noble Army Hospital, I must again ask that you comply with . . . the deputy commander's request. I shall expect your reply not later than 15 April, 1970.

A copy of the above-quoted letter was not sent to Mrs. Boatman.

The grievance procedure set forth in the negotiated agreement between the parties provides that "The dispute or grievance shall first be taken up by the aggrieved employee, the steward if requested, and the appropriate supervisor. . . ." If a grievance is not settled at the first step the employee must elect whether he wishes to process the grievance through the negotiated grievance procedure or the "army grievance procedure." Mrs. Boatman's grievance was processed through the negotiated grievance procedure. Steps 2 and 3 of the negotiated grievance procedure provide for union participation in all phases of the processing.

The first allegation in the complaint alleges that the respondent's disparaging of the ability and integrity of the complainant's president violates Section 19(a)(1) of the order. Section 19(a)(1) prohibits an agency or activity from engaging in conduct which would "interfere with, restrain, or coerce" an employee in the exercise of the rights assured by the executive order, such rights being enunciated in Section 1(a) of the order. The stipulation reveals that the complained of letter was sent directly by the respondent to the complainant's representative in the latter's capacity as president of the Local without any evidence of an intention to make the contents public. While the respondent's observations on "leadership responsibility" may have been personally offensive to the complainant's president, I find no basis for concluding that such expressions of opinion made to an officer of the complainant in and of themselves constitute interference with employee's Section 1(a)(1) rights or that the sending of the letter interfered with the Section 1(a) rights of employees. In the circumstances, I find that the content of the respondent's letter to the complainant's president, also an employee of the activity, contains no explicit or implicit threats of penalty or reprisal which might have tended to impede his future activity as a union representative or any statement which might interfere with, restrain, or coerce an employee in the exercise of rights assured by Section 1(a) of the order. Accordingly, I find that the complaint, insofar as it alleges a violation of Section 19(a)(1) based on alleged disparagement of the ability and integrity of the complainant's president, should be dismissed.

It is also alleged in the complaint that the respondent violated Sections

19(a)(1)(5) and (6) by hinting to an employee that she would be better advised to present her future grievances directly to management without the participation of the complainant. The stipulation reveals that in its letter to Mrs. Boatman in addition to notifying her that the reprimand was being withdrawn, thereby removing the essential cause of the grievance, the respondent's commanding officer stated that his decision was in no way based on the information presented by the complainant's representative and informed her that the same result would have been obtained without the accompanying effort and time involved with the grievance had she dealt directly with management.

It is the stated policy of the executive order to maintain constructive and cooperative relationships between labor organizations and management officials. In furtherance of that goal the order provides for the selection of a labor organization as the exclusive representative of a group of employees in an appropriate unit and Section 19(a)(6) makes it violative to "refuse to consult, confer, or negotiate with a labor organization" that has been so selected by the employees. The scope of this mandate is indicated by Section 10(e), which provides, in pertinent part,

> The labor organization shall be given the opportunity to be represented at formal discussions between management and employees or employee representatives concerning grievances, personnel policies and practices, or other matter affecting general working conditions of employees in the unit.

Once a bargaining representative has been designated by a majority of the employees in an appropriate unit, the obligation of the agency or activity to deal with such representative concerning grievances, personnel policies and practices, and other matters affecting working conditions of all employees within the unit becomes exclusive and carries with it a correlative duty not to treat with others. To disregard the exclusive representative selected by a majority of employees and attempt to negotiate or deal with certain employees individually concerning grievances, personnel policies and practices, or other matters affecting general working conditions of employment in the unit violates the essential principles of exclusive recognition and undermines the exclusive representative's status under the order. Employees have a right, and agencies and activities the obligation, to process grievances through an exclusive representative as provided for in a negotiated agreement.

In the subject case, Mrs. Boatman had elected to pursue her grievance through her exclusive representative in accordance with the provisions of the parties' agreement. Despite this selection, when the respondent notified Mrs. Boatman that the reprimand was being withdrawn, it informed her that the same result could have been obtained had she dealt with manage-

ment. The reference to avoiding the efforts and time involved in the grievance implies that it would be less burdensome to resolve grievances by dealing directly with management rather than through the exclusive representative. The respondent therefore clearly urged the bypassing of the exclusive
representative in the adjustment of any future grievance and at the same
time implicitly suggested to the employee that there would be an easier
adjustment of grievances if she dealt directly with management. Such a suggestion is inconsistent with the exclusive representation relationship described above and runs counter to the very practice and philosophy of exclusive recognition. Thus, the existence of an exclusive relationship requires,
as a minimum, that an agency or activity refrain from inviting employees to
deal directly with management as to grievances.

Accordingly, I find that the above-described conduct constitutes an
attempt to bypass and undermine the status of the exclusive representative
selected by the employees and therefore constitutes a failure to consult,
confer, or negotiate in violation of Section 19(a)(6) of the order. I find
further that by implicitly promising Mrs. Boatman more favorable and expeditious resolution of her grievances when the grievance procedure under
the parties' agreement is bypassed in favor of direct discussions with management, the respondent has interfered with the Section 1(a) rights of
employees in violation of Section 19(a)(1) of the order.

As noted above, the respondent's March 23 letter to the complainant's
president stated, in part, that:

> The action that I am taking is *not* as a result of the (grievance) meeting,
> as I consider that your presentation in that meeting did more to jeopardize
> Mrs. Boatman's position than help it.

I have concluded that in all the circumstances the contents of the letter
to the complainant's president do not constitute an improper interference
with employee rights in violation of Section 19(a)(1). However, I find
that in conveying to the complainant's representative, who was processing
the grievance, the clear message that the adjustment of Mrs. Boatman's
grievance was made strictly on the basis of unilateral considerations, and
was not the result of good faith efforts by both the complainant and the
respondent, the respondent violates Section 19(a)(6) of the order. In the
negotiating of an agreement an agency or activity would not be viewed to
be bargaining in good faith with the exclusive representative if it took the
position that it would decide terms unilaterally rather than as a result of the
bargaining process. Likewise, in the processing of grievances pursuant to a
negotiated grievance procedure, good faith is not demonstrated, where, as
here, an activity informs the exclusive representative that a grievance has
been decided not on the basis of the undertakings of the grievance procedure but on the activity's own personal judgments. This, in my view, con-

stitutes a refusal to consult, confer, or negotiate as required by the executive order.

With respect to the Section 19(a)(5) allegation contained in the complaint, that provision by its terms refers to matters related to the according of appropriate recognition rather than to the conduct of the bargaining relationship, as is involved herein. Accordingly, the Section 19(a)(5) allegation contained in the complaint should be dismissed.

CONCLUSION

By urging the bypassing of the exclusive representative and suggesting that grievances be processed directly with management and that the adjustment of the grievances might be achieved more easily if the exclusive representative is bypassed in favor of direct discussions with management, the activity has violated Sections 19(a)(1) and (6) of Executive Order 11491.

The activity further failed to consult, confer, or negotiate with the exclusive representative in violation of Section 19(a)(6) by stating to the complainant that a grievance had been adjusted on the basis of unilateral considerations apart from the undertakings of the negotiated grievance procedure.

THE REMEDY

Having found that the respondent has engaged in certain conduct prohibited by Sections 19(a)(1) and (6) of Executive Order 11491, I shall order the respondent to cease and desist therefrom and take specific affirmative action . . . designed to effectuate the policies of the order.

ORDER

Pursuant to Section 6(b) of Executive Order 11491 and Section 203.25(a) of the regulations, the Assistant Secretary of Labor for Labor-Management Relations hereby orders that the United States Army School/Training Center, Fort McClellan, Alabama shall

1. Cease and desist from:

(a) Soliciting employees represented by the American Federation of Government Employees, AFL-CIO, Local 1941 to deal directly with management with respect to the resolution of their grievances.

(b) Promising employees benefits in order to restrain them from utilizing the negotiated grievance procedure and their exclusive representative.

(c) Refusing to negotiate in good faith in the processing of grievances pursuant to the provisions of an agreement with the exclusive representative of the employees.

(d) In any like or related manner interfering with, restraining, or coercing its employees in the exercise of rights assured by Section 1(a) of Executive Order 11491.

2. Take the following affirmative action in order to effectuate the purposes and provisions of the order:

(a) Upon request, consult, confer, or negotiate in good faith with American Federation of Government Employees, AFL-CIO, Local 1941, in the processing of grievances.

(b) Post at its facility copies of the attached notice. . . .

Dated: May 14, 1971   /s/ W. J. Usery, Jr.
        Washington, D.C.   Assistant Secretary of Labor
                                for Labor–Management Relations

Discussion Questions

1. List the unfair labor practices allegedly committed by the respondent.
2. How many illegalities did the Assistant Secretary find the respondent had committed?
3. Which provisions in Executive Order 11491 were involved in this case?
4. Did disparagement of the union president's ability and integrity by the respondent's letter constitute an unfair labor practice?

CHAPTER 5

[1] Sanford Cohen, *Labor in the United States,* 3rd ed. (Columbus, Ohio: Charles E. Merrill Publishing Company, 1970), p. 494.

[2] LRX 232(a), sec. 5 (Washington, D.C.: BNA, Inc., 1967).

[3] *Ibid.*

[4] 21 GERR 5153–5154 (RF-27) (Washington, D.C.: BNA, Inc., 1971).

[5] LRX 618, sec. 5 (Washington, D.C.: BNA, Inc., 1967).

[6] GERR (No. 436) (E-1–4) (Washington, D.C.: BNA, Inc., Jan. 24, 1972).

[7] LRX 72(a), sec. 20 (Washington, D.C.: BNA, Inc., 1966).

[8] *Ibid.*

[9] GERR (No. 398) (E-1–3) (Washington, D.C.: BNA, Inc., April 26, 1971).

[10] LRX 102, sec. 31 (Washington, D.C.: BNA, Inc., 1967).

[11] LRX 255 (Washington, D.C.: BNA, Inc., 1963).

[12] LRX 265, sec. 14 (Washington, D.C.: BNA, Inc., 1961).

[13] 21 GERR 5133–5136 (RF-26) (Washington, D.C.: BNA, Inc., 1971).

6 | Impasse and Grievance Resolution Techniques

WHEN parties are unsuccessful in resolving bargaining differences, what is termed an *impasse* results, accompanied by the danger of a strike or work stoppage; this consequence is more readily predictable in private than in public employment because of the general legislative ban on unilateral strike action in the latter realm. The normal techniques for the resolution of impasses in both the public and private sectors include mediation, fact finding, and arbitration.

Mediation involves the efforts of a third party intermediary to maintain communication between the adversaries who may feel that further discussions are useless. The mediator suggests solutions for the troublesome issues to the parties, but his recommendations are not binding and may be rejected summarily.

If offers of mediation are refused, or if the mediator's efforts prove fruitless, the process of fact finding may then be utilized. A Twentieth Century Fund report describes this process:

> Fact finding has been most effective in both the public and private sector where it has been conducted by an individual or by a panel (usually three in number) qualified as impartial, judicious-minded experts in labor relations whose standing and character attest to their competence and lack of bias. . . . Once the sifting and winnowing have disclosed the true facts to the panel's satisfaction—as opposed to what the parties may have alleged during negotiations—the fact finders will frequently essay a mediatory role. They will try to disabuse one or the other or both parties of false notions or assertions and try to get the parties themselves to agree on settlement terms . . . concessions by one or the other or both sides may be offered and agreement may be reached. Or willingly or reluctantly they may submit to the panel's terms as being the best possible way out of their dispute. If, however, the time allotted for such further negotiations does not bring results, the fact finders must make their conclusions public and hope that public opinion will make the unwilling party or parties accept them.[1]

343

Unfortunately, not all fact-finding reports are publicized and even when they are, public opinion is not easily aroused to exert maximum pressure for an equitable settlement. Moreover, compliance with the fact finders' suggestions is not mandatory, with the result that, as with mediation, the adversaries may veto this form of third-party intervention.

Arbitration is another technique for ironing out negotiation impasses as well as the grievances that arise later into the administration and application of the collective agreement. It differs from mediation and fact finding in that the parties are required to conform to the arbitration decision.

Voluntary arbitration is normally the terminal step in negotiated grievance procedures whereby an impartial third party is selected by the labor organization and employer to impose a mandatory settlement. Lists of arbitrators are furnished on request by either the American Arbitration Association or the Federal Mediation and Conciliation Service (FMCS). Again, either one person or a panel or board is selected to investigate, hear, and submit a final ruling—which can be appealed to the courts only if the arbitrator(s) exceeded the authority conferred by the contract and decided nonarbitrable issues.

Compulsory arbitration, rarely utilized in the United States because of widespread opposition from both the employer community and organized labor, operates with a governmentally appointed party or board that is authorized to intervene and impose an obligatory award.

In the federal government, in the event of a bargaining impasse, the assistance of the FMCS can be requested. Mediation is considered the primary means of resolving impasses and the parties involved are expected to participate in the mediation process in such a way as to make it work. When the efforts of the FMCS or another mediator fail, however, the issues involved can be referred to the Federal Service Impasses Panel by the labor organization or public management, or both.

Gilroy and Sinicropi have summarized the legal framework for public sector grievance and impasse resolution that has developed:

> At the federal level, Executive Order 11491 requires that all negotiated agreements include grievance procedures. These procedures are the exclusive system to be used for grievances over interpretation and application of the agreement and may include arbitration as a final step in the procedure. . . . At the state and local level, most jurisdictions have not clearly defined a framework for handling employee grievances. Where such legislation has been enacted, arbitration of grievances is generally authorized. By August, 1971, at least twenty-seven states had enacted legislation relating to the resolution of grievance disputes. . . . In contrast to the federal level where Executive Order 11491 and the Postal Reorganization Act essentially provide the legal framework for impasse resolution, the state, county, and municipal framework is marked by bewildering variety. . . . The federal level stresses voluntary arrangement supported by mediation through the Federal Mediation and Con-

ciliation Service (FMCS), fact finding, and arbitration. The postal system relies heavily on "outside neutrals," while the executive order stresses a permanent impasse structure including the Federal Service Impasses Panel and the Federal Labor Relations Council.[2]

The cases in this chapter will attempt to illustrate the diversity apparent in the impasse and grievance resolution approaches at the various levels of government.

Section 1. The Validity of Binding Grievance Arbitration Clause of Contract

In private employment, upon the filing of a grievance by a union member, the negotiated grievance procedure is implemented. The number of steps—three, four, or even five—depends on the size of the union and the firm involved. Large organizations, because of more levels of supervision and/or union officialdom, require the greater number of steps. The final step in most grievance procedures is binding arbitration by an individual, a panel, or a board. The procedure in public employment is basically the same and, as will be demonstrated next, similar issues arise. For example, in both spheres, a troublesome dispute may develop over whether an issue that is involved in a grievance is arbitrable. In other words, does the arbitrator have the jurisdiction to make an award concerning a certain contract provision when the parties disagree on its interpretation and application? In the public sector, also, the presence of a state statute that apparently limits negotiability may raise a question as to whether the arbitration award is binding or merely "advisory."

In the Matter of Arbitration Between

Placentia Unified School District *and* **Placentia Unified Education Association**[3]

Interim Award
February 22, 1971

(Before Edgar A. Jones, Jr., Impartial Arbitrator)
Laurel W. Simpson   Clyde Williams

I. FINDINGS OF FACT

Representatives, respectively, of the Board of Education of the Placentia Unified School District and of the Negotiating Council of the Placentia Unified Education Association (PUEA), after negotiating over salaries, fringe benefits, working conditions, and certain operating policies during the summer, on September 15, 1970, "Informally agreed," as the district's cover-page description put it, "upon a fifteen-page document containing eleven articles and an appended policy statement concerning leaves of absence for illness or injury. The next day the PUEA representative council ratified the informal agreement. That was then followed on September 23, 1970, by unanimous ratification of the agreement by the Board of Education . . . worded thus:

> Ratified salary schedules, fringe benefits, and working conditions for all certificated personnel in the Placentia Unified School District and other related personnel maters, for the 1970–1971 fiscal year.

The board's coverage to the agreement also stated that, "It should be noted that if any emergencies occur in the implementation of these policies, immediate action will be taken by the Board of Education as provided on p. 14."

That last reference was to Article XI, which in Section A provides that "no change, alteration, or modification of these Articles I through XI shall take place during the 1970–1971 fiscal year, unless there is mutual agreement of the Board of Education and the negotiating council, *except in the case where the Board of Education determines that an emergency exists.*" (Emphasis added.)

Section B declares in mandatory terms that in "such emergency" the board "shall notify the negotiating council of the nature of the emergency and the anticipated changes that will be required to be made due to the emergency." Section D of Article XI mandatorily provides that "These policies shall be reviewed by the negotiating council and the board's representative periodically as necessary."

In Article IV the parties jointly declare that the policy of the district "shall be to develop and practice reasonable and effective means of resolving difficulties which may arise among employees, to reduce potential areas of grievances, and to establish and maintain recognized two-way channels of communication between district employees." That article essentially details three progressive steps for the resolution of an employee's "problem or grievance," involving, in turn, the "immediate supervisor"; the "superintendent's designated representative"; and an "administrative decision" of the superintendent. Finally, if the grievant remains unsatisfied, pursuant to Section 7, *he may request* in writing through the district superintendent to have the grievance reviewed by a panel of three members whose representation shall include:

1. *Option I.*
   (a) One member selected by the Board of Education.
   (b) One member selected by the grievant.
   (c) One member mutually agreed upon by the board and grievant;

or, in lieu of the above-mentioned panel, *the grievant may select to submit his grievance* to the three (3) member panel as follows:
2. *Option II.*
   (a) One member selected by the Board of Education.
   (b) One member selected by the grievant.
   (c) One member mutually agreed upon and selected from a list of five members supplied by the American Arbitration Association with background in school law.

The panel's review of the grievance and its subsequent findings shall be rendered in writing within five (5) working days after the panel has been confirmed *and binding decision regarding the grievance.* . . . Three weeks *after* the Board of Education had already ratified its agreement with the PUEA the district requested a legal review of it by the Orange County counsel. On October 23, Deputy County Counsel Ragnar R. Engebretsen responded with a five-page letter with twenty-one suggested changes to be made in the agreement.

The deputy counsel declared that the county counsel's office believed "that much of the wording in the existing document goes beyond the requirements of the Winton Act, either as it exists or as it has been amended, effective November 23, 1970." He then cautioned the board that it should not conclude that all of the twenty-one suggested changes in his letter "must be followed." But, he added, "not to do so would both unduly limit the district's ability to act and, because of the nature of the concessions made therein, provide a wedge usable by CTA in discussions with other districts."

Among his suggestions he gave specific advice concerning the provision contained in the Article IV "grievance procedure" as the seventh and final step of that procedure, creating options I and II whereby "a panel of three members" might be composed at the option of the grievant (see its terms set forth in full above). That panel is to "review" the grievance and issue "findings" in writing which "shall constitute a final and binding decision regarding the grievance."

This provision for finality prompted the deputy counsel to observe the following:

> There is a *distinct possibility,* based upon the experiences from other districts, that the decision made by such a panel *could, in fact, be contrary to board rules and regulations.* While grievance procedures provide that a grievance pertains only to the interpretation of board rules and policy, panels constituted as outlined here in the proposed (*sic*) procedure *could, because of the equities involved, reach decisions contrary to existing rules.* For this reason, and others, we would suggest any decision made by such a panel be advisory to the governing board which should have the power to make final decisions.

When the president of PUEA, Mr. Clyde Williams, on November 30, 1970, wrote to request designation by the Board of Education of its representative to sit under option II, the Superintendent of Schools, Dr. Murrell M. Miller, responded, on December 4, that he had been directed by the board to inform Mr. Williams "that the findings reached by the panel will be advisory only." This the board attributed to the county counsel's opinion and its own "study of the board's responsibility, rights, and authority as granted under laws of the state of California." It had concluded as a consequence "that such action would be illegal." It deemed that that conclusion by it constituted an "emergency under Article XI, Section B, warranting deviation from the Section A requirement that "no change, alteration, or modification of these Articles I through XI shall take place during the 1970–1971 fiscal year, unless there is mutual agreement of the Board of Education and the negotiating council, except in the case where the Board of Education determines that an emergency exists."

On that same date, December 4, the information bulletin issued by the office of the superintendent quoted board member Dr. Ralph P. Ruth as declaring for the board that the legality of the previously ratified agreement "is yet to be answered as far as court cases are concerned," that board's view was that the provision for binding arbitration was unlawful and to comply with it would create "an educational emergency," and that therefore the panel's "decision will be *advisory only,* because to do anything to the contrary would be contrary to law in our opinion." . . .

On December 16, Mr. Williams duly filed a demand for arbitration with the American Arbitration Association declaring the "nature of the dispute" thus: "The Association claims that Horst Meyer and Felipe Vela were inequitably assigned and overloaded." The "remedy sought" was "Relief from overload through a full, complete, and unencumbered conference preparation period with retroactive pay to contract date."

In the information bulletin, dated January 12, 1971, the board appended a "detailed chronology of events related to the status of grievance procedures" (dated January 11, 1971) that, as it saw it, "clarifies the position of the board in this matter." In sum, this "chronology" declared that the September 23, 1970 ratification by the teachers and then by it of the agreement did not create a contractual relationship—"At no time was it considered to be a collective bargaining agreement or master contract of any kind"—although it conceded that the contents of the agreement "were informally agreed upon in good faith by both parties." The chronology noted that after both parties had "agreed upon" the policies contained in the agreement "the material" was sent to the Orange County counsel "for legal advice and interpretation." The response of the counsel prompted the board to decide that it would "cooperate" in the grievance procedures but that a decision of the panel "would be advisory only." Although the county counsel's response was explicit that "not . . . all of the suggestions made must be followed," and did not declare that the suggested change from binding to advisory would bind the board, the board's chronology nevertheless stated that its unilateral abrogation of the express "final and binding" clause of the agreement was because "The board was following the advice of their legal counsel which they are required by law to do." Finally, the chronology asserted the validity of its interpretation of the "emergency" exception set forth in Article XI of the agreement, and asserted that it "has been consistently misinterpreted by the teachers' organization."

When the district and the PUEA had selected the undersigned impartial arbitrator to chair the grievance panel (through resort to the American Arbitration Association), by letter of January 15, Mr. Clyde Williams gave notice that, "An integral element of the case is the arbitrability of the case and in particular if the interpretation rendered by the panel relative to the grievance will be binding on the parties or only advisory." On that same date Mr. Laurel W. Simpson, also by letter, stated the position of the board that any decision would have to be "advisory" rather than "final and binding."

When the panel convened on February 4, Mr. Simpson appeared as the sole representative of the board and the district as well as its designated panel member. Noting that Mr. Williams was present as the PUEA panel member, he objected to the presence of Mr. Tom Brown of the California Teachers Association, arguing that only the panel of three should "review" the record and reach whatever "advisory" recommendation the panel might adopt. He also noted that Mr. Williams had filed another grievance, subsequent to the instant one on behalf of teachers Meyer and Vela. Mr. Simpson argued that therefore this panel should proceed to render an advisory recommendation and leave to a subsequent panel in a succeeding proceeding to rule on Mr. Williams' grievance in that regard.

The panel chairman ruled that the affected teachers—grievants in this proceeding—were entitled to representation by Mr. Brown before the panel. He explained that it is normal procedure in arbitration for persons to appear as advocates before a tripartite panel composed of an impartial chairman and the partial designees of the respective parties to the dispute. Observing the apparent need for the board or district to have legal representation present during the proceedings, the chairman withheld his ruling on arbitrability pending opportunity for Mr. Simpson to arrange for the presence of a representative of the county counsel.

The chairman did observe, however, that it was routine in arbitration for contested issues of arbitrability to be determined at the outset by a majority vote of such a panel as this. In concluding the first session on February 4, he also indicated that when the panel resumed in its second session there would be a ruling by him on arbitrability since the teachers were entitled to have that issue resolved before proceeding further into what they felt would otherwise be a futile, time-consuming, and expensive proceeding from which little or no benefit could be derived by them. The chairman also indicated that, while he believed himself legally empowered to issue such an award without further delay on February 4, the board having previously had contact with its counsel, the chairman was concerned to assure that there exist the appearance as well as the substance of due process in this proceeding. Therefore he recessed the hearing expressly so that the board or district could arrange for legal counsel to be present prepared to argue the issue of arbitrability.

The hearing resumed on February 19. Deputy County Counsel Ragnar R. Engebretsen was present. The chairman explained his view of the legal posture of the proceeding and, after discussion among those present, ruled that the grievances were arbitrable, which is to say, that the jointly ratified agreement of the parties provided for final and binding arbitration of the grievances, and that the board could not unilaterally abrogate that joint commitment. The board's panel designee, Mr. Simpson, then declared that he was unauthorized to proceed further on that basis. The chairman recessed the hearing pending the PUEA's resort to the Superior Court of California for an order enforcing the panel's award that the Meyer-Vela grievances are arbitrable and compelling the board to proceed to arbitrate as provided by Article IV of the agreement.

Finally in the sequence of events leading up to this arbitration it should be noted that the Superior Court for Los Angeles County, on October 20, 1970, issued its memorandum of intended decision in the widely publicized case of *Hayes* v. *Association of Classroom Teachers—Los Angeles, et al.,* and three other consolidated cases. . . . That litigation arose out of the efforts of the L.A. City Board of Education and its teachers to end a situation of acute tension and work stoppage so as to reach accord concerning the terms and conditions of employment in the city schools for the teachers. In a decision that the trial court itself clearly recognized to be highly contentious, the court held that the Winton Act, delineating the powers of the Los Angeles City Board of Education (and of the Placentia Board and other boards throughout the state) does not confer upon a board of education the power and authority to enter into a contract with a negotiating council of teachers that contains, among other provisions, one that provides for submission of grievances for resolution by a jointly selected impartial arbitrator whose decision, as the L.A. City Rule 3700, Article VI, Section 10(g) phrased it, "shall be final and binding on the district, the Board of Education, the negotiating council, and any employee or employees involved in the arbitration proceedings." The trial court categorized that clause as an invalid delegation of authority.

II. ANALYSIS AND CONCLUSIONS

A basic and quite misleading misconception of the role and function of an impartial arbitrator is reflected in much of the current discussion about the lawfulness of final and binding arbitration of grievances of employees arising in the course of work in the public sector, including public school teachers. It is given typical expression in this instance in the opinion letter of the county counsel's office which observed on

> distinct possibility, based upon the experiences from other districts, that the decision made by such a panel (chaired by an impartial arbitrator) could, in fact, be contrary to board rules and regulations. While grievance procedures provide that a grievance pertains only to the interpretation of board rules and policy, panels constituted as outlined here in the proposed procedure could, because of the equities involved, reach decisions contrary to existing rules.

The United States Supreme Court in *United Steelworkers* v. *Enterprise Wheel and Car Corp., 363* U.S. 593, 597 (1960) has defined the legal role of the arbitrator as the courts see it and as arbitrators, with infrequent exceptions, practice it: "An arbitrator is confined to interpretation and application of the collective bargaining agreement; he does not sit to dispense his own brand of industrial justice."

So it is that where the contracting parties have incorporated a provision in their agreement, one that has become caught up in contention arising out of its application, an arbitrator will seek to deduce and effectuate their mutual intention in adopting it. He will strive to remain faithful to their joint will. His "own brand" of justice only comes into focus when they have purposely refrained from detailing their own intent and instead have indicated their desire that he achieve justice in the particular case, as in the common circumstance when he is explicitly authorized to determine if discipline has been meted out for "just cause." Yet even then it is not simply his own sense of rectitude that he plumbs. He tries to reckon what would have been accepted by the parties as "just," given the circumstances of the employment and of the community attitudes toward the kind of conduct involved, had they sought to negotiate a disposition of precisely this kind of disciplinary problem.

There has always been debate among employers, unions, or governmental regulatory agencies about the continued viability of the institution of collective bargaining in the private sector. . . . But careful studies among employers, unions, and their respective attorneys have disclosed overwhelming acceptance (1) of the utility to the securing of stability of production and employee morale of resort to arbitration for the prompt resolution of employee grievances; (2) of the preference of arbitral processes to the time-consuming, and typically and unfortunately, the inexperienced ministrations of the courts in labor disputes arising during the terms of collective agreements; and (3) of the national emergence of a corps of several hundred experienced and widely acceptable professional labor arbitrators who perform their functions sufficiently well as to prompt informed disputants repeatedly to turn jointly to them for their services in dispute resolution. . . .

Thus the adverse inference contained in the county counsel's opinion letter is unwarranted in the experience of those who have worked with grievance arbitration in recent years. Actually, regardless of the merits of the conclusions stated in it, a fair reading of that letter discloses that in major part it amounted to tactical advice on negotiating with teachers' representative, not only to advance the benefit of the Placentia Board, but even for that of other education districts in Orange County not parties to this agreement.

It is notable that the opinion did *not* say that this agreement was unlawful, only that it went beyond the minimal requirements of the Winton Act in its negotiated concessions. But those negotiations had already been concluded by the responsible representatives of the parties and the resultant agreement had been duly ratified by each.

The kind of advice proffered in the opinion letter would certainly have been relevant to the board during negotiations. That was the time to have sought it. In private sector collective bargaining someone performing the functions illustrated in these circumstances by the county counsel is present at the bargaining table or on the other end of a telephone line making precisely the same kinds of suggestions contained in the opinion letter. But it is unlawful in the private sector as failure to bargain in good faith for an employer to refuse to abide by (or even to refuse to sign) an agreement already "informally" concluded, for the asserted reason that his attorney has since advised him that the prevailing law didn't require him to make as many concessions as he had done, or that other employers might be embarrassed by the extent of them, or that there is a "distinct possibility" that applications of the terms "could, in fact, be contrary to board rules and regulations." This reasoning is as specious in the public sector as it is held to be in the private sector. The courts do not assume otherwise lawful terms will be unlawfully applied, and most assuredly do not do so in determining whether a provision for binding grievance arbitration should be enforced. Yet in suggested change No. 11, the county counsel's opinion letter of October 23 was unable to muster any more substantial reason than that to disapprove of binding arbitration of grievances. And it is noteworthy that, even then, he did not advise the board that it could not lawfully abide by its prior commitment, although the board later expressed itself, on January 12, as regarding his advice to be binding on it.

Turning to the specifics of the dispute at hand, the threshold question of arbitrability is one that is frequently submitted to arbitrators for decision even though there may be a basic legal question underlying its resolution. The issue at this phase of the proceeding is this: may one party to a jointly negotiated and ratified agreement later and unilaterally abrogate its commitment to submit employee grievances to final and binding arbitral decision. The board purported to transpose that evident bilateral obligation to submit into an occasion for the exercise of its discretion to accept or reject an "advisory" report. It expressly relied on the county counsel's opinion letter discussed above. Aside from the fallacious tactical grounds advanced by the county counsel and discussed above, the board's power so to take its action stands or falls with the conclusion that existing state law denies or confers upon boards of education the power to submit to final and binding decisions of employee grievances by impartial arbitrators.

The modern legal thrust in public employment generally throughout the country is to sanction grievance arbitration. This trend is increasing with the realization both that the range and specifics of the administrative issues being resolved by submission to grievance arbitration bear a remarkable resemblance to those that have long since been the grist for private sector arbitration and that arbitrators appear to apply essentially the same standards developed in the private sector. . . . The trend is solidly buttressed by the elemental link between the relinquishment or prohibition of the right of employees to strike and the alternative resort for dispute resolution to arbitration. Public employees are currently not legally entitled to strike. Where grievance arbitration has existed in the private sector, a marked decrease has occurred in "wildcat" strikes—those that are unlawful because of contractual or stautory prohibition. With the surge of "job actions" in the public sector, including teachers, the moral should be wholly visible: where courts may by reasonable interpretations do so, they should presume lawful rather than unlawful statutory delegation of the power of public employer bodies, including boards of education, to submit grievances for final and binding arbitration.

Unfortunately the trial court in the recent *L.A. City Board of Education* case raised the contrary presumption . . . and the seeds thus judicially sown will grow to plague Los Angeles grievously unless the appellate process reacts quickly and sensitively. It is too bad that that trial court did not either have before it or heed the emerging pattern of sympathetic statutory interpretation in the country at large.

Earlier judicial authority reflecting community attitudes rejecting the idea of negotiating for such things as grievance arbitration by public employees through their elected representatives is simply being bypassed by more recent judicial interpretations. Older notions about "delegability" and "plenary power" are being replaced by more contemporary ideas. "The major legal threat—and puny it is—to compulsory and binding arbitration is the doctrine of illegal delegation," write Professors Harry Wellington and Ralph Winter in their recent exhaustive study of the structuring of collective bargaining in public employment. "The constitution of each state gives legislative power to the legislature. The question is, to what extent can the legislature delegate that power? Of course, it can delegate power over wages and conditions of employment of municipal employees to municipal legislatures." Wellington and Winter, "Structuring Collective Bargaining in Public Employment," 79 *Yale Law Journal* 605, 834 (1970). Beyond that, the notion of illegal delegability is receiving short shrift in the most recent decisions of the state supreme courts. Thus the Pennsylvania, Rhode Island, and Wyoming supreme courts have each in recent months had occasion to treat that notion with the back of the judicial hand. The Wyoming Supreme Court succinctly disposed of this conventional but "puny" legal threat by declaring that, as is true in the industrial private sector, arbitrators are empowered to *execute* the law, not to *make it*. *Wyoming* v. *City of Laramie*, 437 2d 295, 304 (1968). The Pennsylvania Supreme Court reasoned, "If the delegation of power is to make law, which involves the discretion of what the law shall be, then the power is nondelegable. If the conferred authority is the power of discretion to execute the law already determined and circumscribed, then the delegation is unobjectionable." *Harvey* v. *Russo*, 71 L.R.R.M. 2817 (1969). The Rhode Island Supreme Court had little difficulty disposing of the asserted problems of invalid delegation for lack of adequate standards to guide the arbitrators and because the delegation was to "private persons." As to the first, the general terms of the enabling statute were "sufficient to meet the constitutional requirements that the delegated power be confined by reasonable norms or standards." As to the "third persons," the court simply held that the arbitrators were acting as public officers or agents of the legislature when they were carrying out their arbitral duties: "each member of boards of arbitration . . . is a public officer and that collectively these officers constitute an administrative government agency." California, even in private sector arbitration, defines arbitrators expressly by statute as "judicial officers" for contempt purposes and empowers them to issue subpoenas, administer oaths, and order depositions to be taken. And California courts have for years been in the forefront of the modern development of labor arbitration as the preferable alternative to economic self-help or judicial administration.

It is obvious that it will serve the public interest greatly to assure that the tensions and frustration of public employees—including teachers—over unresolved grievances be channeled away from "job actions"—regardless of their legality—and into the ameliorating "therapy of arbitration," as the Supreme Court has described a major utility of labor arbitration.

As Arvid Anderson, chairman of New York City's Office of Collective Bargaining and a former public member of Wisconsin's Employment Relations Board, one of the nation's foremost authorities in reference to these problems, has realistically observed, "If the public wants arbitration as a means of resolving public employee disputes, the courts will find new answers to overcome traditional legal obstacles."

These views of courts and critics have shown the insubstantiality of the board's and its advisor's conclusion that it lacked statutory authority when it entered into the "final and binding" commitment. Having carefully reviewed the history of the negotiations between the parties to the agreement, and the belated and specious concerns about lawfulness, the conclusion must be that the board had the power to enter into its original commitment, could not unilaterally withdraw from, will be bound and not merely "advised" by the ultimate award of this arbitration panel on the merits of the Meyer-Vela grievances at issue, and must perforce proceed in this arbitral proceeding without further delay.

III. AWARD

A. This matter was heard on February 4 and 19, 1971, at the offices of the Placentia Unified School District, Placentia, California. Each party was afforded ample opportunity to present evidence and argument, and each availed thereof. . . .

B. The award is that the Meyer-Vela grievances are properly before this arbitration panel for resolution by final and binding decision on the merits. The district and the Board of Education are herewith directed to appear and proceed with the hearing and disposition of the subject grievances. Jurisdiction of those grievances is retained by this panel pending judicial enforcement of this award.

/s/ Clyde Williams

/s/ Edgar A. Jones, Jr.
Chairman

Discussion Questions

1. What were the two main issues in this case?
2. Discuss the importance of the Winton Act to the resolution of the disputed issues.

3. Did the arbitration panel accept the argument that the contract "could, in fact, be contrary to board rules and regulations?"
4. Why are grievance arbitration clauses especially significant in the public as against the private sector?
5. Describe the recent judicial treatment of the notion of "illegal delegability."

Section 2. Arbitrability of Alleged Contract Violations

In private employment, the standard arbitration clause in the collective agreement provides that disputes dealing with the interpretation and application of contractual provisions are to be submitted to arbitration. As far as the role of the judicial branch is concerned, "When a party seeks enforcement of an arbitration clause, the court's only job is to determine whether the contract contains a promise to arbitrate the dispute." [4] After that determination is made, the arbitrator, not the courts, will determine the merits of the dispute.

One difference that has developed between the public and private sector in this regard is that in the latter the courts generally determine the issue of arbitrability, whereas in the former—as will be demonstrated subsequently—labor relations agencies can make such rulings.

In the Matter of

The City of New York (petitioner) *and* Social Service Employees Union, Local 371, District Council 37, AFSCME, AFL-CIO (respondent)

Decision No. B–4–72

Docket No. BCB–95–71

(Office of Collective Bargaining. Board of Collective Bargaining)

DECISION AND ORDER

On May 25, 1971, Social Service Employees Union, Local 371 (the union) filed with the Office of Collective Bargaining a request for arbitration (Case No. A–163–71), claiming alleged violations of a contract. On June 7, 1971, the city filed a petition contesting arbitrability. The union's answer to the petition was filed on June 21, 1971.

The controversy centers upon the layoff of 266 provisional caseworkers in the Department of Social Services which the union maintains was in violation of a collective bargaining agreement ("contract") between the parties and of a supplemental agreement entered into as the result of the recommendations of a reorganization and workload committee which was established, pursuant to the terms of the contract, to deal with problems relating to the reorganization of the Department of Social Services. Both the contract and the supplemental agreement had a terminal date of December 31, 1970.

The city's challenge to arbitrability is based on three main points:

1. That the union relies in whole or in part on contract provisions relating to the departmental reorganization, whereas the layoffs complained of had nothing to do with reorganization but were caused solely by general budget reductions.

2. That the actions complained of occurred *subsequent* to termination of the agreement containing the provisions relied upon by the union

3. That no waivers other than that of the union were filed.

In support of the first main point the city contends that since the contract provisions cited by the union were not intended to deal with the type of condition the union complains of, those provisions were not violated. In response, the union alleges that specified acts of the city violated cited sections of the contract dealing with the subject matter of the controversy proposed for arbitration and that the contract provides for the arbitration of controversies relating to the application or interpretation of the contract. The city does not deny that there is a contract between the parties, or that a controversy relating to the interpretation of the contract exists, or that the contract requires that the parties submit controversies as to the application or interpretation of the contract to arbitration. Instead the city argues for an interpretation of the contract in its favor, namely, that the provisions cited by the union relate only to reorganization of the departments and then proceeds to explain how and why the layoffs were made; that is, that they were not connected with the reorganization but were necessitated by budget cutbacks. The interpretation of contract terms and the determination of their applicability in a given case is a function for the arbitrator and not for the forum dealing with the question of the arbitrability of the underlying dispute. We have defined the basis for the determination of questions of arbitrability in *Matter of Office of Labor Relations and Social Service Employees Union,* Decision No. B–2–69, as follows:

> In determining arbitrability, the board must decide whether the parties are in any way obligated to arbitrate their controversies and, if so, whether the obligation is broad enough in its scope to include the particular controversy presented.

We find, accordingly, that the city's first point does not constitute a bar to arbitrability.

The second main point raised by the city's petition is that while the union's request for arbitration is based, in part, upon the provisions of the supplemental agreement, the effective period of the supplemental agreement had terminated at the time when the acts complained of occurred and that those acts therefore could not have been in violation of the provisions of the supplemental agreement.

The supplemental agreement incorporates by reference the grievance and arbitration provisions of the major contract. Both agreements terminated on December 31, 1970. The record before us, as revealed by the pleadings, establishes the fact that both agreements are interrelated and intended by the parties to prescribe the union-employer relationship between them. We, therefore, read the two agreements together as constituting the collective bargaining agreement between the parties establishing a bargaining relationship for the period ending December 31, 1970.

The pleadings show that subsequent to that date and during the period in which the acts complained of occurred, the parties were engaged in negotiations for a new contract. Since, therefore, the acts complained of occurred during a period governed by the status quo provision of the NYCCBL, this matter is governed by the interpretation of that provision in the *MEBA* case (Decision No. B–1–72). In the cited case, we decided, with some reservation not pertinent here, that all of the terms and conditions of a prior contract are continued in effect by operation of law during the statutory status quo period and those disputes relating to alleged violations of such terms and conditions are subject to arbitration in accordance with the grievance and arbitration provisions of the prior contract. We hold, therefore, that the city's second point does not constitute a bar to arbitration.

The third main point of the city's challenge to arbitrability is that the union has only filed a waiver on its behalf and that in the absence of waivers filed by employees arbitration is barred under the terms of Section 1173–8.0(d) of the NYCCBL. The specific issue regarding the circumstances controlling the need for union or employees' waivers was treated at length in *Matter of the City of New York and New York City Local 246, SEIU, AFL-CIO* (Decision No. B–12–71). That decision, insofar as it is here pertinent, reads as follows:

When the grievance sought to be arbitrated is "uniquely personal" to the grievant (*Brown* v. *Sterling Aluminum Products Corp.*, USCA 8th Cir., 1966, 63 L.R.R.M. 2177, 2180) and involves "an ascertainable aggrieved employee" (*Soho Chemical Co.*, 1963, 141 NLRB No. 72, 52 L.R.R.M. 1390) the board will require that the grievant and the union sign the written waiver before the matter may be further processed." (Cf. *Textile*

Works v. *Lincoln Mills,* 353 U.S. 448, 40 L.R.R.M. 2113, concurring opinion, "The district court had jurisdiction over the action since it involved an obligation running to the union—a union controversy—and not uniquely personal rights of employees sought to be enforced by a union.") However, "whenever the right sought to be enforced is not uniquely personal to the individual but is a right possessed by the bargaining unit as a whole, only the union as the sole representative of that unit would normally have the standing to enforce the right." (Cf. *Brown* v. *Sterling Aluminum Products Corp., supra.*)

. . .

In sum, it is our view that under the NYCCBL, if a factual situation demonstrates that the issue involves an alleged violation or a right possessed by the bargaining unit as a whole, or by the union as exclusive representative, the union's waiver is sufficient to warrant proceeding to arbitration of the dispute.

The rights asserted by the union in this matter derive exclusively from the contract between the parties. The first asserted right is based upon the job security provisions of the contract dealing with provisional caseworkers. Since provisional employees have no job tenure rights under civil service law, it is our opinion that, in the absence of any challenge regarding the authority to enter into the agreement, the right being asserted here exists solely by virtue of the contract.

As the union complains of layoffs in violation of the agreement, the narrow issue appears to concern job rights. The questions whether or not such rights are tied to the term of the agreement or, by reason of the statutory status quo imposed on the city and the union, survived the term of the agreement, are questions peculiarly adaptable to the province of an arbitrator and resolvable in that forum. The union is seeking to enforce job rights it may have under the expired contract. Therefore, we require submission to arbitration of the general issue of whether the union is entitled to stay any action violative of those rights under the expired agreement between the parties.

The second right asserted by the union refers to the section of the supplemental agreement dealing with caseload. Any rights which may exist in this area, are, again, derived exclusively from the contract and a dispute arising thereunder is subject to arbitration.

In both instances it is factually demonstrated that the grievance is a union grievance affecting all or a substantial number of employees in the bargaining unit. Under such circumstances, as we said in the *MEBA* case, *supra,* the only waiver required is by the union and not by the employee.

Therefore, we find that the city's third point challenging arbitrability does not constitute a bar to arbitration.

ORDER

Pursuant to the powers vested in the Board of Collective Bargaining by the New York City Collective Bargaining Law, IT IS HEREBY ORDERED that the petition filed by the city of New York be, and the same hereby is, dismissed; and IT IS FURTHER ORDERED that upon the filing of an appropriate waiver by the union, that this proceeding be, and the same hereby is, referred to an arbitrator to be agreed upon by the parties, or appointed pursuant to the consolidated rules of the Office of Collective Bargaining.

Dated: January 26, 1972
      New York, N.Y.

/s/ Arvid Anderson
    Chairman

/s/ Eric J. Schmertz
    Member

/s/ William Michelson
    Member

/s/ Thomas J. Herlihy
    Member (Alternate)

Discussion Questions

1. Which contract provision did the union allege had been breached by management?
2. Discuss the city's position that the dispute was nonarbitrable.
3. How did the board rule on the city's arguments?
4. A grievance may be a union grievance or an individual grievance. Of what significance is this distinction?

Section 3. Arbitration of a Discharge Grievance

Normally discharge cases are resolved by utilizing the contract's grievance procedure with a final determination by an appointed arbitrator or panel or board of arbitrators. In the absence of specific contractual reasons for discharge actions, the standard usually applied is that of "just" or "reasonable" cause. These criteria are utilized in both the public and private sectors. The following case involves a fact situation in which the discharged employee was not provided with due process after being terminated, according to contractual requirements, and therefore filed a grievance challenging his termination, which necessitated the empaneling of an arbitration board to issue a binding award.

In the Matter of

Erie Metropolitan Transit Authority *and* **Amalgamated Transit Union Local Division 568**

Discharge Grievance
John J. Woods
February 18, 1972

OPINION OF THE CHAIRMAN

BACKGROUND

This grievance came before a board of arbitration for decision pursuant to Article III of the October 1, 1969 agreement between the above parties. It challenges the discharge of driver John J. Woods on September 17, 1971.

At a hearing in Erie on January 6, 1972, both parties had full opportunity to present evidence. Posthearing briefs were waived by agreement. Oral argument was presented by counsel for each party on February 2, 1972, and the board then met to decide the case in executive session. By letter dated February 3, 1972, the parties formally were advised of the board's award, with board member Doyle dissenting. This opinion by the chairman sets forth his analysis of the evidence and contractual issues.

Apart from the ultimate issue of proper cause for discharge, this case involves a significant procedural problem under Article IV, Section 2(c), of the October 1, 1969 agreement, reading:

> In the event the authority considers the alleged misconduct or violation of the rules as sufficient grounds for severe discipline or discharge, or the holding off of the employee from his duties, except in the case of embezzlement of money, use of intoxicants while on duty, and other violations of the criminal statutes, *no such action shall be taken without first giving the employee a hearing* which shall be held within ten (10) days after the date he is charged with the alleged offense. *At a reasonable time prior to the hearing, the employee shall be apprised in writing of the precise charge against him.* At the investigation or hearing, he may be accompanied by representatives of his own choosing who shall be permitted to question witnesses and otherwise represent the individual involved. *He shall have a reasonable opportunity to secure the presence of witnesses of the occurrence under investigation, and the authority shall produce the actual witnesses of the occurrence upon which the authority bases its charge.* The authority shall furnish the accused employee, if he so requests, with a stenographic transcript of the testimony, or, if the accused employee so desires, he may obtain his own reporter. If the

employee is dissatisfied with the disciplinary action taken, he may treat it as a grievance and the matter referred to arbitration to be conducted in accordance with procedure outlined in Article III of this agreement. (Emphasis added.)

Grievant Woods, 46 years of age, was hired by the authority on August 27, 1968. About 2:32 P.M. on September 17, 1971, he was scheduled to relieve another driver on the No. 4 run at the corner of 14th and State Streets; the run proceeds south on State Street from Perry Square and covers about eight miles in various directions before returning finally to the open-air terminal maintained on the west side of Perry Square. Before going to 14th and State, Woods had lunch in a nearby bar and consumed three bottles of ale in addition to his food. Shortly thereafter he went to 14th and State and sat down on some pipes protruding above the sidewalk near the curb at the corner to await arrival of the bus. Mrs. Dolores Gower was a passenger on the bus and her report of the events which followed led to the discharge here under review. Mrs. Gower testified at the hearing and a written statement which she had prepared earlier also was presented in evidence. Since her testimony did not differ materially from the substance of her written statement, the latter is herewith reproduced:

> On Friday, September 17, 1971, I was a passenger on board an Erie Metropolitan Transportation Authority bus—the East 6th St. East 26th St. route to be specific. I had boarded the bus at Perry Square from which we departed at the scheduled time of 2:25 P.M.
>
> We proceeded south on State St. and subsequently arrived at the intersection of State and 14th Sts. My position on the bus was behind and to the right of the driver, on the "side seat" and next to the front doors of the bus.
>
> As we approached the aforementioned intersection, I noticed the "relief" driver sitting on three (3) "pipes" which protrude approximately sixteen (16) inches from the sidewalk cement, directly in front of the traffic light standard. As the bus slowed for its stop, this driver motioned for the bus to continue on—(in jest, I presumed).
>
> The driver operating the bus at the time, brought it to a stop, set the air brakes, put the gears in neutral, removed his belongings and alighted from the bus.
>
> As the waiting driver arose and started to board the bus, I became aware of his unsteady gait—and noticed also, that he climbed the steps with some difficulty.
>
> I might add here—I also realized that the "relief" driver, was Mr. John Woods—a speaking acquaintance—(but Mr. Woods did not, at the time recognize me).

Mr. Woods seemed to stagger as he groped for a handhold and then sat *heavily* down onto the driver's seat. Because of his actions, which did not seem to be those of a sober person, I paid particularly close attention to his motions from then on. He proceeded, with some difficulty to adjust his seat, then attempted twice to release the air brakes, and evidently believing he had done so, stepped on the accelerator and prepared to move on—however, the engine merely revved—so Mr. Woods, for the third time, attempted to release the air brakes, and after a few moments finally succeeded, after which he again raced the engine before he realized he had not as yet, placed the gear in first. With a great amount of "groping"—the brakes were released, gears in position and the driver moved the vehicle forward.

In my position, not only could I view the driver's movements easily, I was also at an advantage to see his face—(i.e., eyes) even though Mr. Woods was wearing sun glasses at the time. I make mention of this, only because I noticed his eyes would close briefly from time to time. To my estimation, Mr. Woods, was indeed, inebriated. As we proceeded on the route, Mr. Woods appeared to have a tendency to "over-drive" the bus.

I think I should inject here, an explanation as to the access of my knowledge of operating this type of vehicle. My knowledge, probably can be considered "first-hand," since, for over a period of twenty years I drove trucks—twelve of those years as a driver of "rigs" (semi-trucks—tractor/trailer)—for a nationally known food processing company—in the State of Washington.

My concern over Mr. Woods' ability to operate the bus in a safe manner increased as we continued on the route. It increased so much, as a matter of fact, I got off the bus two stops *before* my usual stop.

As I walked to my home, I considered the situation seriously, being greatly concerned with the fact that on the return run this bus would be picking up students as well as regular passengers. The possibility of an accident involving so many people was evident—and the further possibility of injuries, maybe deaths, and the resulting litigations left me with no alternative other than to report the matter to EMTA authorities. This decision was made only because of my concern for the safety of others—and *not* to place any individual in ill-aura or his means of livelihood in jeopardy.

Therefore, on the same day, at a few minutes after 3 o'clock P.M., I placed a call to the office of the EMTA and asked for Mr. Bob Ennis. The secretary informed me Mr. Ennis was out but would be returning shortly, and politely requested my name and number for Mr. Ennis to return my call.

Approximately fifteen to twenty minutes later, Mr. Ennis *did* return my call and I explained the entire situation to him, adding that I regretted *any* and *all* hardships it might cause anyone or any anguish which might result, should that be the case, as this was definitely *not* my intent. My *entire* and only concern was to *prevent,* if possible, any trouble(s), accidents, and/or injuries.

I also explained to Mr. Ennis, that I felt I could judge whether or not a person was intoxicated because as a previous tavern owner, I had been exposed to this type of "affliction" quite often.

This, to my recollection, is an accurate account of the events which occurred on that day, and should clarify any misconceptions which may have arisen.

The "Bob Ennis" mentioned in the above statement was Transportation Superintendent Robert J. Enas, with whom Mrs. Gower says she had become acquainted through her use of the EMTA facilities. Superintendent Enas did not testify as to the detail of his conversation with Mrs. Gower, but it seems clear that, in the course of their telephone conversation, she gave him the substance of the report later set forth in her hand-printed statement.

Superintendent Enas did recollect, specifically, that Mrs. Gower gave him the impression that Woods had "wavered" in walking to the bus, had "groped" for the handrail in entering the bus, and had appeared to be in no condition to drive by reason of intoxication. In any event, according to Enas, he took Assistant Superintendent Michael with him to Perry Square to await arrival there of Woods' bus. The bus drew in around 4:05 and exactly what happened thereafter is unclear under the testimony.

Driver Woods says that he brought the bus to a stop not far from where he saw Enas and Michael standing, discharged his passengers, and then loaded passengers boarding at that point. Then, while he was still seated in the driver's seat, Superintendent Enas entered and asked him if he was feeling all right and he replied that he was. Enas then suggested that he was drunk, which Woods denied. Enas asked if he had had anything to drink and Woods replied that he had had a "couple" of ales. Enas rejoined that a couple of ales would not make a man as drunk as Woods appeared to be, and suggested that Woods take a "blood test" which Enas already had arranged at the nearby City Hall. Woods strongly denied that he was intoxicated and refused to take the test. Enas then told Woods that he was discharged. Woods recollected that the conversation up to this point had taken place inside the bus.

Superintendent Enas recollected that the discharge occurred on the sidewalk after he had requested Woods to leave the bus. Both Enas and Assistant Superintendent Michael testified that Woods appeared to be unsteady in leaving the bus, and Michael said that he "lurched" as he did so. Both testified that Woods thereafter leaned against a nearby utility pole for support. They recalled that Woods then went aboard the next bus (which had arrived at the terminal on the same run) and attempted to get some of his former passengers (who had been placed on board by Michael) to sign witness cards for him. Woods finally left, walked to the main office of EMTA at 14th and Peach Streets, and contacted Union Representative Howells. The latter suggested that he come back there at 7 P.M. when Division President Francis Roach was expected to arrive. Woods met Roach at around 7 P.M.

Both Enas and Michael in effect said they thought that Woods was intoxicated because he seemed unsteady on his feet and his speech seemed slurred. They signed a written statement around 5 P.M. on September 17, 1971, reading:

> On Friday, September 17, 1971, at approximately 3:20 P.M., I received a call from a lady passenger. She stated to me that the driver of the East 26th St. bus leaving Perry Square at 2:25 P.M. was intoxicated. When he got into the bus and sat down he had quite a time getting the bus in gear and also jerked the bus starting out. She also said he was acting very strange and should be checked as she didn't believe he was in any condition to drive.

> The Assistant Superintendent, Mr. Michaels, and myself went to Perry Square to check the driver, Mr. Woods. He was due into the Park at 3:50 P.M. to go East 26th Street. He came in at 4:05 P.M. just 15 minutes late. After he discharged the passengers I asked him to get off the bus. In getting off the bus, he showed me a couple signed witness cards and in a somewhat muffled tone said he has these cards. We couldn't understand what else he said. I asked him if he had been drinking and he answered, he had a couple of beers with lunch. I told him a couple beers would not have this bad of an effect. I told him he was in no condition to drive a bus. When he got out of the bus, he was so unsteady on his feet that he had to lean against a light post to steady himself. I also told him that I had it arranged for him to take an intoximeter test at the Police Station if he would consent to it but he refused. I then told him I had no choice but to discharge him for driving while being under the influence of intoxicating beverages.

Woods firmly denied that he was intoxicated but agreed that he had had "about three" bottles of ale at lunch. He not only denied that he had left the bus *prior* to his discharge, but also said that his reason for leaning against the nearby utility pole later was that he was so angry, at having been discharged preemptorily, that he backed a little bit away from where Enas and Michael were standing, folded his arms, and leaned against the pole while seeking to control his emotions. He said that it was not until he had stood alone for a few minutes that he was able to suppress his anger. Then he boarded the next bus, to which some of his passengers had been moved, to obtain witness cards which he indicated he later had lost.

There is no suggestion in the evidence that Woods has a drinking problem, or that he ever before had appeared to be intoxicated while at work. He is the first EMTA driver who was discharged for intoxication. In earlier cases involving liquor problems (perhaps half a dozen in ten years) employees have been removed from duty or suspended and the problems seemingly have been solved.

Woods is a big man, about 6 feet, 3 inches tall, and well built. He weighed about 240 pounds on September 17, 1971. The union urges that he could not have become intoxicated merely by drinking three bottles of ale at lunch. In its judgment, the fact that he was not intoxicated is confirmed by his having driven for an hour and a half without any incident, in reasonably good time, as well as by the manner in which he conducted himself after the discharge took place. Most important, however, the union stresses that there was a failure to give Woods a statement of the charges against him and to accord him a full hearing under Article IV, Section 2 (c) before imposing discharge.

The authority relies on testimony, and the written statements, of Gower, Enas, and Michael to establish that Woods was intoxicated. It emphasizes that he refused to take a "balloon test" (which already had been arranged) and did not present as witnesses either the driver he had relieved on September 17, or the one whose bus he later had boarded at Perry Square, to testify that he seemed to them to be sober. It also stresses that he did not later go to his own doctor for an examination to establish that he was not intoxicated.

When an employee is intoxicated while at work, says the authority, the provisions of Article IV, Section 2(c) do not apply so as to bar immediate discharge without a hearing. Although Article IV, Section 2(c) does not refer to being intoxicated, but rather to "drinking on the job," the authority stresses that the exception to the notice and hearing requirement in Section 2(c) also applies to infractions where "other violations of the criminal statutes" are involved. Driving a bus while "under the influence of liquor" clearly is a violation of Pennsylvania law, in the authority's view, and so falls within this exception.

The authority also cites a provision in its "Bus Rules" issued to all drivers when first employed. Under the heading of "Personal Conduct—Habits," it includes,

5. The following acts are prohibited:
   (a) *The use of intoxicating liquors while on duty, or the excessive use of same at any time, or reporting for duty showing evidence thereof.* (Emphasis added.)
   (b) Constant frequenting of drinking places when off duty where intoxicants are supposed to be sold.

(c) Carrying intoxicants about the person while on duty.
(d) Carrying intoxicants on the company's property at any time.
(e) Gambling in any form.
(f) Smoking or chewing tobacco while operating bus.
(g) Smoking tobacco while off duty in any of the company's buildings, except where specially permitted.

The union questions the applicability of the bus rules (which were developed in 1956 by the predecessor, Erie Coach Company) and urges that the issue of proper cause for discharge should be decided only under applicable terms of the parties' agreement. It sees no doubt that Article IV, Section 2(c), requires a written charge and a hearing within ten days of the alleged offense in all discharge cases. The only relevant exception to the requirement that the hearing take place *before* discharge, it says, applies to use of intoxicants "while on duty," which does not apply here. The authority's assertion that Woods committed a misdemeanor (by driving while "under the influence of liquor"), according to the union, cannot control in any event because Article IV, Section 2(c) plainly requires a written charge and a hearing; the exception therein relates only to whether the holding of a hearing must be *before* the driver is removed from service. This meaning seems entirely clear to the union, when the paragraph in question is read in the context of Article IV as a whole. Any exception to the procedural requirements of Article IV, Section 2(c) thus should be construed narrowly.

The authority replies to this argument by stressing that a discharged employee who does not receive a written charge and hearing under Article IV, Section 2(c) is not totally deprived of a hearing. Rather, it says, the "hearing" takes place in the grievance procedure and in arbitration, where necessary, after he files a grievance. The authority urges, on the basis of an exchange during cross-examination of Division President Roach, that this indeed is the agreed interpretation of this provision. And in any event, it suggests that Division 568 waived any right to raise such a procedural objection by not pressing immediately for a hearing under Article IV, Section 2(c), and by seeming later to concur in the unusual and leisurely procedure followed in considering the grievance. In this connection it stresses that (1) Superintendent Enas told Division President Roach of the discharge in a telephone conversation around 5 P.M. on September 17, (2) the union agreed not to meet on Woods' grievance until October 18, at which time it was shown Mrs. Gower's written statement, (3) after the meeting on October 18 the union was given a copy of Superintendent Enas' written statement, and (4) Grievant Woods was available to participate in the October 18 grievance meeting if the union desired.

FINDINGS

The most significant problem in this case involves interpretation and application of Article IV, Section 2(c). It is appropriate, however, to treat several other matters raised by the evidence before passing on to the key procedural question.

The parties disagree as to whether the "Bus Rules" properly might apply in situations of this sort. These rules were issued initially by the predecessor company in 1956, and so originally were not the rules of the authority. Nonetheless it is clear that the authority adopted the existing rules when it took over this property and each new driver thereafter was given a copy of the rules when initially employed. In these circumstances there is no real doubt that the bus rules provide relevant standards of conduct for the authority's drivers.

Rule 5(a) thus applies here, and the evidence shows that Woods reported for duty "showing evidence" of excessive use of alcohol. This finding supports imposition of appropriate discipline whether or not Woods properly could have been found to be "under the influence of liquor" so as to have committed a misdemeanor within the meaning of the Pennsylvania law. (There is no suggestion that Woods ever has been so charged by the Erie police.)

A next question (apart from any procedural issue) is whether Woods' offense, in light of all relevant factors, could be deemed of such aggravated nature as to warrant discharge. The evidence reveals that in earlier instances when employees reported for work "showing evidence" of excessive use of alcohol, discharge was not imposed; the employee simply was sent home. The rules do not specify automatic discharge in all such cases. The rules in any event are subordinate to the collective bargaining agreement to the extent that proper cause for any specific discipline must be established in the grievance procedure. And since the charge ultimately placed against Woods was that he drove his bus while "under the influence" of intoxicating liquor, the authority would have to shoulder the usual burden of proof in establishing such a charge.

It is against this background that the difficult procedural question under Article IV, Section 2(c) must be evaluated. The evidence leaves no doubt that (1) discharge was invoked without any written statement of the charge against Woods, (2) there was no hearing within ten days of the charged offense, and (3) Woods had no opportunity, with a representative of his own choosing, to hear and question the witnesses against him until the arbitration hearing.

Unless the detailed "due process" provisions of Article IV, Section 2

(c) do not apply at all in situations such as the present, it seems manifest that the discharge must be set aside as improvidently imposed.

The critical language in Article IV 2(c) is by no means unambiguous and the precise interpretive problem never before has been raised in this collective bargaining relationship. Neither party seems to claim that there has been any practice in applying the clause which might provide an accepted interpretation, although Division President Roach testified that in one earlier discharge for intoxication a hearing was held *after* the discharge and the penalty then reduced to a suspension.

The authority puts a good deal of weight on parts of the testimony of Division President Roach under cross-examination, and the following excerpts from his testimony are particularly pertinent in this regard:

Q. Mr. Roach, you have testified in chief that there was no hearing given to Mr. Woods. What do you mean by hearing?

A. By hearing, I mean that the company at no time presented a charge against Mr. Woods, or gave him a chance to face his accusers at a hearing.

Q. Is it your position that the labor contract existing between the union and the authority requires that?

A. Well, I would think so, yes.

.   .   .

Q. It is your position that you may not discharge a bus driver who is under the influence of liquor so as to affect his driving?

A. Is it my position that you may not discharge a bus driver who is under the influence of liquor so as to affect his driving?

Q. Yes.

A. No, that is not my position.

Q. What is your position? I just want to get it.

A. *I think they could discharge a driver, but I think they must then, once he is discharged, there are certain procedures they must do. He certainly has some rights to defend himself.*

Q. I am just exploring. Isn't this arbitration we are having now the kind of hearing you are thinking of when you say he didn't have a hearing?

A. *It didn't have to go to that extent; but now that we could not get it any other way, yes, this arbitration.* (Emphasis added.)

The authority urges that these answers reveal that Division President Roach really accepts its interpretation that the detailed "due process" requirements of Article IV, Section 2(c) do not truly apply in a case such as the present and that the discharged employee receives the only "hearing" he is entitled to in the grievance procedure, if he files a grievance.

The impartial member of this board is unable to embrace this argument. Division President Roach is not versed in the law and hardly could

be thought to speak with final authority in dealing with an intricate interpretive problem. The whole of his testimony, in any event, made plain his
belief that a hearing should have been given Woods long before the case
got to arbitration. As early as October 18, 1971, Roach and other union
representatives had complained that no written charge had been given to
Woods and that no hearing had been held. (Superintendent Enas, on September 17, and General Manager Burke, on September 20, both earlier had
told Roach in effect that there really was not any point in discussing Woods'
discharge. Then on October 18, the authority representatives told Roach
and International Representative Smith that Woods was "done.")

When Article IV is read as a whole there is support for at least three
interpretations of Section 2(c) in respect to cases such as the present. In
addition to the interpretation urged by the authority, Section 2(c) reasonably may be read to permit immediate discharge (where one of the three
exceptions applies) but also to require a written charge promptly thereafter
with a hearing then held within ten days. This procedure seemingly was
followed in one earlier discharge involving intoxication. The exception in
Section 2(c) also may be read, however, to apply *only* to "holding off of
the employee from his duties." Under such an interpretation, the employee
could be relieved from duty immediately, then given a written charge and
hearing within ten days, before any final decision as to "severe discipline
or discharge" was reached.

The union supports the second of the foregoing three interpretations
on the basis that this result comports best with the comprehensive program
for dealing with all discipline problems set forth in Article IV as a whole.
It notes that Section 2(a) contemplates that an employee shall be informed
of *any* alleged misconduct or violation of the rules "as soon as possible."
Section 2(b) then deals with *all* cases in which the authority considers the
alleged infraction as "sufficient grounds" for severe discipline or discharge,
and broadly states that no such action shall be taken without *first* giving the
employee a hearing, ten days after he is charged with the alleged offense.
In the union view, the mandatory requirements for a written charge and
full hearing apply to *all* cases which come under Section 2(c), and the
exception is intended only to eliminate the requirement that the hearing
take place *before* discharge is imposed. The union deems it inconceivable
that the parties—while erecting comprehensive and careful procedural safeguards to deal with all types of discipline in Article IV as a whole—nonetheless would eliminate entirely the written charge and hearing requirements
as to the most serious types of alleged infractions with which an employee
might be charged. Finally, the union emphasizes, the grievance procedure
set forth in Article IV, Section 1(a) and (b) at no point requires any
"hearing" of the sort contemplated in Section 2(c).

Ambiguities in contract language sometimes may be clarified by reference to negotiating history, or to an interpretation adopted in practice. Neither party here refers to negotiating history, however, and the one earlier instance cited by the union, where a hearing of some sort was held after a discharge, cannot reasonably be held to establish an accepted practice. This board thus must seek to find a meaning in the ambiguous language which is consistent with the language in question and also most reasonable and practical in light of other provisions of the collective agreement.

Article IV unmistakably was designed to provide a comprehensive procedural system covering disciplinary matters, so as to attain at least two basic objectives in the administration of discipline: (a) essential fairness to all employees, and (b) assurance to the authority that its officials would not impose discipline precipitately and in ignorance of relevant facts.

The authority, both as a responsible employer and an important public agency, indubitably has a considerable stake in following procedures which aim at these goals. Where discharge is imposed without any actual hearing before arbitration, the employee not only seems deprived of the "due process" which Section 2(c) seeks to provide, but the authority's disciplining officer often may be placed in the position of applying, and then defending, a discharge imposed without full opportunity to learn and evaluate all relevant facts.

As between the interpretation advanced by the authority, and that advocated by the union, therefore, the impartial member of this board believes the union's view to be more reasonable and practical, and more consistent with the basic thrust and purpose of Article IV as a whole. Indeed, it is virtually inconceivable that the parties—had this question come up specifically in their negotiations—would have written Section 2(c) in such manner as to support the authority's position clearly.

Since this is the opinion of the impartial member of this board, however, it may be appropriate here to note that he prefers the third of the above noted possible interpretations as appearing both more practical and more consistent with the language and purposes of Article IV. Notably, the critical language reads,

In the event the authority considers the alleged misconduct or violation of the rules as sufficient grounds for severe discipline or discharge, *or the holding off of the employee from his duties, except in the case of embezzlement of money, use of intoxicants while on duty, and other violations of the criminal statutes,* no such action shall be taken without first giving the employee a hearing which shall be held within ten (10) days after the date he is charged with the alleged offense. (Emphasis added.)

The writer of this opinion believes this language quite properly may be read to mean that the three exceptions listed apply *only* to "the holding off of the employee from his duties" and not to the *final* decision to discharge or to impose discipline. Under this interpretation an employee whom the authority reasonably believes has (1) embezzled, (2) used intoxicants while on duty, or (3) otherwise violated a criminal statute, could be removed from duty immediately, then given a written charge and a hearing before the final decision as to discipline. Such a procedure would permit the authority to act decisively, in terminating any opportunity to further pursue criminal conduct, but also would protect it from imposition of severe discipline without full opportunity to learn all the facts. The employee, of course, would be assured "due process" before any final disciplinary action were taken. There is basis for this interpretation in the precise grammatical structure of the sentence in issue; while the phrase "or the holding off of the employee from his duties" appears immediately after the words "severe discipline or discharge," it is separated from them by a comma.

Although the impartial member of the board thus believes that this interpretation of the ambiguous language would be the most plausible of the three noted in the board's executive discussion, it cannot be made the basis for decision here since (1) neither party appears to embrace it, (2) there was insufficient opportunity for either party to present argument concerning it, and (3) the only evidence as to earlier practice (albeit sketchy and unclear) tends to support the union's interpretation.

Thus for present purposes it is enough to say that the union's interpretation is supportable, and more so than that of the authority. Accordingly it is found that Article IV, Section 2(c) was not properly applied and Grievant Woods should have received a written statement of the charges against him promptly and a full hearing should have been held within ten days.

The appropriate remedy for the failure to observe Section 2(c) is to set aside the discharge. This is not to suggest, however, that Grievant Woods can escape with no penalty for his conduct on September 17, 1971, in violation of Rule 5(a). Even absent the specific rule, he showed such palpably poor judgment in drinking a very substantial amount of ale in a public bar almost immediately before going on duty, and in actually driving his bus with a strong odor of alcohol about him, that his conduct in any event would have warranted discipline. In balance, therefore, a majority of the board has deemed it sound to sustain a sixty-calendar day suspension as proper discipline under the particular facts of this highly unusual case.

As noted in a February 3, 1972 letter advising the parties of the substance of the board's award herein, board member Doyle dissents from the decision setting aside the discharge. Board member Sternstein, while not joining in the chairman's reasoning in this opinion, concurs in the final result.

/s/ Sylvester Garrett
Impartial Member and Chairman

AWARD

After full consideration of the evidence and argument presented in this case, the Board of Arbitration designated pursuant to Article III of the August 1, 1969 agreement between the above parties awards as follows:

1. The discharge of Grievant Woods is set aside for failure to comply with Article IV, Section 2(c) of the agreement.

2. A sixty-day suspension of Grievant Woods for his infraction of September 17, 1971 is found to be proper.

3. Grievant Woods shall be reinstated promptly and made whole for all earnings lost after November 16, 1971 up to the time of his reinstatement pursuant to this award. In calculating earnings lost by Woods after November 16, 1971, the authority is entitled to deduct from the earnings which he would have received in the employ of the authority those amounts which he earned in other employment after November 16, 1971.

/s/ Herman Sternstein
Union Member (Concurring)

/s/ Thomas E. Doyle
Authority Member (Dissenting)

/s/ Sylvester Garrett
Neutral Member and Chairman

Discussion Questions

1. What is the most significant problem in this case?
2. Why were the 1956 "Bus Rules," although challenged as not applicable by management, ruled relevant by the arbitrators?
3. Summarize the fact situation leading to the grievance.
4. Was Woods' offense of such an aggravated nature as to warrant discharge?
5. Discuss the three possible interpretations of Section 2(c). Which one did the arbitrators accept?

Section 4. Fact Finding Under Executive Order 11491

In the federal government when an impasse develops in negotiations the issue or issues involved can be referred to the Federal Service Impasses

Panel after mediation has been undertaken and is unsuccessful in resolving the disagreement. Section 18 of the order describes the recommended procedure:

> *Negotiation impasses.* When voluntary arrangements, including the services of the Federal Mediation and Conciliation Service or other third-party mediation, fail to resolve a negotiation impasse, either party may request the Federal Service Impasses Panel to consider the matter. The panel, in its discretion and under the regulations it prescribes, may consider the matter and may recommend procedures to the parties for the resolution of the impasse or may settle the impasse by appropriate action. Arbitration or third-party fact finding with recommendations to assist in the resolution of an impasse may be used by the parties only when authorized or directed by the panel.

In the following case the panel decided that fact finding with recommendations was the appropriate method for solving the problem that arose in negotiations between the Federal Aviation Administration (FAA) and the American Federation of Government Employees (AFGE).

In the Matter of

Federal Aviation Administration (Dulles International Airport) Washington, D. C. *and* **American Federation of Government Employees, AFL–CIO Local Union No. 2303**

Case No. 70 FSIP 12 [5]

(United States of America before the Federal Service Impasses Panel)

PANEL REPORT AND RECOMMENDATIONS
FOR SETTLEMENT

A request to the Federal Service Impasses Panel (hereinafter referred to as the panel) was filed by John F. Griner, national president of the American Federation of Government Employees, AFL-CIO (hereinafter referred to as the union), on December 1, 1970, alleging that an impasse had been reached on two issues in negotiations with the management of Dulles International Airport, Federal Aviation Administration (hereinafter referred to as the employer).

On December 14, 1970, the panel determined that resolution of the impasse required fact finding. Accordingly, it appointed David T. Roadley (hereinafter referred to as the fact finder) to conduct a fact-finding hearing on two issues—merit promotion policy and parking.

A notice of hearing was issued to the parties on December 19, 1970.

The fact finder conducted a prehearing joint conference at the offices of the panel on January 8, 1971. During the conference the parties indicated a desire to jointly reexamine their position on merit promotion policy.

A fact-finding hearing was conducted on January 13, 1971, at the offices of the panel in Washington, D.C. Appearances were made for and on behalf of each party. Witnesses were introduced, qualified, and examined. Documentary evidence was introduced, accepted by the fact finder, and made a part of the hearing record. Both parties waived the filing of posthearing briefs and elected to stand on the record and on their respective closing arguments.

There was no question raised concerning either representation or negotiability.

At the outset of the hearing the parties informed the fact finder that mutual agreement had been reached on the issue of merit promotion policy whereupon that issue was withdrawn.

I. *History of Current Negotiations*

a. Background—The Parties—Their Relationships. The union is the exclusive bargaining representative of all nonsupervisory wage board employees of the employer assigned to and working at Dulles International Airport. There are approximately 189 workers in the bargaining unit which is comprised of maintenance worker and mobile lounge operator classifications.

The Bureau of National Capital Airports, a unit of the Federal Aviation Administration, operates the only two civil airports owned and managed by the U. S. Government, that is, Washington National Airport and Dulles International Airport. At the Dulles International Airport, located at Chantilly, Virginia, there are approximately 343 workers including the 189 in the bargaining unit.

The union was recognized by the employer in October of 1964. The initial labor agreement was negotiated and executed in 1966 or 1967 under the authority of Executive Order 10988. The second labor agreement covered the period February 19, 1968, to June, 1969.

b. Negotiations on Current Labor Agreement. Negotiations began on March 3, 1969, and continued through forty joint sessions. The discussion concerned ninety pages of union proposals, embracing thirty-eight articles. The contract was extended on a month-to-month basis subsequent to the June, 1969 expiration date. On October 1, 1969, the employer informed the union that it would not agree to any extension beyond October 30, 1969, although it would continue to guarantee the union exclusive recognition rights.

c. Voluntary Arrangements—Mediation Assistance—Unsettled Issues. On March 5, 1970, the union requested the assistance of a mediator from the Federal Mediation and Conciliation Service. At this point there were seven issues in dispute.

Merit Promotion Policy
Discipline
Parking
Hours of Work
Overtime
Office Space
Grievances

Federal Mediator Mills met with the parties on March 21 and March 22, 1970. At the end of the sessions, all but three issues had been resolved.

Hours of Work
Merit Promotion Policy
Parking

Federal Mediator Fidandis met with the parties on July 1, 1970, at which time the hours of work issue was resolved. The union then announced it would seek the assistance of the panel.

d. Moratorium on Negotiations—Sign-off on Agreed Articles. Following July 1, 1970, negotiations came to a standstill primarily because negotiators were not available. On October 8, 1970, the parties executed a one-year agreement which is effective for one year from the date of approval, January 7, 1971. They agreed, however, that the two remaining issues—merit promotion policy and parking—would be submitted to the panel and that their further action would be in accordance with the "rulings of the panel."

II. The Parking Issue

a. The Expired Labor Agreement. The labor agreement, which was terminated on October 30, 1969, contained no provisions on parking spaces or privileges for either bargaining unit employees or union officials.

b. Union's Proposals—Counterproposal—Impasse Issue.

1. Union proposals. The union's initial proposal on parking was presented in two parts, Section 1 covering parking space and privileges for bargaining unit employees, and Section 2 covering parking space and privileges for a union official.

2. Counterproposals. In the ensuing discussions, mutual agreement was reached on that part of the parking proposal which provided for a parking facility for a union official while on official business with management.

The new parking provision in the current labor agreement is as follows:

Article XXVII—Parking. The employer agrees that the union president shall be allowed to utilize the reserved visitor parking places immediately adjacent to the Terminal Building when meeting with management. If more than the hour legal parking time is needed, arrangements will be made with the police for the needed additional time. If visitor parking space is not available, a police vehicle space not being used shall be made available to the union officer.

3. *The impasse issue.* The sole remaining issue concerns the union's proposal on parking space and privileges for bargaining unit employees which is set forth below.

Article XXVII—Parking. Section 1. The employer agrees that exclusive areas will be designated for parking as close to the assigned work areas as feasible for all unit employees. Prior to deciding on any change in the parking plan, the employer agrees to meet with the union to discuss parking arrangements.

This proposal (a rephrasing of an earlier union proposal) was rejected on March 21, 1970, by the employer who elected to stand on its offer to provide parking space only for the union official.

III. *Position of the Union*

The union states that for several years prior to October 1969, employees enjoyed reserved parking space immediately adjacent to the buildings or locations wherein they were employed. Management assigned this space and, to ensure control, issued each employee a decal for which the employee paid a nominal fee of 75 cents.

On October 2, 1969, the employer, without negotiations with the union, changed this parking space arrangement and raised the decal fee to $7.50 per annum, effective at the beginning of the new fiscal year.

The union contends that the change in policy was without good and sufficient reason although it acknowledges that there was some "meager consultation" on the policy change prior to the publication of the new policy. The union believes no bona fide attempt was made by the employer during the long negotiations to find an equitable solution, nor has the employer made proposals for some "alternate solution."

Witnesses testifying on behalf of the union pointed out that there is no public transit system to or from the airport other than relatively expensive airline passenger limousine service, and employees are completely dependent upon car pools or private automobile transportation to maintain their daily work schedules or respond promptly to "call back" requests. Therefore, parking spaces were necessary.

The union asserts that special reserved parking facilities are essential to the work of the employees, particularly when they are called back after a tour of duty and during heavy snow storms when snow removal delays temporarily eliminate available and accessible parking spaces.

The union also points out that, contrary to the new policy which allegedly covers all employees at Dulles International Airport, some airline employees, concessionaire employees, and airport management officials still enjoy reserved parking privileges.

The local union president testified that he had received seven or eight written complaints and had heard of numerous verbal complaints, although another union witness could not recall a situation where he was unable to find a parking space.

Finally, to further support its contentions, the union attempted to show discriminatory treatment in management administration of the October 2, 1969, parking policy by providing "special" spaces to certain employees.

IV. *Position of the Employer*

The employer contends that there was a clear and pressing need for a change in employee parking policy at the facility, citing the following reasons:

1. There had been a continuing increase over the years in the total number of employees at the airport, particularly in the food service concessionaire group, which required additional parking spaces in limited available parking areas.
2. The employer was under pressure, due to the failure of the expected growth rate of passenger utilization of the airport, to operate efficiently at the lowest possible cost.
3. Employees at the Washington National Airport, the other airport facility operated by the employer, had been paying for parking space for several years.

The contemplated change was discussed with responsible union officials in advance of the announcement date. Management asserts there were few, if any, complaints or serious objections from the vast majority of employees after the policy was published.

With respect to the increased fee, the employer explained that it costs $31.29 a year to maintain, illuminate, and police each employee parking space; thus the $7.50 represents only part of the actual annual cost. The new policy, moreover, treats all employees alike and is in line with the management's responsibility to maintain efficient operations at the least possible expense to the government.

Contrary to the union's allegations concerning its arbitrary negotiating posture on this issue, the employer states that it had responded to the union's proposal with an accommodating arrangement to provide special parking for union officials while at the airport. Finally, the employer points out, it has given the union practically everything it demanded in the new contract.

V. *Discussion*

The parties made earnest efforts in direct negotiations to reach agreement on terms and conditions for a new labor agreement, and availed themselves of third-party mediation assistance in an effort to resolve all issues in dispute.

The impasse issue—parking—is properly before the panel as contemplated and provided for in Sections 16 and 17 of Executive Order 11491 and in accordance with the published procedures of the panel.

The substance and rights provided in the new labor agreement represent substantial and significant improvements or additions over the terms and conditions of the expired labor agreement.

In late September, 1969, the employer called in and discussed with union representatives a proposed parking policy change memorandum, together with the reasons for the change.

In an October 2, 1969 memorandum addressed to all government, air carrier, tenant, and concessionaire employees, the employer announced that, effective November 1, 1969, all no-cost parking privileges would be discontinued.

The union's contention that "special" reserved spaces were allocated for management personnel was not borne out by the evidence. There have always been nine spaces reserved for management and operating officials; since the policy change, there is one less space reserved for this group.

Although a study has been conducted at the request of higher airport authority, there is no present plan to establish special reserved parking space for nonbargaining unit employees.

VI. *Panel Conclusions and Recommendations for Settlement*

After a review of the entire record, the panel concludes that:

1. The parties have completed the negotiation of a significantly improved labor agreement, including a new provision for parking facilities for a union official.

2. The parking policy change was neither arbitrary nor discriminatory in design or application.

3. The parking spaces now available for bargaining unit employees are adequate.

4. The increased charge for decals (permits) is reasonable and was justified in light of the showing of a need to recoup some of the cost of providing and maintaining a parking space.

For the reasons set forth above, the panel recommends this dispute be settled as follows:

1. The union's proposal for reserved parking space for bargaining unit employees be withdrawn.

2. The parties enter into a joint letter of understanding which will permit the union to reopen the current labor agreement on the sole matter of "bargaining unit employee reserved parking space" if the employer later determines to establish reserved employee parking spaces for nonbargaining unit employees.

By direction of the panel.
Signed at Washington, D.C., on this twenty-sixth day of February, 1971

/s/ David T. Roadley
Executive Secretary
Federal Service Impasses Panel

Discussion Questions

1. Discuss the issues the fact finder was authorized to resolve.
2. Summarize the union arguments supporting its position.
3. How did the employer respond to these contentions?
4. What were the panel's conclusions and recommendations for settlement?

Section 5. Fact Finding at the State Level

Restated, the definition of fact finding is that it is a process whereby the positions of labor and management in a particular dispute are reviewed by an impartial third party or panel in order to focus attention on the major issues and to resolve differences as to facts. The fact finder or fact-finding panel merely report a determination of the facts on the theory that they are so clear that the parties will perceive a solution of their differences. More frequently, the finding of facts is coupled with a recommendation for settlement. Where a recommendation is made, particularly a public recommendation, pressure is exerted on the parties to accept it.

Regarding the scope of fact finding at the state level, Gilroy and Sinicropi summarize the situation as follows:

> Unlike the private sector, where factfinding is limited primarily to so-called national emergency disputes, the public sector relies more heavily on this technique in negotiation impasse resolution. At least twenty-three states authorize the use of factfinding. . . . The normal procedure is that factfinding may be initiated by either party, a tripartite or neutral panel is utilized, and recommendations for settlement are made by that panel. The recommendations are either made public following the decision,

or delayed pending further negotiation based on those recommendations.
. . . As with mediation, there is considerable variation in the relation-
ship of factfinding to other procedures within states. For example, in
Montana, factfinding is the only impasse procedure specified in the law.
. . . At least twelve of the twenty-three states authorizing factfinding pro-
vided other procedures beyond factfinding.[6]

In the subsequent Rhode Island case, a single fact finder reports on his
investigation of a dispute between a teachers' labor organization and the
State Board of Regents.

In the Matter of

American Federation of Teachers, Local 2012, AFL-CIO *and* **State
Board of Regents**

Case No. FF–7203

(State of Rhode Island and Providence Plantations)

INTRODUCTION

Pursuant to a request filed on behalf of the American Federation of
Teachers, Local 2012, AFL-CIO (hereinafter referred to as Local 2012),
the Rhode Island State Labor Relations Board provided conciliation and
fact finding per the request, under provisions of Title 36, Chapter 11, Section 8 of the General Laws of the State of Rhode Island, 1956, and appointed Earl E. Bushman, Jr., Esq., as the conciliator and fact finder in
this matter.

Thereafter, due notice was mailed to the interested parties and a
conference was scheduled and held on Monday, August 28, 1972 at 1:30
P.M. in Room 132, 235 Promenade Street, Providence, Rhode Island.

In an effort to possibly resolve the impasse by further conciliation
and to obtain more detailed information, a further conference was scheduled for and held on September 7, 1972 at 1:30 P.M. at the location of
the initial conference.

Appearing in behalf of Local 2012 was John H. Hines, Jr., Esq.,
and Mr. Edward P. Conaty, assistant commissioner of education, who
appeared in behalf of the State Board of Regents.

At the original conference, it was agreed by the representatives of
both parties, that prior to the petition for conciliation and fact finding an
impasse had developed in regard to the three provisions of a labor contract covering the year 1972–1973. One of the provisions which had
reached an impasse referred to vacation days, and this particular issue

had been resolved prior to the date of the initial conference. Therefore, at the time of the conference on August 28, 1972, there remained two provisions on which an impasse remained; they were as follows: (a) freezing of in-service training increments; (b) wages.

In an effort to clarify the nature of the proposals and counterproposals put forth by the parties and the recommendations of the fact finder, I feel compelled to set out in some detail the course of the previous collective bargaining negotiations in regard to the members of this unit, as well as the monetary benefits previously attained by certain members of the unit. There are nine basic classifications within this unit, but the employees classified as "coordinators" number approximately seventeen and the number of employees classified as "consultants" number approximately thirty-five employees. Therefore, it is apparent that the number of these two classifications, when combined, constitute almost, if not in fact, a majority of the entire collective bargaining unit. From factual information elicited at the conference, the conciliator and fact finder have computed that the consultants, by reason of pay adjustments and pay raises, have accrued a level of salary increase which amounts to approximately 33 percent during the last twenty-six month period. This, of course, included a 4 percent across-the-board wage increase granted to all employees of this bargaining unit in November of 1971.

As a result of a study commission's recommendation, Local 2012 sometime in December of 1971 proposed a flat across-the-board increase in conformity with the recommendations of the study commission. The State Board of Regents rejected the proposal because of insufficient funds available at that time, but agreed to adjust the pay scale of the *coordinators* by granting them a 5 percent increase with no benefits to any other member of the collective bargaining unit. This proposal was rejected by the membership of Local 2012. Therefore, the negotiator for Local 2012 held a conference with Dr. Burke, commissioner of education, and stated to this fact finder, that at this conference Dr. Burke had inferred or hinted, but not definitely promised, that when collective bargaining negotiations were undertaken relative to the 1972–1973 contract, he would try to convince the State Board of Regents to grant the same increase to the consultants in addition to all other benefits that might be derived from collective bargaining beneficial to the entire membership of the collective bargaining unit. However, no direct testimony was presented as to the degree of Dr. Burke's commitment or even as to his authority, if any, to make such a statement.

Disregarding this fact, however, the fact finder feels compelled to state that it is his conviction that the ratification by the unit membership of the proposal to raise only the pay grade of the coordinators was achieved by the union representative based on his relating to the consultants that it was his understanding that they would be given the same preferential treatment when the new labor contract was negotiated. The fact is that the membership of Local 2012 did ratify this proposal, under the terms of which only the coordinators received any monetary benefit, and the coordinators pay scale was immediately increased following the ratification of this proposal.

WAGES

FINDINGS OF FACT

In the early part of this year, 1972, the negotiators for Local 2012 submitted a proposal for consideration by the State Board of Regents which in regard to wage provisions stated that all members of the collective bargaining unit were to receive an increase equivalent to a 5½ percent across-the-board raise in pay and that the consultants would receive an additional across-the-board 5 percent increase. This proposal also stipulated that the State Board of Regents would be allowed to deny in-service training to any employee of this collective bargaining unit if said employee had not commenced such in-service training prior to the signing of the proposed labor contract. The State Board of Regents rejected this offer and made a counterproposal, which was in effect, an entirely new pay plan, which, with the exceptions of six specific pay grades, amounted to pay increases ranging from approximately 5⅓ percent to 6.8 percent but averaging out to approximately 6.3 percent for all members of the collective bargaining unit. It rejected in total any additional benefits for the consultants and requested that all members of the collective bargaining unit not engaged in taking in-service training at the time of the execution of the new labor contract be denied the right to elect to take in-service training in the future. This counterproposal was rejected by the union membership, and at that time the request for conciliation and fact finding was instituted.

At the termination of the second conference held by the conciliator and fact finder, the representative of the State Board of Regents agreed to submit to the State Board of Regents the following proposals submitted by Local 2012:

(a) Local 2012 wanted a 5½ percent across-the-board increase, plus an additional increase of 5 percent for the consultants, or

(b) The new pay plan offered by the State Board of Regents, plus a 3½ percent increase for the consultants and retention of in-service training privileges.

The State Board of Regents rejected both of these proposals as submitted by the counsel for Local 2012.

This fact finder has given careful consideration to the proposals of both parties and after careful deliberation, he has concluded as follows in regard to the issue of wages:

RECOMMENDATIONS

That the pay plan proposed by the State Board of Regents be adopted, on condition, however, that the increase to every employee of the collective bargaining unit be an amount not less than a sum equivalent to a 7 percent increase over the present salary scale now in effect regarding all employees of the collective bargaining unit.

IN-SERVICE TRAINING INCREMENTS

FINDING OF FACT

The fact finder is unaware of any current labor contract referable to employees of the State of Rhode Island wherein there is a provision denying to any employee the right to commence in-service training at any time as long as the employee obtains prior approval of the state agency regulating this procedure. The fact finder feels very strongly that the State of Rhode Island is the derivative benefactor of this type of program either in increased productivity among some employees or an enhanced degree of professionalism among its executive or professional employees.

RECOMMENDATIONS

The fact finder recommends no change in the provisions in the existing labor contract in regard to the increments flowing to employees who have successfully completed the prescribed in-training programs.

The recommendations referable to wage or salary increases as set out herein remain subject to approval of all provisions under Stabilization Act of 1970, as amended.

Rhode Island State Labor Relations Board
By:

/s/ Earl E. Bushman, Jr.
Conciliator and Fact Finder

Discussion Questions

1. What were the key issues in this case?
2. Summarize the recommendations of the fact finder.

Section 6. Arbitration Under Executive Order 11491

Under Executive Order 10988, in effect from 1962 to 1969, the arbitration of issues under negotiation was not permitted. In fact, the report of the President's Task Force on Employee-Management Cooperation clearly demonstrated the intent that the agencies and employee organizations in the federal service should make every effort to resolve any differences between them wherever possible without third-party intervention. The report indicated that impasses in negotiations between government officials and employee organizations that had been granted exclusive recognition should be solved by means other than arbitration and that methods for helping to bring about settlements should be devised and agreed to on an agency-by-agency basis. However, "advisory" arbitration was ultimately allowed, whereby the Secretary of Labor, after viewing the parties' preferences as to who the arbitrator should be, made the final selection himself. The advisory nature of the award allowed agency management to reject its findings. Most of the awards involved decisions as to the appropriateness of bargaining units, questions of voting eligibility, and majority status determinations for exclusive recognition.

Executive Order 11491 abolished advisory arbitration and in Sections 13 and 14 developed guidelines for the utilization of arbitration procedures not unlike those in use in the private sector.

In the Matter of

International Association of Machinists and Aerospace Workers *and*
U.S. Kirk Army Hospital, Aberdeen, Md.

FLRC No. 70A–11 [7]

(United States Federal Labor Relations Council, Washington, D.C.)

DECISION ON NEGOTIABILITY ISSUE

BACKGROUND

During the course of bargaining, the union submitted a proposal that the "union shall have the right and shall discuss with the employer any dispute or complaint concerning the interpretation or application of this agreement, or any policy, regulation, or practice now or hereinafter enforced wherein the employer has discretion," with any such dispute or complaint subject to a two-step appeal procedure and binding arbitration. The hospital claimed that the proposal was non-negotiable. Upon referral, the Department of the Army concurred in the hospital's position, determining that the proposal, insofar as it would apply the binding arbitration procedures to a union dispute or complaint over "any policy, regulation, or practice now or hereinafter enforced wherein the employer has discretion," violated Sections 13 and 14 of the order. The union appealed to the council, and the council accepted the petition for review of this issue under Section 11(c)(4) of the order.

CONTENTIONS OF THE PARTIES

The union asserts that its proposal is consistent with the order, essentially because (1) the proposal, if applied to employee grievances, would be negotiable, and union disputes and employee grievances should be considered alike under the order; (2) the proposal does not seek arbitration of changes or proposed changes in the agreement or agency policy, which is alone prohibited in Section 14; and (3) similar provisions have been included in contracts covering other Department of Defense units.

The agency contends, however, that the order carefully limits the arbitration of union disputes to controversies involving the interpretation or application of an existing agreement, and that the union's proposal extends beyond these limits and is therefore non-negotiable. Furthermore, according to the agency, the provisions in other agreements relied upon by the union, which "slipped past" the management review process, are not dispositive as to negotiability under the order.

OPINION

The question for decision is whether, under Sections 13 and 14 of the order, binding arbitration procedures may be applied to a union dispute or complaint over not only the "interpretation of application" of an agreement, but also of "any policy, regulation, or practice" within the discretion of management.

Sections 13 and 14 provide in relevant part as follows:

> Section 13. *Grievance procedures.* An agreement with a labor organization which is the exclusive representative of employees in an appropriate unit may provide procedures, applicable only to employees in the unit, for the consideration of employee grievances and of disputes over the interpretation and application of agreements. The procedure for consideration of employee grievances shall meet the requirements for negotiated grievance procedures established by the Civil Service Commission. A negotiated employee grievance which conforms to this section, to applicable laws, and to regulations of the Civil Service Commission and

the agency is the exclusive procedure available to employees in the unit when the agreement so provides.

Section 14. *Arbitration of grievances.* (a) Negotiated procedures may provide for the arbitration of employee grievances and of disputes over the interpretation or application of existing agreements. Negotiated procedures may not extend arbitration to changes or proposed changes in agreements or agency policy. Such procedures shall provide for the invoking of arbitration only with the approval of the labor organization that has exclusive recognition and, in the case of an employee grievance, only with the approval of the employee. The costs of the arbitrator shall be shared equally by the parties. . . .

A reading of these provisions clearly establishes that two separate and distinct types of controversies may be subject to binding arbitration procedures, namely, (1) "employee grievances," and (2) "disputes over the interpretation or application of existing agreements." Arbitration of the first type of controversy, that is, employee grievances, may be invoked only with the approval of the union *and* the employee, while arbitration of the second type of controversy, commonly referred to as "union disputes," needs only the approval of the union itself. Also employee grievances, as distinguished from union disputes, must specifically comply with the requirements for negotiated procedures prescribed by the Civil Service Commission.

Apart from the literal wording of Sections 13 and 14, the background of these provisions shows that the arbitration of union disputes was intended to be considered in a manner separate from the arbitration of employee grievances. Under Section 8(b) of Executive Order 10988, which preceded Executive Order 11491, negotiated procedures were sanctioned only for the advisory arbitration of individual employee grievances. In reviewing the need for changes in these provisions, the report accompanying Executive Order 11491 observed that "current proposals would permit the parties to an agreement to include arbitration procedures for the resolution of disputes over the interpretation and application of the agreement *as well as* for the resolution of employee grievances" (emphasis supplied); and the report recommended the adoption of such disputes procedure, stating: "Arbitration should be made available for the resolution of disputes over the interpretation and application of an agreement." This recommendation, as so limited, was adopted in the final order and was explained in the report as follows:

Agreements may contain employee grievance procedures which meet CSC requirements, may make them the only grievance procedures available to the employees in the unit, and may provide for arbitration (with union and employee consent and cost-sharing by union and agency). Agreements may also contain procedures for consideration of disputes over interpretation and application of agreement, including arbitration of such disputes with consent of the union (cost-sharing by union and agency). . . .

It is plain from the foregoing that union disputes were designed and regarded as distinct from employee grievances for arbitration purposes, under Sections 13 and 14, and, since the proposal involved in this case concerns the arbitration of a union dispute or complaint, rather than an employee grievance, it must meet the special requirements for the arbitration of such disputes.

As already indicated, the arbitration of union disputes is expressly confined under Sections 13 and 14 to disputes over the interpretation or application of an existing agreement. While Section 14 also prohibits the extension of arbitration "to changes or proposed changes in agreements or agency policy," these provisions simply establish a further condition to any arbitration which may be negotiated, whether of employee grievances or union disputes. Obviously nothing in that specific prohibition presumes to enlarge the *scope* of union disputes which may be subject to arbitration, that is, "disputes over the interpretation or application of existing agreements."

In our opinion, it is clear, therefore, that the arbitration of union disputes over the "interpretation or application" of "any policy, regulation, or practice" within the employer's discretion, as here proposed by the union, is violative of Sections 13 and 14 of the order and is not negotiable. Although other contracts may have included such provisions, as claimed by the union, this circumstance cannot alter the express language and intent of the order and is without controlling significance in this case.

Accordingly, based upon the foregoing and upon careful consideration of the entire record, we find that the agency's determination as to the non-negotiability of the union's proposal was proper and, pursuant to Section 2411.18(d) of the council's rules of procedure, the determination is sustained.

By the council.

Issued: March 9, 1971

/s/ W. V. Gill
Executive Director

Discussion Questions

1. What was the main issue in this case?
2. What two types of arbitration proceedings are permitted in the federal government?
3. Discuss the decision rendered by the council.

Section 7. The Constitutionality of a State Statute Providing for Compulsory Arbitration of Labor Disputes in Municipal Police and Fire Departments

Compulsory arbitration has been defined as a process "wherein the disputants are required by law or governmental regulation to submit disputes and abide by the award. The term does not cover arbitration voluntarily agreed to by the parties even though the acceptance of the results may be compulsory and enforceable by the courts." [8]

A number of states have laws providing for compulsory arbitration, but there is considerable variety as to the classes of employees covered, arbitrable subjects, and the obligatory or advisory nature of the final award.[9]

Compulsory arbitration statutes exist in eleven states (Florida, Illinois, Maine, Michigan, Nebraska, Pennsylvania, Rhode Island, South Dakota, Vermont, and Wyoming), with mandatory awards in all but Florida and Illinois.[10] In Pennsylvania, either party may invoke binding arbitration in police or firemen's disputes. The Rhode Island statute imposes compulsory arbitration upon the parties when negotiation impasses involve police and firemen. The terminal step in fire fighter disputes in Vermont makes binding arbitration compulsory. The constitutionality of compulsory arbitration statutes in Michigan, Pennsylvania, and Rhode Island has been challenged, but upheld, by state courts.[11]

Dearborn Fire Fighters Union, Local 412, IAFF v. City of Dearborn
Civil Action No. 171–115 [12]
(State of Michigan, Circuit Court for the county of Wayne)

OPINION

On or about December 16, 1970, plaintiff commenced this suit for specific performance or in the alternative, mandamus to enforce an arbitration award against the defendant. On December 16, 1970, this court issued a temporary restraining order compelling compliance. Such order was extended by the court at a hearing on January 11, 1971.

In the meantime, both parties filed motions for a summary judgment. The motions were argued on January 11, 1971, with leave granted to both parties to submit and exchange briefs.

The uncontroverted facts appeared to establish the following: plaintiff's union is the recognized, exclusive bargaining representative of Dearborn firemen under applicable Michigan law (Act 336 P.A. of 1947 as amended by Act 379 P.A. of 1969 as amended). On or about June 15,

1970, the union initiated binding arbitration proceedings and selected its delegate to an arbitration panel pursuant to Act 312 P.A. 1969, MCLA 423, 231 MSA, which act provides for compulsory arbitration of labor disputes in municipal police and fire departments.

The city declined to appoint its statutory arbitration panel member despite requests that it do so made to the city both by the plaintiff and by the chairman of the Michigan Employment Relations Commission. When the city persisted in its declination, the chairman of the Employment Relations Commission, pursuant to the statute, on July 23, 1970, designated Dr. Charles M. Rehmus as impartial chairman of a panel of arbitration in the dispute between the plaintiff and the defendant.

The panel convened and conducted hearings on or about August 10, 13, 14, and October 6, 1970. On November 11, 1970, Dr. Rehmus and Joseph R. Kovach, the union's delegate to the panel, issued an award effective July 1, 1970, a copy of which was attached to the complaint. When the city failed, neglected, or refused to implement the award, plaintiff formally requested defendant's compliance, citing the binding effect of the award under the statute. . . . On December 1, 1970, defendant's counsel informed plaintiff that the defendant would not comply with the award absent a court order compelling it to do so. To this date, there has been no implementation of the award by the city.

The city in its brief now states that it believed that Act 312 was unconstitutional and by its silence refused to appoint a panel member to the arbitration panel. The city contends that subsequent to November 11, 1970, it maintained that the purported panel had no power to issue an award since it was improperly constituted, and in fact recommended litigation in order to test the constitutionality of Act 312.

The plaintiff filed its motion for summary judgment under GCR 1963, 117(2) and (3) for the reason that the defendant has failed to state a valid defense to the claim asserted against it and there is no genuine issue as to any material fact, and plaintiff is entitled to a judgment as a matter of law.

The defendant filed a counter motion for summary judgment on the grounds that plaintiff in its complaint failed to state a claim upon which relief could be granted. More specifically, defendant alleges,

1. Act 312 Public Act 1969, MCLA 423.231, et seq. (hereinafter referred to as Act 312) is unconstitutional.

2. The purported panel of arbitrators was not properly constituted under Act 312 in that the Michigan Employment Relations Commission had no authority to appoint a panel chairman and the purported panel had no authority to act until two other delegates had been appointed and had failed themselves to designate a chairman.

3. The purported panel of arbitrators failed to adhere to the clear man-

date of Section 6 of Act 312 requiring that the hearing be concluded within thirty days of its commencement.

The court is of the opinion that a summary judgment should be granted in this case under Michigan General Court Rules 117(2) and (3), since only a question of law is involved and both parties agree that there is no genuine issue of fact.

The principal question presented is whether Act 312 P.A. 1969 is constitutional.

The pertinent sections of Act 312 read as follows:

Compulsory Arbitration of Labor Disputes in Municipal Police and Fire Departments

An act to provide for compulsory arbitration of labor disputes in municipal police and fire departments; to define such public departments; to provide for the selection of members of arbitration panels; to prescribe the procedures and authority thereof; and to provide for the enforcement and review of awards thereof.

Section 1. Provision for Compulsory Arbitration

It is the public policy of this state that in public police and fire departments, where the right of employees to strike is by law prohibited, it is requisite to the high morals of such employees and the efficient operation of such departments to afford an alternate, expeditious, effective, and binding procedure for the resolution of disputes, and that end the provisions of that act, *providing for compulsory arbitration, shall be liberally construed.* (Emphasis supplied.)

. . .

The defendant city of Dearborn contends that Act 312 is unconstitutional for the following reasons:

(a) Act 312 violates Article VII, Section 22, and Article VII, Section 34, of the 1963 Michigan Constitution by taking away from municipal governments the power vested in them over an essentially local concern and delegating that power to private persons who are not subject to the electorate, nor to any governmental body or public official.

(b) Act 312 violates Article III, Section 2 of the 1963 constitution of the state of Michigan in that said act constitutes an improper delegation of legislative and administrative power to private persons.

(c) Act 312 violates Article IX, Section 2 of the 1963 constitution of the state of Michigan and the Fourteenth Amendment of the United States Constitution in that the act deprives local units of government and their constituents of property without due process of law.

The cases demonstrate that there is a general presumption of statutory validity.

Justice Kelly, in the case of *Gartland S.S. Co.* v. *Corporation Securities Commission,* 339 Mich. 661, in upholding the constitutionality of P.A. 1952, No. 183, wrote on p. 673:

In determining the question before us and in interpreting the legislature's intent in the passage P.A. 1952, No. 183, we cannot presume that the legislature intended to enact an unconstitutional law. . . . And, in *Rouse, Hazard & Co.* v. *Wayne Circuit Judge,* 104 Mich. 234 (27 L.R.A. 577, 53 Am. St. R. 457), this court adopted that principle when we said (p. 239): "The power of declaring laws unconstitutional should be exercised with extreme caution, and never where serious doubt exists as to the conflict. In cases of doubt, every possible presumption, not clearly inconsistent with the language and the subject matter, is to be made in favor of the constitutionality of the act."

Similar language is found in the case of *Cady* v. *City of Detroit,* 289 Mich. 499, 505. The court there stated,

A statute will be presumed to be constitutional by the courts unless the contrary clearly appears; and in case of doubt every possible presumption not clearly inconsistent with the language and the subject matter is to be made in favor of the constitutionality of the legislation. . . . Every reasonable presumption of intendment must be indulged in favor of the validity of an act, and it is only when invalidity appears so clearly as to leave no room for reasonable doubt that it violates some provision of the constitution that a court will refuse to sustain its validity. A statute is presumed to be constitutional and it will not be declared unconstitutional unless clearly so, or so beyond a reasonable doubt. . . .

In *People* v. *Breen,* 326 Mich. 720, a 1950 case, it was held that courts interfere with discretion of the legislature enacting police regulations only where the regulations adopted are arbitrary, oppressive, or unreasonable. *Parkes* v. *Bartlett,* 236 Mich. 460, held if a matter is a proper subject of legislation and the measures adopted are appropriately related to the object and have an obvious tendency to accomplish it, the courts will not disturb the legislative discretion.

Defendant contends that Act 312 is unconstitutional because it divests municipal governments of power vested in them under Article VII, Sections 22 and 34 of the 1963 Michigan Constitution. It is claimed that is done by "taking away from municipal governments the power vested in them over an essentially local concern and delegating that power to private persons who are not subject to the electorate, nor to any governmental body or public office."

Article VII, Section 22 is merely a restatement of the home rule provisions which earlier appeared in Article VIII, Section 21 of the 1908 Constitution. Article VII, Section 34 is a new section merely intended, according to the constitutional convention comment, "to extend to counties and townships within the powers granted to them" liberal construction of their powers similar to that of other local governments.

The same basic language continues to appear in Article VII, Section 22, which subordinates home rule powers to the "general laws" of the state and permits each city and village "to adopt resolutions and ordinances relating to its municipal concerns, property, and government *subject to the constitution and the law.*" (Article VII, Section 22, emphasis supplied.)

. . .

The defendant in its brief states, "The city concedes that labor relations is a matter of state concern and is properly within the purview of the state legislature. The city also recognizes the seriousness of the problem of strikes in public employment. The right of public employees to bargain collectively and the duty of public employers to respond by good faith bargaining cannot be questioned." The city in its brief goes on to add, "However, the legislature can—in fact, must—search for constitutional solutions to the serious problems of labor relations in the public sector."

Defendant argues in its brief that in the area of public and private sector, labor relations are and should be of local concern over which the state may not legislate.

In the specific area of regulation of public and private sector labor relations, the Michigan Supreme Court has rejected contentions similar to those made here by the defendant; that these are local concerns over which the state may not legislate. *Local Union No. 876* v. *State Labor Board,* 294 Mich. 629 (1940); *City of Detroit* v. *Division No. 26 of Amalgamated Assoc.,* 332 Mich. 237 (1952); *School District for the City of Holland* v. *Holland Education Assoc.,* 380 Mich. 314 (1968).

The legislature's powers to regulate labor relations in the public sector has been reaffirmed in the Michigan Constitution of 1963, Article IV, Section 48, which provides that, "The legislature may enact laws providing for the resolutions of disputes concerning public employees, except those in the classified Civil Service."

From the foregoing constitutional provisions, it seems too clear for argument that there has been reserved by the constitution in the legislature the express power to enact laws for the resolution of public disputes concerning public employees, as in this instance.

The Michigan courts have repeatedly upheld the constitutionality of various sections of the Public Employment Relations Act, Act 336 of 1947 as amended by Act 379 of 1965, as being within the legislature's purview. (*Holland School District* v. *Educational Assoc.,* 380 Mich. 374; *Board of Control of Eastern Michigan University* v. *Labor Mediation Board,* 18 Mich. App. 435; *Regents of University of Michigan* v. *Labor*

Mediation Board, 18 Mich. App. 489; *City of Escanaba* v. *Michigan Labor Board,* 19 Mich. App. 273; *School District of Dearborn* v. *Labor Mediation Board,* 22 Mich. App. 222)

Defendant relies on and discusses the case of *Simpson* v. *Paddock,* 195 Mich. 581, as authority for its position. The *Simpson* case has been overruled by the later labor case of *Fire Fighters Assoc.* v. *Village of Grosse Pointe Park,* 303 Mich. 405, and the subsequent constitutional amendments.

It is obvious from the cases cited herein, as well as Article IV, Section 48 and the reserved authority of Article VII, Section 22, that the legislature has authority to pass laws of general concern, including those pertaining to labor relations. Act 312 does not interfere with the city of Dearborn's home rule powers of control of local government.

Defendant next contends that Act 312 violates Article II, Section 2 of the state constitution "in that said act constitutes an improper delegation of legislative and administrative power to private persons."

The law is clear that where the standards are sufficient, there is no unlawful or improper delegation of legislative authority.

The city in its brief concedes the sufficiency of standards in Act 312. It argues, however, that the act constitutes an improper delegation of legislative and administrative power to private persons. The recent decision of the Michigan Supreme Court in *City of Pleasant Ridge* v. *Governor,* 382 Mich. 225, upholds the compulsory arbitration statutes relative to the route of Interstate 596. The local arbitration board provided under Act 312 was not a continuing board or body with a fixed term for its officers. It constituted an *ad hoc* determination. There was found to be no improper delegation of legislative authority which affirms the validity of such arbitration.

Defendant next asserts that Act 312 violates Article IX, Section 2 of the state constitution "by indirectly but undeniably surrendering the power to tax." It contends that the arbitrators' award is tantamount to the imposition of a tax. The cited constitutional section says, "The power of taxation shall never be surrendered, suspended, or contracted away."

There is nothing in Act 312 or the award entered that either imposes a tax or diminishes the city taxing authority. Act 312 does not in any way violate Article IX, Section 2 of the state constitution relative to the power to tax.

Defendant pleads but presents no argument that Act 312 denies due process. The statute prescribes careful procedures and constraints. Judicial review is provided. There is no merit to the contention.

The defendant submits two final contentions regarding the arbitration panel. It alleges that the panel was not properly constituted since it had no authority to appoint a chairman and that the panel consisting of only the chairman and the union delegate had no authority to act; also, that the hearing in the instant case was not concluded within thirty days of its commencement, in contravention of Section 6, Act 312. These defenses come too late. The defendant is estopped to raise them. The city could not sit idly by, having been appraised of each step of the arbitration proceedings, and take no action. Stated another way: one who is silent when he ought to speak cannot speak when he ought to be silent. In the case of *Oliphant* v. *Frazho,* 381 Mich. 630, 638 states, "The state as well as individuals may be estopped by its actions, conduct, silence, and acquiescence is established by a line of well-adjudicated cases. . . ." As indicated, the city in this instance is "estopped by its silence and acquiescence."

· · ·

Act 312 . . . provides for compulsory arbitration where policemen and firemen are prohibited by law from striking. The section states, "It is requisite to the high morals of such employees and the efficient operation of such departments *to afford an alternative, expeditious, effective, and binding procedure for the resolution of disputes, and to that end the provisions of this act providing for compulsory arbitration shall be liberally construed."* (Emphasis supplied.)

In view of the foregoing this court finds Act 312 of Public Acts 1969 to be constitutional. It cannot be said that the statutory provisions assailed by the defendant are violative of the constitution on any of the grounds asserted by it. The plaintiff has complied with the procedures of the act and is entitled to the relief sought. The motion for summary judgment of the plaintiff will be granted, and the countermotion filed by the defendant for a summary judgment will be denied.

No costs of public question being involved.

Dated: February 26, 1971   /s/ Theodore R. Bohn
      Detroit, Mich.   Circuit Judge

Discussion Questions

1. Discuss the key issue in this case.
2. What were the defendant's main arguments against the compulsory arbitration statute?
3. How did the court rule on these objections?
4. Describe the case law on the subject.

CHAPTER 6

1 *Pickets at City Hall* (New York: The Twentieth Century Fund, 1970), pp. 23–29.

2 Thomas P. Gilroy and Anthony Sinicropi, *Dispute Settlement in the Public Sector: The State of-the-Art,* U.S. Department of Labor (Washington, D.C.: U.S. Government Printing Office, 1972), pp. 20–21.

3 GERR (No. 395) (E-1–5) (Washington, D.C.: BNA, Inc., April 5, 1971).

4 LRX 20, sec. 9 (Washington, D.C.: BNA, Inc., 1970).

5 21 GERR 6013–6015 (RF-21) (Washington, D.C.: BNA, Inc., 1971).

6 Gilroy and Sinicropi, *op. cit.,* pp. 10–11.

7 21 GERR 7005–7006 (RF-13) (Washington, D.C.: BNA, Inc., 1971).

8 LRX 15, sec. 2 (Washington, D.C.: BNA, Inc., 1970).

9 LRX 16(a), sec. 2 (Washington, D.C.: BNA, Inc., 1970).

10 Gilroy and Sinicropi, *op. cit.,* p. 12.

11 *Ibid.,* pp. 12–13.

12 GERR (No. 3920) (E-1–4) (Washington, D.C.: BNA, Inc., March 3, 1971).

7 | The Strike Weapon

IN the private sector, when negotiations fail and impasse resolution techniques are unsuccessful in efforts toward a settlement, the parties resort to economic weapons: the strike or the lockout. The right to strike is limited only when a work stoppage in a basic industry, if permitted, would jeopardize the national health, welfare, or security. Then, the emergency strike provisions of the Railway Labor Act—if the dispute is in the railroad or airlines industry—or the Taft-Hartley Act become operative. The President appoints so-called emergency boards and injunctions are imposed to forestall the strike action for a period of time, during which the parties are required to return to the bargaining table to attempt a peaceful settlement of their differences.

In public employment, by and large, federal, state, and municipal legislation has prohibited strike action by public employees. The prevalent attitude toward such activities by public employees is illustrated in a letter written by President Franklin D. Roosevelt to the president of the National Federation of Federal Employees on August 16, 1937, in which he said,

> Particularly, I want to emphasize my conviction that militant tactics have no place in the functions of any organization of government employees. . . . A strike of public employees manifests nothing less than intent on their part to prevent or obstruct the operations of government until their demands are satisfied. Such action, looking toward the paralysis of government by those who have sworn to support it, is unthinkable and intolerable.

The Supreme Court of the United States clearly enunciated the proposition that public employees did not have a right to strike and that the injunctive processes might properly be used to prevent or halt such strikes in the case of *United States* v. *United Mine Workers,* 330 U.S. 258, 67 S. Ct. 677 (1947). This case has never been overruled or modified. Its judicial standard has been followed generally in most of the other state jurisdictions where it has been held repeatedly that strikes by public employees are, or should be, prohibited and that injunctions should be granted to halt or prevent them. Only Hawaii, Pennsylvania, and Vermont allow

397

a limited strike right to some public employees and then only if the public health, welfare, or safety is not endangered.

At this juncture, a review of judicial decisions seems appropriate. One of the most frequently cited cases is the *Norwalk Teachers' Association* v. *Board of Education,* 138 Conn. 269, 83 A.2d 482, 485 (1951). The teachers' association sought a declaratory judgment to determine their rights to organize as a union and to strike. The action followed a refusal by 230 of the association members to return to their teaching duties. The work stoppage was settled, however, through subsequent negotiations. In answering the question of the legality of strikes the court stated,

> Under our system, the government is established by and run for all of the people, not for the benefit of any person or group. The profit motive, inherent in the principle of free enterprise, is absent. It should be the aim of every employee of the government to do his or her part to make it function as efficiently and economically as possible. The drastic remedy of the organized strike to enforce the demands of unions of government employees is in direct contravention of this principle. . . . In the American system, sovereignty is inherent in the people. They can delegate it to a government which they create and operate by law. They can give to that government the power and authority to perform certain duties and certain services. The government so created and empowered must employ people to carry on its task. These people are agents of the government. They exercise some part of the sovereignty entrusted to it. They occupy a status entirely different from those who carry on a private enterprise. They serve the public welfare and not a private purpose. To say that they can strike is the equivalent of saying that they can deny the authority of government and contravene the public welfare.

In *Board of Education* v. *Redding,* 32 Ill. 2d 567, 207 N.E.2d 427, 430 (1965) and *New Jersey Turnpike Authority* v. *AFSCME,* 83 N.J. Super. 389, 200 A.2d 134, 138 (1964), the courts used similar logic in ruling against the right to strike. The former case involved a strike and peaceful picketing by thirteen custodial employees of Community Unit School District, No. 2, Bond County, Illinois. The Circuit Court of Bond County refused to grant an injunction, sought by the Board of Education, on the grounds that the school board failed to show irreparable damage and that the employees' action was a valid exercise of constitutional rights. The Supreme Court of Illinois reversed the lower court, holding that the injunction should have been granted. The court held that,

> [T]here is no inherent right in municipal employees to strike against their governmental employer. The underlying basis for the policy against strikes by public employees is the sound and demanding notion that governmental functions may not be impeded or obstructed, as well as the concept that the profit motive inherent in the principle of free enterprise is absent in the governmental functions.

The court proceeded to express the opinion that as agents of the state, the school employees exercise part of the "sovereign power" of the state and hence have no right to strike.

In the New Jersey case the Turnpike Authority sought a declaratory judgment on whether the turnpike employees, as employees of the state, had a right to strike. Declaring that no such right existed, the court stated that "any such action, the intended result of which is the disabling of government, is inimical to the public interest and will not be tolerated."

Advocates of strike action in the public sector have questioned the relevance of above-mentioned "sovereignty theory" and, in fact, have described it as a legal fiction. They have received support in the form of the decision in *Board of Education* v. *Public School Employees Union,* 45 N.W. 2d 797 (1951), in which a Minnesota court stated that to prohibit public employees from striking is "to indulge in the expression of a personal belief and then ascribe to it legality on some tenuous theory of sovereignty or supremacy of government."

Chief Justice DeBruler of the Indiana Supreme Court, dissenting in *Anderson Federation of Teachers* v. *School City of Anderson,* 251 N.E.2d 15 (1969), argued against a complete ban on strikes by public employees:

> It is true that a strike by public employees may result in some amount of disruption of the agency for which they work. In the absence of legislation dealing with this subject we believe that it is a judicial function to determine whether the amount of the disruption of the service is so great that it warrants overriding the legitimate interests of the employees in having effective means to insure good faith bargaining by the employer. This is a minimum requirement before a court can declare a strike by public employees illegal.

The justice is expressing the minority view that collective bargaining is not meaningful unless resort to economic force is possible and that some public sector strikes would not create immediate emergencies.

In any event, Gilroy and Sinicropi summarize the present state of affairs:

> There is no across-the-board right of public employees to strike in any state or in the federal sector. . . . No one writing in the area argues that there should be, at least not before the exhaustion of other procedures. On the other hand, very few argue that strikes can be completely prevented by outlawing them.[1]

Section 1. A Ban on Strikes by Federal Employees

Executive Order 11491 and the Taft-Hartley Act both contain provisions that prohibit strike action by federal government employees. Section 305 of the latter states, "It shall be unlawful for any individual employed by the United States or any agency thereof including wholly owned government corporations to participate in any strike. . . ."

The same clause also imposes penalties for violations:

Any individual employed by the United States or by any such agency who strikes shall be discharged immediately from his employment, and shall forfeit his civil service status, if any, and shall not be eligible for reemployment for three years by the United States or any such agency.

Section 19 of the order entitled "Unfair Labor Practices," indicates in paragraph b(4) that: "A labor organization shall not call or engage in a strike, work stoppage, or slowdown; . . . or condone any such activity by failing to take affirmative action to prevent or stop it; . . . ." It should be noted that the United States experienced a postal strike in 1971 involving several hundred thousand postal employees. However, because of the large numbers of workers involved, and the substantial degree of public support for their grievances and demands, the imposition of sanctions did not ensue in the interest of political expediency. The following case is, thus far, the definitive decision in this area.

United Federation of Postal Clerks v. Winton M. Blount, as Postmaster General of the United States

United States District Court for the District of Columbia, Civil Action
No. 3297–69 [2]
Decided March 31, 1971

Before J. SKELLY WRIGHT, circuit judge, GEORGE E. MacKINNON, circuit judge, and JOHN H. PRATT, district judge.

PER CURIAM

This action was brought by the United Federation of Postal Clerks (hereafter sometimes referred to as clerks), an unincorporated public employee labor organization which consists primarily of employees of the Post Office Department, and which is the exclusive bargaining representative of approximately 305,000 members of the clerk craft employed by defendant. Defendant Blount is the Postmaster General of the United States. The clerks seek declaratory and injunctive relief invalidating portions of 5 U.S.C. Section 7311, 18 U.S.C. Section 1918, an affidavit required by 5 U.S.C. Section 3333 to implement the above statute, and Executive Order 11491, F.F.R., Chap. II, p. 191. The government, in response, filed a motion to dismiss or in the alternative for summary judgment, and plaintiff filed its opposition thereto and cross motion for summary judgment. A three-judge court was convened pursuant to 28 U.S.C. Section 2282 and Section 2284 to consider this issue.

THE STATUTES INVOLVED

5 U.S.C. Section 7311(3) prohibits an individual from accepting or holding a position in the federal government or in the District of Columbia if he "(3) participates in a strike . . . against the government of the United States or the government of the District of Columbia. . . ."

Paragraph (c) of the appointment affidavit required by 5 U.S.C. Section 3333, which all federal employees are required to execute under oath, states, "I am not participating in any strike against the government of the United States or any agency thereof, and I will not so participate while an employee of the government of the United States or any agency thereof."

18 U.S.C. Section 1918, in making violation of 5 U.S.C. Section 7311 a crime provides,

> Whoever violates the provision of Section 7311 of Title 5 that an individual may not accept or hold a position in the government of the United States or the government of the District of Columbia if he . . . (3) participates in a strike, or asserts the right to strike, against the government of the United States or the District of Columbia . . . shall be fined not more than $1,000 or imprisoned not more than one year and a day, or both.

Section 2(e)(2) of the Executive Order 11491 exempts from the definition of a labor organization any group which: "asserts the right to strike against the government of the United States or any agency thereof, or to assist or participate in such a strike, or imposes a duty or obligation to conduct, assist, or participate in such a strike. . . ."

Section 19(b)(4) of the same executive order makes it an unfair labor practice for a labor organization to: "call or engage in a strike, work stoppage, or slowdown; picket any agency in a labor-management dispute; or condone any such activity by failing to take affirmative action to prevent or stop it. . . ."

PLAINTIFF'S CONTENTIONS

Plaintiff contends that the right to strike is a fundamental right protected by the Constitution, and that the absolute prohibition of such activity by 5 U.S.C. Section 7311(3) and other provisions set out above thus constitutes an infringement of the employees' First Amendment rights of association and free speech and operates to deny them equal protection of the law. Plaintiff also argues that the language to "strike" and "participates in a strike" is vague and overbroad and therefore violative of both the First Amendment and the due process clause of the Fifth Amendment. For the purposes of this opinion, we will direct our attention to the attack on the constitutionality of 5 U.S.C. Section 7311(3), the key provision being challenged. To the extent that the present wording of 18 U.S.C. Section 1918(3) and Executive Order 11491 does not reflect the actions of two statutory courts in *Stewart* v. *Washington,* 301 F. Supp. 610 (D.C.D.C. 1969) and *NALC* v. *Blount,* 305 F. Supp. 546 (D.C.D.C. 1969), said wording, insofar as it inhibits the *assertion* of the right to strike, is overbroad because it attempts to reach activities protected by the First Amendment and is therefore invalid. With this *caveat,* our treatment of the issue raised by plaintiffs with respect to the constitutionality of 5 U.S.C. Section 7311(3) will also apply to 18 U.S.C. Section 1918, the penal provision, and for Form 61, the affidavit required by 5 U.S.C. Section 3333. For the reasons set forth below, we deny plaintiff's request for declaratory and injunctive relief and grant defendant's motion to dismiss.

I. PUBLIC EMPOYEES HAVE NO CONSTITUTIONAL RIGHT TO STRIKE

At common law no employee, whether public or private, had a constitutional right to strike in concert with his fellow workers. Indeed, such collective action on the part of employees was often held to be a conspiracy. When the right of private employees to strike finally received full protection, it was by statute, Section 7 of the National Labor Relations Act, which "took this conspiracy weapon away from the employer in employment relations which affect interstate commerce" and guaranteed to employees in the private sector the right to engage in concerted activities for the purpose of collective bargaining. . . . It seems clear that public employees stand on no stronger footing in this regard than private employees and that, in the absence of a statute, they too do not possess the right to strike.

The Supreme Court has spoken approvingly of such a restriction, see *Amell* v. *United States,* 384 U.S. 158, 161 (1965), and at least one federal district court has invoked the provisions of a predecessor statute, 5 U.S.C. Section 118p–7, to enjoin a strike by government employees. *Tennessee Valley Authority* v. *Local Union No. 110 of Sheet Metal Workers,* 233 F. Supp. 997 (D.C.W.D. Ky. 1962). Likewise, scores of state cases have held that state employees do not have a right to engage in concerted work stoppages, in the absence of legislative authorization. See, for example, *Los Angeles Metropolitan Transit Authority* v. *Brotherhood of R.R. Trainmen,* 54 Cal. 2d 634, 355 P.2d 905 (1960); *Board of Education* v. *Redding,* 32 Ill. 2d 567, 207 N.E.2d 427 (1965); *Alcoa* v. *International Brotherhood of Electrical Workers,* 203 Tenn. 13, 308 S.W.2d 476 (1957). It is fair to conclude that, irrespective of the reasons given, there is a unanimity of opinion on the part of the courts and legislatures that government employees do not have the right to strike. . . .

Congress has consistently treated public employees as being in a different category than private employees. The National Labor Relations Act of 1935 and the Labor Management Relations Act of 1947 (Taft-Hartley) both defined "employer" as not including any governmental or political subdivisions, and thereby indirectly withheld the protections of Section 7 from governmental employees. Congress originally enacted the no-strike provision separately from other restrictions on employee activity, that is, such as those struck down in *Stewart* v. *Washington* and *NALC* v. *Blount, supra,* by attaching riders to appropriations bills which prohibited strikes by government employees. See, for example, the Third Urgent Deficiency Appropriation Act of 1946, which provided that no part of the appropriation could be used to pay the salary of anyone who engaged in a strike against the government. Section 305 of the Taft-Hartley Act made it unlawful for a federal employee to participate in a strike, providing immediate discharge and forfeiture of civil service status for infractions. Section 305 was repealed in 1955 by Public Law 330, and reenacted in 5 U.S.C. Section 118p–7, the predecessor to the present statute.

Given the fact that there is no constitutional right to strike, it is not irrational or arbitrary for the government to condition employment on a promise not to withhold labor collectively, and to prohibit strikes by those in public employment, whether because of the prerogatives of the sovereign, some sense of higher obligation associated with public service, to assure the continuing functioning of the government without interruption, to protect public health and safety, or for other reasons. Although plaintiff argues that the provisions in question are unconstitutionally broad in covering all government employees regardless of the type or importance of the work they do, we hold that it makes no difference whether the jobs performed by certain public employees are regarded as "essential" or "nonessential," or whether similar jobs are performed by workers in private industry who do have the right to strike protected by statute. Nor is it relevant that some positions in private industry are arguably more affected with a public interest than are some positions in the government service. While the Fifth Amendment contains no equal protection clause similar to the one found in the Fourteenth Amendment, concepts of equal protection do inhere in Fifth Amendment principles of due process. *Bol-*

ling v. *Sharp,* 347 U.S. 487 (1954). The equal protection clause, however, does not forbid all discrimination. Where fundamental rights are not involved, a particular classification does not violate the equal protection clause if it is not "arbitrary" or "irrational," that is, "if any state of facts reasonably may be conceived to justify it." *McGowan* v. *Maryland,* 366 U.S. 420, 426 (1961). Compare *Kramer* v. *Union Free School District,* 395 U.S. 621, 627–628 (1969). Since the right to strike cannot be considered a "fundamental" right, it is the test enunciated in *McGowan* which must be employed in this case. Thus, there is latitude for distinctions rooted in reason and practice, especially where the difficulty of drafting a no-strike statute which distinguishes among types and classes of employees is obvious.

Furthermore, it should be pointed out that the fact that public employees may not strike does not interfere with their rights which are fundamental and constitutionally protected. The right to organize and to select representatives for the purpose of engaging in collective bargaining is such a fundamental right. . . . But, as the Supreme Court noted in *Local 232* v. *Wisconsin Employment Relations Board, supra,* "The right to strike, because of its more serious impact upon the public interest, is more vulnerable to regulation than the right to organize and select representatives for lawful purposes of collective bargaining which this Court has characterized as 'fundamental right' and which, as the Court has pointed out, was recognized as such in its decisions long before it was given protection by the National Labor Relations Act," 336 U.S. at 259.

Executive Order 11491 recognizes the right of federal employees to join labor organizations for the purpose of dealing with grievances, but that order clearly and expressly defines strikes, work stoppages, and slowdowns as unfair labor practices. As discussed above, that order is the culmination of a long-standing policy. There certainly is no compelling reason to imply the existence of the right to strike from the right to associate and bargain collectively. In the private sphere, the strike is used to equalize bargaining power, but this has universally been held not to be appropriate when its object and purpose can only be to influence the essentially political decisions of government in the allocation of its resources. Congress has an obligation to ensure that the machinery of the federal government continues to function at all times without interference. Prohibition of strikes by its employees is a reasonable implementation of that obligation.

II. THE PROVISIONS ARE NEITHER UNCONSTITUTIONALLY VAGUE NOR OVERBROAD

Plaintiff contends that the word "strike" and the phrase "participates in a strike" used in the statute are so vague that "men of common intelligence must necessarily guess at their meaning and differ as to their application," *Connolly* v. *General Construction Co.,* 269 U.S. 385, 391 (1926), and are therefore violative of the due process clause of the Fifth Amendment. Plaintiff also contends that the provisions are overly broad. While there is no sharp distinction between vagueness and overbreadth, an overly broad statute reaches not only conduct which the government may properly prohibit but also conduct which is beyond the reach of governmental regulation. A vague statute is merely imprecise in indicating which of several types of conduct which could be restricted has in fact been prohibited.

These concepts of "striking" and "participating in a strike" occupy central positions in our labor statutes and accompanying case law, and have been construed and interpreted many times by numerous state and federal courts. "Strike" is defined in Section 501(d) of the Taft-Hartley Act to include "any concerted stoppage of work by employees . . . and any concerted slow-down or other concerted interruption of operations by employees." On its face this is a straightforward definition.

It is difficult to understand how a word used and defined so often could be sufficiently ambiguous as to be constitutionally suspect. " 'Strike' is a term of such common usage and acceptance that 'men of common intelligence' need not guess at its meaning." *Connolly* v. *General Construction Co., supra,* at 341.

Plaintiff complains that the precise parameters of "participation" are so unclear that employees may fail to exercise other, protected First Amendment rights for fear of overstepping the line, and that in any event, "participates" is too broad to withstand judicial scrutiny. Plaintiff urges that Congress is required to more specifically define exactly what activities are to be caught up in the net of illegality.

The government, however, represented at oral argument that it interprets "participate" to mean "striking," the essence of which is an actual refusal in concert with others to provide services to one's employer. We adopt this construction of the phrase, which will exclude the First Amendment problems raised by the plaintiff in that it removes from the strict reach of these statutes and other provisions such conduct as speech, union membership, fund raising, organization, distribution of literature, and informational picketing, even though those activities may take place in concert during a strike by others. We stress that it is only an actual refusal by particular employees to provide services that is forbidden by 5 U.S.C. Section 7311(3) penalized by 18 U.S.C. 1918. However, these statutes, as all criminal statutes, must be read in conjunction with 18 U.S.C. Sections 2 (aiding and abetting) and 371 (conspiracy). We express no views as to the extent of their application to cases that might arise thereunder as it is practically impossible to fashion a meaningful declaratory judgment in such a broad area.

This case does not involve a situation where we are concerned with a prior construction by a state supreme court, but rather one in which we are faced with interpretation to be given a federal statute in the first instance by a federal court. Under such circumstances, federal courts have broad latitude, the language of the statute permitting, to construe a statute in such terms as will save it from the infirmities of vagueness and overbreadth. *Kent* v. *Dulles,* 357 U.S. 116 (1958). This principle of interpretation is equally true of cases which involve rights under the First Amendment. *United States* v. *CIO,* 335 U.S. 106, 120–122 (1948); *Chaplinsky* v. *New Hampshire,* 315 U.S. 568, 573–574 (1942). Such construction of the word "strike" and the phrase "participates in a strike" achieves the objective of Congress and, in defining the type of conduct which is beyond the reach of the statute, saves it from the risk of vagueness and overbreadth.

Accordingly, we hold that the provisions of the statute, the appointment affidavit and the executive order, as construed above, do not violate the constitutional rights of those employees who are members of plaintiff's union. The government's motion to dismiss the complaint is granted. Order to be presented. . . .

/s/ J. Skelly Wright
U.S. Circuit Judge

/s/ George E. MacKinnon
U.S. Circuit Judge

/s/ John H. Pratt
U.S. District Judge

Discussion Questions

1. What constitutional arguments does the plaintiff utilize in support of the right to strike by government employees?
2. Do public employees have a constitutional right to strike? Discuss the court's answer to this query.
3. Trace the development of the right to strike for private employees.
4. Did the Court believe that a distinction between "essential" and "nonessential" public jobs was important in ruling on (a) the merits of strike action or (b) a differentiation between public and private employment?
5. How does the Court dispose of the contention that the statutory antistrike provisions are unconstitutionally vague and overbroad?

Section 2. A Ban on Strikes by State Employees

Rhode Island is typical of those states that have more than one statute to cover different classifications of public employees in the exercise of their collective bargaining rights. It has five laws encompassing, respectively, state employees, municipal employees, teachers, firemen, and policemen. The case to be discussed here involves teachers who have engaged in strike activity.

School Committee of the Town of Westerly v. Westerly Teachers Association
Supreme Court of Rhode Island, No. 1874–M. P.[3]

OPINION

KELLEHER, J. Last September when the public school bells rang to announce the beginning of a new school year, there was one group whose response was something less than unanimous. It was the school teachers. In several communities they appeared at the schoolhouse doors not to teach but to picket. A phrase was heard which until recently was usually uttered by those engaged in the private sector of employment. It was "no contract, no work."

The town of Westerly was one such community. On September 1, 1971, the school committee and the Westerly Teachers Association had entered into a collective bargaining agreement concerning the "hours, salary, working conditions, and other terms and conditions of professional employment of the teachers." The contract was for a two-year period and contained a wage reopening clause for the 1972–1973 school year. Subsequent wage negotiations proved fruitless. Arbitrators were appointed pursuant to the relevant provisions of G. L. 1956 (1968 Reenactment) Chap. 9.3 of Title 28, the School Teachers' Arbitration Act. However, since the arbitrators' unanimous decision related to "matters involving the expenditure of money," it was not binding and was rejected by the school committee. Matters reached an impasse in late August, 1972.

September 5, 1972 was teachers' orientation day. A substantial number of the teachers failed to attend the scheduled meetings. The next day was the first day of school. The students appeared but, once again, the teachers were conspicuous by their absence from the classrooms. At 10 A.M., the committee closed the schools and shortly thereafter a complaint was submitted to a justice of the superior court. He then issued an ex parte temporary restraining order which enjoined the strike and ordered the teachers to return to work. On September 7, 1972, the association sought from us certiorari and a stay of the superior court's order. We issued the writ but denied the request for a stay. Thereafter, the strike ended and school began in Westerly.

Our issuance of the writ has been motivated by the fact that within recent times, each and every time the public schools of our state have resumed operations after summer vacation, teachers in many of the public school systems have refused to return to their classrooms claiming they have a right to strike. We have agreed to review the issuance of the superior court's restraining order because it is intertwined with an issue of substantial public interest which is capable of repetition yet evading review. . . . In doing so, we are reassessing a position first taken in *City of Pawtucket* v. *Pawtucket Teachers' Alliance,* 101 R.I. 243, 221 A.2d 806 (1966). The holding first expressed in 1958 states that striking by public school teachers is illegal and subject to being enjoined. We see no reason why this principle should be modified.

There is no constitutionally protected fundamental right to strike. In 1926, Mr. Justice Brandeis wrote that neither the common law nor the Fourteenth Amendment conferred the absolute right to strike. *Dorchy* v. *Kansas,* 272 U.S. 306, 47 S. Ct. 86 (1926). It was pointed out in *United Federation of Postal Clerks* v. *Blount,* 325 F. Supp. 879 (D.D.D.C. 1971), *aff'd,* 404 U.S. 802, 92 S. Ct. (1971), that at common law no employee whether private or public had a constitutional right to strike in concert with fellow workers because such an association was often regarded as an illegal conspiracy which was punishable under the criminal law. The conspiracy weapon was removed and the private employees' right to strike became fully protected with the passage of Section 7 of the National Labor Relations Act. . . . In the years that have ensued since the first Pawtucket school teachers' case, there has not been any instance where any court has held that public employees have a constitutional right to strike.

The diffusion of knowledge through the use of the public school system so that the advantages and opportunities afforded by education will be made available to the people is the constitutional responsibility of the state. Article XII, Section 1 of the Rhode Island Constitution. This responsibility is carried on at the local level by the school committee as an agent of the state.

The state has a compelling interest that one of its most precious assets—its youth—have the opportunity to drink at the font of knowledge so that they may be nurtured and developed into the responsible citizens of tomorrow. No one has the right to turn off the fountain's spigot and keep it in a closed position. Likewise, the equal protection afforded by the Fourteenth Amendment does not guarantee perfect equality. There is a difference between a private employee and a public employee, such as a teacher who plays such an important part in enabling the state to discharge its constitutional responsibility.

The need of preventing governmental paralysis justifies the "no-strike" distinction we have drawn between the public employee and his counterpart who works for the private sector within our labor force.

A thorough compilation of cases covering all facets of a public employee's right to strike can be found in Annot., 37 A.L.R. 3d 1147 (1971). A study of this annotation makes it perfectly clear that a judicial or legislative interdiction against strikes by public employees does not constitute involuntary servitude or an unwarranted impingement on one's constitutional rights be they of free speech, assembly, due process, or equal protection.

The teachers argue, however, that in the time that has elapsed since the first Pawtucket school teachers' case, the United States Supreme Court has treated public employees in such a way as to afford them rights previously denied them. They point to the holdings in *Keyishian* v. *Board of Regents,* 385 U.S. 589, 87 S. Ct. 675 (1967) and *Garrity* v. *New Jersey,* 385 U.S. 493, 87 S. Ct. 616 (1967).

In *Keyishian,* the Supreme Court described the classroom as the "market place of ideas" and invalidated the New York teachers' oath and loyalty law on the basis that their vagueness and ambiguity posed an unconstitutional threat to the teachers' right of free speech. The *Garrity* case dealt with a criminal conviction based upon evidence given by some defendants after they had been told that if they exercised their right against self-incrimination during an investigation of their conduct as policemen they might be discharged. These cases are of no assistance to the teachers because here there is no effort being made to inhibit the give-and-take that goes on in the classroom between teacher and pupil nor are we concerned with any violation of the Fifth Amendment right. . . .

Having failed in their efforts to persuade us that the right to strike has been elevated to constitutional status, the teachers point to various actions taken by the General Assembly and take the position that they have an implied right to strike. They embark on this effort by first pointing out that the General Assembly in its several enactments according collective bargaining rights to various groups of public employees has specifically stated that they shall not have the right to strike and then stress the absence of any such language as it concerns the teaching profession. The teachers look upon the legislative silence as implicit permission to go on strike. We disagree.

The School Teachers' Arbitration Act became law during the January, 1966 session of the General Assembly. We need only set forth the following excerpt:

28–9.3–1. Declaration of policy—purpose.

.   .   .

It is hereby declared to be the public policy of this state to accord to certified public school teachers the right to organize, to be represented, to negotiate professionally, and to bargain on a collective basis with school committees covering hours, salary, working conditions, and other terms of professional employment, provided, however, that nothing contained in this chapter shall be construed to accord to certified school teachers the right to strike.

While this section fails to contain an express prohibition against a strike, it certainly does not give the public school teachers the right to strike. On such a vital issue, we will not attribute to the General Assembly an intent to depart from the common law unless such an intent is expressly and unmistakably declared. . . . If the legislature wishes to give the public school pedagogues the right to strike, it must say so in clear and unmistakable language. Accordingly, we find no legislation implicitly granting such a right to the teachers of this state.

The sentiments we have just expressed relative to the implicit right to strike apply equally as well to the teachers' contention that their dispute with the school committee was subject to the anti-injunction provisions of Section 28–10–2. In the first Pawtucket school teachers' case we rejected this argument. The only additional comment that might be made is that if striking public employees are to be given the advantages of the anti-injunction statute, such action will have to result from legislative action rather than judicial construction.

The teachers' inability to enjoy the benefits of the legislation which severely limits the superior court's jurisdiction to enjoin a labor dispute does not mean that every time there is a concerted work stoppage by public employees, it shall be subject to an automatic restraining order. Rule 65(b) of Super. R. Civ. P. specifically states that no temporary restraining order shall be granted without notice to the adverse party unless it clearly appears from specific facts by affidavit or verified complaint that irreparable harm will result before notice can be served and a hearing held.

We must concede that the mere failure of a public school system to begin its school year on the appointed day cannot be classified as a catastrophic event. We are also aware that there has been no public furor when schools are closed because of inclement weather, or on the day a presidential candidate comes to town, or when the basketball team wins the championship. The law requires that the schools be in session for 180 days a year. . . . There is a flexibility in the calendaring of the school year that not only permits the make-up of days which might have been missed for one reason or another but may also negate the necessity of the immediate injunction which could conceivably subject some individuals to the court's plenary power of contempt.

It is true that the issuance of an interlocutory injunction lies within the sound discretion of the trial justice. The temporary restraining order was entered in the case at bar upon the verified complaint of the chairman of the school committee in which it is averred that schools had not opened as scheduled and that irreparable harm would be sustained by the students, parents, and citizens of Westerly. We think that in the light of what we have just said such a declaration will no longer justify ex parte relief. In making such a statement, we wish to make it clear that we are not faulting the trial justice. We are well cognizant that the temporary restraining order now before us was entered subsequent to the entry of another temporary restraining order by another justice of the superior court in a case involving a strike by the teachers in the Chariho School District. We stayed that order whereupon the district's school committee withdrew its complaint.

Counsel for petitioners and respondents concede that the trial justice in the pending cause made it clear that he had signed the restraining order solely in the interest of having a uniformity of practice in the issuance of restraining orders, both of which were requested within hours of each other.

Ex parte relief in instances such as teacher-school committee disputes can make the judiciary an unwitting third party at the bargaining table and potential coercive force in the collective bargaining processes. We embrace the position taken in *School District* v. *Holland Education Ass'n.,* 380 Mich. 314, 157 N.W.2d 206 (1968), where it was held that the trial court, before giving affirmative relief, should normally conduct a hearing where it would review what has gone on between the disputants and then determine whether injunction should issue and, if so, on what terms and for what period of time.

In conclusion, we would emphasize that the solution to the complex problem involving public schools, teachers, and collective bargaining rests within the capable hands of the members of our legislature. They will not want for proposed answers. During its January, 1969 session, the General Assembly created a "Commission to Study the Ways and Means of Avoiding and Resolving Impasses Which Arise During Contract Negotiations Between School Teachers' Organizations and School Committees." The commission's report was published on March 2, 1970. A majority of the commission recommended compulsory and binding arbitration on all matters. Another commissioner asked for a qualified right to strike while two others declared that "teachers have an ethical, moral, and professional right to withhold their services." One commission member took a neutral position by endorsing neither the majority report nor any of the minority reports. The diverse opinions expressed within the commission are ample proof that the policy to be followed is the one which must be laid out by the members of the Senate and House of Representatives.

The petition for certiorari is granted; the temporary restraining order is quashed *pro forma,* and the papers in the case are returned to the superior court.

MR. CHIEF JUSTICE ROBERTS, dissenting.

The majority has asserted that "there is no constitutionally protected fundamental right to strike." Moreover, the majority states that since there is no constitutional right to strike, the teachers must obtain this right in a clear and unmistakable grant from the legislature. From these contentions, I must dissent.

The right to strike was never explicitly granted to any employees, public or private. The labor union and strike arose out of economic struggle and not by the action of any legislature. Chief Justice Taft recognized the right of employees to strike long before the National Labor Relations Act . . . was passed. He described the development of the strike as follows:

> Is interference of a labor organization by persuasion and appeal to induce a strike against low wages under such circumstances without lawful excuse and malicious? We think not. Labor unions are recognized by the Clayton Act as legal when instituted for mutual help and lawfully carrying out their legitimate objects. They have long been thus recognized by the courts. They were organized out of the necessities of the situation. A single employee was helpless in dealing with an employer. He was dependent ordinarily on his daily wage for the maintenance of himself and family. If the employer refused to pay him the wages that he thought fair, he was nevertheless unable to leave the employ and to resist arbitrary and unfair treatment. Union was essential to give laborers opportunity to deal on equality with their employer. They united to exert influence upon him and to leave him in a body in order by this inconvenience to induce him to make better terms with them. They were withholding their labor of economic value to make him pay what they thought it was worth. The right to combine for such a lawful purpose has in many years not been denied by any court. The strike became a lawful instrument in a lawful economic struggle or competition between employer and employees as to the share or division between them of the joint product of labor and capital. *American Steel Foundries* v. *Tri-City Central Trades Council,* 257 U.S. 184, 208–209, 42 S. Ct. 72, 78 (1921).

Nowhere in the NLRA or other labor legislation does Congress expressly grant to employees the right to strike. Rather, in my opinion, this legislation was enacted for the protection of a right already possessed. Such protection was necessary to curb the repressive attitude of many state courts toward labor organizations and their activities. I reiterate that the legislation did not create any new rights for employees, for such rights would still exist if Section 7 of the NLRA were repealed. . . . The fact is that Section 7 of that act makes no mention of the right to strike. In Section 13 thereof reference is made to the right to strike as follows: "Nothing in this act, except as specifically provided for herein, shall be construed so as either to interfere with or impede or diminish in any way the right to strike, or to affect the limitations or qualifications on that right." Obviously, Section 13 is a rule of construction. . . . It is my opinion that the NLRA recognized the rights which labor already had and was intended to afford those rights extensive legislative protection.

Having concluded that the right to strike accrues to labor not by legislative grant, but by the irresistible thrust of socioeconomic forces, I turn to the question of whether the right to strike is within the protection of the constitutional guarantees. The Supreme Court has long recognized that the right of labor to organize and to bargain collectively is a fundamental right with constitutional protection. *NLRB* v. *Jones & Laughlin Steel Corp.,* 301 U.S. 1, 33–34, 57 S. Ct. 615, 622–623 (1937). Obviously, the right to strike is essential to the viability of a labor union, and a union which can make no credible threat of strike cannot survive the pressures in the present day industrial world. If the right to strike is fundamental to the existence of a labor union, that right must be subsumed in the right to organize and bargain collectively. *Bayonne Textile Corp.* v. *American Federation of Silk Workers,* 116 N.J.Eq. 146, 152–153, 172 A. 551, 554–555 (1934).

I am persuaded that if the right to organize and to bargain collectively is constitutionally protected, then the right to strike, that is, for persons similarly situated to act in concert to promote and protect their economic welfare, must be an integral part of the collective bargaining process.

That being so, it follows that it must be within the protection of the constitutional guarantees of the First Amendment. The collective bargaining process, if it does not include a constitutionally protected right to strike, would be little more than an exercise in sterile ritualism.

I find further support for the proposition of the right of employees to strike in the First and Fifth Amendments to the Constitution of the United States. The First Amendment's protection of freedom of speech and freedom of association has been extended to union organizational activities. *Thomas* v. *Collins,* 323 U.S. 516, 532, 65 S. Ct. 315, 323–324 (1945); *Hague* v. *CIO,* 307 U.S. 496, 59 S. Ct. 954 (1939). Moreover, the right to select a bargaining representative has been declared to be a property interest protected by the Clayton Act. *Texas & N.O. R.R.* v. *Brotherhood of Ry. & S.S. Clerks,* 281 U.S. 548, 571, 50 S. Ct. 427, 434 (1930). Such property interest would also be protected by the due process clause of the Fifth Amendment. In view of the fact that the protection of the First and Fifth Amendments is not alien to labor activity, I would conclude that the penumbra of those amendments protects individual workers while acting in concert to further their economic goals. Such activity by necessity includes the right to strike.

Being of the opinion that the right to strike is constitutionally protected, I turn to the question whether public employees, by reason of such employment, have forfeited that right. I think not. No waiver of constitutional rights is contemplated by public employment. *Keyishian* v. *Board of Regents,* 385 U.S. 589, 605–606, 87 S. Ct. 675, 685 (1967); *Garrity* v. *New Jersey,* 385 U.S. 493, 500, 87 S. Ct. 616, 620 (1967).

In the first place, I cannot agree that every strike by public employees necessarily threatens the public welfare and governmental paralysis. Merely because a group of employees is working for the government, it does not follow that their collective withholding of the services performed will have a substantial adverse effect upon the interests of society. The fact is that in many instances strikes by private employees pose the far more serious threat to the public interest than would many of those engaged in by public employees. It is elementary that the services performed by people employed in the private sector are in many instances so essential to the orderly operation of society that the health, safety, and welfare of the community would be substantially endangered were they to strike. It is not difficult to visualize the adverse effect on the public interest of a strike by the employees of a privately operated hospital or of a public utility. On the other hand, it could be extremely difficult to conjure up such a threat to the public interest arising out of a strike of the employees of a recreation department of a municipality or of the clerical staff of a state agency. In short, it appears to me that to deny all public employees the right to strike because they are employed in the public sector would be arbitrary and unreasonable.

Underlying the argument of those who say public employees have no right to strike is the notion that one cannot strike against the sovereign. This idea finds its basis in the same philosophy which dictates that one cannot sue the sovereign. The doctrine emanates from the concept of English law that the King could do no wrong and that the sovereign was above the courts. In recent years, sovereign immunity in tort law has been extensively criticized as an anachronism, and many states, including Rhode Island, have through their highest courts abandoned the doctrine in whole or in part. *Becker* v. *Beaudoin,* 106 R.I. 562, 261 A.2d 896 (1970). Perpetuation of the doctrine of sovereign immunity in tort law led to a great many inequities, its application effecting many incongruous results. Similarly, the application of the doctrine that one cannot strike against the sovereign leads to unfair results. Clinging to a doctrine that prohibits employees of the government the right to strike denies those individuals their constitutional right while applying an idea that is archaic and no longer logically supportable.

In asserting my conviction that public employees have a constitutionally protected right to strike, I am not overlooking the police power of the state. I am fully aware that the legislature has the inherent power to exercise the police power to protect the health, safety, and welfare of society. The police power may be invoked not only to prohibit strikes on the part of public employees but, where the effect of a strike would be to threaten the public interest, to forbid strikes by employees in the private sector. But surely the police power may be exercised where a strike on the part of public employees would curtail an essential public service. . . .

I subscribe, then, to the proposition that the right to strike is fundamental and is an integral part of the collective bargaining process. I further hold that the right to strike as an inherent component of the collective bargaining process is constitutionally protected for the benefit of those employed in the public sector as well as those employed in the private sector. I recognize, however, that the state may, by a valid exercise of the police power, proscribe an exercise of the right to strike with respect to those employed in areas of the public service where to permit its exercise would be to make probable an adverse effect on the public health, safety, or welfare.

Discussion Questions

1. Did the U.S. Supreme Court in the *Keyishian* and *Garrity* cases confer the right to strike on public employees?
2. Why did the Court disagree with the claim that teachers have an implied right to strike under Rhode Island law?
3. What criticism is normally directed at ex parte proceedings?
4. Discuss the positions taken in the dissenting opinion.

Section 3. The Suspension of Dues Checkoff Following a Prohibited Strike Activity

The dues checkoff is defined as "an arrangement whereby the employer deducts employees' union dues from their wages and remits the dues to the union. It is generally regarded as a form of union security. . . ." [4] Under federal law, the individual employee must provide written authorization for this action by the employer to remain in force for more than one year or beyond the expiration date of the collective bargaining agreement, whichever occurs first. Because the ban on strikes by public employees exists in almost all jurisdictions, suspension of the checkoff arrangement has been proposed as a penalty to be imposed on public employee unions which have unlawfully taken strike action.

In the Matter of

Michigan Civil Service Commission (plaintiff-appellant) v. Local 1342 AFSCME, AFL-CIO (defendant-appellee)

Docket No. 8793

Michigan Civil Service Commission (plaintiff-appellant) v. Local 567, AFSCME, AFL-CIO (defendant-appellee)[5]

Docket No. 9028

(State of Michigan Court of Appeals Division 2)

Before V. J. BRENNAN, P. J. FITZGERALD, and J. J. LEVIN. BRENNAN, P. J. This is an appeal by the Michigan Civil Service Commission from adverse rulings in the circuit courts of Wayne and Lapeer counties. The two cases were consolidated on this court's own motion.

Local Unions 1342 (State Liquor Wholesalers) and 567 (Lapeer State Home) were organized as affiliates of Council 7 of the American Federation of State, County, and Municipal Employees, AFL-CIO. They were organized pursuant to the "employee relations policy" of the Civil Service Commission which provides in part

> *Recognition:* The Civil Service Commission, as a public agency charged by the constitution with the regulation of all conditions of employment, and with responsibility for the public interest of all citizens equally, will grant recognition to employee organizations coming within the definition stated in this policy. Recognition shall continue so long as such organization satisfies the criteria for such recognition.

The definition of an employee organization is defined as:

> *Employee Organization:* Any lawful association, organization, or union composed of employees in the Michigan State Classified Service, having as its primary purpose the improvement of conditions of employment; but not including any organization (1) which asserts the right to strike, or which imposes a duty or obligation to conduct, assist, or participate in any such strike.

B. THE LABOR ORGANIZATION STATUS OF PATCO
UNDER SECTION 2(e)

The record clearly supports the hearing examiner's finding that
[PAT]CO, by its conduct and activities in February, March, and April,
[196?], assisted or participated in a strike against the government of the
[Unit]ed States within the meaning of Section 2(e)(2) of the executive
[order]. The hearing examiner properly rejected PATCO's contentions that
[it did] not in any way authorize, assist, or participate in the controller's
[walkout"]; that the controllers were acting individually rather than con-
[certed]ly; and that the controllers' work stoppage was justified because of
[unsafe] and dangerous conditions.

[I] find, therefore, in agreement with the hearing examiner, that PATCO
[called] the controllers' strike, assisted or participated therein, and con-
[doned] the strike by failing to take effective affirmative action to prevent
[or sto]p it. I, therefore, conclude that as a result of these acts, PATCO
[lost its] status as a labor organization within the meaning of Section 2(e)
[by] the order.

C. THE UNFAIR LABOR PRACTICE ISSUES

[Th]e evidence supports the examiner's findings that PATCO engaged
[in cond]uct violative of Section 19(b)(4) of the executive order in that
[it called] or engaged in a strike, work stoppage, or slowdown, or condoned
[such act]ivity by failing to take affirmative action to prevent or stop it.
[Wh]ile the conduct engaged in by PATCO clearly falls within the
[prohibiti]on contained in Section 19(b)(4), PATCO argues that no vio-
[lation of] Section 19(b)(4) can be found since the very conduct in which
[it engage]d served to deprive it of its status as a labor organization within
[the mean]ing of Section 2(e)(2). Thus, the argument continues, if PATCO
[is n]ot to be a labor organization within the meaning of Section 2(e)
[of the e]xecutive order (essentially because it called or engaged in a
[strike), it] cannot be held accountable for a violation under Section 19(b)
[which pro]hibits "labor organizations" from engaging in certain practices
[inc]luding or engaging in a strike. Acceptance of this argument would
[in effect] nullify Section 19(b)(4) of the executive order. Therefore,
[this argume]nt must be rejected.

[Acco]rdingly, I adopt the finding of the hearing examiner that PATCO
[violated S]ection 19(b)(4) of the executive order. Also, I accept the
[hearing ex]aminer's finding that PATCO's conduct in this situation, while
[violative o]f Section 19(b)(4) of the executive order, does not also
[constitute] a violation of Section 19(b)(1) since it has not been shown
[that the stri]ke constituted interference, restraint, or coercion of employees

In September and October of 1968, both unions allegedly engaged
in some prohibited strike activity. Thereafter, the commission issued show
cause orders to each union ordering them to show cause why recognition
should not be withdrawn. After hearings, at which extensive testimony was
taken, the commission determined that the prohibited activity had in fact
occurred. Although the commission might have withdrawn recognition,
instead it ordered that the unions were no longer to be provided with
payroll deduction of dues (dues checkoff). It is the position of the defendant unions that in so doing the commission exceeded its authority. We
agree.

The pertinent section of the employee relations policy dealing with
dues checkoff provides "Dues Collections: Recognized employee organizations will be provided with the payroll deduction system for the collection
of dues."

It is undisputed that the locals were "recognized employee organizations" both before and after the order suspending dues checkoffs.

The commission contends, however, that the order was proper on
two grounds. First, the commission urges that since dues checkoff is a
condition of employment, it may properly make this type of order under
its constitutional power to "regulate all conditions of employment in the
classified service." Const. 1963, Art. 11, Sec. 5. Secondly, it is argued that
the power to withdraw complete recognition contains within it the power
to exact penalties short of nonrecognition.

Neither of the commission's arguments meets the issue in this case.
We are not concerned here with whether the commission could have included a revocation of dues checkoff in its policy nor are we concerned
with the commission's authority to exact a different, although more severe,
penalty. We are faced, rather, with the unequivocal language in the commission's own policy statement to the effect that recognized employee
organizations will be provided with dues checkoffs and with the undisputed
fact that nowhere in the rules and regulations of the Civil Service Commission is there provision for a suspension of dues checkoff as a possible
penalty for engaging in strike activity. Accordingly, what was said in the
concurring opinion of Mr. Justice Edwards in *Dillon* v. *Lapeer Training
School,* 364 Mich. 1, 26 (1961) is applicable here: "An executive agency
must be rigorously held to the standards by which it professes its action
to be judged. See *Securities & Exchange Commission* v. *Chenery Corp.,*
318 U.S. 80, 87, 88, 63 S. Ct. 454. Accordingly, if dismissal from
employment is based on a defined procedure, even though generous beyond the requirements that bind such agency, that procedure must be
scrupulously observed. See *Service* v. *Dulles,* 354 U.S. 363. This judicially
evolved rule of administrative law is now firmly established and if I may

add, rightly so." Quoting with approval from *Vitarelli* v. *Seaton*, 359 U.S. 535, 546, 547 (1959).

Since the standards by which the commission professes itself to be judged do not provide for suspension of dues checkoff as a penalty for engaging in certain activities and since suspension is inconsistent with the commission's policy statement that recognized employee organizations will be provided with dues checkoff, we believe that the order suspending them was arbitrary and cannot stand. MCLA Sec. 24.108 Stat. Ann. 1969 Rev. Sec. 3.560(21.8).

For the foregoing reasons, the judgment in favor of the defendants is affirmed.

Discussion Questions

1. What sanction can be imposed on an "employee organization" that conducts a strike in contravention of the Michigan statute?
2. How did the commission attempt to justify its suspension of dues checkoff rights for the two unions?
3. Why did the court disagree with the commission's action in this case?

Section 4. The Nullification of a Representation Petition Due to a Prohibited Walkout

Section 2(e)(2) of Executive Order 11491 excludes from its definition of "labor organization" any organization that engages in an unlawful strike against the federal government by stating,

> "Labor organization" . . . does not include an organization which (2) asserts the right to strike against the government of the United States or any agency thereof, or to assist or participate in such a strike, or imposes a duty or obligation to conduct, assist, or participate in such a strike. . . .

In the spring of 1970, the Professional Air Traffic Controllers Association (PATCO), the labor organization representing airport controllers, led a strike against the FAA. The upcoming case illustrates the ramifications of such activity vis-à-vis PATCO's role as a labor organization.

In the Matter of

**Professional Air Traffic Controllers Organizati
National Association of Government Employe**
and **Federal Aviation Administration (activity),
Controllers Organization, Inc. (petitioner), N
Government Employees, Inc.; American Fed
Employees; Air Traffic Control Association, I
of Federal Employees; and International A
and Aerospace Workers (inte**

Case No. 46–1698(C

Case No. 46–1593(F

(United States Department of Labor Befo
for Labor–Management F

DECISION AND OI

On October 5, 1970, Hearing Examine
port and recommendations in the above-en
Professional Air Traffic Controllers Orga
engaged in a strike in violation of Section
11491 and was, as a result thereof, disqu
within the meaning of Section 2(e)(2) o
PATCO engaged in violative conduct, the
that it be required to take certain affirm
. . . report and recommendations. . . .
the complainant, National Association
(NAGE); the activity, Federal Aviation
intervening Air Traffic Control Associati
with supporting briefs, to the hearing ex
tions.

The Assistant Secretary has rev
examiner made at the hearing and finds
mitted. The rulings are hereby affirmed
examiner's report and recommendatio
ject case, including the exceptions, s
adopt the findings and recommendati
extent that they are consistent with th

PA
197
Unit
orde
it di
"sick
certe
unsaf

called
doned
or sto
lost its
(2) of

Th
in cond
it called
such act
Wl
prohibiti
lation of
it engage
the mear
is found
of the e
strike) it
which pr
such as ca
effectively
the argum
Acco
violated S
hearing ex
violative c
constitute
that the st

within the meaning of the executive order. In addition, the hearing examiner correctly concluded that the evidence does not warrant a finding that PATCO committed independent acts of interference, restraint, or coercion against individual controllers.

D. PATCO'S REPRESENTATION PETITIONS

On February 18, 1970, PATCO filed a petition for certification as exclusive bargaining representative for a nationwide unit of all "non-supervisory Air Traffic Control Specialists," with certain specified exclusions. PATCO also has filed several other petitions requesting certification as exclusive representative of employees in various bargaining units less than national in scope. I do not find it necessary to enumerate each of these "local" petitions as my decision on the nationwide petition will be applied to all petitions filed by, or in behalf of, PATCO. As discussed above, after filing its nationwide petition PATCO participated in and condoned a work stoppage, which I find disqualified it as a labor organization entitled to the rights afforded by the order. Consequently, I find that the strike and the attendant disqualification under Section 2(e)(2) operated to nullify any petitions filed by PATCO. Therefore, I will not accept as valid any presently pending or future petitions or showings of interest filed by, or in behalf of, PATCO until such time as I have found it to be in compliance with this decision and order. Moreover, I conclude that further processing of the present petitions will not effectuate the policies of the order. Accordingly, I shall order that all pending PATCO petitions be dismissed. Similarly, any PATCO requests or motions to intervene presently pending before the Department of Labor will be dismissed. And lastly, if PATCO has any unfair labor practices complaints pending as of the date of this decision and order these too shall be dismissed. However, any individuals named in any such complaints may refile complaints in their own names notwithstanding the timeliness proviso of Section 203.2 of the regulations, provided that each such complaint is refiled within thirty days of its dismissal.

E. THE UNFAIR LABOR PRACTICE REMEDY

This executive order attempts to balance two principal aims: (1) that employees (here, the controllers) are entitled to representation by the organization of their choice; and (2) that labor organizations be deterred effectively from violating the provisions of the executive order.

Despite the flagrant nature of the violation, I believe that permanent debarment of PATCO as an employee representative might deprive controllers of their freedom of representation to an unwarranted extent. However, I feel that some period of debarment is required for two reasons: (1) to provide PATCO with an adequate opportunity to comply with the affirmative provisions of my remedial order, and (2) to serve notice on all labor organizations that the United States government will not condone violations of the executive order.

Accordingly, until such time as the Professional Air Traffic Controllers Organization, Inc., affiliated with the National Marine Engineers Beneficial Association, AFL-CIO (PATCO-MEBA) can demonstrate to my satisfaction that it has complied with my decision and order, and that it will comply in the future with the provisions of the executive order, I shall not permit it to utilize the procedures available to a labor organization within the meaning of Section 2(e) of the executive order. In this regard, I shall not entertain any submission by PATCO-MEBA to this effect until sixty days from the date of posting or mailing, whichever is later, of the . . . notice to members and employees. . . .

I find that the nature of the violative conduct in which PATCO engaged dictates that it establish new showings of interest in order to participate, either as petitioner or intervenor, in future representation matters.

Any new showings of interest should be in the form of authorization cards which reflect PATCO's affiliation with the National Marine Beneficial Association, AFL-CIO (MEBA) and the cards must be dated at least ten days after the posting or the mailing of notices to employees or members, whichever is later.

I shall order that PATCO-MEBA cease and desist from the conduct herein found violative, and that it post for a period of sixty consecutive days an appropriate notice to employees and members, signed by its present national president and board chairman, in all of its national and local business offices and meeting places. Further, to ensure that all controllers are made aware of the content of this notice, I shall (1) require PATCO-MEBA to mail a copy of the signed notice to each of its members at his last known home address and (2) require the Federal Aviation Administration to post the notice at places where it customarily posts information to its controllers. Accordingly, within fourteen days of the date of this decision and order, PATCO-MEBA shall furnish FAA with sufficient copies of the signed notice to meet FAA's posting requirement.

The record reflects that the dues deduction agreement between FAA and PATCO presently is suspended. It is my opinion that the suspension should be continued during the period in which PATCO-MEBA is barred from filing petitions or complaints. Therefore, I shall order that FAA and PATCO-MEBA be precluded from entering into or giving effect to any dues deduction agreements with FAA during the period of bar. This prohibition shall apply also to the PATCO locals having exclusive and formal recognition granted under Executive Order 10988.

ORDER

Pursuant to Section 6(b) of the executive order and Section 203.25 (a) of the regulations, the Assistant Secretary of Labor for Labor-Management Relations hereby orders that:

1. All pending petitions and unfair labor practice complaints filed by or on behalf of PATCO be dismissed and that before the filing of any future petitions or complaints PATCO-MEBA demonstrates to the satisfaction of the Assistant Secretary that it has complied with this decision and order, and will comply in the future with the provisions of Executive Order 11491.

2. All of PATCO's pending requests of motions for intervention in representation proceedings currently before the Department of Labor be dismissed.

3. Future showings of interest submitted by PATCO-MEBA be in the form of authorization cards dated at least ten days after the posting or the mailing of notices to employees or members, whichever is later.

4. PATCO-MEBA, its officers, agents, and representatives, shall

(a) Cease and desist from:

(1) Calling or engaging in any strike, work stoppage, or slowdown against the Federal Aviation Administration or any other agency of the government of the United States, or from assisting or participating in any such strike, work stoppage, or slowdown.

(2) Condoning any such activity by failure to take effective affirmative action to prevent or stop it.

5. FAA and PATCO-MEBA are prohibited from entering into or giving effect to any dues deduction agreements during the period that PATCO-MEBA is barred from utilizing the procedures established under Executive Order 11491.

6. PATCO-MEBA take the following affirmative action to effectuate the purposes and provisions of the executive order:

(a) Post at its national and local business offices and in normal meeting places copies of the . . . notice signed by the national president and board chairman of PATCO-MEBA. . . . Said copies of the notices shall be posted for a period of sixty consecutive days in conspicuous places, including all places where notices to members are customarily posted. Reasonable steps shall be taken by PATCO-MEBA to ensure that said notices are not altered, defaced, or covered by other material.

(b) Mail a copy of said notice to each of its members at his last known home address.

(c) Furnish sufficient copies of said notice to the Federal Aviation Administration for posting at places where it customarily posts information to its controllers. Notices should be furnished to FAA within fourteen days of the date of this decision and order.

(d) At such time as PATCO-MEBA believes that it can meet the requirements as a labor organization under Section 2(e) of the executive order, but in no event sooner than the expiration of the sixty-day posting period, it may furnish to the Assistant Secretary of Labor for Labor-Management Relations a specific account, in writing, of the steps it has taken to comply with this decision and order, as well as steps it has taken to ensure future compliance with Executive Order 11491 and the regulations pertaining thereto. PATCO-MEBA shall serve copies of such account simultaneously upon all other parties to this proceeding and furnish the Assistant Secretary with a statement that such service has been made. Other parties will have five days from service of PATCO-MEBA's account within which to file comments with the Assistant Secretary.

Dated: January 29, 1971   /s/ W. J. Usery, Jr., Assistant Secretary of
     Washington, D.C.   Labor for Labor-Management Relations

Discussion Questions

1. What arguments did PATCO present to defend itself against the illegal strike charges?
2. Discuss the approach PATCO utilized in denying that its strike action was an unfair labor practice.
3. What rationale did the Assistant Secretary follow in temporarily, rather than permanently, suspending PATCO's right to process a representation petition?
4. What additional sanctions were imposed on PATCO in its capacity as a labor organization?

Section 5. Penalties for Illegal Work Stoppage by Police Officers

New York's Taylor Law, in Section 210(1), prohibits strikes in public employment by stating, "No public employee or employee organization shall engage in a strike, and no public employee or employee organization shall cause, instigate, encourage, or condone a strike." [7]

A public employee who strikes in violation of this provision is subject to discharge or other disciplinary action by the appropriate authorities. The case to be discussed here involved an illegal strike action by New York City policemen in January, 1971, and an appeal from the sanctions imposed.

Edward J. Kiernan et al. v. John V. Lindsay et al.
United States District Court, Southern District of New York, *ul Civ.*
2978 DNE [8]

MULLIGAN, C. J. The plaintiffs, New York City patrolmen suing on behalf of themselves and others similarly situated, bring this action seeking a declaratory judgment of unconstitutionality and an injunction against the enforcement of New York Civil Service Law Section 210(2) (McKinney Supp. 1970) on the ground that the section is violative of the Fourteenth Amendment to the United States Constitution.

The defendants, the city of New York and a number of its officials, cross-moved to dismiss pursuant to Rule 12(b)(1) and (6) of the Federal Rules of Civil Procedure on the grounds that the court lacks jurisdiction over the subject matter of the action, and that the complaint fails to state a claim upon which relief can be granted. In their briefs they also argued that even if the court should find that jurisdiction exists, it should abstain from exercising it in this case.

The action arose out of a violation of the Taylor Law, N.Y. Civ. Serv. Law Section 210 (McKinney Supp. 1970) consisting of an alleged six-day strike by New York City policemen in January, 1971. Following the procedures mandated by that law, the Mayor of the city of New York determined that specific patrolmen in the New York City Police Department had violated the Taylor Law on one or more of the six days on which the strike occurred (January 14–19, 1971). He imposed the penalties prescribed by Civil Service Law Section 210(2) and notified each of the offending patrolmen that he would be on probation, serving without tenure, for a period of one year, and the City Comptroller, having been notified of the Mayor's determination, would deduct from the compensation of such patrolmen two days' pay for each day he was determined to be absent in violation of the law. At the time that this case was argued the deductions from compensation had been made, and the probationary period had commenced.

Under the provisions of Section 210(2)(h) every patrolman who received such notice may file an objection with the Mayor stating why he believes that the determination was incorrect. Virtually all of the 21,000 patrolmen involved have filed an objection. Based solely on the affidavit submitted, the Mayor may sustain or deny the objection. However, if a question of fact arises, a hearing will be held at which the patrolman must demonstrate by a preponderance of the evidence that he did not violate the section. All these determinations are judicially reviewable pursuant to Article 78 of the Civil Practice Law & Rules. N.Y. Civ. Serv. Law Section 210(2)(h) (McKinney Supp. 1970). Both sides concede that if a hearing were to be held for each of the 21,000 patrolmen, it would take an extremely long time to complete the procedure, and it is possible that the last man would not be heard until some years after the one year probation period had expired.

It is the imposition of the pay and probationary penalties without a prior adversary hearing which the plaintiffs principally claim to be deprivation of due process of law as guaranteed by the Fourteenth Amendment of the United States Constitution.

At the plaintiffs' request, a three-judge court was convened pursuant to 28 U.S.C. Section 2282 and Section 2284. Since the motion papers were supplemented by affidavits, the matter was treated as a motion for summary judgment, Fed. R. Civ. Proc. 12(c), argument was heard on the merits and on the jurisdictional and abstention objections. We shall first examine the jurisdictional question.

Plaintiffs contend that this court has jurisdiction over their claims for injunctive relief and for declaratory relief pursuant to 28 U.S.C. Section 2201 and Section 2202 under both 28 U.S.C. Section 1331, general federal question jurisdiction and 28 U.S.C. Section 1343(3), which confers original jurisdiction on the district courts over cases involving a deprivation of the privileges and immunities protected in 42 U.S.C. Section 1983. We shall consider the jurisdictional bases separately.

Section 1331

Title 28 U.S.C. Section 1331(a) is the general federal question statute. It requires not only that the suit arise under the Constitution, laws, or treaties of the United States, but also that the "matter in controversy" exceed "the sum or value of $10,000." Since a resolution of plaintiffs' claim that the imposition of the Taylor Law penalties without a prior hearing is a deprivation of due process of law depends entirely on the construction of the Fourteenth Amendment of the Constitution, there can be no dispute that a federal question is involved.

Defendants do claim, however, that the plaintiffs, despite the allegations in their complaint, have failed to demonstrate the amount in controversy exceeds $10,000, and therefore no jurisdiction exists. In determining the question we must examine the various penalties imposed to see if the monetary requirement has been met.

Civil Service Law Section 210(2)(g) provides that any public employee determined to have participated in an illegal strike "shall have deducted from his compensation . . . an amount equal to twice his daily rate of pay for each day or part thereof that it was determined that he had violated this subdivision." Since the strike in question lasted only six days, the highest actual monetary loss to be suffered by any individual patrolman, under this aspect of the statutory penalties, is conceded by the plaintiffs to be only $600.

Since the individual patrolmen cannot aggregate their claims in order to reach the $10,000 requirement, *Snyder* v. *Harris,* 394 U.S. 332 (1969); *Hague* v. *CIO,* 307 U.S. 496 (1939); *Local 1497, National Federation of Federal Employees* v. *City and County of Denver,* 301 F. Supp. 1108 (D. Colo.), appeal dismissed, 396 U.S. 273 (1969), it is apparent that the monetary penalty alone will not support Section 1331 jurisdiction.

If the jurisdictional monetary amount is to be satisfied, it must be based on a valuation of that portion of the Taylor Law penalties which provide that a public employee determined to have been engaged in an illegal strike will be placed "on probation for a term of one year following such determination during which period he shall serve without tenure." N.Y. Civ. Serv. Law Section 210(2)(f) (McKinney Supp. 1970). The meaning and effect of this provision is hotly disputed by the parties.

The defendants maintain that the two terms "probation" and service "without tenure" are synonymous and that the sole consequence of this sanction is that the patrolman loses the right to an adversary hearing before dismissal under Section 434a–14.0 of the administrative code of the city of New York if there is a charge of misconduct after he has been placed on probation. The corporation counsel has taken the position on behalf of the city that there has been and will be no adverse effect on plaintiffs' rights to promotion, retirement, sick leave, health insurance, or any other fringe benefit to which he might otherwise be entitled. In fact, numerous patrolmen on Taylor Law probation have been promoted according to the city and this does not seem to be contested. The plaintiffs on the other hand equate the probation under the Taylor Law with that defined in Section 63 of the Civil Service Law under which the test for dismissal is the suitability and fitness of a new appointee or promotee for the position he occupies as a probationer. This they claim gives the commissioner of police absolute and unfettered discretion to determine at any time that a Taylor Law probationer is unfit for future employment for any reason. This of course would jeopardize the patrolman's livelihood and all of the benefits he had acquired during his tenure.

In determining the attributes of Taylor Law probation, we are not assisted by any case in New York State which has decided or even considered the questions. However, we are persuaded that the failure of the New York legislators to repeat the language of the prior Condon-Wadlin Act [C. 790, Section 108(5)(c) (1958)] McKinney's N.Y. Sess. Laws 1008 (repealed 1967) which provided that the probationer had to serve without tenure "and at the pleasure of the appointing officer of body" was significant. Without clear and unmistakable language to the contrary we

428 · THE STRIKE WEAPON

would hesitate to construe the statute to permit the obliteration of benefits accrued during years of service by administrative whim. The posture of the city in this case negates any such Draconian approach, and we cannot reasonably conclude at this juncture that this probation entails anything more than the loss of the right to a hearing prior to discharge for misconduct during the probationary period. Certainly the plaintiffs have not demonstrated by a preponderance of the evidence that the drastic interpretation they urge is justified under state law. In a comparable situation Chief Judge Lumbard's caution is most appropriate, "In addressing this question of state law . . . the role of the federal court is a modest one." *United States ex rel. Harrington* v. *Mancusi,* 415 F.2d 205, 209 (2d Cir. 1969).

Our next inquiry must of course be whether this one year suspension of tenure meets the $10,000 test of Section 1331. In an equity action initiated in a federal court, the plaintiffs have the burden of establishing by a preponderance of the evidence that they have satisfied the jurisdictional requirement. *McNutt* v. *General Motors Acceptance Corp.,* 298 U.S. 178, 189 (1936). Moreover, plaintiffs do not meet this burden if the right they seek to protect is incapable of monetary valuation. "It is firmly settled law that cases involving rights not capable of valuation in money may not be heard in federal courts where the applicable jurisdictional statute requires that the matter in controversy exceed a certain number of dollars. The rule was laid down in *Barry* v. *Mercein,* 46 U.S. (5 How.) 103. . . . "The words of the Congress are plain and unambiguous. . . . 'There are no words in the law, which by any just interpretation can be held to . . . authorize us to take cognizance of cases to which no test of money value can be applied', 46 U.S. at 120," *aff'd without consideration of the jurisdictional question,* 393 U.S. 316 (1969). See *Rosado* v. *Wyman,* 414 F.2d 170, 176–177 (2d Cir. 1969), *rev'd on other grounds,* 397 U.S. 397 (1970); *Goldsmith* v. *Sutherland,* 426 F.2d 1395 (6th Cir.), *cert. denied,* 400 U.S. 960 (1970); *Post* v. *Payton,* 323 F. Supp. 799, 804 (E.D.N.Y. 1971); *Ackerman* v. *Columbia Broadcasting System,* 301 F. Supp. 628, 633–634 (S.D.N.Y. 1969).

Plaintiffs urge that even though their rights may be intangible, there should be no difficulty in determining that their monetary value exceeds the jurisdictional requirement. The cases relied upon are distinguishable. For example, in *Gobites* v. *Minersville School District,* 24 F. Supp. 271 (E.D. Pa. 1938), *aff'd,* 108 F.2d 683 (3rd Cir. 1939), *rev'd on other grounds,* 310 U.S. 586 (1940), plaintiffs' children were denied the right to attend public school because of their refusal to salute the flag. The alleged right not to salute could be measured "by the cost of obtaining an equivalent education at private institutions." 24 F. Supp. at 275. In *City of Mem-*

phis v. *Ingram*, 195 F.2d 338 (8th Cir. 1952), a municipal corporation in Tennessee sought to enjoin a county officer in another state from the demolition of a bridge and roadways to it in Arkansas. While exact valuation of the pecuniary loss was not required, the initial cost of the approach roadways and the bridge were found to far exceed the jurisdictional level. *Eison* v. *Eastman,* 421 F.2d 560 (2d Cir. 1969), *cert. denied,* 400 U.S. 841 (1970), involved an action by a landlord against a city rent and rehabilitation director challenging the constitutionality of the rent control law. The court found that the controversy involved the value of two buildings free from rent control as against being subject to control and the capitalized value of the rent reduction far exceeded the $10,000 limitation. These cases all involved the application of formulae which could reasonably calibrate the matter in controversy in dollars. There is no possible norm to measure in dollars the injury flowing from the suspension of tenure for one year.

A second category of cases involving actual discharge of employees, *Martin* v. *Ethyl,* 341 F.2d 1 (5th Cir. 1965); actual expulsion from a union, *Giordano* v. *RCA,* 183 F.2d 558 (3rd Cir. 1950), *Friedman* v. *International Ass'n of Machinists,* 220 F.2d 808 (D.C. Cir.), *cert. denied,* 350 U.S. 824 (1955); or an actual loss of pension funds, *George* v. *Lewis,* 228 F. Supp. 725 (D. Colo. 1964) are equally unavailing since all have involved an actual rather than a potential loss of money. Here, no actual loss occurs until misconduct is charged and a dismissal takes place. There is no allegation or suggestion that such has ever been threatened.

Finally, plaintiffs' reliance on cases such as *Berk* v. *Laird,* 429 F.2d 302 (2d Cir. 1970), where injunctive relief against federal officers is sought, is also unavailing here. In such cases there is no state remedy and the plaintiff would have been without redress unless the federal forum were provided. This facet of the jurisdictional problem was emphasized by Judge Edelstein in his dissenting opinion in *Boyd* v. *Clark, supra,* 287 F. Supp. at 567–569; see also *Cortright* v. *Resor,* 325 F. Supp. 797, 808–811 (E.D.N.Y. 1971), *rev'd on other grounds,* 447 F.2d 245 (2d Cir. 1971). That the state courts in New York could entertain this action is not questioned here. That they should, will be developed *infra.*

In cases where the state has concurrent jurisdiction, the jurisdictional requirement of $10,000 should be strictly construed. "Due regard for the rightful independence of state governments, which should actuate federal courts, requires that they scrupulously confine their own jurisdiction to the precise limits which the statute has defined." *Healy* v. *Ratta,* 292 U.S. 263, 270 (1933).

Plaintiffs have failed to demonstrate that the New York courts would construe the Taylor Law in accordance with their claims and thus have not sustained their burden of establishing that the monetary jurisdictional requirements of Section 1331 have been met. We, therefore, conclude that we have no jurisdiction under that section.

Section 1343(3)

Plaintiffs also allege that the imposition of "probation" without a prior hearing is a deprivation of Fourteenth Amendment rights and therefore jurisdiction is conferred by 28 U.S.C. Section 1343(3) which confers original jurisdiction over civil actions authorized by 42 U.S.C. Section 1983. We believe that this is clearly not a case involving personal liberty within Section 1343(3). This circuit has recently given full consideration to the question of the applicability of the statute to a discharge from public employment in *Tichen* v. *Harder*, 438 F.2d 1396 (2d Cir. 1971) where a newly appointed probationary teacher brought an action against state officials because of an alleged arbitrary dismissal without any hearing or notice of hearing. In finding no Section 1343(3) jurisdiction the court found that her dismissal did not infringe upon any nonproperty rights protected by the first eight amendments, and "in absence of a clear, immediate, and substantial impact on the employee's reputation which effectively destroys his ability to engage in his occupation, it cannot be said that a right of personal liberty is involved." *Id.* at 1402. Here plaintiffs claim that the imposition of the penalties infringe upon their right to free speech and assemblage guaranteed by the First Amendment. The mere allegation that the power of dismissal "chills" First Amendment rights without any substantiation in fact is not persuasive. We cannot assume an abuse of the power of dismissal without misconduct. In fact, as indicated above, the announced position of the city is decidedly contrary. We see no evidence at all of any "chilling" effects except for the vague and conclusory statements of the complaint and affidavit not supported by any facts. We deem it to be too frivolous and unsubstantiated to support Section 1343(3) jurisdiction. *Bell* v. *Hood*, 327 U.S. 678, 682 (1945).

Moreover, there can obviously be no "clear, immediate and substantial impact" on reputation so as to effectively destroy plaintiffs' ability to engage in their occupation. They have not been discharged. They have been fined and placed in an undefined probationary status. They are all working and some have even been promoted. We cannot read *Tichen* as limited to probationary employees. While the plaintiff in *Tichen* was probationary and had not achieved a professional reputation, the holding clearly required a finding of an effective deprivation of livelihood looking to the circumstances of the dismissal and not the mere fact of dismissal in order to find an impact on personal liberty. In *Birnbaum* v. *Trussell*, 371 F.2d 672 (2d Cir. 1966) where 1343 jurisdiction was upheld, Dr. Birnbaum was discharged from the staff of a municipal hospital without a hearing. He was accused of anti–Negro bias, and all other municipal hospitals were advised and instructed not to hire him. It is clear that the discharge of even tenured municipal employees is by itself insufficient to give 1343 jurisdiction unless there are collateral circumstances establishing clear, effective, and substantial obstacles to future employment such as the blackballing techniques employed in *Birnbaum*. The instant situation is clearly distinguishable and we find no 1343 jurisdiction. . . .

Even though we have held that this court lacks jurisdiction of this matter, we further believe that even assuming it existed, we should abstain from exercising it here. While the doctrine of abstention has been narrowly limited, it is still applicable in two situations both of which are present here.

The first involves a case where the state statute is susceptible to a construction which would avoid or modify the constitutional question presented to the federal court for resolution. *Zwickler* v. *Koota,* 389 U.S. 241, 248–249 (1967). The constitutional question here is "due process" under the Fourteenth Amendment. We must recognize that the due process concept is not subject to precise definition or exact calibration.

As the Supreme Court has indicated in *Hannah* v. *Larche,* 363 U.S. 420, 442 (1960):

> As a generalization, it can be said that due process embodies the differing rules of fair play, which, through the years, have become associated with differing types of proceedings. Whether the Constitution requires that a particular right obtain in a specific proceeding depends upon a complexity of factors. The nature of the alleged right involved, the nature of the proceeding, and the possible burden on that proceeding, are all considerations which must be taken into account.

See also *FCC* v. *WJR,* 337 U.S. 265 (1949); *Kelly* v. *Wyman,* 294 F. Supp. 893 (S.D.N.Y. 1968), *aff'd,* 397 U.S. 254 (1970). In this case, while there is no uncertainty as to the penalty of lost pay, we have pointed out there is no case which has even discussed the attributes of a Taylor Law probation. We have held that the plaintiffs have failed to establish by a preponderance of the evidence that it does result in a deprival of benefits which have a monetary value, and hence we have no jurisdiction. More importantly, the metes and bounds of Taylor Law probation should be fixed by state court adjudication before we prematurely decide the sensitive constitutional issue of due process. . . . There is no question that New York has provided for a declaratory judgment remedy when the constitutionality of a state statute is challenged. . . . In addition to these differences as to probationary sanction, the parties have disagreed in their briefs as to the scope of an Article 78 proceeding which the Taylor Law provides. (N.Y. Civ. Serv. Law Section 210(2)(h). As a matter of fact, no Article

78 proceeding under this statute has been commenced by any offended public employee. To the extent therefore that the sanctions are defined and the scope of the Article 78 hearing is clarified in the state court, the constitutional question, if not avoided, will be modified. *Coleman* v. *Ginsberg,* 428 F.2d 767 (2d Cir. 1970).

The second recognized area for the application of the abstention doctrine occurs where the exercise of jurisdiction would disrupt state administrative processes. . . . The administrative process in this case involves the complex relationships between the state of New York and the public employees of that state. *Zwickler* v. *Koota,* 389 U.S. at 256 (Harlan, J. Concurring). We should not unnecessarily intrude in such relationships. *Coleman* v. *Ginsberg, supra,* 428 F.2d at 769.

The Taylor Law is not a casual piece of state legislation. It presents a comprehensive, substantive, and procedural program for determining the rights and obligations of public employees and their public employers. Its statement of policy is instructive. N.Y. Civ. Serv. Law Section 200:

> The legislature of the state of New York declares that it is the public policy of the state and the purpose of this act to promote harmonious and cooperative relationships between government and its employees and to protect the public by assuring, at all times, the orderly and uninterrupted operations and functions of government. These policies are best effectuated by . . . (e) continuing the prohibition against strikes by public employees and providing remedies for violations of such prohibition.

It is clear that a most vital and sensitive part of the program involves the procedural due process to be provided in the event of a strike and the imposition of sanctions. As we have elaborated herein, a basic issue of the nature of the probation sanction has never been litigated in the state court. No case has arisen where the procedures for hearing and review have been put into effect. The state has set up an elaborate apparatus and no state litigation has tested it in action. We therefore believe that federal intervenion is highly inappropriate. *Reetz* v. *Bezanich,* 397 U.S. 82 (1970).

We conclude that we have no jurisdiction under either Section 1331 or Section 1343(3) and that in any event abstention should be our proper rule.

We therefore grant judgment dismissing the complaint herein.

Dated: November 24, 1971
      New York, N.Y.

/s/ William Huges Mulligan
U.S. Circuit Judge

/s/ David N. Edelstein, Chief Judge
U.S. District Court

/s/ Frederick P. Bryan
U.S. District Judge

Discussion Questions

1. What penalties were imposed upon the policemen for their strike action?
2. Why did the court lack jurisdiction in this case?
3. Discuss the constitutional questions involved in this case.
4. Distinguish the facts in this proceeding from those in the cases cited.
5. What is the "abstention" doctrine?

Section 6. Statutory Strike Notice to Municipal Employees Required to Effectuate a State Antistrike Statute

In private employment the Taft-Hartley Act requires that an employer or union that wishes to modify or terminate an existing contract must give notice of such intent to the other party sixty days before the expiration date of the contract. Serious negotiations are to commence forthwith and if after thirty days no agreement has been reached, appropriate state and federal mediation services must be notified. If mediation efforts prove unsuccessful, a strike or lockout may occur at the end of the sixty-day period, except in national emergency disputes. Therefore, the notice referred to here is in reality a strike notice by one side to the other. A number of states require strike notices and prestrike waiting periods in intrastate commerce labor disputes. The following case involves a statutory strike notice that an employer must send to his striking public employees in order to make operative the Ohio antistrike statute.

Goldberg v. City of Cincinnati et al.
Ohio Supreme Court, No. 70–434, Decided June 23, 1971 [9]

Before SCHNEIDER, Acting C. J., POTTER, DUNCAN, CORRIGAN, STERN and LEACH, JJ., concur.

POTTER, J., of the Sixth Appellate Division, sitting for O'NEILL, C. J.

Appeal from the Court of Appeals for Hamilton County.

Appellee, Mitchell B. Goldberg, brought this action as a taxpayer's suit, seeking to enjoin the appellant, city of Cincinnati, from paying increased compensation to certain municipal employees who belong to a number of unions comprising District Council No. 51 of the State, County, and Muncipal Employees Union. The city had been negotiating with the union and made an offer of increases in wages and other benefits. The employees rejected the offer and, on January 5, 1970, went on strike.

The city filed case No. A244947 in the Hamilton County Court of

Common Pleas and a permanent injunction was issued against the strike. The employees continued their strike and let it be known that they would remain away from their jobs until a satisfactory agreement had been reached.

Subsequently, the city's various appointing authorities notified the employees that they were deemed to have resigned their positions. These notices were sent pursuant to Section 4.7311 of the personnel policy and procedures of the city of Cincinnati.

On February 5, 1970, the City Manager signed a memorandum of settlement with the union representative, providing for the wage increases and other benefits here in question. The City Council passed a wage adjustment ordinance on February 11, 1970 (Ordinance No. 37–1970, effective February 8, 1970), which substantially conformed to the recommendation of the city manager and the memorandum of settlement.

On February 9, 1970, appellee Goldberg filed the instant action. His petition alleged, in essence, that the strike was in violation of R. C. Chapter 4117, the Ferguson Act, and prayed for an injunction against the payment of any increased compensation, direct or indirect, in the form of salary, wages, or any other benefits, to the striking employees which exceeded that received by them immediately before the strike. This restriction was prayed to continue for at least one year from the date of their appointment, reappointment, employment, or reemployment following such strike.

Appellant's action for injunctive relief was heard by the court of common pleas, and judgment dismissing the petition was entered on February 17, 1970. Before the trial court, the parties stipulated that there had been a strike by the municipal employees against the city for the purpose of obtaining higher wages and other benefits. It was also uncontroverted that notices provided for in R. C. 4117.04 were not sent to the striking employees. The trial court ruled that the Ferguson Act, which prohibits granting a pay increase to employees who violate Chapter 4117, was not self-executing; and that the city had not invoked the provisions of the Ferguson Act because of its failure to mail the notices provided for in R. C. 4117.04.

The court of appeals reversed the judgment of the trial court, holding that the notice provision of R. C. 4117.04 was inapplicable to the instant case. The court reasoned that while R. C. 4117.04 defines what conduct by municipal employees constitutes a strike and provides for the mailing of strike notices to employees engaging in such conduct, the stipulation that the employees had been on strike rendered the sending of the notices unnecessary. The court of appeals entered its judgment enjoining the city from paying any compensation to the employees involved in excess of that received by them immediately prior to the strike, for at least one year from the date of appointment, reappointment, or reemployment of such persons. Pursuant to the entry of the court of appeals, the city determined who had been on strike, and reduced their wages to the prestrike level. The cause is before this court pursuant to our allowance of a motion to certify the record. . . .

HERBERT, J. Appellant's basic contention is that the Ferguson Act is not self-executing. In particular, they argue that public employees are not deemed to be on strike within the meaning of the Ferguson Act unless they have been sent the notice provided for in R. C. 4117.04.

Appellee asserts that the Ferguson Act is self-executing, in that the sanctions provided for in R. C. 4117.03 and 4117.05 apply automatically where public employees are engaged in the type of concerted activity defined as a strike in R. C. 4117.01(A) and 4117.04. Appellee argues that the notice provision in R. C. 4117.04 is nothing more than a procedural safeguard designed to give public employees an opportunity to request a hearing to establish that they were not engaged in a strike.

It is uncontroverted that the employees in question were engaged in a strike, and that notices pursuant to R. C. 4117.04 were not sent by the employees' superiors.

In R. C. 4117.01, the general definition of the terms "strike" and "public employee" are set forth.

As used in Sections 4117.01 to 4117.05, inclusive, of the revised code:

> "Strike" means the failure to report for duty, the willful absence from one's position, the stoppage of work, or the abstinence in whole or in part from the full, faithful, and proper performance of the duties of employment, for the purpose of inducing, influencing, or coercing a change in the conditions, compensation, rights, privileges, or obligations of employment, or of intimidating, coercing, or unlawfully influencing others from remaining in or from assuming such public employment. Such sections do not limit, impair, or affect the right of any public employees to the expression or communication of a view, grievance, complaint, or opinion on any matter related to the conditions or compensation of public employment or their betterment, so long as such expression or communication is not designed to and does not interfere with the full, faithful, and proper performance of the duties of employment.
>
> (B) "Public employee" means any person holding a position by appointment or employment in the government of this state, or any municipal corporation, county, township, or other political subdivision of this state, or in the public school service, or any public or special district, or in the service of any authority, commission, or board or in any other branch of public service.

The general prohibition against public employee strikes is found in R. C. 4117.02, which states:

No public employee shall strike. . . . No person exercising any authority, supervision, or direction over any public employee shall have the power to authorize, approve, or consent to a strike by one or more public employees, and such person shall not authorize, approve, or consent to such strike.

The Ferguson Act also contains specific sanctions against those employees violating its proscription:

R. C. 4117.05 provides: . . . Any public employee who violates Sections 4117.01 to 4117.05, inclusive, of the revised code, shall thereby be considered to have abandoned and terminated his appointment or employment and shall no longer hold such position, or be entitled to any of the rights or emoluments thereof, except if appointed or reappointed.

R. C. 4117.03 reads as follows: . . . A person violating Sections 4117.01 to 4117.05, inclusive, of the revised code, may be appointed, or reappointed, employed, or reemployed, as a public employee, but only upon the following conditions:

(A) His compensation shall in no event exceed that received by him immediately prior to the time of such violation;

(B) His compensation shall not be increased until after the expiration of one year from such appointment or reappointment, employment or reemployment;

(C) Such person shall be on probation for a period of two years following such appointment or reappointment, employment or reemployment, during which period he shall serve without tenure and at the pleasure of the appointing officer or body.

The contentions of the parties to this appeal center upon R. C. 4117.04, which provides:

Any public employee who, without the approval of his superior, unlawfully fails to report for duty, absents himself from his position, or abstains in whole or in part from full, faithful, and proper performance of his position for the purpose of inducing, influencing, or coercing a change in the conditions, as compensation, rights, privileges, or obligations of employment or of intimidating, coercing, or unlawfully influencing others from remaining in or from assuming such public employment is on strike provided that notice that he is on strike shall be sent to such employee by his superior by mail addressed to his residence as set forth in his employment record. Such employee, upon request, shall be entitled to establish that he did not violate Sections 4117.01 to 4117.05, inclusive, of the revised code. Such request must be filed in writing, with the officer or body having power to remove such employee, within ten days after regular compensation of such employee has ceased. In the event of such request such officer or body shall within ten days commence a proceeding for the determination of whether such sections have been violated by such public employee, in accordance with the law and regulations appropriate to a proceeding to remove such public employee. Such proceedings shall be undertaken without unnecessary delay.

At common law, strikes by public employees are uniformly illegal. The courts have prohibited such concerted activity by public employees because of its interference with the paramount public interest in the unimpeded performance of essential governmental functions. . . .

In order to further safeguard the public interest by preserving a continuum of governmental services, Ohio and other states have enacted legislation which not only reiterates the common law prohibition against public employee strikes, but also fashions stringent disciplinary measures. . . .

In the case at bar, the first issue presented is whether in view of the existence of common law doctrines forbidding public employee strikes at the time of enactment of the Ferguson Act, all strikes by public employees automatically come within the purview of that legislation. One persuasive clue is to be found in the wording of R. C. 4117.03 and 4117.05, wherein the sanctions of the act are set forth; both sections express the applicability of the disciplinary provisions contained there in terms of persons "violating R. C. 4117.01 to 4117.05." Moreover, there is nothing in the language of Chapter 4117 suggesting that the General Assembly intended to preempt the entire area of the law concerning public employee strikes. For example, the act does not purport to affect the power of the court of common pleas to enjoin common law strikes by public employees.

In view of the continued viability of the historic common law interdiction of public employee strikes, and the express language in R. C. 4117.03 and 4117.05 directing their disciplinary impact against persons violating Chapter 4117, it is reasonable to conclude that the occurrence of a common law strike does not, *ipso facto,* constitute a strike in violation of the Ferguson Act.

R. C. 4117.02(A) sets out a definition of the term "strike," and R. C. 4117.02 provides that public employees shall not strike. However, it is clear that only R. C. 4117.04 contains an operative provision for determining when a public employee is on strike in violation of the act. Significantly, the definition of "strike" appearing in this section, is, for practical purposes, identical to that found in R. C. 4117.01(A).

Under R. C. 4117.04, the ultimate question turns upon the effect of the language "provided that notice he is on strike shall be sent to each employee by his superior by mail addressed to his residence and set forth in his employment record." In our opinion, a proper analysis of this language is essential to any determination of when a public employee is on strike within the meaning of R. C. Chapter 4117.

An investigation of the legislative history of this enactment proved fruitful. As introduced by Senator Ferguson in the 97th General Assembly, Section 6 of S.B. 261 provided:

Section 6. Notwithstanding the provisions of any other law any person holding such a position who, without the lawful approval of his superior, fails to report for duty or otherwise absents himself from his position, or abstains in whole or in part from full, faithful, and proper performance of his position shall be deemed on strike, provided, however, that such person, upon request, shall be entitled, as hereinafter provided, to establish that he did not violate the provisions of this act. Such request must be filed in writing, with the officer or body having power to remove such employee within ten days after regular compensation of such employee has ceased. In the event of such request such officer or body shall within ten days commence a proceeding for the determination of whether the provisions of this act have been violated by such public employee, in accordance with the law and regulations appropriate to a proceeding to remove such public employee. Such proceedings shall be undertaken without unnecessary delay.

As can be seen, the General Assembly, for reasons of its own, significantly altered a vital provision of Senator Ferguson's bill. In its original form, the bill left no room for argument. The proviso, delimited by the word "however," related solely to an employee's request to obviate the stigma of guilt by association. The burden to assert the protection was entirely upon the employee, and the procedure under that proviso did not work as a condition precedent to the existence of the statutory strike. However, as the bill emerged in its final form, it had been distinctly revised to state that a public employee was engaged in the statutory strike provided the required notice was given.

The appellee contends further, and the court of appeals held, that the sending of notices pursuant to R. C. 4117.04 advising each of the employees in question that they were on strike was unnecessary because the employees had informed the city they were on strike. While the public employees in question did engage in a common law strike against their public employer, they cannot be considered to have engaged in a Ferguson Act strike where the notices required by R. C. 4117.04 were not sent. It must be emphasized that R. C. 4117.04 expressly contemplates actual written notice to each employee that he is on strike. There is good reason for strict compliance with this condition. Even in the case of employees who are reinstated, the effects of their violation of the Ferguson Act are severe and continue in force for as long as two years after reinstatement.

Appellee raises the further argument that the public employees continue their strike in violation of a permanent injunction and should not be permitted to retain the benefits achieved through such conduct. We are not here deciding what discipline the trial court should dispense for a violation of its injunction. This appeal is not from a judgment in that action. The record before us shows that the withholding of funds was ordered upon the basis of a found violation of the Ferguson Act, not as punishment for contumacious behavior.

Appellee contends also that a public employer has no discretion as to whether to "invoke" the Ferguson Act by sending notice to the employees that they are on strike, and argues that the failure of the city of Cincinnati to send such notices in the instant case should not, as a matter of public policy, vitiate the force of the Ferguson Act. As we have pointed out, the Ferguson Act itself imposes the notice condition. The question of a public employer's clear legal duty to employ the act must be raised at a proper time and in a far different manner than was selected here.

In view of our holding that a public employee is not engaged in a strike in violation of the Ferguson Act unless the notice required by R. C. 4117.04 is sent, and since the court of appeals necessarily based its decision solely upon a purported violation of the Ferguson Act, the judgment of the court of appeals must be reversed and the judgment of the court of common pleas is affirmed in accordance with this decision.

Judgment reversed.

Discussion Questions

1. Of what significance is the fact that the statutory strike notices required by the Ferguson Act were not sent to the strikers?
2. Why had the court of appeals held that the mailing of strike notices was unnecessary?
3. Describe the statutory sanctions to be imposed on striking public employees.
4. What was the gist of the appellee's arguments?
5. Why did the Ohio Supreme Court reverse the appellate court ruling?
6. Without strike notices being sent by the city, what kind of strike did the court consider had actually occurred?

CHAPTER 7

[1] Thomas P. Gilroy and Anthony Sinicropi, *Dispute Settlement in the Public Sector: The State of-the-Art,* U.S. Department of Labor (Washington, D.C.: U.S. Government Printing Office, 1972), p. 61.

[2] GERR (No. 395) (F-1–3) (Washington, D.C.: BNA, Inc., April 25, 1971).

[3] GERR (No. 491) (E-1–5) (Washington, D.C.: BNA, Inc., Feb. 19, 1973).

[4] LRX 672, Sec. 33 (Washington, D.C.: BNA, Inc., 1961).

[5] GERR (No. 398) (F-1) (Washington, D.C.: BNA, Inc., April 26, 1971).

[6] 21 GERR 5033–5035 (RF-17) (Washington, D.C.: BNA, Inc., 1971).

[7] 51 GERR 4116 (RF-47) (Washington, D.C.: BNA, Inc., 1972).

[8] GERR (No. 432) (E-1–4) (Washington, D.C.: BNA, Inc., Dec. 27, 1971).

[9] GERR (No. 408) (E-1–3) (Washington, D.C.: BNA, Inc., July 5, 1971).

INDEX